Britain in the Far East

Britain in the Far East:
A survey from 1819
to the present

Peter Lowe

Senior Lecturer in History,
Manchester University

Longman
London and New York

Longman Group Limited

Longman House
Burnt Mill, Harlow, Essex, UK

Published in the United States of America
by Longman Inc., New York

First published 1981

British Library Cataloguing in Publication Data

Lowe, Peter
  Britain in the Far East.
  1. East Asia – Foreign relations – Great
  Britain
  2. Great Britain – Foreign relations –
  East Asia
  3. Eastern question (Far East)
  I. Title
  950'.3   DS518.4   79-42619

  ISBN 0-582-48730-7
  ISBN 0-582-48731-5 Pbk

Set in 10/11pt VIP Times Roman
Printed in Singapore by Kyodo Shing Loong Printing Industries Pte Ltd

Contents

List of maps

Maps 1 and 5 are redrawn from *The Cambridge History of China*, vol. 10, ed. J. K. Fairbank, Cambridge U.P., 1978; Map 2 is redrawn from P. Lowe, *Great Britain and the Origins of the Pacific War*, Oxford U.P., 1977.

Preface

The aim of this work is to provide a succinct general survey of British policy in the Far East with the emphasis placed primarily upon policy towards China and Japan; South-East Asia is discussed, particularly in the nineteenth century and the period after 1941, when it is more important to assess developments within the pattern of British advance and retreat in the Far East. In chronological terms the stress has been placed on the first half of the twentieth century as revealed in chapters 4–10; the first three chapters consider the establishment of the British role during the nineteenth century and the final chapter is in the nature of an epilogue on the rapid decline of British interests in the region following the conclusion of the Second World War.

Anyone writing a general account must be deeply conscious of his obligation to those who have laboured before him. I have tried to produce a synthesis based on the principal studies to have emerged in recent years; the extent of the compression has sometimes been considerable, as is unavoidable given the period under discussion. I was originally stimulated while studying the Far East by reading G. F. Hudson's *The Far East in World Politics*; if I have achieved at least some of his lucidity, I shall be well satisfied.

It should be noted that Chinese names are arranged according to the Wade-Giles system. Japanese names have been rendered with the surname or family name preceding the personal name.

Acknowledgements

I would like to thank the staffs of the John Rylands University Library of Manchester, the Library of the School of Oriental and African Studies, London University, and the Library of University College, Cardiff, for their assistance in the preparation of this work. I am grateful to the following for kindly allowing me to make use of their doctoral theses or for making other information available to me: Dr Jeffrey Brider, Dr Clive Christie, Dr Gordon Daniels, Dr Paul Haggie, Dr James Hoare, Dr Harold Kane, and Dr Richard Sims. Over the years I have derived much encouragement from discussing far eastern issues with Mr Evan Edwards, Dr Ian Nish, and Mr Richard Storry and I would like to express my appreciation to them. Mrs Margaret Gissop has yet again coped admirably with the task of typing the work for me: I am grateful for her zeal and efficiency. The Japan Foundation generously gave me a short-term visitor's award, which made it possible for me to travel extensively around Japan and to meet a number of my Japanese colleagues. I am grateful to the Japan Foundation for facilitating my visit, in the course of which I also went to Thailand and Hong Kong. Lastly I must state that I am responsible for any errors that remain.

Peter Lowe
Manchester
December 1979

Introduction

In 1800 Great Britain occupied a strictly limited role in the Far East. British trade with China was assuming more significance with the growth of the insatiable demand for tea in Britain and with the ominous beginnings of the expansion of the opium traffic from India. The East India Company wished to see commerce flourish beyond the restricted conditions laid down by the Chinese government at Canton. In 1793 Lord Macartney visited China and was received by the Ch'ien-lung emperor in Peking; the meeting was of an amicable nature, despite difficulties over the ceremony of the kowtow, which was regarded as peculiarly embarrassing by Europeans. However, the meeting took place on the basis of traditional Chinese superiority and it was clear that trade would function in Canton on the lines already established.[1] In 1816 Lord Amherst endeavoured to see the Chia-ch'ing emperor without success. There were no British contacts with Japan in 1800, since Japan was firmly protected by the seclusionist policy implemented in the early years of the Tokugawa shogunate. The East India Company possessed a foothold in the Malayan peninsula where Penang had been acquired in 1786; Britain was engaged in rivalry with the Dutch, which was to be serious until the 1820s and which was to linger for some fifty years afterwards.[2] British interest in Burma was beginning to develop as a consequence of British dominance in India. In 1900 British interests in China were more important than those of any other single power and were largely concentrated in Shanghai and the Yangtze valley; the British lead over other powers was by then declining and was not as striking as it had been a generation before. Nevertheless Britain was in front of others in terms of economic interest down to 1914. In Japan Britain had been extremely active in opening up Japan in the later 1850s and 1860s and possessed more influence than any other country over the development of Japan before 1914.[3] The most obvious contrast in looking at the map of the Far East in 1900 and comparing it with that of 1800 lies in the incorporation of Burma, Malaya and British Borneo within the British Empire. This was a development that took from the 1820s to the 1890s to be accomplished, the two principal phases of growth of British influence and authority occurring in the 1820s and subsequently in the 1870s and the 1880s; the 1870s are usually regarded as the crucial period in the case of

Malaya, although one historian has argued that the 1820s can be considered more of a turning-point.[4]

Therefore, in the nineteenth century British might was growing until the last decade of the century and as regards Malaya, British authority was still expanding in the 1890s. In the twentieth century Britain was largely preoccupied with grave crises in Europe and with the repercussions of these crises. In the nineteenth century British ambitions in and towards China had been the most dynamic element in the formulation of British policy in the Far East as a whole. In the twentieth century down to 1945 the emerging powerful and ultimately devastating challenge from Japan was the vital theme in British policy.[5] Originally Britain and Japan were allies from 1902 to 1923. In the 1930s they were involved in a grave collision of interests, leading to the Pacific war in 1941, which in some respects can be viewed as an Anglo-Japanese war rather than as an American-Japanese war: British economic and territorial interests in the Far East were greater than those of the United States and Japanese animosity was heavily concentrated on Britain between 1937 and 1941.[6] However, in another sense Britain was not central to the vital decisions taken at the climax of the far eastern and Pacific crisis in 1941; the United States assumed the direction of western policy towards Japan, and Britain did not participate in the Washington talks in 1941, the failure of which led directly to the Japanese attacks on Malaya and Pearl Harbor.[7] Britain's formal empire in the Far East was not deeply shaken until the Japanese successes in swiftly conquering Malaya, Burma, and Borneo in 1941–42. Opposition to British rule in Burma had admittedly been growing since the First World War and had become strident in the 1930s, when the British gave Burma a constitution as a prelude to self-government. In Malaya nationalism was slower to develop before 1941, although it was marked and vociferous in the case of the Chinese population. The Pacific war demolished the image of the invincibility of colonial empires and Britain's task after 1945 was to negotiate the end of empire. Burma became independent outside the British Commonwealth in 1948 and Malaya secured independence within the Commonwealth in 1957; British territories in Borneo shortly joined with Malaya to form the state of Malaysia. The British role in the Far East rapidly declined after 1945, and, in a meaningful sense, ended with the military involvement in supporting Malaysia against Indonesia during the curious period of confrontation in 1963–64.[8] British economic interests continued to be important in the late 1970s but British defence was restricted to an essentially nominal presence at Hong Kong.

What was the nature of British imperialism in East and South-East Asia? Why did it develop as it did? In a famous article published in 1953 J. Gallagher and R. Robinson argued persuasively for continuity in British imperialism throughout the nineteenth century. To consider imperialism only by the criterion of formal control was 'rather like judging the size and character of icebergs solely from the parts above the water-line'.[9] Gallagher and Robinson believed that Britain's political and economic role in the world expanded in formal and informal terms throughout the century and that the mid-Victorian era was not one of hostility to the development of empire as formerly maintained.[10] The aim was to enhance the prospects for trade in the best way possible and this did not necessitate the extension of formal control: 'Once entry had been forced into Latin America, China and the Balkans, the task was to encourage stable governments as good investment risks, just as in weaker or unsatisfactory states it was considered necessary to coerce them into more co-operative attitudes.'[11] In a later article Oliver MacDonagh rightly drew attention to the consistent criticisms of the abuse or alleged abuse of British power expressed by mid-Victorian radicals such as Richard Cobden, John Bright, and Henry Richard.[12] Cobden castigated developments in Borneo, Burma, and China.[13] D. C. M. Platt has pointed out that for most of the nineteenth century the British government did not wish to involve itself too deeply in trade matters and that Britain did not seek to erect an exclusive sphere of influence in China; indeed Lord Elgin was told in 1858 that, 'Her Majesty's Government have no desire to obtain any exclusive advantages for British trade in China but are only desirous to share with all other nations any benefits which they may acquire in the first instance, specifically for British commerce.'[14] It is clear that Britain wished to open up as many parts of the Far East as she could to the beneficial effects of trade – in China, Japan, Burma, Malaya, Siam – and that British policy-makers hoped that Britain would secure as large a proportion of total trade as possible. Free trade would apply but the assumption was that Britain would obtain a prominent share. The British government did not believe that it should become involved in the business of individual firms or in advocating individual commercial projects; however, this attitude was modified under the spur of growing competition in the 1880s and was virtually abandoned after 1898.[15] Sir John Jordan, the British minister in Peking from 1906 to 1919, spent much of his time advancing business projects, above all railway concessions, but without wishing to become too deeply immersed in individual firms.

J. A. Hobson, the left-wing liberal writer and publicist, put forward an original interpretation of imperialism in 1902 in his book *Imperialism : a Study*; Lenin largely adopted Hobson's analysis while refining it in a Leninist direction.[16] Hobson believed that investors were basically responsible for the acquisition of colonies in tropical regions; they were at the back of the activities of the more overt practitioners of imperialism – the arms manufacturers, missionaries, army officers, administrators.[17] Hobson wrote:

Aggressive imperialism, which costs the taxpayer so dear, which is of so little value to the manufacturer and trader, which is fraught with such grave incalculable peril to the citizen, is a source of great gain to the investor who cannot find at home the profitable use he seeks for his capital, and insists that his Government should help him to profitable and secure investments abroad.[18]

Hobson contended that the solution to the unhealthy preoccupation of investors with imperialist profits lay in the employment of such capital within the domestic economy to remedy the urgent social wrongs of low wages and slums.[19] How great was British investment in the Far East and what did Britain gain in terms of increased trade?

In 1902 British business investments in China have been estimated by C. F. Remer at 150 m. US dollars; by 1914 this had risen to 400 m. US dollars and by 1931 to 963 m. These investments comprised between 30 per cent and 40 per cent of total business investments in China in the period indicated.[20] To these figures have to be added the foreign holdings of government obligations in China. In 1902 Britain contributed 110 m. US dollars; in 1914 207 m. US dollars; and in 1931 211 m. US dollars. These constituted almost two-fifths of the total foreign holdings during this period.[21] British imports from China amounted to about £9.5 m. on average in the period 1854–63, to nearly £12 m. from 1864 to 1873, and to over £13 m. from 1874 to 1883.[22] British exports to China were over £3 m. on average between 1854 and 1863; just over £8 m. from 1864 to 1873; and nearly £8½ m. from 1874 to 1883.[23] Between 1884 and 1893 British exports to China overtook imports, the value of the former being £8.5 m. to £7.5 m. for imports. Thereafter the balance of trade swung heavily in favour of Britain: in 1913 British exports to China amounted to £19.5 m. and imports to under £5.5 m.[24] Tea and raw silk were originally prominent in Chinese exports to Britain, but these declined in value after 1890 as Indian tea displaced Chinese tea in the British market. Cotton goods were the most important British export to China in the second half of the nineteenth century, usually constituting about 65 per cent of exports.[25] The proportion was falling at the beginning of the twentieth century: between 1898 and 1913 British cotton textiles averaged 35 per cent of China's imports.[26] Opium was a major British export until the end of the nineteenth century; in 1857 31,907 chests were imported into Shanghai. In 1878 opium amounted to 45 per cent of Chinese imports. By 1898 opium imports had fallen to slightly under 50,000 piculs, valued at 29 million taels*; this was approximately 14 per cent of the value of Chinese imports.[27] The British share of China's shipping was appreciable, comprising 60 per cent in 1899 and 41 per cent in 1913. Over half of the coastal shipping was British in 1913 and British vessels carried over 60 per cent of the total value of cargoes. Before 1880 the British comprised over 50 per cent of the foreign population of China; in 1899 the proportion was 32 per cent. In 1865 the British population of Shanghai was 60 per cent of the total foreign population; in 1900 it was 40 per cent. The British population of the treaty ports of China totalled 8,966 in 1913 to which has to be added about 5,000 in Hong Kong.[28]

According to figures cited by Herbert Feis, British foreign investment in Japan (long-term publicly issued British capital investment) amounted in 1914 to almost £63 m.[29] Japan was not as important for British trade as China. British exports to Japan were worth nearly £4 m. in 1880, just

---

*One picul = 133⅓ lbs (60.453 kgs). One tael = 1.208 English ounces of pure silver.

over £4 m. by 1890, and £15 m. in 1913 (the latter including Korea, Formosa, and Kwantung). Japanese exports to Britain amounted to less than £2 m. per year before 1902; in 1913 Japanese exports were worth almost £4½ m.[30] The principal imports from Britain were cotton piecegoods, machinery, metals, woollens, and chemicals; from 1896 to 1913 Japan offered a better market than China for machinery, metals, electrical goods, and chemicals.[31] Between 1900 and 1913 the nature of trade with Japan varied: British exports included more machinery, iron and steel, and woollen piecegoods, while cotton goods declined.[32] The various parts of the British Empire contributed significantly; raw cotton was supplied by India, rubber by Malaya, wool by Australia, and timber and pulp by Canada. The British Empire provided about 26 per cent of Japan's total imports in 1913 and took over 8 per cent of Japan's exports; the direct British share constituted almost 17 per cent and 5 per cent respectively.[33]

In Malaya, the Straits Settlements were distinctly poorer than the Federated Malay States. In 1913 the revenue of the former was 12 m. Malayan dollars while the Federated Malay States provided 44 m. Malayan dollars. Tin was originally the backbone of the Malayan economy: in 1904 56 per cent of the world's total production came from Malaya. The rubber industry grew dramatically after the introduction of rubber seeds from Brazil via Kew. By 1914 the rubber acreage was 1,168,000 and exports amounted to 46,652 long tons. In 1904 the foreign trade of the Straits Settlements was worth £64 m. and in 1914 over £107 m. Rubber exports by 1914 were worth about £11 m. and tin about £7 m.[34] British exports to Malaya totalled over £3 m. in 1900 and over £7 m. in 1913. Imports from Malaya amounted to £7 m. in 1900 and to over £19 m. in 1913.[35]

In Burma rice was the foundation of the economy. The oil industry began to develop at the end of the nineteenth century and by 1913 production had reached about 277 m. gallons with exports of 22 m. gallons valued at £142,000. British exports to Burma totalled nearly £3 m. in 1900 and nearly £6 m. in 1913. British imports from Burma totalled more than £2 m. in 1905.[36]

Thus, to sum up the economic position before 1914, the China market had not fulfilled the hopes of those who had ardently urged the opening of China in the middle of the nineteenth century. China was too poor and self-sufficient in essentials to offer the vast commercial expansion talked about by the more naive politicians and merchants. Money could certainly be made in China, as the success of Jardine, Matheson and of the Hong Kong and Shanghai Bank exemplified. However, collectively the commercial prospects in China were not as promising as had been hoped. Japan was less lucrative than China and Japan's rapid modernisation resulted in a change in the pattern of trade with Britain. Malaya was the most valuable single area for British investment, which was originally attributable to tin and subsequently to rubber as well.

Therefore, how significant was the economic motive in precipitating

British expansion in the Far East? It is rarely possible to say that one aspect alone is responsible for a great historical development. Economic interests and aspirations were certainly important, particularly in China. A combination of political, strategic and economic motives contributed to the process of expansion. The part played by individual initiative was often fundamental: the man on the spot had considerable freedom in the nineteenth century when communications with superior authority and particurlarly with London were slow and cumbersome. Captain Elliot and Sir John Bowring in China, Rutherford Alcock and Harry Parkes in Japan, and Sir Harry Ord and Sir William Jervois in Malaya frequently had to cope with situations as best they could or as they saw fit. The latter point in the previous sentence can be separated from the former point; officials in the Far East in the nineteenth century thought of themselves as pioneers performing a great work and one imperfectly comprehended in London or Calcutta. Stamford Raffles revealed this attitude and one of his successors in Malaya, Sir Andrew Clarke, went on record in the 1890s as saying with reference to his own work in Malaya twenty years earlier that the minds of men in London sometimes had to be made up for them by the man on the spot.[37] As D. K. Fieldhouse has aptly remarked, 'almost any European living on or beyond the frontier of "civilized" government became a compulsive empire-builder'.[38] The strategic factor of safeguarding interests or possessions from other powers was frequently significant. Britain was suspicious of the intentions of France, Russia and Germany at various times in China during the nineteenth century; rivalry with France influenced British attitudes in the 1860s and 1870s towards China and Japan and was extremely important in the final annexation of Burma in the 1880s; there were recurring anxieties about foreign interest in Malaya from the 1870s to the 1900s. Of all the elements concerned, the strategic aspect was probably the most important in determining colonial annexations or consolidation. In China and Japan the economic incentive was initially the most effective in stimulating British advance: economic and strategic considerations combined to explain the new emphasis on spheres of interest in China from 1898. In the twentieth century, British policymakers confronted by the rise of an increasingly bellicose Japan after 1931 realised that Britain could not abdicate responsibility for defending British interests in China because of the presence of the British Empire in India and South-East Asia. Appeasement of Japan at the expense of China and of British interests in China would simply encourage Japan to demand more and would decisively discredit Britain in the eyes of the inhabitants of India, Burma and Malaya. The accuracy of this assessment was borne out by the consequences of the collapse of the British forces in South-East Asia in 1941–42; Malaya and Burma were conquered by the Japanese army and the leaders of Congress in India launched the 'Quit India' movement in the summer of 1942. The strategic motive in the twentieth century meant that Britain's informal empire in China had to be defended in order to sustain the formal empire in India and South-East Asia. It was in many ways remarkable, after the savage blows suffered by

Britain at the hands of Japan, that India and Malaya elected to remain within the British Commonwealth when they obtained independence and that only Burma, to the personal regret of the Burmese leader General Aung San, chose finally to sever the ties with the successor to the British Empire.

Chapter 1

The opening of China and British expansion in South-East Asia, 1818–1853

The most important developments in Britain's role in the Far East in the first half of the nineteenth century occurred in China. This is not to underestimate the significance of the acquisition of Singapore in 1819; the rivalry with the Dutch leading to the treaty of 1824; or the encroachment upon Burma. These aspects were certainly to contribute in a major way to the subsequent growth of Britain's formal empire in South-East Asia and will be considered later in this chapter. However, China was the principal magnet; Britain took the chief part in opening up China, a process that was accelerated by the first Anglo–Chinese war of 1840–42 and the ensuing treaty settlement. The clash between Britain and China represented the confrontation between two wholly diverse and uncomprehending civilisations — between the brash dynamism of the Industrial Revolution and the serene confidence of Confucian superiority. The experience comprised a protracted and painful realisation of occidental superiority for China and the Chinese government was faced with numerous other problems: the western menace, spearheaded by Britain, simply appeared as one of the difficulties and not the most dangerous.

China in the nineteenth century had entered a phase of decline characteristic of the later stages of dynasties in her ancient history. The Ch'ing (Manchu) dynasty enjoyed its greatest success in the reigns of the K'ang-hsu (1662–1722) and Ch'ien-lung (1736–96) emperors. In the eighteenth century China was vigorous and assertive; it was a period of cultural flowering. Decline had, however, already set in during the latter part of the reign of the Ch'ien-lung emperor. From the beginning of the nineteenth century all the familiar features of dynastic decline were revealed: less competent rulers, growing corruption throughout the government, the neglect of public works, maltreatment of the peasantry. These traditional manifestations were accompanied by a new and more threatening development — rapid population growth. It has been estimated that China's population grew from approximately 100 million at the beginning of the Ch'ing dynasty in 1644 to about 430 million by 1850. Population growth thus provided the most revolutionary ingredient to the transformation of China and one that was only dimly appreciated by those in government.[1] The Ch'ing court and officials believed that the difficulties with which they were contending, in the domestic and foreign contexts, were evanescent and could be surmounted. The British and other foreigners were regarded as insolent barbarians who did not understand their place in the Confucian world. China was the true centre of world civilisation and the further a country was from Peking, the less civilised it was by definition. The new strength of the occidental powers was not grasped.

British trade with China was centred in the southern port of Canton from 1760 to 1834. The Ch'ing government permitted trade to function on terms that allowed the Chinese authorities to control what happened without themselves being in direct contact with the foreign merchants. Chinese traders known as the 'cohong' constituted a monopoly and dealt with the foreigners; the members of the cohong were responsible to the superintendent of maritime customs at Canton, described by western merchants as the 'hoppo'.[2] British trade was conducted by the East India Company as a direct extension of the Company's authority in India.[3] The balance of trade was heavily in favour of China for many years. Tea and textiles were sold by the cohong in exchange for commodities such as woven cloth. The tea trade grew rapidly in the last quarter of the eighteenth century, as the British acquired a taste for this form of refreshment. Tea sales increased enormously and in 1785 over 15 million pounds of tea were sold: the increased consumption was facilitated by the sharp reduction in tea duties effected in 1784. The entire basis of the East India Company rested on tea sales in the final stages of the Company's history.[4] The term 'country trade' was used to describe commerce between India, the East Indies, and China. This commerce was crucial to the functioning of the China trade. The East India Company issued licences to private merchants in India to pursue trade with China: this system was used to supply the necessary finance for the tea trade. India sent items such as cotton and opium to China, obtaining in return lower valued commodities such as sugar and tutenag (zinc, prominent in S.E. Asian trade). The financial benefit lay clearly with India, the surplus amounting to approximately £1 million in the early nineteenth century.[5] It was this favourable balance that acted as a counterweight to the trade of the East India Company, therefore paying for the tea purchases. The principal arrangement used to finance the complex triangular trade was for the Company to exchange bills on the court of directors in London or on the government of Bengal for the specie from country merchants, these bills being much desired by the merchants as a method of sending their funds to Britain or India.[6] Tea supplies were carried only in Company ships. The system was supported by both sides, because the Company could finance its activities and the country merchants could abstract their profits.[7]

According to figures cited by Michael Greenberg for the year 1828, total British imports at Canton were 20,364,600 Spanish dollars; of this figure 4,518,957 dollars were on the Company's account and 14,364,600 on private account. Nearly half of the Company's imports came from the west (2,189,237 dollars, including 1,764,217 dollars in woollens) and virtually all of the eastern items (2,329,720 dollars) comprised Indian raw cotton. The eastern goods totalled 15,590,136 dollars, of which raw cotton constituted 3,480,083 dollars and opium 11,243,496 dollars. The exports from Canton amounted to 18,136,052 dollars, rather more than half of this being on private account. Tea comprised almost all of the Company's exports. Out of 9,656,767 dollars exported on private account, 6,094,646 dollars was in silver.[8]

In 1813 the East India Company's monopoly in India was terminated by the British government: the Company was permitted, however, to keep control of the China trade for a further twenty years. The most radical change in the nature of trade in the 1820s and 1830s was brought about by an enormous expansion in opium sales. Small quantities of opium had been imported into China in previous centuries, despite the attempts of the Ch'ing authorities to prevent it. There were two kinds of opium produced in India – Patna and Malwa; the former was regarded more highly by consumers of opium. The East India Company sold opium to private traders, who were thus responsible for conducting the trade. Between 1800 and 1818 the opium trade averaged 4,000 chests a year,* based on Macao.[9] After 1820 demand for opium grew and the trade more than quadrupled, so that by 1836 the import trade totalled over 34,000 chests.[10] Profits were so tempting that the country merchants extended their activities; one of the most prominent was William Jardine, a name that was to become renowned in far eastern trade through the great firm of Jardine, Matheson. The opium traffic caused a drastic reversal in the terms of trade for China. Between 1800 and 1810 China had gained approximately 26 million dollars in her balance of payments; between 1828 and 1836 China faced a deficit of 38 million dollars.[11] British commercial circles were agitating for the expansion of trade and for the British government itself to adopt a more resolute approach in dealing with China. Pressure was consistently exerted by Manchester merchants for the end of the East India Company's monopoly of tea and for complete freedom in pursuing trade with China.[12]

The termination of the East India Company's monopoly in 1833 inevitably brought the British government into direct dealings with the Chinese authorities. A British superintendent of trade was appointed at Canton; the foreign secretary, Lord Palmerston, appointed Lord Napier to the post. Palmerston wished to foster British trade with China but did not desire conflict with China, not realising that conflict would be unavoidable for the simple reason that the Ch'ing emperor saw no necessity for direct relations with the government of King William IV. Since China was the 'Middle Kingdom', the centre of true civilisation, it was impossible to have a direct diplomatic relationship of the character Palmerston was accustomed to in Europe. China was superior to other countries and would graciously determine the amount of trade to be permitted and the

*The quantity of opium in a chest varied according to the type; for Malwa a chest was 133⅓lbs, for Patna a chest was 160lbs.

rules of the game. Palmerston instructed Napier to inform the Chinese viceroy of his arrival and to pursue trade matters from then on. Napier reached Canton in July 1834, and endeavoured to fulfil his instructions. The governor-general, Lu K'un, refused to accept communications from Napier and instructed him to leave Canton. Contrary to Palmerston's wishes, Napier decided to employ force. It is worth noting that Napier frequently saw the British merchants and that he was especially friendly with William Jardine; he lived in Jardine's house and Jardine assisted him by conveying messages to the Chinese.[13] In one of the first manifestations of the famous 'gunboat' approach to diplomacy in China, Napier ordered two warships to advance up the Pearl river. Lu K'un proceeded to blockade the river and prepared to use force himself. Napier initially tried to withstand the blockade. After seventeen days, he forfeited the support of the British community, except for the loyal Jardine, and retreated to Macao, where he died in October 1834.[14] The immediate result of this episode was to encourage the Chinese in the illusion that they could afford to take a vigorous line with the British. The merchants in Canton predictably urged a forthright response. In a petition to the king they stated 'that the most unsafe of all courses that can be followed in treating with the Chinese government, or any of its functionaries, is that of quiet submission to insult, or such unresisting endurance of contemptuous or wrongful treatment, as may compromise the honour, or bring into question the power of our country'.[15] Representations were also made by Liverpool and Manchester merchants. Palmerston was back at the Foreign Office after the brief interregnum of the Peel government of 1834–35; he appointed Captain Charles Elliot, then assistant superintendent at Macao, to the post of superintendent with instructions to follow a policy midway between belligerence and weakness. Elliot was imbued with self-confidence but miscalculated the problems he faced. A period of sparring between Elliot and the new governor-general, Teng T'ing-chen, ensued with Elliot trying to advance the British position without confrontation. Teng similarly wished to avoid concessions but was worried at the threat of British naval action.[16]

As opium sales continued to expand, so the Ch'ing authorities became alarmed at the moral and economic consequences. The effects upon those consuming opium were becoming more apparent in the provinces adjacent to Canton; equally significant were the repercussions on the Chinese economy with the outflow of silver. Chinese officials were corrupted by the insidious nature of the opium trade: the commander of the fleet supposedly suppressing the trade, for example, permitted opium to be carried in return for suitable rewards. It is possible, as Frederick Wakeman has suggested, that profits from opium were reaching the Ch'ing court, having been sent from Canton.[17] However, this cannot be proved. The Tao-kuang emperor, who had reigned since 1820, decided that the troublesome barbarians must be put in their place more effectively and Lin Tse-hsu, the governor-general of Hupei and Hunan, was appointed in December 1838 to suppress the opium trade. Lin was a highly capable

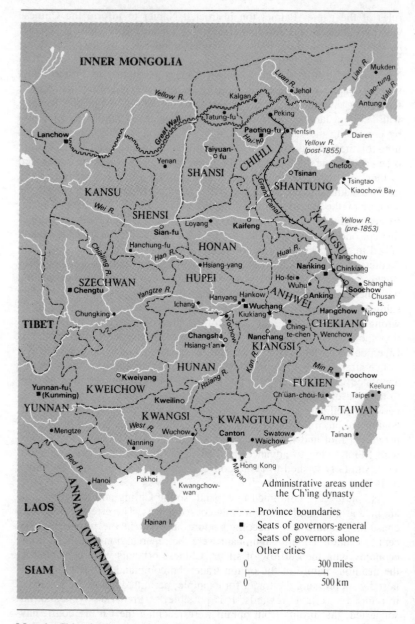

Map 1. China in the nineteenth century

Confucian official of honesty and integrity who advocated a policy of firm suppression of the opium traffic, including a mixture of rehabilitation and punishment for addicts. He maintained that foreign traders should be warned and punished if they proved recalcitrant. In March 1839 Lin told the hong merchants that they must at once secure the transfer of opium stocks to him for destruction: he threatened drastic action if his instructions were not complied with.[18] He also determined to arrest one of the most prominent British merchants, Lancelot Dent. Elliot interpreted Lin's action as the prelude to war.[19] He left Canton and proceeded to Macao where he found a blockade of the foreign factories in progress. Worried at the danger to the foreign community in Macao, Elliot believed he would have to compromise. He issued a guarantee of financial support to the British merchants and advised them to surrender the opium to Lin. Once again it appeared that the tough Chinese policy had been vindicated by British submission. Lin's moment of triumph was short-lived, however: war was shortly to break out and was to lead to his disgrace. British traders were alarmed at the new vigour with which Chinese policy was being implemented by Lin and were irate at the inadequate British response. The opium business of James Matheson declined steadily and Matheson deplored the fact that Elliot 'had adopted the novel course of assisting the [Chinese] Government in this, against his own Countrymen'.[20] The consequences were bound to be serious and Matheson contended that Elliot's policy of appeasement would encourage the Chinese to commit themselves too far, thus giving rise to conflict.[21] In fact, Palmerston and Elliot disliked the existing situation and deprecated the smuggling of opium; they wished to see the problem solved by negotiation between the two governments with the opium trade recognised as legal by China.[22]

In July 1839 a Chinese peasant was killed by a group of drunken British seamen; another of the not unfamiliar crises involving conflict with Chinese law had arisen. Lin wanted the murderer surrendered but Elliot wished to complete a thorough investigation. Lin implemented a blockade of Macao with the aim of compelling British acquiescence. On 4 September 1839 Elliot ordered an attack on the Chinese naval squadron in order to obtain supplies; the first shots of the approaching war had been fired.[23] Lin's suspicions of Elliot had been growing and he deduced that the British representative was in active collusion with opium interests. Lin therefore decided to send a letter containing 'moral advice' to Queen Victoria. It is an admirable example of the Chinese sense of indignation at the infamous opium trade and of the traditional air of Confucian superiority. Lin wrote:

A communication: magnificently our great Emperor soothes and pacifies China and the foreign countries, regarding all with the same kindness. If there is profit, then he shares it with the peoples of the world; if there is harm, then he removes it on behalf of the world. This is because he takes the mind of heaven and earth as his mind.

The kings of your honorable country by a tradition handed down from generation to generation have always been noted for their politeness and submissiveness . . .

But after a long period of commercial intercourse, there appear among the crowd of barbarians both good persons and bad, unevenly. Consequently there are those who smuggle opium to seduce the Chinese people and so cause the spread of the poison to all provinces. Such persons who only care to profit themselves, and disregard their harm to others, are not tolerated by the laws of heaven and are unanimously hated by human beings. His Majesty the Emperor, upon hearing of this, is in a towering rage . . .

The barbarian merchants of your country, if they wish to do business for a prolonged period, are required to obey our statutes respectfully and to cut off permanently the source of opium . . . After receiving this dispatch will you immediately give us a prompt reply regarding the details and circumstances of your cutting off the opium traffic. Be sure not to put this off . . . [24]

In November 1839 conflict occurred between the British and Chinese fleets, after Elliot decided to oppose Lin's ultimatum to accept the Chinese government's instructions or risk destruction. A ship of the Royal Navy fired on Chinese junks:[25] war was imminent. The British were overwhelmingly superior in leadership, morale, technology, and tactics. The Chinese forces were incompetent and the strength of their forces was much less than was claimed on paper. British merchants exerted pressure on London; William Jardine helped to finance a campaign intended to convince public opinion of the peculiar horrors faced by British nationals on the China coast[26] and co-ordinated representations to Palmerston urging a tough policy at Canton including a blockade of Chinese ports to secure reparations, a commercial treaty, the opening of four new ports, and the occupation of several islands like Hongkong.[27] Palmerston had already decided to dispatch an expeditionary force to blockade Canton and the Peiho. Palmerston wanted the ports of Canton, Amoy, Foochow, Shanghai, and Ningpo opened, so that British nationals could live and trade there; he wanted British consuls to operate in the ports, compensation for the opium destroyed, the end of the hong system, and the cession of an island to facilitate trade.[28] Elliot was in favour of positive action but feared that Palmerston's wish to send a ship to the Peiho could produce an escalation of the situation and preferred to concentrate on the Yangtze.[29] In the House of Commons Palmerston's policy was castigated by the Conservative opposition; Gladstone commented, 'A war more unjust in its origin, a war more calculated to cover this country with permanent disgrace, I do not know and I have not read of.'[30]

The Opium War began formally in June 1840. British strategy aimed at bypassing Canton and taking Chusan island. It was clear that the war would be primarily naval in character, since it was impossible for British armies to advance into the interior of China.[31] Chusan was swiftly captured; the advance of the British towards the Peiho alarmed the imperial court and it was decided to negotiate. The Tao-kuang emperor felt that Lin Tse-hsu must be sacrificed and the imperial commissioner was dismissed.[32] Ch'i-shan, the governor-general of Chihli, was appointed to succeed Lin. Ch'i-shan realised that Britain was too powerful to be repulsed by the methods employed by Lin and favoured a more subtle approach, amounting to managing the barbarians diplomatically. Elliot

believed strongly in the need for Britain to acquire an island to promote
trade; he emphasised to Ch'i-shan his determination to take Hong Kong.
Ch'i-shan tried to avert the concession but reluctantly concurred in the
convention of Chuenpi (January 1841); it was also agreed that an indemnity would be paid to Britain and that the Canton trade would function
as Britain wished.[33] The emperor felt that the concessions demanded
were too great; he approved the resumption of hostilities and ordered
reinforcements to Canton. In London Palmerston was dissatisfied at
Elliot's conduct of the negotiations and regarded Hong Kong as manifestly less satisfactory than Chusan. Elliot was dismissed by Palmerston
– 'I gave you specific demands and furnished you with the means of
obtaining them . . . You have disobeyed and neglected your instructions'[34]
– and replaced by Sir Henry Pottinger, who had served in the Indian army
and had been political agent in Sind; he was not to enjoy particularly
fruitful relations with the merchant community but apparently met with
the approval of his subordinates.[35] The emperor dismissed Ch'i-shan and
appointed three officials instead – I-shan, Lung-wen, and Yang Fang.
Chinese reinforcements were poured into Canton. Elliot, still in command
pending Pottinger's arrival, sent his fleet upriver. Yang Fang was compelled to accept the re-opening of trade but was overruled by his fellow
officials when they arrived. In a naval engagement on 21 May 1841 the
Chinese fleet of war junks was destroyed and a number of shore batteries
captured.[36] Pottinger reached Hong Kong on 10 August 1841. A British
expedition including twenty-five ships of the line and troopships had
advanced to Singapore. Chusan was swiftly recaptured in military operations directed by General Sir Hugh Gough on 1 October 1841; Ningpo
was captured soon afterwards. The emperor's cousin, I-ching, was
appointed to head military operations against the British; in the subsequent fighting the inept Chinese forces were quickly routed by the British.[37]

The Tao-kuang emperor recognised that negotiations would have to
take place but he hoped to minimise concessions. He sent the elderly
I-li-pu to command the forces in Chekiang: Ch'i-ying was appointed in
April 1842 to negotiate a settlement.[38] He succeeded in persuading the
emperor that concessions must be made and he was empowered to conclude a treaty. The treaty of Nanking was signed on 29 August 1842,
under the terms of which China agreed to pay twenty-one million dollars
as an indemnity; the ports of Canton, Amoy, Foochow, Ningpo, and
Shanghai were to be opened to trade and British consuls established in
each port; the island of Hong Kong was to be ceded; British prisoners
were to be released; representatives of the two governments were to confer, supposedly on equal terms; the hong system was ended; transit duties
on British goods were to be of a moderate nature. Pottinger considered
the retention of Hong Kong to be imperative and he acted contrary to his
orders in obtaining the island in perpetuity. He was one of the first to
grasp the potential of the magnificent natural harbour of Hong Kong.[39]
The treaty of Nanking was of great historic importance, marking the

beginning of the modern treaty port system as it was to endure for a century until swept away by Japanese imperialism in 1941. It was the first major success for western imperialism in China and was soon to be followed by growing pressure from France, the United States and Russia. However, Britain had not gained as much as she thought. The Chinese emissaries had not reported the full details to the emperor and the British desire for equality of status in diplomatic terms was not appreciated. Far more remained to be accomplished before the British wish for full facilities to develop trade could be said to have been obtained.

Britain wanted to see the principles of free trade triumph on the China coast. British merchants should be able to pursue their activities without hindrance and for this purpose they must be free to move around the treaty ports if they wished and be subject to British law, as applied under the authority of British consuls. This desire ironically suited the Ch'ing government, once the decision had reluctantly been taken to accept the treaty of Nanking. Allowing British nationals (and those of other western nations) to function under their own laws reduced contact with Ch'ing officialdom and accordingly limited the danger of friction: the barbarians would be left to discipline their own. As J. K. Fairbank has pointed out, this was analogous to the 'loose rein' policy frequently deployed in dealing with the barbarians of Inner Asia.[40] Ch'i-ying held that the most successful way of handling the British was to pretend to be friendly while delaying talks and further concessions for as long as was practicable. British merchants wished to secure internal free trade within China and to avoid taxation other than in the treaty ports. The new regulations on trade, replacing the old Canton system, were published on 22 July 1843. British consuls would assume responsibility for British ships; the consuls would exercise authority over British subjects. The supplementary treaty of the Bogue was signed on 8 October 1843 by Pottinger and Ch'i-ying.[41] Under the treaty British trade was restricted to the five ports in which residence was authorised. Contacts between Hong Kong and Canton were recognised; smuggling was to be jointly discouraged; and provisions for extraterritoriality and for extradition of criminals were approved. A most favoured nation clause was incorporated under which concessions made to other powers would be extended to Britain. Opium was not referred to in the treaties of Nanking and the Bogue: Britain wanted opium to be legalised but this was unacceptable to the emperor and so it was not referred to. The opium trade continued to flourish and by 1860 some 60,000 chests were being imported annually. James Matheson instructed his opium-ship captain, in April 1843, to act cautiously, remarking that, 'The opium trade is now so very unpopular in England, that we cannot be too cautious in keeping it as quiet and out of the public eye as possible.'[42]

The new treaty ports were opened in stages. Canton was opened on 27 July 1843; Amoy on 2 November and Shanghai on 17 November 1843; Ningpo on 1 January 1844; and Foochow in June 1844. Treaties with the United States of America and France were signed in July and October

1843. The treaty ports gradually developed, catering for a combination of diplomats, traders and missionaries. Foreign communities developed around the bund (or foreshore), which was clearly most accessible for commercial purposes and also more defensible. By 1850 approximately five hundred occidentals lived in the treaty ports. Men were in the large majority; about half of the foreign populace was British, a substantial proportion coming from India.[43] In Shanghai in the mid-1850s about seventy firms were engaged in trade and there were over three hundred foreign residents with eight consulates and thirty-six Protestant missionaries.[44] The treaty ports were dependent on shipping links for communication with Britain: mail deliveries took two to three months across the isthmus of Suez; the Cape route took a month longer.[45] The most prominent British firms were Jardine, Matheson and Company and Dent and Company; American merchants were starting to become more active. The large firms dominated shipping and controlled banking and insurance. A big firm like Jardine's employed a large staff of British and Chinese and would deal with various commodities such as tea, silk, and textiles. British consuls in the treaty ports were concerned with encouraging trade. This involved verifying ships' papers; checking imported goods; establishing the standard of coinage; and coping with the problems of British seamen. As regards relations with the Chinese officials, the consul was responsible for renting land and houses, preventing smuggling, and extraditing criminals.[46]

At Canton considerable difficulties were experienced in asserting the treaty rights recently secured. The authorities at Canton were hostile and resentful of the foreign presence while the British merchants wished to see trade expand without hindrance and behaved with increasing arrogance, if not contempt, towards the Chinese. Sir John Francis Davis, an old China hand with more knowledge of Canton and conversant with the language, succeeded Pottinger as superintendent and governor of Hong Kong in 1844. Davis was a patient but determined man; he believed Britain should firmly press for free admission to Canton, in accordance with treaty stipulations. He was critical of the attitude shown by the British community, writing to Palmerston, 'I am not the first who has been compelled to remark that it is more difficult to deal with our own Countrymen at Canton than with the Chinese government...'[47] Palmerston was not concerned with the British merchants as such but rather with the principle involved. He wrote to Davis in December 1846, 'I have only to say that wherever British subjects are placed in danger, in a situation which is accessible to a British Ship of War, thither a British Ship of War ought to be, and will be ordered not only to go, but to remain as long as its presence may be required for the protection of British interests.'[48] The foreign secretary maintained that a balanced policy had to be pursued:

We shall lose all the vantage ground we have gained by our victories in China if we take a low tone. We must especially care not to descend from the relative position which we have acquired. If we maintain that position morally, by the tone of our intercourse, we shall not be obliged to recover it by forcible acts; but if we permit the Chinese either at Canton or elsewhere, to resume, as they will no doubt always be endeavouring to do, their former tone of superiority, we shall very soon be compelled to blows with them again.[49]

In April 1847 Davis launched a joint military and naval expedition to capture the Bogue forts, an aim that was accomplished with relative ease. The British demand to enter the city gates of Canton was conceded within a period of two years.[50] Palmerston was for the moment satisfied with the outcome; if the Chinese were recalcitrant again in the future, then further armed action would be necessary.[51] Growing complications in Europe, including the numerous revolutionary upheavals of 1848, meant that Britain was not likely to intervene decisively in China immediately. It was simply a lull before the next storm arose. The Royal Navy instead concentrated on tackling the menace of pirates off the China coast, an activity in which British naval personnel were to be engaged for the next century.[52]

On the eve of the second war between Britain and China in the 1850s, Britain had been reasonably successful in building upon the foundations and opportunities provided in the treaties of 1842 and 1843. British traders could not be satisfied with the limited achievements, however, and the Ch'ing government, which still regarded the British as an irritant rather than a fundamental threat, was not prepared to make more concessions. A renewal of conflict could be anticipated and sooner rather than later.

The development of Britain's interest in South-East Asia in the modern period dates from the extension of the East India Company's involvement in the China trade, with the subsequent acquisition of trading ports in the Malayan peninsula. Penang was acquired in 1786, largely at that time for naval reasons:[53] Penang was attractive owing to its proximity to the Straits of Malacca and because it was within an acceptable sailing distance of the Coromandel coast. The acquisition has to be seen in the light of Anglo-Dutch commercial rivalry and the East India Company's wish to prevent Dutch expansion.[54] Penang was not geographically well situated to attain the Company's objectives, for it was not sufficiently central and the presence of pirates in appreciable numbers handicapped shipping. The decisive impetus in expanding the British stake in Malaya was provided by the dynamic Stamford Raffles, the first of the vigorous proconsular figures to guide British destinies in the Far East in the nineteenth century. Raffles was born in 1780 and had joined the East India Company as a clerk, where he showed a prodigious capacity for work, combined with a restless mind, always full of diverse schemes. He had a profound belief in Britain's expansive mission, fuelled by the exciting era of the Revolutionary and Napoleonic wars and the concomitant struggle against the French and the Dutch. In 1805 Raffles was dispatched to Penang with the rank of assistant secretary. He threw himself energetically into the task of mastering the Malay language, which he succeeded in achieving rapidly, and soon became an expert in Malay culture.[55] Raffles impressed the governor-general in Calcutta, Lord Minto, and in 1810 was appointed agent to the Malay States. He set up his headquarters at Malacca and devoted his attention to taking over Java and making it part of the East India Company's possessions. He succeeded in dominating Java and held it until it was returned to the Netherlands at the end of the Napoleonic wars, being thus frustrated in his aim of erecting a permanent British base in Java. In 1819 he landed on the island of Singapore at the tip of the Malayan peninsula; he determined to retain the island and persuaded the local Malay chief to cede it.[56] He wrote, 'What Malta is in the West, that may Singapore become in the East.'[57] Anglo–Dutch rivalry resumed after 1815. After lengthy negotiations, the treaty of London was signed in 1824 under the terms of which Singapore was retained by the East India Company and Malacca was taken over.[58]

In Penang the East India Company's settlement developed encouragingly in the early years. It became a significant trading centre, where British and Indian goods were exchanged for such commodities as rice, tin, spices, pepper and rattans. Penang was not self-sufficient in food, however, and was dependent on the neighbouring state of Kedah. For administrative purposes Penang, Malacca and Singapore were governed from Bengal. In 1826 the presidency of the Straits Settlements was set up but this was ended in 1830. The Straits Settlements then became a residency under the authority of the governor and council of Bengal. Singapore was made the capital in 1832 and rapidly grew in importance.[59] By 1824 the population was over 10,000; by 1829 this figure had risen to almost 18,000; by 1845 to over 52,000; and by 1860 to 81,000. Chinese constituted a high proportion of the immigrants from the 1830s onwards and by the mid-1860s Chinese comprised 65 per cent of Singapore's population.[60] In the later years Indians increased rapidly and by the 1860s had overtaken the Malays as the next most important ethnic group after the Chinese. In 1860 the total population of the Straits Settlements was nearly 274,000; Penang comprised about 125,000; Singapore 81,000 and Malacca 68,000.[61] The Straits Settlements were ruled by a governor and a council under the jurisdiction of the governor-general of India in Calcutta. After the Charter Act of 1833 the efficiency of the administration in the Straits Settlements declined as a result of excessive centralisation.[62] Singapore's contribution to far eastern trade was impressive: in 1824 the commerce of Singapore amounted to over 13 m. Mexican dollars, to nearly 19 m. dollars in 1829–30, to almost 24 m. dollars in 1849–50, and to over 38 m. dollars in 1855, the latter figure being approximately £9 m.[63] Merchants had feared that the opening of new ports in China would diminish the role of Singapore but there was no justification for such apprehension. Singapore functioned according to the principles of free trade advocated by Raffles; from the beginning Singapore was free from all duties.[64] In 1867 Singapore had some sixty European companies

Overleaf **Map 2.** South-East Asia and the western Pacific before 1945

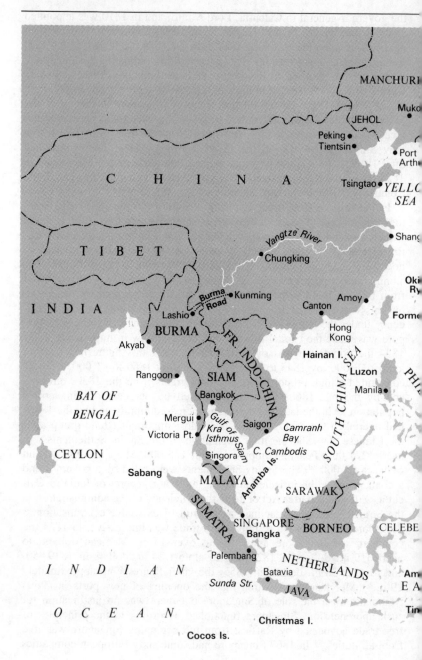

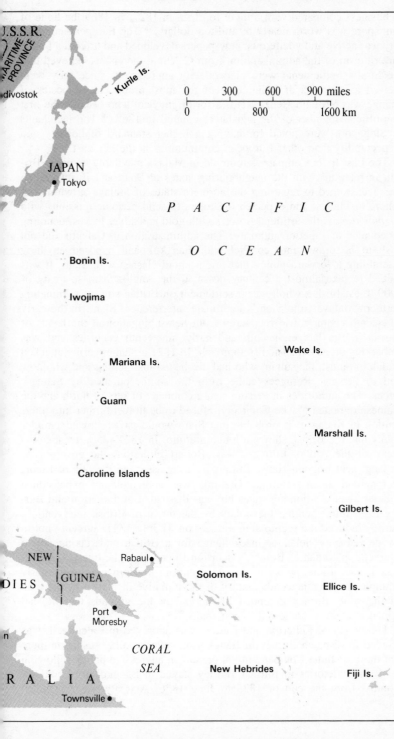

U.S.S.R.

MARITIME PROVINCE

divostok

Kurile Is.

0   300   600   900 miles

0   800   1600 km

JAPAN

● Tokyo

P A C I F I C

O C E A N

Bonin Is.

Iwojima

Wake Is.

Mariana Is.

Guam

Marshall Is.

Caroline Islands

Gilbert Is.

NEW

DIES

GUINEA

Rabaul ●

Solomon Is.

Ellice Is.

Port
Moresby ●

CORAL

n

SEA   New Hebrides

Fiji Is.

R A L I A

Townsville ●

in business compared with a mere fourteen in 1827. In 1869 the trade of Singapore was worth nearly 59 million dollars.[65] The European community was active and vociferous; newspapers developed and offered a forum for criticism of the administration from Calcutta; merchants believed that the Straits Settlements were inadequately appreciated, since they were viewed as outposts of India. One of the most prominent advocates of change was William Henry Reid, a forthright Scot who became the first non-official member of the legislative council in 1867.[66] The merchants in Singapore were noted for having a higher standard of honesty and respectability than other European communities in the Far East.[67]

The East India Company's foothold in Malaya inevitably involved Britain in relations with the neighbouring states of Siam and Burma. Siam was accustomed to regarding the northern states of Malaya as within her sphere of interest and expected the rulers to send periodic missions with the *bunga mas*, the artificial flowers with gold and silver leaves, denoting acceptance of superior authority. The administration in Calcutta did not wish to be drawn into conflict with Bangkok and opposed anything resembling a forward policy that might entail clashes with Siam. It was indeed to take almost a century down to the Anglo–Siamese treaty of 1909 to establish a wholly clear settlement on Britain's terms eliminating northern Malaya from Siam's legitimate interference. Siam, in the early nineteenth century, had recovered from her subjugation at the hands of Burma in the late eighteenth and early nineteenth centuries and was embarking on an expansionist approach. In 1821 a Siamese army attacked Kedah to punish the sultan, who had disobeyed instructions and who now fled to Penang. Refugees came from the south, pursued by Siamese forces. The authorities in Penang sent a company of sepoys north and the Siamese retreated.[68] The Company refused to be drawn further into intervention in Kedah: it is probable that Siam would have followed a milder policy had the British shown a tough attitude. In 1824–25, after the outbreak of the Anglo–Burmese war, Robert Fullerton, the governor of Penang, sent Captain Henry Burney as an emissary to the raja of Ligor, seeking aid against Burma. The raja was contemplating expansionist policies against adjoining states but was dissuaded by Fullerton and Burney from implementing the policy by the threat of British intervention. Burney induced the raja to sign a treaty on 31 July 1825, agreeing not to invade Perak or Selangor in exchange for a British undertaking not to intervene in Kedah.[69] Burney's decision to conclude the treaty was contrary to the official policy of non-intervention: it affords one of the early examples in the nineteenth century of the initiative displayed by the man on the spot. Burney defended his action on the grounds that he had helped to avert a Siamese invasion south.[70]

The policy of Fullerton and Burney was approved in Calcutta. It was decided to dispatch Burney to Bangkok in order to allay suspicion there that the East India Company might pursue an aggressive policy following the British victories in Burma. Burney stayed in Bangkok for about six months, from the end of 1825 to June 1826. A treaty was concluded under which Perak was protected from attack by both signatories; the autonomy of the sultan was recognised and it was left to the sultan to decide whether or not to send the *bunga mas* to Bangkok. The commercial clauses were rendered as vague as possible by the Siamese and the opportunities for fostering British trade were less encouraging than had been hoped. Burney could not persuade Siam to withdraw her garrison from Kedah; instead he conceded that the sultan should be taken from Penang so as not to constitute a menace to Siam.[71] It was further agreed that there would be no political intervention in the states of Trengganu and Kelantan and that British merchants should be able to trade.[72] Siam had no intention of observing the agreement on Perak. In 1826 a treaty was signed between the East India Company and the sultan of Perak, stipulating British assistance should his position be threatened, that the sultan would not communicate with other states on political issues, and that the *bunga mas* would not be sent to Siam.[73] Afterwards the Siamese forces withdrew from Perak. The Perak treaty was not originally recognised formally by the authorities in Calcutta, who deemed it unduly interventionist; however, time enhanced its importance and it was accepted as binding in 1844, 1853 and 1874.[74] Kelantan and Trengganu opposed Siamese attempts to control them. Between 1858 and 1862 a struggle took place in Pahang, following a quarrel in the ruling family of the state. The governor of the Straits Settlements, Colonel Orfeur Cavenagh, authorised a bombardment of the sultan of Trengganu's fort in 1862; this had the effect of discouraging further Siamese intervention.[75] Relations between the British and Siamese remained cool, as was unavoidable in a situation where Britain was by implication, if not overtly, challenging Siamese power. An improvement was temporarily effected at the time of the Bowring mission to Bangkok in 1855, which will be considered in the next chapter.

The growth of British intervention in Burma followed the establishment of a common frontier between Burmese and Indian territories after 1784, in which year King Bodawpaya of Burma conquered the kingdom of Arakan.[76] Trouble did not immediately arise, because Burma was more interested in expanding against Siam. The calibre of government declined owing to Bodawpaya's preoccupation with religious matters; the efficiency of government fell away and taxation became more onerous.[77] Difficulties developed in 1811–12, when Arakan was invaded from British-ruled Chittagong by a dissident Arakanese leader. The Burmese government believed British officials to have inspired the invasion: this was incorrect, although undoubtedly errors had been committed by the British authorities in Bengal. Burma soon afterwards assumed a hostile attitude and began intervening in border areas. In 1819 King Bagyidaw succeeded to the Burmese throne. Assam was occupied and the Burmese demanded the return of Assamese leaders who had sought refuge with the British. Burma attacked Manipur and Chahar; Chittagong itself was menaced. The East India Company declared a protectorate over Chahar and Jaintia. War clearly loomed and was precipitated by a clash over an island in the River Naaf, accentuated by conflict between British and Burmese forces in Chahar. War was declared by the authorities in Calcutta on 5 March 1824[78] and a British force captured Rangoon in May 1824. This dramatic success could not properly be followed up owing to the monsoon, which began in June. The British troops were weakened by disease but managed to repel Burmese efforts to recapture Rangoon until reinforcements from India materialised. Aided by the Mons and Karens, traditional opponents of centralised Burmese rule, the British force proceeded towards the Burmese capital in 1825–26; Burma decided to make peace. Under the terms of the treaty of Yandabo, signed on 24 February 1826, Burma was forced to pay an indemnity of 10 million rupees (about £1 million); Tenasserim, Arakan, Manipur, and Assam were ceded to Britain. It was agreed that Burma would not attack Siam, would admit a British resident, and would make a commercial treaty.[79]

Relations between the British and the Burmese worsened from 1830 onwards. The court resented the concessions extorted from Burma and wished to reverse the outcome of the war of 1824–26. After a successful rebellion in 1837, Prince Tharrawaddy assumed power. He disliked the presence of Burney, the British resident, and contested the validity of the treaty of 1826.[80] War seemed near, particularly as the British were committed militarily in China and in Afghanistan. War did not occur, however, because the king followed his brother into insanity and Burmese officials realised that they could not rely on the loyalty of the population of Lower Burma.[81] British rule in the strategic coastal area of Tenasserim brought stability to the region and helped to reduce the danger of armed conflict between Burma and Siam. In Arakan British rule met with a serious rebellion in 1836; economic circumstances improved, however.[82]

The second Anglo-Burmese war, in 1852, resulted from British ire at fines imposed on the captains of two British ships for allegedly breaking port rules. The governor-general of India, Lord Dalhousie, did not desire war but was prepared, if necessary, to face this situation;[83] two naval vessels were dispatched to Rangoon to demand redress and the removal of the offending Burmese official. The Burmese government acted in a conciliatory way but unfortunately more trouble occurred over shipping matters. The British implemented a blockade of the coast in January 1852; the naval commander, Commodore Lambert, acted in an arrogant manner. Dalhousie rebuked Lambert but maintained that war was inevitable. The British expeditionary force was better prepared that its predecessor of 1824 and the campaign advanced competently. Martaban, Rangoon and Bissein were captured in April–May 1852. Dalhousie urged the government of Lord Aberdeen to accept the annexation of Lower Burma; Prome and Pegu were taken in October–November 1852. King Pagan was overthrown early in 1853 and replaced by one of his half-brothers, Mindon Min. The Burmese army retreated and the British assumed control of

Lower Burma; it took three years to restore order. The borders of Tenasserim province were extended to incorporate the Karen regions between the Lower Salween and Sittang rivers. Pegu province was carved out of the remainder of the territory.[84] Thus British control of much of Burma had been achieved, largely due to the dynamic policy pursued by Dalhousie. Another generation passed by before the remainder of Burma came under British rule.

British interest in the large island of Borneo developed during the eighteenth century as part of the rivalry between the East India Company merchants and the Dutch and a British post was established at Banjermasin in 1812. The East India Company's representative was Alexander Hare, who was solely concerned with enriching himself; his behaviour discredited Raffles, who had supported him, and the Company.[85] In 1816 the Company vacated Banjermasin to be promptly succeeded by the Dutch. Raffles made some headway in combating endemic piracy and in establishing British interest in Borneo in 1812–15 but his ambitious designs were curbed by the new governor-general, Lord Moira, who was less enthusiastic about expansion than Lord Minto had been.[86] In the 1820s, down to the Java war in 1825, the Dutch consolidated their hold; after the war, however, financial exigencies compelled drastic economies.[87] Piracy was rife around the Malayan coast and in the Indonesian archipelago. It had long been present in the region and was rendered more lucrative by the profits to be made from slavery and cargoes; it was encouraged by certain rulers and highly placed native officials.[88] The European powers would not co-operate to suppress piracy, as the failure to implement the relevant provisions of the Anglo–Dutch treaty of 1824 exemplified. The arrival of James Brooke in 1839 marked the onset of vigorous measures against the pirates and the beginning of a close association between the Brooke family and Borneo that was to last for a century. Brooke came from the Bengal civil service and had fought in Assam. On a visit through the Malay archipelago in 1830, Brooke was entranced by the islands, and when he inherited a large sum from his father he equipped himself with a yacht and crew and went to Borneo in 1839,[89] subsequently securing the governorship and full cession of Sarawak in return for assistance given during a quarrel in the ruling family. Brooke, with Admiral Cochrane, acted firmly to suppress piracy. He had urged the British government to accept the island of Labuan, which contained valuable coal deposits. Palmerston decided that Labuan should be accepted from the sultan of Brunei and that a commercial treaty should be signed with the sultan.[90] Labuan was acquired in 1846. In 1849 Brooke and Admiral Collier eliminated a new upsurge of piracy, much of which resulted from the activities of Chinese pirates.[91] The Dutch disliked Brooke's activities and once again worked to build up Dutch strength in Borneo. However, British interests were solidly established in Borneo, despite the failure of Labuan to develop into as significant a port as had been hoped originally and the controversial final phase of Brooke's career, when he was involved in defending himself against a venomous press campaign.

Therefore, in China and in South-East Asia British interests were being more rapidly advanced by methods of formal and informal imperialism by 1853. The British contribution to the opening of Japan was about to materialise.

Chapter 2

The opening of Japan and expansion in China, 1853–1868

Japan faced the same challenges as China in the middle of the nineteenth century. The established system of government under the Tokugawa shogunate was breaking down and the foreign powers were demanding that Japan open her ports to foreign residence and trade. After profound internal convulsions, Japan was to prove herself capable of surmounting the dangers of decline and embarked upon the process of modernisation that was to transform her into a major power within an astonishingly short period. Japan had enjoyed prolonged peace and stability under the Tokugawa shogunate which had aimed to freeze the new situation resulting from the military triumph secured at the beginning of the seventeenth century. An effective method of centralised feudalism was developed, reinforced through ubiquitous surveillance in Edo (Tokyo) and the numerous han (domains). Each daimyo (lord of a han) was expected to spend one year in two in the shogunal capital of Edo; his wife and family remained in Edo when he returned to his han. Apart from one or two brief phases of suspension or modification, this system, known as sankin kotai, prevailed until the 1860s and proved efficacious for a long time in preventing dangerous intrigue against the Bakufu (military government). Tokugawa Japan was changing far more rapidly, however, than was realised by the shogun and his advisers. The samurai (warrior class) had little or no fighting to do in the period of unprecedented peace and stability inaugurated by the Tokugawa and became, to a considerable extent, a class of administrators, whilst being expected to be proficient in the martial arts. The merchants became more significant but were looked down upon as inferiors, according to the Confucian theory that influenced Japan deeply under the Tokugawa. The economy and society of Japan were changing swiftly. Certain of the tozama han – the outer han originally opposed to the Tokugawa in 1600 – notably the south-western han of Choshu and Satsuma, were becoming restless and assertive, thus posing a latent and ultimately overt threat to the power of the Bakufu.[1]

In the 1630s Japan had adopted a policy of stringent seclusion from contact with foreign powers.[2] The Tokugawa were apprehensive at the possibility of the Spanish, Dutch, English, and Portuguese combining with domestic opponents to overthrow the Bakufu. Limited and carefully controlled trade was permitted only at the southern port of Nagasaki in

Kyushu, where a Dutch trading settlement existed on the artificial island of Deshima; Chinese vessels also visited Nagasaki, which was important for providing a centre from which Chinese and western ideas would penetrate Japan with significant effects on Japanese intellectuals. Japan was largely left alone by the foreign powers until the Napoleonic period, when occasional British, French, or Russian ships appeared off the home islands of Japan and met with a hostile reception. Most Japanese in central government and in the han wanted to perpetuate foreign exclusion, while the more perceptive realised that it would not be feasible to do so for much longer. They were aware of foreign interest in China and were alarmed to hear of the first Anglo–Chinese war and of the treaty of Nanking. The moment of reckoning arrived in 1853 when Commodore Matthew E. Perry of the United States navy arrived bearing a letter from President Millard Fillmore requesting the opening of diplomatic and commercial relations. Perry paid a return visit in 1854 to ascertain the Japanese response. The Bakufu officials did not wish to open Japanese ports to trade but appreciated the unpleasant implications of refusal. Their decisions were inevitably linked closely with the frequently tortuous path of internal politics.[3] Lengthy exchanges and arguments between the representatives of the Bakufu and the foreign emissaries took place, for Britain, France, and the Netherlands were as interested as the United States in establishing relations.[4]

British traders started to show intermittent rather than constant interest in the potentialities of trade with Japan in the early nineteenth century. The East India Company was not particularly concerned, yet ships flying the colours of the Company visited Japan in 1813–14; this was attributable to the ambitious Stamford Raffles.[5] In 1834 Palmerston desired information on the possible development of trade but it is unlikely that he devoted attention to Japan,[6] since China was infinitely more attractive. In August 1845 Captain Belcher arrived in Nagasaki and wished to foster the British role in the manner often shown by the zealous man on the spot. Dr John Bowring intended visiting Japan but was prevented by his preoccupation with China and, to a lesser extent, with Siam. The Foreign Office produced a memorandum on relations with Japan in August 1845 revealing ignorance of Japan and of the most effective method of developing relations; it regarded Japan as being clearly subordinate to China in the scale of priorities but maintained that the country could nevertheless offer attractive possibilities in commercial terms.[7] Admiral Sir James Stirling visited Japan in 1854 and signed the Stirling convention which stipulated the opening of Nagasaki and Hakodate for repairs, provisions, and supplies; Japanese laws would apply to British ships. Stirling did not pursue trade aspects; the Foreign Office thought Stirling was correct not to press further at this juncture but the Board of Trade and Bowring dissented.[8] Both sides experienced difficulty in coping with translation.[9] In further negotiations Stirling tried to expand Britain's role; he entertained far-reaching schemes, which were deemed too advanced by the Foreign Office and the Admiralty. His successor,

Map 3. Japan in the nineteenth century

Admiral Seymour, showed more skill and patience in conducting exchanges.

The crucial decade in the opening of Japan extended from 1858 to 1868. Lord Elgin arrived in Japan in the summer of 1858 to sign a major treaty, critical of British policy towards China in the preceding twenty years, which he felt had too frequently been characterised by resort to force. The same view was held by the foreign secretary, Lord Clarendon, when he issued Elgin with his instructions in 1857. Elgin insisted on proceeding to Edo to negotiate, believing this to be essential in putting the discussions on the correct basis of formality. In the course of the negotiations he agreed to follow the same procedure as had governed the treaty concluded earlier in 1858 by Townsend Harris on behalf of the United States. Elgin signed the treaty on 26 August 1858. Nagasaki, Kanagawa (Yokohama), and Hakodate were to be opened for commercial and residential purposes as from July 1859; Niigata or an alternative port on the Japan Sea would be opened from January 1860 and Hyogo (Kobe) from January 1863. Foreign residence in Edo and Osaka would be permitted from January 1862 and January 1863. A representative of the British government would be allowed to live in Edo and consuls could be appointed at the ports opened to trade. Extraterritorial rights were extended with consular authority, religious toleration, and most favoured nation provisions. Tariffs were laid down but could be revised after five years. The treaty was generally welcomed by the British government and by British public opinion. British merchants regarded the trade prospects in Japan with some enthusiasm.[10]

Discontent was growing in Japan, as revealed in the activities of vociferous samurai and rebellious peasants. The Bakufu itself was divided and weak, especially after the assassination of the strong man, Ii Naosuke, in 1860. The imperial court at Kyoto was being brought into the centre of the political scene; the popular slogan of the later 1850s and early 1860s was 'Revere the emperor; expel the barbarian'. Confucian scholars had contributed to the growing belief that many of Japan's troubles resulted from the usurpation of power by the shogun and that the disappearance of the Bakufu would lead to a dramatic recovery in Japan's position. Under the emperor Japan would be able to regain unity and strength and to expel the insolent foreigners. Within various han men from a lower samurai background were in the ascendancy and were forcing the pace of change. Originally such men were bellicose in their attitudes to foreigners. Under the pressure of events, however, the more astute among them modified their views in the early and mid-1860s and believed that Japan must come to terms with the west and implement modernisation; this offered the only route for preserving the independence of Japan. Some remained conservative in their attitudes to institutions within Japan and thought of true feudalism being restored once the Bakufu had been removed.[11]

The British consul at Canton, Rutherford Alcock, was appointed to the post of consul-general for Japan in December 1858 and reached Japan in June 1859. Alcock's background was unconventional for a diplomat but not unusual for the pioneering era of intense western activity in the Far East. He was originally qualified in medicine and had served as a consul for fifteen years in four of the treaty ports on the China coast. A shrewd and capable diplomat, he believed British policy in China had vacillated between bullying and weakness; he detested the opium trade. Alcock favoured a policy of firmness in dealing with Chinese, for he considered that this engendered respect; he believed that the same reasoning applied to Japan.[12] In the main he proved a successful minister in circumstances that were often dangerous and provocative. The foreign secretary, Lord Malmesbury, emphasised that tact was essential in dealing with the Japanese and that the government would be satisfied with 'gradual progress'.[13] Malmesbury indicated that apart from fostering relations with Japan, Alcock should carefully observe Russian activities in the Far East. Alcock entirely agreed with the views of the Foreign Office. The flavour of his attitude is illustrated in the advice he gave to the consul at Hakodate:

Firmness tempered with moderation and great patience are essential conditions to success with the Japanese officials. . . Rights secured by Treaty are never lightly to be abandoned, even when they appear to be of secondary importance; and when they bear directly upon material interests the faithful observances of its conditions must be steadily insisted upon. There are many modes of insisting, and firmness is quite compatible with courtesy. Neither are all rights of equal importance, nor all times equally fitting for their assertion.[14]

Alcock was largely left to his own devices, since it took six months to obtain replies to his reports to the Foreign Office.

The officials of the Bakufu warned Alcock and his fellow diplomats of the unrest and instability within Japan and of the danger of widespread attacks on foreigners by hostile samurai. Alcock at first felt that the Tokugawa authorities were exaggerating the extent of unrest for their own purposes; he thought that a minority of devious daimyo constituted the core of the problem and acted accordingly.[15] The Bakufu was endeavouring by diplomatic means to sustain Japanese sovereignty and to postpone opening ports or making more concessions to the powers. Alcock was involved in a number of clashes in 1861–62, including two attacks on the property of the British legation and the murder of two British army officers. In the light of the developing ferment in Japan, Alcock revised his opinion on the menace to occidentals, believing that Japan could be on the verge of civil war with all the horrors and disputes this would entail.[16] Several more ports were due to be opened but it was agreed that these would stay closed until January 1868 (the ports concerned were Osaka, Edo, Hyogo, and Niigata). A series of attacks on British nationals and property occurred. Perhaps the best known episode took place in September 1862 when an Englishman named Richardson rode in front of part of the procession of the daimyo of Satsuma: he was promptly cut down by the loyal samurai. The anti-foreign incidents gave rise to vigorous protest. The leading tozama han of Satsuma and Choshu were involved in clashes with the foreign powers in 1862–63. In retaliation the

Royal Navy bombarded the dissident han in 1863 and 1864. The foreign
secretary, Lord John Russell, wished peaceful methods to be pursued but
authorised the use of force if necessary.[17] The action of the navy was
condemned by those consistent critics of Palmerstonian methods, Richard
Cobden and Charles Buxton, for causing unnecessary suffering and destruction,[18] although the effect of the naval actions in which Britain was
concerned was to clear the air and to lead to a deeper respect for British
achievements in Satsuma and Choshu.

In January 1865 Harry Parkes was appointed British minister in succession to Alcock. Parkes was an excellent example of the Victorian
pioneering spirit. He was born in Walsall in 1828 and orphaned at the age
of five; his elder sister had married Karl Gutzlaff, the distinguished missionary and adviser to British diplomats. Parkes went to Macao in 1841
and was to spend most of his life in the Far East. He served in a consular
capacity in several of the ports on the China coast[19] and knew little of
Japan when he was appointed but he was eminently practical and direct in
his approach and felt that Japan should be treated in the same manner as
China. In the words of Gordon Daniels, 'Parkes thought Orientals should
be taught by treaties and disciplined by force'.[20] Industrious, tough, and
impetuous, Parkes did not suffer fools gladly and liked his own way. He
intended to see that the existing treaties were properly fulfilled by Japan
and to seize any opportunities that arose for gaining more concessions; he
believed that a vigorous naval demonstration was called for and that the
repercussions on the dissident han and samurai would be beneficial. His
Dutch and French colleagues concurred and an expedition comprising five
British warships, three smaller French vessels, and one Dutch ship sailed
to Hyogo in November 1865.[21] Despite previous doubts he had entertained, Parkes held that the shogun could be trusted and that the best
policy for Britain to pursue was to support the Bakufu in the looming
struggle against its opponents. The naval action persuaded the Bakufu to
open talks on tariffs. Parkes wished to rationalise the tariff structure,
which was chaotic. He favoured a uniform five per cent tariff, based on
commodity price averages of the past eight to ten years and freedom for
everyone to follow commercial activities at the open ports. Parkes
resisted pressure from British chambers of commerce for the abolition of
virtually all taxes on imports, since he regarded the proposal as most
unwise and open to manipulation; only coal, foreign clothing, and grain
were approved as duty free.[22] Thus Parkes had revealed a more flexible
and moderate side to his character than normally met the gaze. The new
tariff arrangements were approved on 25 June 1866.

The confrontation within Japan between the adherents and opponents
of the Bakufu came to a climax between 1866 and 1868. The two outstanding tozama han of Satsuma and Choshu formed an alliance in 1866
after a period of rivalry and suspicion between them. This alliance gave an
immense stimulus to the opposition to the shogunate. British policy was
to remain neutral in the internal struggle; explicit instructions to this

effect were sent to Parkes,[23] who saw the need to possess accurate intelligence on the fast-evolving situation; for this purpose two able junior
members of the British legation, Algernon Mitford (afterwards Lord
Redesdale) and Ernest Satow travelled extensively around Japan. Their
memoirs sometimes convey the impression that Britain was more sympathetic to Choshu and Satsuma and more antagonistic towards the
Bakufu than was the case in reality.[24] Parkes welcomed the choice of
Hitotsubashi Keiki as the new shogun upon the death of Iemochi in 1866;
he had obtained information from leading figures in Satsuma depicting
the previous shogunal regime in a poor light and he welcomed the re-
emergence of Keiki, whom he met in January 1867; it was agreed that
Japan would co-operate with the powers in carrying out a survey of port
facilities at Osaka and that a proclamation should be issued opening the
ports of Osaka and Hyogo on 1 January 1868.[25] Parkes was impressed
with Keiki's intelligence and seeming honesty and was inclined to support him, while perturbed at the actions of Russia and France, particularly
the latter. The French minister, Leon Roches, was sedulously working to
extend French power; France was giving economic and military assistance to the shogun.[26] Rivalry between Parkes and Roches therefore persisted. In true Victorian manner Parkes thought that Japan required a
dominating personality at the helm to prevent anarchy.[27]

In January 1868 the final brief but savage civil war started between
the Bakufu and its supporters on the one side, and the imperialist
forces, dominated by Satsuma and Choshu, on the other side. The western powers proclaimed neutrality in the struggle: originally the British
government had hoped for a compromise between the contending fac-
tions but it was now felt that an imperial victory had become unavoidable and that the Bakufu was moribund.[28] Harry Parkes considered
neutrality the only feasible policy, writing to the Foreign Office on
5 January 1868 that, 'there is always the danger of many civil passions
being let loose when once the sword is drawn, especially in a semi-
civilised country'.[29] More incidents of attacks on foreigners occurred,
including one onslaught by two ronin (wandering samurai) on Parkes
himself while he was journeying to the imperial palace to see the
emperor on 23 March 1868. Parkes reacted more calmly than might
have been anticipated. He left the question of punishment to the Japanese government but indicated that an imperial statement of condemnation might be issued; Parkes described the attack as more of an affront
to the emperor than to the British minister.[30] The civil war was quickly
over, culminating in a decisive victory for the imperial forces dominated
by Satsuma and Choshu. Sporadic resistance by supporters of the
Tokugawa continued, including bitter fighting in Aizu and Hokkaido,
where an attempt was made by Admiral Enomoto to hive off the northern island as an outpost of Tokugawa rule.[31] Enomoto surrendered in
1869 and was soon to serve the new Meiji government. Parkes welcomed the outcome and the opportunity for Japan to reform herself on a

basis of harmony and co-operation with the western powers. British policy towards the internal struggles, as laid down in London, called for neutrality and Parkes followed the policy loyally. The British Foreign Office wished to encourage the development of a Japanese middle class, which would hopefully connote stability and moderate politics.[32]

In China British trade flourished after the signature of the Nanking treaty and larger numbers of merchants and missionaries entered the newly opened ports. Sir John Davis, who succeeded Pottinger as superintendent of trade and governor of Hong Kong in 1844, accurately observed that, 'The vicinity of Shanghai to the Grand Canal gives it advantages which will make it the first of the 4 new Ports.'[33] Raw silk was being exported, about one quarter of the Indian opium production imported, and there was a growing demand for British cotton. British trade more than doubled in value from 1844 to 1845, rising from less than £1 m. to over £2.25 m.[34] Shanghai was in fact to develop within a relatively short period into the great metropolis of the Far East. Certain of the British who entered the treaty ports behaved in a high-handed and insolent manner towards the Chinese, causing Davis additional problems.[35] Trouble was experienced with one or two merchants, with missionaries, and with sailors. The ports of Ningpo and Foochow were disappointing for trade and Davis's successor, Sir George Bonham, thought that new ports should be found.[36] Palmerston felt that renewed efforts would have to be made to secure the opening of more ports. Pressure was growing in Britain for admission to the interior of China, the Manchester chamber of commerce being to the fore in pressing this aspect. Palmerston showed signs of exasperation with the Chinese, minuting on one occasion:

I clearly see that the Time is fast coming when we should be obliged to strike another Blow in China... These half civilized governments, such as those of China, Portugal, Spain, America require a Dressing every eight or ten years to keep them in order. Their Minds are too shallow to receive an Impression that will last longer than some such period, and warning is of little use. They care little for words and they must not only see the Stick but actually feel it on their Shoulders before they yield to that only argument which to them brings conviction, the *Argumentum Baculinum*.[37]

The new British superintendent of trade and governor of Hong Kong after Bonham was Dr John Bowring, a former radical MP and secretary of the Peace Society. Bowring was an admirer of the doctrines of Jeremy Bentham and was a personal friend of Richard Cobden. Financial embarrassment had compelled his resignation from Parliament; he had subsequently been appointed consul at Canton before becoming superintendent of trade and governor of Hong Kong. Despite Bowring's association with the peace movement, he became an enthusiastic advocate of extending Britain's informal empire in East and South-East Asia and did not hesitate to contemplate the use of force. Research based in part on Chinese records has modified the traditional view that Bowring came to consider the use of force because of the obduracy of the mandarins with whom he was dealing. Bowring was impetuous and peppery and wished to expand Britain's position as rapidly as he could.[38] The fundamental constituents of the situation, as twenty years previously, were that Britain wished to see China granting more concessions in facilitating trade and that China wanted to minimise foreign encroachment. The imperial government in Peking had other difficult problems to contend with, problems that were of a grave character in threatening the continuance of Ch'ing rule. The decline of the Ch'ing was graphically underlined by the cluster of rebellions that developed comprising the huge Taiping insurrection and the more localised risings of the Nien in the north-east and the Moslem rising in Kansu and the west. Of these the most serious was the Taiping rebellion. The Taiping movement differed from previous rebellions in Chinese history in standing not simply for the elimination of the Ch'ing dynasty but for the inculcation of the bizarre Taiping variety of Christianity in place of Confucianism, which had provided the cement of Chinese society for 2,000 years. The Taipings were led by Hung Hsiu-ch'uan, who came from the Hakka minority in Kwangsi province. Hung had been unsuccessful in his attempt to pass the first stage of the Confucian examinations and this personal reverse had the effect of at least partly disturbing his sanity. He was motivated by an intense hatred of the Ch'ing and all they stood for and inspired by a sense of personal mission to liquidate the Manchu 'devils and imps'. Deeply influenced by one of the early Protestant missionary tracts translated into Chinese and distributed on the China coast, Hung believed himself to be the younger brother of Jesus Christ sent by God to convert China to Christianity. The Taiping conception of Christianity was an egregious mixture of half-understood Christian ideas, of the cloudy thoughts of Hung and his co-leaders, and of traditional Chinese beliefs. The Taiping rebellion began around 1850 in the south-western province of Kwangsi and spread rapidly. By 1853 the Taipings had captured the former southern capital city of Nanking and established there the capital of the T'ai P'ing T'ien-kuo or 'Heavenly Kingdom of Great Peace'. The survival of the Ch'ing dynasty seemed doubtful.[39]

British attitudes to the Taipings varied considerably. British officials displayed interest in the rebellion in that it could assist Britain in putting pressure on the Peking government. Sir John Bowring, as he had now become, maintained that instability 'invites us to avail ourselves of the changes which are inevitable'.[40] It was possible that the Taipings might inflict military defeat on the Ch'ing forces and succeed to the 'mandate of heaven'. Officials mostly reserved judgement on the desirability of this outcome; scepticism was engendered by the weird character of Taiping ideology. Missionaries not surprisingly greeted the advent of the Taipings with enthusiasm, believing that their prayers had been answered and that China was about to cast off its ancient philosophy and embrace Christianity. Closer acquaintance with Taiping tenets and the growing divisions among the Taipings, following the bloody upheavals within the leadership in 1856, caused missionaries to regard them with developing animosity. Merchants hoped that the Taipings would encourage commerce but, as always, the hoped-for expansion of the China market was not to be justified by events.[41] Official British policy, as drawn up in London, decreed a cautious approach and a line of neutrality. Bowring felt that the success of the Taipings would connote 'the establishment of difficulties greater than we had to struggle before the Opium War'.[42] Bowring was imbued with a fervent sense of mission and wished to move swiftly. He wrote to the foreign secretary: 'Now at all events I *have* an end and an object, *to open China* and if you will support me, and I have such colleagues as the U.S. have now sent, we *will open* China. *Aye*! and with the keys of peace.'[43] Bowring's hopes were frustrated, however, for the Royal Navy was not in a position to supply more than limited aid and the Ch'ing authorities, despite the embarrassments caused by the prevalence of rebellion, would not concede what Bowring desired. He worked with some success to improve relations with the other treaty powers, with whom relations had been previously characterised by suspicion and hostility; these were now allayed, to some extent at least.[44]

Bowring wanted to see a resident British minister in Peking; consular access to local viceroys; the modification of the tariff; the legalisation of the opium trade; co-operation to combat piracy; and a clear system to deal with emigration. The outbreak of the Crimean war in 1854 precluded the adoption of a more vigorous policy by Britain. The next impetus to the advance of British interests was provided by the *Arrow* incident and its consequences.[45] The *Arrow* was a Chinese lorcha vessel under the command of a British national, Thomas Kennedy. On 8 October 1856, off an island in the river opposite the British factories at Canton, the *Arrow* was boarded by a number of Chinese police and twelve Chinese members of the crew were removed to a Chinese vessel. The *Arrow* was registered in Hong Kong but did not hold an up-to-date licence. The British flag was not flying and was not removed by the Chinese officials, as was alleged. The *Arrow* was evidently engaged in piracy. The British consul at Canton was Harry Parkes. Young, ambitious, and imbued with the determination to expand British interests in China and in the Far East generally,[46] he decided to seize the opportunity presented by the affront to British prestige in the *Arrow* incident and to demand an apology from the Chinese authorities. Parkes insisted on the return of the arrested seamen and was supported in the stand he had taken by Bowring. Parkes was involved in a scuffle with Chinese officials and adopted a tougher attitude in retaliation.[47] The Chinese were recalcitrant and Parkes maintained that a resolute approach was essential. At the end of October 1856 a British naval party took action in Canton and the residences of officials were bombarded. The crisis had escalated and, as Bowring observed, '...the question...has now assumed a character seriously involving all our present and future rela-

tions with China'.[48] The British government fully agreed with the
attitude adopted by Bowring and Parkes, although there was opposition
in the House of Commons and a formidable combination of Lord John
Russell, Cobden, Gladstone and Disraeli castigated Palmerston's policy.[49] The prime minister defended Bowring and Parkes with typical
zest but was defeated in the vote. Palmerston was unfair in his bitter
condemnation of the viceroy of Kwangtung, Yeh Ming-ch'en, for Yeh
was a loyal and efficient servant of his government and not the sadistic
barbarian described by Palmerston.[50] The British trading community in
China supported Bowring's conduct and his approach was endorsed in
parliament by Gregson, the chairman of the East India and China
Association.[51] After his defeat Palmerston appealed to the country in
one of the most personalised elections of the nineteenth century and
won a resounding victory.

In April 1857 Lord Elgin was appointed high commissioner to replace Bowring. Troops were sent to reinforce Elgin's mission and Elgin
was instructed to secure treaty revision. Napoleon III decided to co-
operate with Britain in compelling China to grant the required concessions and plans were drawn up for Anglo–French naval co-operation
on the China coast. At the end of December 1857, after a period of
fruitless discussion between Elgin, Gros (the French emissary) and Yeh,
military operations took place. The Anglo–French forces attacked Canton; Yeh Ming-ch'en was captured and sent to India, where he died
soon afterwards, after apparently starving himself to death.[52] The local
Chinese militia attempted to regain Canton without success. Anglo–
French forces assumed responsibility for the occupation of Canton; the
next objective was to coerce Peking,[53] where Elgin wished to see a British minister in residence, not simply to fulfil the long-standing aims of
British policy but to ensure more effective control over British nationals. The more Elgin saw of many British people and their attitudes to
the Chinese the less he liked them and the more disillusioned he
became. He remarked that, 'I have seen more to disgust me with my
fellow-countrymen than I saw during the whole course of my previous
life.'[54] The Ch'ing administration was still hostile to the appearance of
a British minister in Peking and for the present Kuei-liang, the principal
Chinese negotiator, persuaded Elgin to agree that this should be optional
in return for which he agreed that the Yangtze could be explored without awaiting treaty ratification.[55] Thomas F. Wade and the youthful
Horatio Nelson Lay were responsible for conducting the negotiations at
Tientsin and the treaty of Tientsin was signed on 26 June 1858. It was
agreed that a British diplomatic representative should reside in Peking;
ten new ports were opened on the China coast, including Nanking and
Hankow; foreign travel was permitted in the interior of China; the likin
tax (internal transit tax) on foreign imports was to be no higher than 2.5
per cent *ad valorem*; an indemnity was paid; foreign missionaries were
to be free to travel throughout China; and the opium trade was legalised. Lord Elgin emphasised the sense of responsibility that should be

demonstrated by British nationals in the wake of the latest stage in opening China. In an address to the British community in Shanghai he said:

Uninvited and by methods not always of the gentlest, we have broken down the barriers behind which these ancient nations sought to conceal from the world without, the mysteries, perhaps also, in the case of China at least, the rags and rottenness of their waning civilisations. Neither our own consciences nor the judgement of mankind will acquit us if, when we are asked to what use we have turned our opportunities, we can only say that we have filled our pockets from among the ruins we have found or made.[56]

The Foreign Office decided that Frederick Bruce, Elgin's younger brother, should take over the post of superintendent of trade. Bruce was ordered to proceed to Tientsin in a British warship and prepare for his first visit to Peking: he was advised not to tolerate equivocation.[57] He duly advanced with the naval expedition to encounter serious resistance from the Chinese forces. Fighting broke out off the mouth of the Peiho at Taku, below Tientsin, in June 1859. The Mongol military commander, Sengerinchin, had strengthened Taku with cannon and was unaware of the foreign emissaries' intended visit. They were not prepared for conflict, however, and the landing force became ignominiously caught in the mud. The Ch'ing court was heartened by this victory. When the news reached London Palmerston wrote to Russell, 'This is a disagreeable Event in China & we must in some way or other make the Chinese repent of the outrage . . . We might send a military-naval Force to attack & occupy Peking & drive the Emperor out of it & put our Plenipotentiaries into it. . .'[58] Bruce was told to obtain an apology from China and that Britain would now demand the right to appoint a minister based in Peking. Military and naval plans were co-ordinated with France. The forces would occupy Chusan, halt grain shipments, and set up bases on the Gulf of Pechihli.[59] Elgin was dispatched to China again in March 1860 to settle outstanding problems and to obtain a definitive solution.[60] He viewed his mission without enthusiasm.

An Anglo–French expeditionary force of nearly 20,000 men was dispatched. The Taku forts were quickly captured and at the end of August 1860 British and French troops entered Tientsin. Elgin relied on Harry Parkes to handle the negotiations,[61] but the impetuous Parkes and a group of British and French officials were captured in September 1860. They were maltreated and several were executed. Attempts were made to force Parkes into making concessions but he resisted the pressure and was released through the intercession of a discerning official. Elgin and Gros decided it was necessary to teach the Chinese a salutary lesson: an ultimatum was delivered demanding swift compliance with Anglo–French terms for monetary compensation to those who had been tortured or to the relatives of the survivors. If the Ch'ing government did not submit, the imperial palace would be burned. The summer palace was duly burned on 18 and 19 October 1860 in an act later regarded as one of peculiar cultural vandalism. In retrospect this is justified; at the time, however, Elgin believed he had no alternative.

On 23 October 1860 the convention of Peking was at last signed. The final negotiations were conducted by Elgin, Gros, and Prince Kung, the able young Manchu official now in the ascendancy at court.[62] China agreed to pay an indemnity of eight million taels to Britain and the same amount to France; Tientsin was opened to foreign trade; and the Kowloon peninsula opposite the island of Hong Kong was ceded to Britain. The allied forces left Peking on 8 November 1860. The events of 1857–60 in China had resulted in a major advance in the western presence and in the development of the treaty port system. The volume of trade was expanding and those responsible for the conduct of commerce growing in numbers.[63] The imperial maritime customs service had begun to function from the middle of the 1850s and was already discharging the wide range of activities for which it was responsible, including the collection of customs dues, the provision of modern harbour and navigation facilities and the building of lighthouses. Horatio Nelson Lay, son of one of the first British consuls, helped to direct the initial organisation of the customs service. Lay was too erratic and too concerned with advancing his own financial interests to survive and was dismissed in 1863.[64] He was succeeded by the man who did more than anyone else to establish and consolidate the maritime customs, Robert Hart. Hart's role will be considered further in the next chapter.

Finally, reference should be made to Sir John Bowring's visit to Bangkok and signature of the important treaty with Siam in 1855. The Singapore chamber of commerce had been active in the late 1840s and early 1850s in pressing for improved trade with Siam and had protested that the Burney treaty of 1826 had been violated.[65] James Brooke was sent to Bangkok in 1850 but his mission was unsuccessful; Brooke bitterly protested at not being formally received at the Siamese court.[66] In 1854 the Foreign Office decided that Bowring should visit Siam (and Japan and Cochin-China if possible) and conclude a commercial treaty.[67] Bowring was accompanied by Harry Parkes and it would appear that Parkes was largely responsible for the actual negotiations, although Bowring made the better impression on the Siamese. In contrast to Brooke's experiences, Bowring's mission was highly successful. The discussions were conducted in a cordial atmosphere; the Siamese authorities were well aware of British power and deduced that it was in Siam's interests to follow a more flexible policy than China had pursued in the previous twenty years. The Bowring treaty inaugurated a new system of export and import duties, marked the development of the rice trade, and included the appointment of a British consul with the creation of extraterritoriality.[68] The treaty constituted the beginning of the rapid commercial development of Siam. The economic and political repercussions for Siam have been termed 'revolutionary'.[69] Siam's chances of retaining independence amidst the threat of occidental imperialism were enhanced by the subtle policy of limited concession accepted by King

Mongkut and his ministers.[70] No significant change to the Burney treaty was made with regard to the Malay states.

Thus between 1853 and 1868 Britain made a major contribution to the process of prising open Japan and China. In both countries the treaty port system was flourishing by 1868, if inevitably more slowly in Japan, and Britain was playing a more dynamic part than any other power in advancing occidental imperialism in East Asia.

Chapter 3

The development of formal and informal empire, 1868–1898

The period after 1868 saw the continued expansion of Britain's role in China and the British contribution to the developing modernisation of Japan. Informal empire therefore extended itself. This period was equally significant in the growth of formal empire in South-East Asia, notably in Malaya and Burma. Since the latter development is more dramatic in affecting British power in the Far East, it will be considered first. It used to be maintained that the quickening rate of imperial acquisition in the 1870s and 1880s originated, in part at least, in the new spirit of imperialism deriving some of its impetus from the revivified faith in the civilising mission of the British Empire proclaimed by Disraeli and applied by his administration between 1874 and 1880. This view has been discredited following the investigation of the archives and private papers of those responsible for policy formulation. It is clear that no sharp break in policy-making occurred in the 1870s and that substantial continuity can be discerned in the policies of the Gladstone and Disraeli governments. In Malaya, west Africa and the southern Pacific decisions pointing towards the acquisition of territories were effectively taken by Gladstone's colonial secretary, Lord Kimberley, and implemented under his Conservative successor, Lord Carnarvon. More important is the fact that vital decisions in precipitating or determining situations were taken by officials in the regions concerned, often acting independently. Much initiative rested with the man on the spot.[1]

In 1867 the Straits Settlements ceased to be administered by the government of India: instead administrative control passed to the Colonial Office. Pressure for this change had been exerted for some years on the grounds that Calcutta was not genuinely interested in the affairs of such insignificant places as Singapore, Malacca, and Penang; a more direct link with London was essential to secure appropriate concern in the well-being of the Settlements.[2] Ironically the last Indian governor, Colonel Orfeur Cavenagh, was personally agreeable and popular; the first Colonial Office governor, Sir Harry Ord, was arrogant and discourteous.[3] When Ord was appointed in 1868, he was instructed not to become involved in relations with the Dutch, since this was the province of the Foreign Office. In general terms Ord was told that: 'Although therefore circumstances may not infrequently arise in which you may be called to act absolutely on your own judgement, yet it is generally undesirable that you should enter into formal negotiations with native princes . . . except in pursuance of an object or a policy approved of by HM's Government.'[4] The problem for the administration in Malaya was to ensure the maintenance of British interests without intervening unduly in the domestic affairs of the native states. A complicating factor of some delicacy involved Britain's relations with Siam. The northern Malayan states of Kedah, Kelantan, and Trengganu were in Siam's sphere of interest; they sent the *bunga mas* to Bangkok, signifying acceptance of Siamese superiority. The precise extent of Siamese influence was unclear and disputes were certain to occur in the future, as they had done in the past. The wider background to developments in Malaya and Burma is related to the increasing manifestations of European imperialism in the Far East. Russia had expanded rapidly in Central Asia, sweeping aside the decadent khanates of the area. In addition, Russia had taken over huge areas in the Amur and Ussuri regions of eastern Siberia. China had previously claimed to control the areas concerned; the numerous other challenges faced by the Ch'ing government in the 1850s meant that there was no alternative to acquiescing reluctantly in Russia's annexation of the Amur and Ussuri regions under the treaties signed in 1858 and 1860. The 'great game' of British and Russian rivalry was principally played on the outer borders of the Indian empire but British alarm at Russian designs would before long extend to China.[5] Of more direct impact in South-East Asia was the swift growth of French ambitions. France had created a protectorate in Cambodia in 1867 and was anxious to extend this further.[6] A rumour of possible German interest in Malaya was to have effect on the mind of Lord Kimberley at one vital point in 1873.[7]

The Malay states were mostly weak in the early 1870s with incompetent and corrupt administrations. Johore and Kedah enjoyed reasonably efficient governments and these were states adjacent to the British settlements and accordingly subject to greater British influence.[8] Johore was ruled by Temenggong Abu-Bakar, who had received a knighthood in 1866. Trengganu was ruled effectively by Sultan Omar. Pahang was seriously weakened by civil strife. The British colonial administration was chiefly concerned with the western states of Perak, Selangor, and Sungei Ujong; these areas were important for tin. The outstanding difficulties involved divisions among the Chinese tin-miners and the dynastic quarrels among the Malay royal houses.[9] The Chinese miners were loyal to competing secret societies and murderous confrontations between them not infrequently occurred. The struggles within Malay royal houses could sometimes prove equally violent and lead to grave disorder. Both problems were prominent in Perak and Selangor in the early 1870s. The governor, Ord, was on leave in Britain when the crisis broke. His deputy, Colonel Archibald Anson, grappled with the complexities, although neither Anson nor the Colonial Office in London understood properly the nature of the situation facing them.[10]

The Selangor incident in June 1871 occurred when an armed clash

Detached by Siam
from Kedah, 1892

PERLIS
1909

SIAM
(THAILAND)

KEDAH
1909

PROVINCE
WELLESLEY
1800

PENANG
1786

PERAK
1874

KELANTAN
1909

TRENGGANU 1909

Kedah, Perlis, Kelantan,
and Trengganu trans-
ferred from Siamese to
British Suzerainty, 1909
(Treaty of Bangkok).

J.W.W.Birch, Resident
of Pahang murdered at
Pasir Salak, 2 Nov. 1875

Peak River

Kuala Lipis

PAHANG
1888

Raub

Kuantan

Pahang River

SELANGOR
1874

Pekan

Kuala
Lumpur

JELEBU
1886

Rompin River

Sungei
Ujong
1874

NEGRI
SEMBILAN
1889

Endau

Rembau
1887

Tinggi
Is.

NANING

Segamat

Malacca

Muar

Kluang

▦ Straits Settlements

▨ Federated Malay States (1896)

▥ Unfederated Malay States

JOHORE
1885

Batu Pahat

Kota
Tinggi

0 ——— 100 miles
0 ——— 200 km

SINGAPORE
1819

Map 4. British intervention in Malaya 1874–1909

took place between a Singapore police party and pirates, following an
attack on a Perak junk. The police action escalated because it was connected with rivalry in the ruling house of Selangor. Anson approved

action by the Royal Navy to uphold British authority in the skirmishes that developed. The British then moved to support one side in the civil war. Against a muddled and confused background, Britain took forward action.[11] Lord Kimberley, the colonial secretary, did not appreciate the position. From the initial report he received from Anson, he believed it had been competently handled. Kimberley did not favour a British advance in Selangor but significantly minuted that measures might be required.[12] It took the Colonial Office a further year to piece together the different elements at work in the western states.[13] A dispute over the succession to the sultanate developed in Perak; there was fighting among Chinese miners in Larut; and civil war in Selangor with the danger of this affecting Sungei Ujong. Sir Harry Ord had returned from sick leave and determined to act firmly, since it was becoming clear that Britain would have to take important decisions on the future relationship between British representatives and the sultanate. The lieutenant-governor of Penang, George Campbell, who had served in India, proposed that the Indian system of appointing 'residents' should be adopted in Malaya.[14] Lord Kimberley was still reluctant to intervene decisively but in the summer of 1873 he changed his mind. The reasons for the change were the seriousness of the war in Larut; discreet pressure from firms with interests in Selangor; and the danger of another foreign power intervening there.[15] British capitalists interested in the Selangor Tin Company conveyed concern over unrest in Malaya.[16] Kimberley was faced with a number of problems simultaneously, therefore, and present in his mind also was apprehension over the growing interest in South-East Asia displayed by France and the United States, with rumours of German and Italian activity, too.[17] Kimberley reflected on matters and wrote to the prime minister, Gladstone, on 10 September 1873:

The condition of the Malay Peninsula is becoming very serious. It is the old story of misgovernment of Asiatic States. This might go on without any very serious consequences except the stoppage of trade were it not that European and Chinese capitalists stimulated by the great riches in tin mines which exist in some of the Malay States are suggesting to the native Princes that they should seek the aid of Europeans ... We are the paramount power in the Peninsula.[18]

Kimberley decided that the new forward policy should be implemented by the new governor, Sir Andrew Clarke. Before Clarke reached Malaya, the retiring governor, Sir Harry Ord, had become involved in the internal struggles in Perak, in effect repeating the pattern of creeping intervention followed by Anson in Selangor two years earlier.[19] Sir Andrew Clarke assumed office on 3 November 1873. Kimberley told Clarke to investigate the situation in the various states and 'I should wish you especially to consider whether it would be advisable to appoint a British officer to reside in any of the [Malay] states.'[20] Kimberley expected Clarke to report back carefully before any decisions were made. Clarke's ideas were different and afford an excellent example of the independent initiative taken by the man on the spot. In a public lecture given some years later Clarke stated:

My instructions were simple. The Colonial Office was thoroughly dissatisfied with the state of affairs in the Peninsula. I was to make it the subject of careful inquiry, and report my views as soon as possible. I fear that in some quarters there lurks a belief in the efficacy of reports . . . It was necessary to act in the first place and to report afterwards. . .[21]

Clarke added that the Malay chiefs responded to the promise of greater stability and prosperity.

Lord Carnarvon took over from Lord Kimberley as colonial secretary with the formation of Disraeli's government in 1874. He regarded the situation in Malaya as less challenging than the problems he faced in the Gold Coast and Fiji.[22] Sir Andrew Clarke immediately grasped the gravity of the problem in Perak on his arrival in Malaya. Piracy had reached disturbing proportions off the coast of Larut. W. H. M. Read, one of the leading merchants, arranged a visit to Singapore by the pretender to the Perak sultanate and Clarke intervened decisively, establishing contact with the disputatious Chinese leaders in Larut as well as with Perak, where Clarke recognised Abdu'llah as sultan and utilised the scheme of appointing residents.[23] Clarke rather than the Colonial Office was determining the rate of progress. Carnarvon defended Clarke's actions in the House of Lords but privately warned Clarke to be cautious: the resident system was experimental.[24] Clarke, however, authorised the appointment of residents in Perak and Selangor on 4 September 1874, his last significant act before handing over to his successor, Sir William Jervois. Jervois was impulsive and believed in a policy of more rapid advance; he felt that Perak should be annexed[25] and put forward his views in a letter to Carnarvon:

It appears to me that the Residential system which implies advice as distinguished from control, is not calculated to meet the requirements either present or future of the case. The Sultan and Rajahs . . . are our obstacles to any just and enlightened system of government . . . we should, as opportunity offers, take possession of these States . . . This may be done without shedding blood and without opposition from the people, except Sultans and Rajahs who profit by the present state of things.[26]

Carnarvon, although shaken, was not at first unsympathetic; however, he had more urgent business to deal with elsewhere. Lord Salisbury, the secretary of state for India, was opposed to annexation in Malaya because of the unsettling effects on relations with other states, notably Burma, Siam, and China.[27] Jervois embarked on expansionist measures without informing Carnarvon; he was working to take over Perak.[28] Carnarvon at once instructed him, via the telegraph, not to advance further: time was needed for the resident system to work and events in Burma and China necessitated a careful policy.[29] Just at this point, news was received of the murder on 2 November 1875 of James Birch, the resident in Perak, who had shown no tact or sense in the way in which he had approached the problem of establishing the resident system.[30] The cabinet reluctantly approved military action but hoped that the scale of operations could be controlled. Carnarvon was disturbed at Jervois's idea on the action required but, as it turned out, the military intervention proved relatively inexpensive and efficacious. As W.D. McIntyre has written, the activities of both Clarke and Jervois illustrate the repercussions of the man on the spot pursuing real forward policies which embarrassed London. Carnarvon appointed residents in three states – Perak, Selangor, and Sungei Ujong; he did not wish to proceed beyond this point but appreciated that intervention usually led to more intervention subsequently.[31]

In the twenty years following the important developments of 1872–75 the resident system was established on a more secure foundation. The resident was an adviser to the ruler and it was stipulated by the governor in 1878 that if a resident overstepped the mark and began to exercise authority then he would be responsible for the ensuing conflict of authority.[32] In Perak, Hugh Low worked sedulously and skilfully to establish the position of resident. He showed enterprise in handling the chiefs, ensuring that they had administrative appointments and a proportion of government revenue collected. Low set up a State Council comprising the sultan, the resident, the leading Malay chiefs, and two or three prominent Chinese businessmen. State legislation was passed by the Council and all fundamental matters involving revenue and appointments were brought before it. Courts of justice were set up with European magistrates presiding.[33] Residents concentrated, in the early years, on visiting the country and reporting to the governor in Singapore. Considerable freedom of decision was possessed by each resident and there was no tight centralisation. Pahang became a protected state in 1888; it took some time to secure effective law and order. In 1895 the Minangkabau states merged to constitute the confederation of Negri Sembilan and a British resident was appointed. Sir Frederick Weld became governor in 1880. He was a man of proconsular outlook and was dominated by a profound belief in the potentialities of Malaya, given a period of stable government.[34] He believed that Malaya could become one of the most important parts of the British Empire; British authority should gradually be extended in Malaya to develop its economic resources and to protect it from aggressive foreign powers – Weld had a minor obsession regarding the prevalence of Russian ships in Malayan waters in 1880–81.[35] France remained the main foreign menace in South-East Asia. The fast-expanding French interest in Indo-China, giving rise to the Sino-French war of 1883–85 and Bismarck's new interest in acquiring colonies stimulated British advance, including the growing British role in Pahang in 1885–86.[36] British economic interests were vocal in urging expansion in Pahang.[37]

The creation of the Federated Malay States in the mid-1890s provided another example of decisions having been taken by the responsible ministers in one British government and of these being implemented by their successors. The colonial secretary in Gladstone's fourth government and in Rosebery's administration was the Marquis of Ripon, with Sydney Buxton as parliamentary under-secretary. Frank Swettenham, the most assertive rising official in Malaya, wished to see the process of British control in Malaya expanded.[38] Charles Lucas, an able official in the Colonial Office, was of the same opinion. Between them they accumulated sufficient evidence to convince the political heads of the Colonial Office of the desirability of the federal scheme; it was necessary for administrative, political, economic, and strategic reasons.[39] It was imperative that the Malay rulers affected should accept the new arrangement voluntarily and without acrimony. Annexation was impossible and undesirable; the new federal scheme would be a sensible half-way house between the existing freedom and complete centralisation. Ripon and Buxton decided that the federal plan should be adopted. At this juncture the Liberals left office, in 1895, and Lord Salisbury formed his third government with Joseph Chamberlain at the Colonial Office. Chamberlain presided over the formal adoption of the plan. Swettenham was entrusted with the task of persuading the sultans concerned to accept federation and he employed all his not inconsiderable talents to convince the sultans, occasionally by sleight of hand, that they would not lose by the transition and that a more efficient form of government would be in the interests of everybody.[40] The sultans of Perak and Selangor accepted at once and the sultan of Pahang after brief reflection. As Eunice Thio has observed, the speed with which the consent of rulers was secured is analogous to Sir Andrew Clarke's action at Pangkor in 1874 and Sir Harold MacMichael's swift establishment of the Malayan Union in 1945.[41] Swettenham's success did much to advance his reputation but Sir Andrew Clarke mordantly commented that the sultans would accept anything the British required of them.[42]

The Federated Malay States officially came into existence in 1896: the states concerned were Perak, Selangor, Pahang, and Negri Sembilan. The scheme was anomalous; the sultan of each state retained sovereignty within the state and external sovereignty was possessed by the Malay rulers. The governor of the Straits Settlements was given the title of high commissioner in his dealings with the Malay states. A resident-general was appointed with the function of maintaining contact with the Malay rulers and with the residents, to be the channel of contact between the resident and the governor and subject to the high commissioner. The Colonial Office hoped that the four Malay states would ultimately comprise separate districts of a single British protectorate with homogeneous administration, treasury and legislature.[43] Swettenham was appointed resident-general to see the new structure off the ground. To glance ahead, in 1897 the Anglo-Siamese convention was signed under which Siam promised not to cede territory in the Siamese northern states or to grant concessions in these areas without discussion with Britain.[44] Britain was anxious at the vague nature of Siamese jurisdiction over the four northern states; Siamese authority in Kelantan and Trengganu was essentially nominal. In 1899 Britain reached agreement with Siam that Kelantan and Trengganu were under the authority of Siam, that Siamese advisers would be appointed, and that concessions to foreign powers were not to be made without Siamese approval. Agreement over Kedah and Perlis was reached in 1905. British policy then changed, however, partly because of the development of German interests in Malaya.[45] It was decided to obtain withdrawal of Siamese claims so as to consolidate the imperial frontier. The northern Malay states of Kedah, Perlis, Kelantan, and Trengganu were brought under British rule as a result of the treaty signed by Britain and Siam in 1909, under which Siam relinquished her rights in the states. The four states of Kedah, Perlis, Kelantan, and Trengganu constituted the Unfederated Malay States with the addition of Johore. Johore had always been in a distinct position, having experienced a close relationship with Britain since 1819. Difficulties had been encountered with the young sultan of Johore at the beginning of the twentieth century, when he wished to follow a more independent policy after Johore had been given a constitution in 1895 with a council of ministers and a council of state. An executive council was set up in 1912 and in 1914 the sultan of Johore accepted a general adviser; British control was consolidated.[46] Each of the Unfederated Malay States had a British adviser, who expected to be consulted by the ruler on all matters of significance. Malaya continued to be divided, somewhat untidily, into the British colony of the Straits Settlements, the Federated Malay States, and the Unfederated Malay States, down to the start of the Pacific war.[47]

In Borneo, the second Raja Brooke, Charles Johnson, took power in Sarawak in succession to his uncle in 1868. The size of the territory had been extended during the 1850s and 1860s. The British government was worried at the emerging international rivalry in Borneo, with Spain and the Netherlands participating in a struggle for influence and with the possibility of other powers becoming active. Concession hunters, including the egregious Austro-Hungarian consul in Hong Kong, Baron von Overbeck, complicated the scene further. The British North Borneo Company was established in 1881 with rights prescribed by the British parliament: the company could not dispose of its interests without the government's approval and the government would supervise contacts with foreign powers.[48] Rivalry grew between Sarawak and the North Borneo Company for control over the possessions of the weak sultanate of Brunei. In the light of the French progress in Indo-China and of Germany's takeover of part of New Guinea and of the Caroline Islands, Britain declared North Borneo and Sarawak to be protected areas and soon afterwards agreements were concluded with the sultan of Brunei and Raja Charles Brooke.[49]

In Burma the effect of British rule in Lower Burma was to break down traditionalism and to encourage the growth of an economy based on wage labour and money. The adoption of the British-Indian court system removed some of the crude features of Burmese justice at the cost of introducing a complex system with corruption in the lower levels.[50] British officials endeavoured to improve the educational system, incorporating teaching in western subjects. Buddhism proved resilient, despite the developing activities of missionaries.[51] In Upper Burma King Mindon Min (1852–78) refused formally to recognise the British occupation of Lower Burma and hoped that the lost territory would be restored to him. Mindon introduced administrative reforms and dispatched envoys to build up the prestige of Burma. Tax reforms were decreed in an attempt to put the finances of the state on a more secure footing and to eliminate corruption. Relations between Mindon and the British were respectful but in the circumstances could not be close. Mindon appointed foreign advisers to assist his government and to act as a form of limited counter-weight to British pressure. Burma was caught in Anglo-French rivalry, the focal point being the wish to gain access to Yunnan province in south-western China, as a means of expanding commerce and of erecting political influence. The French approach was through the Mekong and Red River valleys; the British approach would be via the Irrawaddy valley.[52] The British authorities in Rangoon believed that future trade prospects between Burma and China were encouraging and they desired a thorough survey of south-eastern China.[53] King Mindon u.ed to induce France to intervene in Burma without success. As the 1870s progressed, British policy towards Burma became more avaricious. A new survey of the route from Bhamo to China was carried out in 1874; A. R. Margary, the British representative, was travelling to meet Colonel Horace Brown, the leader of the expedition, when he was murdered on 21 February 1875 in the Kachin country near the Chinese border. The Chinese action was taken to fulfil orders that Margary should not be permitted to travel through Yunnan. Colonel Brown narrowly escaped massacre at the hands of the Chinese. The Burma government in Mandalay was in no way to blame and acted correctly throughout.[54] In the context of British relations with China, the Margary affair led to the Chefoo convention of 1876, connoting the extension of the treaty port system; this aspect will be considered below.

In September 1878 King Mindon died without having made arrangements for a smooth transfer. It would seem that his choice as successor was the Nynungyan prince but the principal queen, Sinpyumashin, seized power in a *coup* and Prince Thibaw was chosen by the triumphant clique as the new king because of his pliable qualities.[55] Many opponents of the new regime were massacred in February 1879. Nynungyan and a brother fled to the British to escape death and British officials contemplated supporting him; Lord Lytton, the viceroy of India, was in favour of a forward policy but was restrained by the other problems he was handling in Calcutta, and preoccupied with the war in Afghanistan.[56] The government in London was opposed to aggressive moves, the prime minister, Lord Beaconsfield, minuting on 31 March 1879, 'I can conceive nothing more unwise at this moment, than an ultimatum to the King of Burma.'[57] The British residency in Mandalay was closed in September 1879, owing to the threat to the staff as relations deteriorated. In the final stages of Thibaw's reign in the 1880s the calibre of administration in Upper Burma worsened markedly and law and order largely broke down. The third war between Britain and Burma was occasioned by an exorbitant fine levied on the Bombay-Burmah Trading Corporation.

However, basic to the fast evolving situation was British weariness at the incompetence and bloodshed of King Thibaw's rule and a belief that Britain had no time to lose in consolidating her position in Burma when France was rapidly extending her role in Indo-China.[58] French dominance had grown from Cochin-China to envelop Annam and Tongking to the north and then Laos. The left bank of the Mekong river constituted the eastern frontier of Shan states, which rendered tribute to Burma[59] and the Burmese government was actively seeking to draw France into Burma: a treaty was signed in January 1885. The French consul, Haas, arrived in Mandalay on 1 June 1885. He immediately negotiated a railway concession for a line from Mandalay to Toungoo and signed an agreement providing for the setting up of a state bank for Burma. The Nynungyan prince had died early in 1885 and there was no other member of the royal family suitable from the British viewpoint to replace Thibaw. Consul Haas had exceeded his instructions and the Ferry government was following a more cautious approach when it fell in March 1885.[60] British officials in Rangoon entertained doubts about annexing Upper Burma because of the subsequent difficulties sure to be encountered in securing acceptance of alien rule. British merchants supported annexation, for this would open up the commercial prospects of Burma and eradicate the French menace. The viceroy and the Salisbury government in London decided upon annexation unless Burma accepted a list of demands, including arbitration on the fine imposed on the British company, the appointment of a British resident at Mandalay, and British control of Burmese foreign policy. King Thibaw's court objected to the last demand, after returning a conciliatory reply on the first two. British troops crossed into Upper Burma in November 1885 and swiftly captured Mandalay and other cities. Thibaw and others from the royal court were arrested and sent to India. Burma was fully annexed to the British Empire and for administrative purposes was governed until 1935 from Calcutta and Delhi.

Siam became a focal point for Anglo-French tension in the last quarter of the nineteenth century, at one stage appearing to threaten war between Britain and France. The French control of Cochin-China and the British presence in Burma meant that Siam was surrounded by competing imperialist powers. Under the kings Mongkut and Chulalongkorn (1851–1910) a shrewd policy of maintaining Siamese autonomy was pursued and in earlier years of expanding the geographical limits of Siam.[61] Britain and France feared that Siam could fall under the domination of the opposing power. There was a powerful motive, therefore, for Britain to settle outstanding issues with Siam, notably frontier demarcation, and in 1889 the Ney Elias commission was appointed to secure the latter objective.[62] Also in 1889 France proposed that Siam should be regarded as a buffer state.[63] Lord Salisbury broadly welcomed the approach and advo-

cated a settlement of Siam's borders on a basis of discussion with the
government in Bangkok. France did not reply and instead dispatched an
emissary, Pavie, as resident minister at Bangkok. French political and
commercial activities were developed.[64] The French foreign minister,
Waddington, asked Salisbury in February 1892 to accept that the upper
Mekong should be the dividing line between British and French interests.
Salisbury rejected the proposal, observing that this would involve an
appreciable extension of French influence. The Salisbury government fell
in 1892 and Lord Rosebery returned to the Foreign Office in Gladstone's
last government. Rosebery emphasised that Britain would adhere to the
territorial rights and interests inherited from the defunct Burmese monarchy.[65] Waddington claimed that Vietnam possessed the land on the left
bank of the Mekong and that the Siamese attitude was mistaken. The
French government decided to assert French power and called upon Siam
to recognise the French claim to the areas affected on the Lower Mekong.
Military measures were authorised in Paris. Siam appealed for British aid;
Rosebery did not wish to exacerbate matters and pursued a conciliatory
policy. However, the French activities on the Mekong provoked a series
of border clashes with the Siamese.[66]

Two Royal Navy ships were ordered to Bangkok in April 1893 to lend
encouragement to the British community there. Three French gunboats
were also sent. The Siamese government ignored Rosebery's advice and
shots were fired at the French vessels. France pressed for the cession of
the strategic area of Luang Prabang between Siam and Laos, and an
indemnity. Britain was deeply disturbed that France would expand and
that French territory would share a common border with Burma. France
gave assurances, in response to representations from Rosebery, that if
Siam complied with French demands a buffer state would be created to
prevent conflict between Britain and France. Rosebery counselled Siamese acceptance and Siam submitted in October 1893.[67] The attempt to
define the border area foundered after a bitter clash between the British
and French emissaries, J. G. Scott and Pavie. Negotiations took place in
June 1895, as a result of which France agreed to guarantee the independence of the Menam valley in return for Britain withdrawing her claims
to land east of the Mekong. The agreement was signed in January 1896;
Britain and France undertook not to establish dominance of Siam.[68] The
Anglo-French *entente* of 1904 finally terminated the quarrel over Siam.

In China the Ch'ing government succeeded in defeating the series of rebellions that confronted it during the middle decades of the nineteenth
century. The defeats were attributable as much to the defects in leadership
among the Taipings and the Niens and the absence of co-ordination and
co-operation between the rebels, as to the work of the government. This
is not to denigrate the arduous activities of the principal servants of the
government responsible for rallying resistance, in particular Tseng Kuo-
fan and Li Hung-chang. Tseng and Li reinvigorated civil and military
authority. The period from the early 1860s to the mid-1870s is known as

the Tung-chih restoration, taking its name from the reign title of the boy emperor. It was one of the evanescent phases of recovery which had occurred previously in the declining years of a dynasty: a temporary revival, holding out the tantalising prospect of a return to the days of glory, of which Mary Wright has written eloquently and brilliantly.[69] It has been observed by Philip Kuhn that the extent of the restoration was less impressive than Mary Wright maintained.[70] However, the vigour of government was briefly established again. Presiding over the government was Yehonala, better known as the dowager empress Tz'u-hsi, who had been the favourite concubine of the Hsien-feng emperor. Tz'u-hsi was possessed of far more intelligence and guile than the average concubine; she soon built up her power and established herself as the principal source of authority under two boy emperors (Tung-chih, 1862–74, and Kuang-hsu, 1876–1908). She was reactionary by inclination and did not understand the challenge of the west and the demands that the growing occidental incursions would make on China. The most important officials in the government were the Manchu, Prince Kung, Tseng Kuo-fan, and Li Hung-chang. Prince Kung was indolent but capable; he was out-manoeuvred by Tz'u-hsi in a power struggle and he was not as important after 1865 as he had been before. Tseng Kuo-fan enjoyed great prestige until his death in 1872. Li Hung-chang was most significant as the trusted adviser of Tz'u-hsi from the early 1870s until his death in 1901. Li was highly intelligent and corrupt. He pandered to the prejudices of Tz'u-hsi and did not fulfil the high ideals of his mentor, Tseng. He supported the policy of 'self-strengthening', connoting the adoption of a combination of traditional Confucian precepts and of western knowledge. The basic aim was for China to develop its strength through the implementation of western technology: the west would ultimately be rebuffed through the fusion of Confucian values with western weapons.[71]

The growth of the British community in the developing treaty ports of China raised the central issue of the relationship between the official representatives of the British government and the variety of British nationals working on the China coast. The British government wished to see trade flourish and wanted to secure the best conditions to promote this objective. At the same time British ministers and officials did not see themselves as being in any sense rubberstamps for the frequently excessive demands of merchants,[72] while the merchant community desired maximum freedom to pursue commercial objectives and viewed the Foreign Office as inept and temporising.[73] Frederick Bruce, the younger brother of Lord Elgin and responsible as minister in the aftermath of the treaty settlement of 1858–60, believed strongly that the British aim should be to encourage happy relations with the Chinese authorities and people.[74] British policy-makers were not sanguine over the size of the trade that was likely to develop in China and believed that merchants exaggerated what could be gained. The China trade was not particularly lucrative in the 1860s and the proportion of British trade with China as a proportion of total British trade had declined between 1800 and 1860; in 1800 British imports and exports to and from China amounted to 10 per cent and 4 per cent respectively as proportions of the total British import-export trade. In the 1860s the proportion was half of what it had been at the start of the century.[75] By 1869 the total China trade was worth between £30 m. and £40 m.; out of the global British export figure of £70 m., approximately £5 m. went to China.[76] Lord Clarendon, foreign secretary in Gladstone's first government in 1868, stated clearly that it was the joint responsibility of Britain and China to minimise problems and to pursue conciliatory methods in settling the differences that existed.[77] Sir Rutherford Alcock, the minister in Peking, followed Clarendon's approach and experienced bitter censure from commercial circles. The latter were deeply hostile to the Alcock convention of 1869, maintaining that insufficient advances had been made. A similar, if less strident view was taken of the Chefoo convention, signed in 1876 following the murder of A. R. Margary on the Yunnan-Burma border. The convention provided for the opening of four other ports and of six ports of call on the Yangtze; an indemnity was also to be paid. Because of the merchant antagonism, Britain did not formally ratify the convention; in the words of Nathan Pelcovits, it was allowed silently to come into effect, except for two provisions concerning likin taxes on opium by the Imperial Maritime Customs and a clause stipulating foreign settlements as the area of likin exemption.[78]

British exports to China averaged as follows between 1869 and 1892: 1869–72 £9.35 m.; 1873–76 £8.22 m.; 1877–80 £7.74 m.; 1881–84 £7.93 m.; 1885–88 £8.57 m.; 1889–92 £8.23 m. Cotton goods exported to China averaged slightly over £5 m.[79] Thus trade remained fairly constant and there was no significant expansion. The foreign population of the treaty ports in 1879 was 3,814 and 351 firms were in business there. Of the foreign merchants, 1,953 were British, the next highest contingents being Americans and Germans. Of the firms, 220 were British with Germans and Americans a considerable distance behind.[80] Of British firms the most prominent were Jardine's and Butterfield's, both of which dominated commerce and shipping. The Hong Kong and Shanghai Banking Corporation was set up in 1867 and was soon to develop a leading role in banking activities and a close relationship with the British government in the late nineteenth and early twentieth centuries. In 1880 the Hong Kong and Shanghai Bank was responsible for floating three Chinese imperial loans.[81] In 1889 the China Association was formed with the purpose of creating greater unity of interest and response among those concerned in trade with China and Japan. William Keswick, a redoubtable figure in British commerce, was elected chairman and R. S. Gundry became honorary secretary.[82] The China Association functioned as a vocal pressure group but without having as much overall impact on the Foreign Office as had been hoped originally.

The attitude of the Foreign Office towards commercial prospects in China was that British firms should seize the opportunities that existed but that British diplomats should not become directly or personally involved in promoting particular projects. As the minister in Peking, Sir Nicholas O'Connor, wrote in 1886, it was not appropriate to 'tout for contracts for your own countrymen'.[83] During the 1880s the Foreign Office became more alarmed at the threat of foreign competition in China, especially of German competition. In 1885–86 modifications were made in British policy by Lord Salisbury and endorsed by his successor, Lord Rosebery. Salisbury told O'Connor that, 'In cases where foreign representatives interfere to the detriment of British commercial interests, you are at liberty to give the latter your support.'[84] Rosebery concurred with Salisbury's instruction but emphasised, however, that the British government could not support projects unless satisfied of their soundness or practicability.[85] O'Connor did not wish to approach the Chinese government personally over commercial or industrial concessions and instead he extended advice informally to British firms as to the best methods of securing concessions. The alarm felt by the Foreign Office in 1886 over foreign competition was exaggerated but the underlying trends were not encouraging for future developments.

The Imperial Maritime Customs service developed rapidly from the mid-1850s and was largely directed, at its higher levels, by British nationals. The Customs service represented admirably the hybrid concept of privileged western participation in the modernisation of China referred to by J. K. Fairbank.[86] Staffed by occidentals and Chinese and with an ideal of efficient common service in the interests of China successfully inculcated, the Customs service was shaped and developed largely through the tenacity and dedication of Robert Hart, who had begun his long career in China in the British consular service. He came to be the personification of the integrity for which the Maritime Customs stood. In his early years in China he had a Chinese concubine by whom he had three children; he delegated the task of supervising their education to his friend and colleague, John Campbell, the London agent of the Customs.[87] Hart later married Julia Bredon and became one of the most respected westerners in China. He always felt concern for the advancement of British interests and his voluminous correspondence contains criticism of the incompetence or lethargy of British ministers and merchants; some of the criticism was justified but allowance has to be made on occasion for personal prejudice. Hart had a profound sense of loyalty and obligation to the Chinese government and he conceived of his role as bridging two cultures and civilisations in the wider interests of the Chinese people. It must be added that Hart did not neglect his own interests and had about £80,000 in London, invested privately by the Bank of England in various stock.[88] Hart was keenly involved in all matters relating to the Maritime Customs; he made a tour of each of the growing number of treaty ports every summer.[89] In his attitude to the western relationship with China, Hart advocated a mixture of firmness and kindness. In a letter to Campbell in August 1873 he wrote:

You have to choose between coercion and assistance. If you decide to assist China to progress, you have again to choose between active assistance and non-interference. As far as we can see, the most likely plan to secure success is to pursue a policy made up of *official non-interference* at the Capital, and mercantile activity in the localities concerned. At the same time, we must not blind ourselves to the fact, that, without official authority from headquarters, there is no certain local security: *the chances are* that application to headquarters for authority will elicit a prohibition and that activity in a given locality will in time become a recognised *fait accompli, but*, while the chances are thus, there is a risk to be run by local action, and that is, that, if it had not official authority at the start, it may when on the point of succeeding, be upset by an official order. You must thus either coerce the central Govt., or let things take their chance: the central Govt. will consent to anything, however damaging, if it sees you are *determined* to have it, and will prohibit anything, however useful, if you bring it before us as a friendly suggestion. I write, of course, in a general way; exceptions will crop up both ends of the line.[90]

Hart was offered the post of British minister in Peking in April 1885, following the sudden death of Sir Harry Parkes. Hart initially accepted but subsequently changed his mind, probably realising that he would not enjoy fixity of tenure at the legation and would have less power than if he remained as inspector-general of the Maritime Customs.[91] He remained in China until 1908 and retained the appointment as inspector-general until his death in 1911.

It has been observed that friction arising from the activities of missionaries was the most important cause of acrimony in Anglo-Chinese relations between 1860 and 1909. The files in the archives of the Chinese office for handling foreign relations, the Tsungli Yamen, include 910 files giving the details of missionary incidents (excluding the Boxer disturbances of 1899–1900).[92] Missionaries went to China imbued, if not intoxicated, with passionate zeal for uplifting the Chinese people and for demonstrating to them the superior qualities of Christianity. Many of them possessed deep idealism and love of the people among whom they worked. Missionaries made a valuable contribution to the dissemination of education and to the amelioration of health standards. However, none of this could sufficiently outweigh the simple fact that they had come to China with the intention of fundamentally transforming Chinese civilization and culture.[93] Christian contact with China did not, of course, begin in the nineteenth century: the Jesuits had visited China in the sixteenth and seventeenth centuries and had made a number of converts. However, the opening of China from the 1830s onwards encouraged large numbers of missionaries to go to China. Some were Catholic missions, especially French. The British Protestant societies were to the fore in dispatching personnel – the London Missionary Society, the Church Missionary Society, and the British and Foreign Bible Society. Robert Morrison of the London Missionary Society was the first to arrive, in 1807. The Bible was translated into Chinese and missionary tracts began to circulate. Catholic and Protestant activities expanded rapidly after 1860, the number of Catholic priests rising from about 250 in 1870 to 886 in 1900. The Protestant missionaries grew in number from 189 in 1864 and had reached 3,445 by 1905.[94] The various denominational societies were financed by contributions from their respective home institutions. The non-denominational China Inland Mission was run on autocratic lines in accordance with the policy of its founder, J. Hudson Taylor.[95] Taylor starkly expressed the missionary's purpose in going to China:

Shall not the low wail of helpless, hopeless misery, arising from one half of the heathen world, pierce our sluggish ear, and rouse our spirit, soul, and body, to one mighty, continued and unconquerable effort for China's salvation? That, strong in God's strength, and in the power of His might, we may snatch the prey from the hand of the mighty, may pluck these brands from the everlasting burnings?[96]

The missionary appeal was considerable to young men and women in Britain and the United States: over 90 per cent of Protestant missionaries at the end of the nineteenth century were British or American.[97] Missionaries inevitably affected ordinary life in the villages into which they advanced. Often they behaved in an arrogant or tactless manner in seeking to alter traditional customs and patterns of conduct. Their relations were bound to be viewed as an attack on gentry leadership and on the village elders.[98] Missionaries sometimes perished or were physically attacked, thus creating more problems for the long-suffering diplomats to resolve.[99] It was perhaps with sympathy for the latter that the Duke of Somerset asked in the House of Lords in 1870 why British missionaries should be travelling to China 'to convert the Chinese in the middle of their country . . . for every missionary almost requires a gunboat.'[100] Diplomats regarded missionaries as responsible for creating or accentuating many of the difficulties with which they contended. Missionaries like the Welshmen, Griffith John and Timothy Richard, devoted their lives to service in China and exemplified the dedication and tenacity of the true 'men of God'.

The progressive British involvement in China necessitated the creation of an effective diplomatic and consular service. The number of treaty ports expanded appreciably (see map 5): five ports had been opened in 1842, a further ten in 1858–60, and a steady stream of new ports were opened subsequently down to the opening of ports in Manchuria in 1910. The China consular service, which was later renamed the Far Eastern Service to incorporate Japan and Siam, was set up in 1843. At first entrance into the service was irregular but after 1854 the position was formalised. The consular service was not attractive as a career, owing to the remoteness of China and inadequate pay and promotion prospects.[101] All those entering into the consular service had to complete a lengthy period of language study and consuls were involved in commercial and legal work. A supreme court for China and Japan at Shanghai was set up in 1865 and a mixed court was created at Shanghai.[102] The consular service included some men of bizarre character or, perhaps to be more accurate, the nature of their work in conditions of isolation brought out the latently eccentric features of their characters. There is a splendid description of Thomas Taylor Meadows, who represented Britain at the

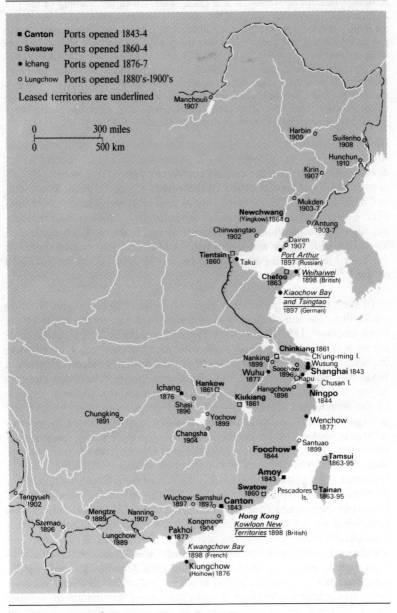

■ **Canton** Ports opened 1843-4
□ **Swatow** Ports opened 1860-4
● Ichang Ports opened 1876-7
○ Lungchow Ports opened 1880's-1900's

Leased territories are underlined

0   300 miles
0   500 km

Manchouli
1907

Harbin
1909

Suifenho
1908

Hunchun
1910

Kirin
1907

Mukden
1903-7

Newchwang
(Yingkow) 1864

○Antung
1903-7

Chinwangtao
1902

Dairen
1907

Tientsin
1860

Taku

Port Arthur
1897 (Russian)

Chefoo
1863

Weihaiwei
1898 (British)

● *Kiaochow Bay
and Tsingtao*
1897 (German)

Chinkiang 1861

Ch'ung-ming I.

Nanking
1899

Wusung

Wuhu
1877

Soochow
1896

Chapu

Shanghai 1843

Ichang
1876

Hankow
1861□

Hangchow
1896

Chusan I.

Shasi
1896

Kiukiang
1861

Ningpo
1844

Chungking
1891

Yochow
1899

Wenchow
1877

Changsha
1904

○Santuao
1899

Foochow
1844

□**Tamsui**
1863-95

Amoy
1843

Swatow
1860

Pescadores
Is.

□**Tainan**
1863-95

Tengyueh
1902

Wuchow Samshui
1897 ○ 1897○

Canton
1843

*Hong Kong
Kowloon New
Territories* 1898 (British)

Mengtze
○ 1889

Nanning
1907

Kongmoon
1904

Szemao
1896

Lungchow
1889

Pakhoi
● 1877

Kwangchow Bay
1898 (French)

Kiungchow
(Hoihow) 1876

Map 5. Growth of the treaty port system

port of Newchwang in the 1860s. Sir Edmund Hornby, the chief justice
of the Shanghai supreme court, wrote of Meadows that he was:

A strange mixture of Humboldt and Livingstone – with the learning of the one and the untiring physical energy of the other . . . He was at once a philosopher and naturalist, and would have been a politician, a lawyer and a diplomatist . . . In person he was tall and gaunt, not unlike the description we have of Don Quixote in figure and manner; while his immense Chinese spectacles set across a powerful nose, his stubble hair, and semi-Chinese costume presented a picture not easily forgotten. It was with some difficulty we forced our way into his residence, a succession of temples, in each of which was a colossal figure of a god, and with whose worship Meadows allowed no interference. The inner apartments were guarded from intrusion by three or four gigantic Mongolian dogs.[103]

Bearing in mind the lonely life and invidious problems with which consuls often had to grapple, it is understandable that eccentricities developed. In the main the consuls performed their work competently and assisted the development of the British role in China.[104] British ministers in China resided in Peking from 1861. In the early years ministers in both Peking and Tokyo were normally appointed from the consular service, although Hart's position was different, as noted above. Each performed his duties with ability and distinction; Alcock and Parkes had served at the Tokyo legation, in Parkes's case for a prolonged period, as discussed below.[105]

In 1868 the Meiji restoration began in Japan. The term itself is rather misleading, for the changes that occurred in Japan in the reign of the Meiji emperor (1868–1912) were to transform Japan from a feudal society to a rapidly modernising state with an industrial sector of growing importance.[106] The emperor's power was not restored: indeed emperors in Japan had usually exercised little effective authority. The Meiji emperor reigned but did not rule: the length of his reign and the impressive nature of the achievement meant that he was regarded with deep respect and perhaps on occasion could influence policy-making. Power in government was wielded by the outstandingly able group of young leaders, predominantly from the han of Satsuma and Choshu, which was responsible for the overthrow of the Tokugawa shogunate. Kido Koin, Ito Hirobumi, Yamagata Aritomo and Inoue Kaoru from Choshu with Okubo Toshimichi, Saigo Takamori (until he left the government in 1872) and Matsukata Masayoshi from Satsuma and Okuma Shigenobu from Hizen established the new government on a durable foundation and guided it through the extremely challenging years after 1868. Within the first decade of the restoration the old feudal order was demolished, the daimyo persuaded to relinquish their power through a generous financial settlement, and the samurai compelled to accept a stringent financial arrangement, in contrast to the daimyo, with the formal termination of samurai status.[107] There were numerous peasant uprisings and manifestations of samurai discontent but there was, however, only one major military challenge to the new government in the form of the localised but grave rebellion in Satsuma in 1877 led by the heroic Saigo Takamori, now wholly

disillusioned with the outcome of the struggles in which he had participated in former years.[108] The new government laid the basis for an effective modern society between 1868 and 1890. Western-type political
institutions appeared in the 1880s, partly modelled on Bismarck's Germany, with a prime minister, cabinet, and eventually the Meiji constitution of 1889, which provided for limited involvement by the lower house
according to a highly restricted male franchise.[109] Modern industries
were set up with government finance before being sold off to the emerging zaibatsu. A modern army and navy were created, the success of the
former being demonstrated in the defeat of the Satsuma rising and the
success of the latter in the rout of the Chinese fleet at the beginning of the
Sino-Japanese war in 1894.[110]

Britain played an important part in relations with Japan throughout the
period of almost a century from the opening of Japan to the outbreak of
the Pacific war. As with China, this reflected the dynamism of a Britain
inspired by industrial prowess. After the salutary defeats inflicted by the
Royal Navy on Satsuma and Choshu in 1863–64 Britain was viewed with
respect. The British minister in Tokyo from 1865 to 1883 was Sir Harry
Parkes, who was blunt, outspoken, and tended to adopt a bullying
approach towards the Japanese: he was a typical product of Victorian
imperialism. While Parkes stood consistently for the assertion of British
interests, he was not manipulated by the British merchants and was sometimes assailed in treaty port newspapers.[111] The treaty ports where British
nationals lived were Nagasaki, Yokohama, and Hakodate. The familiar
features of the treaty port system developed, as in China, and foreigners
lived along lines of similar privilege. As also in China, the merchants
were vociferous in demanding a resolute British policy. All Japanese disliked extraterritoriality and fervently desired the end of the treaty ports.
Nationalism was growing fast, although Harry Parkes was slow to grasp
what was happening.[112] Japanese leaders wanted to achieve the revision
of the unequal treaties and the phasing out of extraterritoriality; tariff
autonomy should also be regained.[113] The prevailing attitude is illustrated
in the words of the court noble, Iwakura Tomomi, who was an important
member of the government after 1868. Iwakura wrote, in April 1869:
'We must guard our country's independence. Foreign troops have been
stationed in our open ports, and even when foreigners who live in our
country violate our laws, we are forced to stand by while agents of their
governments exercise jurisdiction over them. Our country has never
before known such shame and disgrace.'[114]

It took more than twenty years of patient discussion and the dispatch of
various missions and emissaries abroad before Japan could make substantial progress in persuading the powers to modify and ultimately terminate
the treaties. Far-sighted members of the government realised in the early
1870s that it would be futile to expect the powers to accept changes until
Japan had suppressed internal dissent, modernised the legal codes, and
established a secure political framework.[115] The progress made by Japan

in an extremely short space of time was most impressive; as Ian Nish has said, the foreign powers recognised in the 1880s that the treaties were not essential and, furthermore, that trade might be hampered rather than promoted by their continuance.[116] Since Britain had more interests in Japan than any other country and had evinced more sympathy for Japan in recent years, Japanese efforts were largely concentrated on convincing the British. In the autumn of 1893 talks took place in London between Aoki Shuzo and the British minister in Tokyo, Hugh Fraser, who was then on leave in London. Eventually a treaty between Britain and Japan was signed on 16 July 1894. Extraterritoriality was to end five years later; an agreed *ad valorem* import tariff was stipulated; and the new tariff was to be introduced one month after ratification, which took place in Tokyo on 25 August 1894.[117] The treaty represented a major breakthrough for Japan and the reduction of internal tensions, which had given rise to the bomb attack on Okuma, the foreign minister in 1889, and to demonstrations against foreigners, as in December 1893. Aoki, the Japanese ambassador in London, reported to the foreign minister, Mutsu, on a discussion with Lord Kimberley, the foreign secretary, in July 1894:

When we signed the treaty two days ago, Lord Kimberley congratulated our cabinet and me, saying that 'the importance of this treaty for Japan far outweighs the defeat of the great armies of China.' From now on we must try to make our government and people act in accordance with 'the laws of Nations and thereby cause civilization to flourish increasingly in our land'.[118]

The treaty with Britain and the treaties with the other powers came into effect in August 1899, after Japan had introduced the revised civil and commercial codes in 1898 and 1899 respectively. The application of the treaties in 1899 marked the end of extraterritoriality. However, tariff autonomy was not obtained: import duties were determined by separate treaties and would terminate after twelve years.[119]

Britain's attitude to Japan in the generation after the restoration of 1868 was a paternalistic one, particularly when Sir Harry Parkes was minister.[120] Parkes was never slow to express his advice, frequently in trenchant terms. In general Britain was sympathetic to the strenuous efforts of the Japanese government in surmounting the formidable range of problems confronting it. The two countries shared a common suspicion of Russia, which was eventually to bring them together in the Anglo-Japanese alliance of 1902. Long before this date Britain intervened in 1885, when there was a threat of Russia taking Port Lazarev (Gensan) on the Korean peninsula. The far eastern squadron of the Royal Navy was sent to Port Hamilton and remained there until 1887.[121] Japanese interest in Korea was constant from the early 1870s until Korea was finally annexed as part of the Japanese empire in 1910. Korea was an ancient, decadent kingdom in the Chinese sphere of interest. In 1872–73 an angry dispute raged in and beyond governing circles in Japan as to whether Japan should send an expedition to Korea to assert Japanese interest; the issue was linked with unstable internal politics and with the wish of some in the government to see the restless energies of discontented samurai expended outside Japan. Conflict did not then take place over Korea, partly because of the pressure exerted by Prince Iwakura on his return to Tokyo from his visit to Europe and the United States. Britain was not in favour of bellicose initiatives by Japan; for the moment this coincided with the consensus in Japanese ruling circles. However, rivalry between Japan and China over Korea resumed in the 1880s, when Chinese policy was skilfully implemented by the Chinese resident, Yuan Shih-k'ai.[122] In 1894 the problem came to a head and war between Japan and China was imminent. Britain offered to mediate; the British minister in Peking proposed that a naval demonstration be organised in the seas around Japan. As in 1904 and 1941, Japan proceeded swiftly to attack. Most foreign opinion underestimated Japan and this was true of a number of British people living in Japan. China was routed and the success of the hectic activity of the Meiji restoration was sharply underlined. Britain was apprehensive that the war might extend into the Yangtze valley and adversely affect British investments in the region. Assurances were forthcoming from the Japanese foreign minister, Mutsu Munemitsu, that foreign rights would be respected and that Japan would restrict action to what was essential.[123] In 1895 the triple intervention took place, when Russia, France and Germany warned Japan not to impose too drastic a settlement on China at the end of the war and indicated that Japan should hand back the leases in the Liaotung peninsula, including the naval base of Port Arthur. Russia was instrumental in organising the triple protest but the German minister took the lead in presenting the warning in Tokyo, which he fulfilled in an unnecessarily offensive manner. This harmonised with Kaiser William II's hysterical fears of the 'yellow peril' but antagonised the Japanese; the memory rankled in Tokyo until 1914, when Japan returned the compliment at German expense.[124] Britain did not participate in or endorse the triple intervention; this in itself helped to improve Anglo-Japanese relations.

Outside the overt political sphere, British firms and nationals made a valuable contribution to the development of the Japanese economy. However, the number of British people living in the treaty ports was always small. In 1859 there were 18 British out of a foreign population of 35 in Yokohama; in 1883 the British comprised 1,094 out of 2,382 in the whole of Japan.[125] The British role was more prominent than that of other states, since Britain's presence in Japan was an extension of Britain's activities in China – the latter was always regarded as more important. British firms were quick to establish themselves in the treaty ports of Yokohama, Nagasaki, Hakodate, Hyogo, Osaka, and Niigata. Many of the firms were ephemeral and it is difficult to ascertain the business engaged in by certain of them. The largest firms engaged in the China trade participated in trade with Japan, too. Jardine, Matheson was the principal firm in Yokohama and William Keswick originally represented the company in 1859. Jardine's was involved in imports, exports, shipping, and insurance. Butterfield and Swire began business in Yokohama in 1867, dealing in importing British textiles and exporting tea. Later Butterfield's imported sugar and became agents for the Blue Funnel Line of Liverpool.[126] In the 1860s cotton and woollen goods, sugar, metals, and machinery were imported while tea, silk, and other commodities were exported.[127] The Peninsular and Oriental Steam Navigation Company developed a regular route to Japan from 1859. Cloths and woollen manufactures were important in British trade in Yokohama after 1868. In the 1870s British merchants encountered growing competition from French, German and American competitors. In 1880 Britain controlled 58 per cent of the import trade in Yokohama. The United States and France had by then taken over Britain's dominance of the silk commerce.[128]

In Nagasaki numerous British firms appeared. Jardine's and Dent's were the most famous, although Dent's went bankrupt in 1866. Other prominent names were Arnold and Company, Glover and Company, and the P. & O. steamship line. Nagasaki was already a major port and trade rapidly developed in the 1860s. The chief imports were sugar, cotton and woollen goods, Chinese herbs, indigo, and vermilion. Exports to Britain included silk, tea, vegetable wax; rice, fish, flour, wax, and seaweed were sent to Hong Kong.[129] The most dynamic firm in Nagasaki in the 1860s and 1870s was Glover and Company. The firm acted as agents for several insurance companies, had its own banking business, and from 1868 acted as agents for the Hong Kong and Shanghai Bank. Thomas B. Glover demonstrated the classic Victorian entrepreneurial skills: he was shrewd and maintained good political contacts, notably with the daimyo of Satsuma,[130] assisting in obtaining foreign ships for the Tokugawa government and the daimyo of Satsuma. The shipbuilding industry at Nagasaki grew with British help.[131] British companies assisted with the foundation of a spinning and weaving factory in 1866 and with developing a coal mine. Shipping grew swiftly after the opening of the Suez canal; however, the British consul reported in 1875 that trade would not improve significantly until internal communications were strengthened.[132]

The port of Hakodate in the northern island of Hokkaido was slow to develop at first, largely because of its geographical isolation. Jardine's and Dent and Company were active in the early years; trade included such diverse items as lumber, seaweed, deer skins and furs, and fish oil.[133] The civil war of 1868–69, which lingered on in Hokkaido, stimulated shipping and commerce. Subsequently trade declined again in the 1870s. British interests were dominant in shipping. Hyogo was opened to trade at the beginning of 1868. Glover and Company were active; Glover believed the prospects for trade were encouraging, because of the proximity to the great trading centre of Osaka.[134] Hyogo soon became a major port and more foreigners came to dwell in the neighbouring port of Kobe. The Hong Kong and Shanghai Bank was established there, as were other banks. British firms were significant in shipping, gas, and paper production. The Kobe Iron Works and a shipyard were set up in 1873. Osaka did not develop fully in the context of foreign trade until the end of the nineteenth century; the chief British contribution was the establishment of the Osaka Iron Works.[135] Niigata was not important, owing to inadequate facilities: the British consul maintained in 1874 that it had a promising future if the government put sufficient effort into developing it.[136]

The foreign trade of Japan in the first phase after 1868 showed a heavy bias in favour of imports: between 1868 and 1880 imports outdistanced exports by an annual average of nearly six million yen.[137] The main imports were cotton and woollen goods, arms, sugar, and rice while the exports consisted largely of silk, silkworm eggs, tea, and vegetable wax. Sir Harry Parkes believed that the growth of the Japanese economy was hampered by shortage of capital, poor communications and fluctuations in paper currency.[138] There were some difficulties in accepting the Japanese statistics as wholly accurate before 1883. However, according to the returns published Britain supplied between 43 per cent and 59 per cent of Japan's imports for each year between 1873 and 1883. Japan's exports to Britain accounted for between 9 per cent and 27 per cent of her total exports. Of Britain's world-wide trade, the proportion concerning Japan was extremely small for this period; British exports to Japan comprised not much more than 1 per cent of her total exports.[139]

Chapter 4

The struggle for China and the making of the Anglo–Japanese Alliance, 1898–1905

Growing uneasiness manifested itself in Great Britain over foreign issues in the later 1890s. It was part of the dawning realisation of a new atmosphere in the world and that the old familiar guidelines of the earlier Victorian era were fast disappearing, a change in approach exemplified in the response of Joseph Chamberlain, the ambitious and vocal colonial secretary. Chamberlain contemplated the making of an agreement with Germany, the dynamic rising force in Europe.[1] The prime minister, Lord Salisbury, was sceptical of the supposed advantages of alignment with Germany but was not as powerful a voice in the cabinet as formerly. Public opinion in Britain was aroused and there was much clamour for a more active policy to defend British interests. The China Association was active in propaganda.[2] Chamberlain was influenced by public pressure, writing to A. J. Balfour on 3 February 1898: 'I wish that you read all the papers just now. If you did, you would, I think, agree with me that grave trouble is impending on the Government, if we do not adopt a more decided attitude in regard to China.'[3] Chamberlain favoured British co-operation with the United States and Germany in persuading Russia to keep open the ports she had occupied and envisaged the possible employment of force if Russia was recalcitrant. It was, however, clear that Russia would insist on taking Port Arthur and Talienwan. Britain's aim was to preserve freedom for trade and a compromise would have been feasible had Russia been prepared to meet her halfway, but Russia desired sole control of Port Arthur for strategic purposes. Balfour, who was in charge of the Foreign Office during Salisbury's absence, exchanged views with Sir Claude MacDonald, the minister at Peking. Balfour considered,

> ... allowing Russia to lease Port Arthur subject to engagements to preserve existing treaty rights, and possibly, though this is doubtful, to refrain from fortifying Port Arthur, we taking as a makeweight a lease of Weihaiwei ... [or] requiring the Russians to abstain from leasing Port Arthur, we engaging to take no port in Gulf of Pechili and not to intervene in Manchuria.[4]

The cabinet spent several meetings in debating whether or not to acquire Weihaiwei. From the strategic viewpoint, the Admiralty regarded the port as of insufficient depth and was doubtful of its merits. In political terms

Weihaiwei lay in an area where German interests were being extended and the danger of antagonising Germany had to be borne in mind. The governing factor was the need to assert Britain's authority and not to accept a subordinate position. It was in this light that the cabinet determined to authorise occupation of Weihaiwei. China assented to the occupation with some reluctance, owing to her fear that other powers would make further demands upon her. MacDonald was personally opposed to the occupation but nevertheless persuaded the Chinese to accept. The events of 1898 were to unleash competition for concessions; Chinese apprehension was, therefore, justified.

The period after 1898 was characterised by the growth of spheres of influence in China, a trend that continued and became more intense down to 1914.[5] Britain was concerned with defending the position of dominance acquired fifty years before; the most tangible examples of her authority lay in her presence in the Yangtze valley and in her determination to ensure that the post of inspector-general of Maritime Customs continued to be occupied by a British national. Britain also wished to pursue the project for a railway running from Burma to Yunnan. Russia and Germany deemed Manchuria and Shantung respectively to be spheres of interest. France secured the lease of Kwangchow Bay in April 1898, and showed greater interest in dominating the provinces of south-eastern China. Railway concessions became focal points for rivalry and tension. One of the most significant concessions involved the projected construction of a line extending from Peking to Canton; American and Belgian firms were interested.[6] It was felt in the Foreign Office that Britain should compete for the concession. *The Times* criticised the weakness and tergiversations in British policy; British statesmen 'cannot be expected, as we know by observation and on authority, to display an intelligent anticipation of events before they occur'.[7] The China Association agitated for British intervention to combat rival powers. In response to this pressure the British government lent increasing support to the two principal spearheads of British capitalism in China, the Hong Kong and Shanghai Banking Corporation and Jardine, Matheson and Company, as part of a general policy of fostering greater British activity.[8]

The French successes stimulated a British demand for concessions from China. These involved the acquisition of land needed to defend Hong Kong; assurances that exclusive rights had not been granted to France in railway or mining concessions; Nanning to be made a treaty port; and recognition of an Anglo–Chinese agreement not to alienate the south-western provinces of Kwangtung and Yunnan; in addition, a railway concession to Britain in the Yangtze was demanded.[9] China agreed to the extension of the crown colony of Hong Kong and a treaty providing for a ninety-nine year lease of the New Territories was signed on 9 June 1898. Britain endeavoured to obtain a railway concession between Pakhoi and Nanning but France was firmly opposed, and in October 1899 China approved a scheme to construct a French line between Nunkuan (Lungchow) and Nanning.[10] Britain was engaged in competition against

France in Yunnan, along the upper sections of the Yangtze, and in north China. Within north China, Britain was active in Shansi and Honan and in Manchuria. The concessions in the former provinces were secured by the Peking Syndicate, which had been established in 1897. Owing to the antagonism of local mining interests, no mining took place in Shansi, however. Through a clause in the agreement, a concession for achieving a connection with the Yangtze was contemplated via the construction of a line from the mines to Siang-yang on the Han river. When further investigations revealed the scheme as not viable, Britain requested a concession running through Kaifeng to Pukow. Negotiations continued until interrupted by the Boxer rising, the British motive being to combat Franco–Russian control of the projected Peking–Hankow railway.[11] The construction of the Northern railway from Tientsin through Taku to Shanhaikuan and beyond was directed by a British engineer, C. W. Kinder. Britain did not react vigorously to the Russian advance but, at the same time, would not recognise Manchuria as a Russian sphere of influence. Salisbury supported the bid by the British and Chinese Corporation for the concession to extend the Northern railway in Manchuria. China welcomed the bid and a loan for £2,300,000 was arranged in June 1898 for the Northern railway to be extended to Newchwang; the loan was a first charge in the lines between Peking and Shanhaikuan. The British and Chinese Corporation had the right to take over the Peking–Shanhaikuan line if default occurred.[12]

Anglo–German exchanges continued and resulted, in September 1898, in the conclusion of a new banking agreement which provided for a British sphere of interest for railway concessions in the Yangtze valley and the provinces to the south, together with the province of Shansi. The German sphere comprised Shantung and the Hoang-ho valley. The Foreign Office was later to have doubts about it, but in the contentious atmosphere of 1898 it had been readily approved. No clear agreement on definition of spheres was reached between Britain and France. British and French firms concluded agreements with reference to concessions in Yunnan and the Hankow–Canton concession. Both governments were suspicious of each other but appreciated that some tacit agreement was required. Talks between the British and Russian governments were held in London in July 1898. Balfour was active in the negotiations and advocated agreement with Russia if possible. On his return from holiday Salisbury took over dealing with the matter. For a mixture of political and financial reasons, Russia was anxious to conclude an agreement. In February 1899 Muraviev suggested that the two countries should mutually recognise spheres of interest in Manchuria and the Yangtze. The British cabinet accepted the proposal and an agreement was formally signed on 28 April 1899.[13] Lord Salisbury worked to improve relations with Russia and deprecated attempts by British firms to infiltrate Manchuria. For this reason he reacted irately to the visit of Admiral Lord Charles Beresford to China in 1898–99. Beresford was sent to China by the Associated Chambers of

Commerce, which desired a report on the economic situation. Beresford created the unfortunate impression that he was on an official mission and indicated to Prince Henry of Prussia, who was also touring the east, that Britain, Germany, the United States, and Japan could combine to exclude Russia from Manchuria.[14] Salisbury wished to follow a cautious policy in the Far East, which would not involve committing British naval strength to the region. The Anglo–Russian agreement created more stability in the immediate future before the outbreak of the Boxer rising caused more turmoil. In the autumn of 1899 the American secretary of state, John Hay, sent the first of the 'open door' notes to the powers. He was alarmed at the foreign rivalry and the erection of spheres of interest; it was necessary to defend American commerce in this situation. Hay urged the continued recognition of international treaties and that competition for dominance among the powers should not be carried too far. With the exception of Russia the powers were generally sympathetic to the American aim but did not wish to commit themselves precisely. Britain believed that the open door should be retained as far as was possible but that the growth of spheres of interest was irreversible.

The Boxer movement was originally a secret society hostile to the Ch'ing dynasty; it began in the late eighteenth century, then went underground to re-emerge in the last two decades of the nineteenth century. It was in essence a protest movement functioning in the curious atmosphere of superstition, xenophobia and crude violence which often distinguishes secret societies. The Boxers changed direction in the later 1890s by dropping their hatred of the Ch'ing rulers and replacing it with an intensified hostility to the foreign presence and all it stood for, a transformation accomplished through bribery from the dowager empress Tz'u-hsi, who had staged an effective return to the exercise of genuine power by her victory over the well-meaning but inept Kuang-hsu emperor following the collapse of the 'One Hundred Days' of reform in 1898. The emperor, inspired by the Confucian reformer, K'ang Yu-wei and his young disciples, tried to introduce substantial reforms affecting the political and economic basis of the Chinese state.[15] This policy was regarded with suspicion by reactionary Manchus and when the devious Yuan Shih-k'ai betrayed the reformers, the triumph of reaction was assured. Tz'u-hsi, embittered and angry at the challenge to her position, crushed the reformers mercilessly. The unfortunate Kuang-hsu was treated most humiliatingly as a prisoner in his own palace and lived a miserable existence until his mysterious demise in 1908, when he died one day before Tz'u-hsi herself. Tz'u-hsi regarded westerners with loathing and associated westernisation with reform. She decided to encourage the xenophobia of the Boxers in the hope that it would spark off an insurrection strong enough to terminate the western presence in China. This illustrates the fact that sixty years after the opening-up of China began seriously with the outbreak of the first Anglo–Chinese war, some Chinese leaders still failed to appreciate the realities of power and thought that China could again assert her superiority.

Larger numbers of foreigners came to live in China in the 1890s; prominent among them were missionaries. Relations between the foreigners and Chinese peasants deteriorated; missionaries and their converts again became the targets for the circulation of rumours on the alleged evil nature of Christianity. The activities of the Boxers occurred principally in the north-eastern provinces of Shantung and Chihli (Hopei); central and southern China were not affected by the disturbances. Boxer agitation grew markedly in 1899–1900. Foreign diplomats were perturbed by the sinister and menacing developments and complaints were made to the Chinese government.[16] In response the court issued an edict on 11 January 1900 calling for the cessation of Boxer activity. The edict was couched in equivocal terms, however; the British, French, German, and American ministers made a vigorous protest against the phraseology employed.[17]

Shortly before the proclamation of the edict, a British missionary was murdered in Shantung. The governor of the province, Yuan Shih-k'ai, detested the Boxers and acted firmly. Two men were arrested, found guilty, and sentenced to death and the local magistrate was dismissed. Yuan's determination was not matched by other leading officials, who deferred to the pressure of the court to view the Boxers with some sympathy. Sir Robert Hart, the head of the Imperial Maritime Customs, noted in a private letter in January 1900 that rumours were proliferating in Peking of a Boxer invasion of the capital city.[18] The situation gradually worsened as the months passed by. The diplomats in Peking believed that naval demonstrations and armed intervention by the powers would be necessary to curb Boxer activity and frighten the court. Baron von Kettler, the German minister, was one of the most vociferous advocates of action. Salisbury was disturbed to hear of the deterioration and was reluctant to consider intervention in China. He advised Sir Claude MacDonald to keep in the background as much as possible and let any suggestions for further action come from others.[19]

At the beginning of June 1900 two Church of England missionaries were murdered; the response of the Tsungli Yamen was one of indifference. MacDonald felt more determined action to be necessary and Admiral Seymour was asked to send reinforcements to the legation guard. In early June the atmosphere in Peking became extremely menacing with the reactionaries at the court gaining ascendancy. MacDonald urgently requested reinforcements from Seymour.[20] The admiral was authorised to take command of operations and he summoned a meeting of other senior naval officers from European countries and the United States to decide action. The Foreign Office was worried that Russia might seize the opportunity to exert undue influence and possibly occupy Peking; Salisbury warned Seymour and MacDonald of the dangers. On 10 June MacDonald urgently appealed to Seymour for assistance: 'Situation extremely grave. Unless arrangements are made for immediate advance to Peking it will be too late.'[21] Seymour at once decided to lead an expedition to Peking, which departed on 11 June. The Chinese authorities opposed an increase in the number of western forces in Peking, while in the city itself order had broken down: Boxer bands were active and Christian converts were a leading target for attack and murder. Imperial decrees were issued calling for the restoration of order but these were ignored and the disturbances showed every sign of degenerating into complete anarchy. The dowager empress hesitated as to the right course of action to adopt: she wished to expel the foreigners if possible but was conscious of the obstacles.

The diplomats proceeded with defensive preparations to resist an attempt to take the legation quarter; it was expected that Admiral Seymour's force would soon arrive. Allied forces had meanwhile attacked the Taku forts and the Tsungli Yamen stated, on 19 June, that it was accordingly no longer possible to guarantee the protection of foreigners: they were advised to depart from Peking within twenty-four hours. The diplomats thought the order should be accepted but that more time was needed to complete arrangements. No reply was received from the Tsungli Yamen and Baron von Kettler was shot when he rode out to the Yamen to seek a reply. On 20 June, when the ultimatum expired, Chinese troops fired upon the legations. The siege had begun and lasted until 14 August. No news could now be received from the western community in Peking and dire rumours spread as to events in the capital. It was believed by many that the community had been massacred and that there were no survivors: the *Daily Mail* published a report to this effect and *The Times* published an obituary of its famous Peking correspondent, Dr G. E. Morrison.[22] Public outrage was stimulated and vociferous demands for condign punishment of the Chinese were heard. In London the Foreign Office was alarmed at the threat of Russia establishing herself in northern China to the detriment of British interests. Salisbury wrote, in a letter to Queen Victoria, that 'Russia not China seems to me the gravest danger at the moment.'[23] Francis Bertie, a leading Foreign Office official, took the view that Britain could do little to stop Russian domination of northern China and should, therefore, concentrate on securing control of the Yangtze.[24] Contingency moves were indeed made for naval action at Nanking if necessary.

Upon learning of the rapid escalation of the crisis in Peking, Salisbury decided to organise a relief force which could be sent to China with the minimum of delay. Owing to the need for urgent action, additional forces could only be provided by Russia or Japan. Japan was willing to supply troops; Aoki, the Japanese foreign minister, stressed that Japan would assist; he told Britain that the danger of Russia exploiting the situation for her own purposes must be obviated.[25] Salisbury was conscious of the dangers of antagonising Russia and held that the most satisfactory method of advancing was to enlist Russian co-operation. Germany was in favour of a vigorous response to the events in China but wished to maintain her independence and not to be used by either Britain or Russia for their own purposes. William II was profoundly upset to hear of Kettler's death and urged drastic action against the evil Chinese. Salisbury pursued discussions with each of the principal powers to secure agreement on common principles to guide action. He was anxious to safeguard the territorial integrity of China, as was the United States; it was this concern that prompted the second of John Hay's 'open door' notes.

In late July and early August the powers exchanged views on the composition and leadership of the international force to be sent to Peking. Germany was most anxious to secure the command for a German national. Britain was not happy at the proposal but the urgency of the time factor and the importance of achieving some unity among the powers persuaded them to accept Field Marshal Count von Waldersee as the commander.[26] It proved impossible to attain a truly unified command and there was much rivalry among the powers. The British commander, General Gaselee, was given explicit instructions on his relationship with Waldersee. Gaselee was always to command British forces, subject to the overall decision on employment in a particular sphere by Waldersee.[27] Before Waldersee left Europe the allied forces advanced and Waldersee was left to handle the resulting situation when he arrived in China. The allied forces moved from the coast to Peking, fighting two battles against Chinese troops on 6 and 9 August 1900. The Russian contingent led the onslaught on Peking and the intrepid international community was rescued on 14 August.

The advancing allied troops fulfilled the Kaiser's exhortation to treat the Chinese with great ruthlessness and to stamp the foreign image irrevocably on the capital, and indulged in extensive rape and pillage. Chinese were handled with great brutality; their lives were regarded as cheap and expendable. Property was seized and much destruction occurred. The behaviour was barbaric and struck the more sensitive Europeans as being ironical, given the chorus of international censure on China for inhumanity displayed by the Boxers. Sir Robert Hart wrote that, 'instead of order terrorism (except in the Japanese quarter) seems the order of the day and looting and commandeering are the only methods the soldiers think of resorting to'.[28] General Gaselee attempted to prevent British troops from participating in the pillage but he found this could not be enforced when other foreign troops behaved as they did. Sir Ernest Satow was appalled by the devastation commenting, 'It was like entering a huge city of the dead where the tombs had been thrown down and enveloped in dust.'[29] Friction predictably developed among the powers with Russia revealing a definite intention of dominating developments as far as she could, proposing that since the Chinese court had fled from Peking, there was no point in keeping forces there after the termination of the siege and that all efforts at a settlement should be postponed until the court returned to Peking. Germany was hostile to the suggestion, for it would virtually eliminate a role for Waldersee, who had still not reached China. Members of the British cabinet felt that there was now a possibility of reaching an agreement with Germany in the interest of both powers. Chamberlain, Balfour, and Lansdowne were all anxious for progress and hoped Germany would recognise British rights in China, while Salisbury preferred a cautious approach with the maintenance of the Anglo–Russian agreement of April 1899.[30] He was suspicious of German motives, and did not regard an agreement with her as being as desirable as did a number of his colleagues while the question still remained as to what Germany would demand in compensation. It appeared most likely that she would wish to assure herself effective control of Shantung. When the detailed negotiations took place in London, Germany proposed a limited agreement which would allow her to share in the Yangtze trade, while Britain desired a broader agreement which could involve Germany in joining to resist Russian consolidation in Manchuria and north China.[31] The eventual agreement, signed on 16 October 1900 stipulated that both powers would aim to maintain the open door in China and they agreed to preserve their existing interests in China; freedom of trade was regarded as concerning the ports and littoral of China. The agreement was as much as could have been obtained but fell short of original British expectations.

In October 1900 the powers had to decide upon the basis of the punishment of China following the suppression of the Boxer rising. France put forward several points to govern policy, the most important of which envisaged punishment of Chinese officials incriminated in Boxer activities and close co-operation among the powers with equal treatment. Sir Ernest Satow, who had exchanged posts with Sir Claude MacDonald, represented Britain at the conferences of diplomats in Peking. Satow interpreted British policy as being 'to act in concert with the rest of the Plenipotentiaries and to save as much of an independent China as is possible under the circumstances'.[32] He believed that the death penalty was appropriate for Chinese officials guilty of close involvement with the Boxers. The representatives worked out their policy and decided against seeking punishment of the dowager empress. The general trend that emerged was against requiring the death penalty for Chinese officials, since it was felt that this could cause interminable argument and thus delay the conclusion of more significant aspects of the settlement. The cabinet disliked the omission of the death penalty but had difficulty in following the detailed discussions in Peking: criticisms of Satow were expressed for not keeping the Foreign Office better informed. Eventually the draft of a joint note was approved, calling for a full apology and acceptance of responsibility by China.

Discussions now commenced with the Chinese government. Satow described the Chinese behaviour as 'objectionable and almost arrogant'.[33] As anticipated, the most contentious immediate problem surrounded punishment of Chinese officials. Britain and Germany advocated a tough approach with the death penalty for those manifestly guilty of encouraging murderous attacks. The other powers showed less enthusiasm for exacting the ultimate penalty. Growing friction developed with Russia, hinging on Russian truculence and British suspicion of Russian motives. With regard to negotiations over an indemnity, Britain did not desire a large indemnity because of the repercussions on the customs service and subsequently on Britain. A committee chaired by Bertie of the Foreign Office concluded that China could not pay more than a maximum of £1.5

million a year; this would service a loan of £30 million at 5 per cent. France supported a substantial indemnity and Russia decided to make a separate indemnity claim. A total indemnity of 450 million taels emerged from the discussions, certainly a larger sum than Britain had contemplated. Britain acted astutely and successfully in the complex exchanges over the indemnity. China accepted the terms finally arrived at on 27 August 1901 and was compelled to accept a larger measure of foreign control over her affairs as a consequence of the Boxer rising. The 'high noon' of western imperialism in China lasted from 1901 until the outbreak of the First World War in 1914.

China was, however, beginning to experience a much accelerated process of change, stimulated by the events of 1900. The first phase of revolution may be dated from the aftermath of the Boxer rising; the ground was now laid for the take-off into the revolutionary era, which has lasted from 1911 to the present time. In the words of Mary Wright:

Rarely in history has a single year marked as dramatic a watershed as did 1900 in China. The weakness laid bare by the allied pillage of Peking in the wake of the Boxer Rebellion finally forced on China a polar choice: national extinction or wholesale transformation not only of a state but of a civilization. Almost overnight Chinese – imperial government, reformers, and revolutionaries – accepted the challenge. Easily three quarters of the foreign non-official observers – journalists, missionaries, businessmen, doctors, teachers – were dumbfounded at the change. Letters flowed home assuring friends and colleagues who had left China only a few years earlier that they simply would not recognize the country today. A few called the changes superficial, but the great majority supported their impression of a vastly altered ambience with specific observations and experiences.[34]

The imperial government realised that the policy of the state had to change and could not continue as it had been prior to 1900. Political, economic, social and educational changes were necessary. In the 1900s the preparatory moves for the introduction of a constitution were taken with the emphasis on local assemblies. Modernisation in the economy was recognised as necessary and western education had to be promoted to supplement, if not replace, the Confucian classics. The most fundamental development was the initial suspension in 1905, and then abolition, of the traditional examination system which, in its essential characteristics, had existed for over 1,000 years. This struck at the long-established basis for the social dominance of the scholar-gentry class and was in itself a revolutionary act. It was ironical that it should have been implemented by the reactionary Tz'u-hsi as a means of endeavouring to bolster her authority after the reverses and humiliation she had suffered in 1900–01. The more perceptive western observers appreciated the new developments but others still comforted themselves with the belief that the Chinese would be unable, at least for a century, to organise themselves so as to offer a challenge to western privilege.

The most important feature of British policy in the Far East in the first decade of the twentieth century concerned the formation of the Anglo-

Japanese alliance, which endured from 1902 until it finally expired in 1923 following the Washington conference. The alliance was significant in the European context. It was initially directed, in 1902–05, against the looming menace of Russia; after 1905 it assumed importance for Britain as part of her strategy of concentrating her naval forces in European waters in preparation for a decisive confrontation with Germany in the era of the Anglo–German naval race. For Japan the alliance was tangible recognition of the remarkable success of modernisation. Japan, which had been treated with such disdain if not contempt by the western powers a generation previously, was now accepted as an equal partner of the greatest empire in the world.

The origins of the Anglo–Japanese alliance are to be found in the common suspicion of Russia and of Russian ambitions in Asia. Such fears were not new; British policy for much of the nineteenth century had operated in terms of rivalry and doubt over Russian aims in Central Asia and in China and areas adjacent to China. Britain was apprehensive of the danger of Russia exerting influence along the borders of India and in northern China, thus constituting a menace to British rule in the Indian sub-continent, and to British commercial ascendancy in China. These apprehensions were much exaggerated but were nonetheless sincerely held. The construction of the Trans-Siberian railway in the 1890s and the weakness of China increased cause for concern. Japan was worried at Russia's meddling in the tangled affairs of Korea and at her infiltration of Manchuria. It was manifestly in the interests of both powers to conclude an agreement but that is not to maintain that the alliance was easy to negotiate or that problems did not have to be surmounted.

The coalescence of Britain and Japan might well have embraced Germany in the early stages of discussion. The first secretary at the German embassy in London, Eckardstein, spoke of the possibility of a triple agreement on several occasions in 1901, when he was conducting official business during the illness of the ambassador, Count Hatzfeldt. Eckardstein was not a trained diplomat, however, and was sometimes indiscreet in his actions.[35] Germany had made it clear to Britain that the Anglo–German agreement of October 1900 could not be applied to Manchuria but this did not prevent Germany from fostering closer contacts with Britain and Japan. In March 1901 Eckardstein advocated, in discussion with Hayashi Tadasu, the Japanese ambassador, that a triple alliance comprising Britain, Japan and Germany should be reached with the purpose of protecting Chinese integrity and the 'open door' doctrine. Hayashi asked the *Gaimusho* if he could open talks with Britain. The foreign minister, Kato Takaaki, authorised the step but Hayashi was warned to advance on a non-committal basis.[36] Hayashi was an Anglophile and had become an ardent advocate of an Anglo–Japanese alliance. The influential *genro*, Yamagata Aritomo, supported making an agreement with Britain, the reason being his alarm at Russian expansion.[37]

The principal official on the British side in negotiating the alliance was

Francis Bertie. The new foreign secretary, Lord Lansdowne, was inexperienced and relied heavily on Bertie for guidance. Bertie was in charge of the Asiatic department of the Foreign Office from 1898 to 1902. A man of pronounced opinions who supported the concept of an alliance with Japan, he was hostile to Russia and was not in favour of an agreement with Germany. Lansdowne met Hayashi on 31 July 1902 and told him that the two countries should consider the far eastern situation should it be 'threatened with serious disturbances'.[38] Lansdowne spoke of his anxiety at Russian policy in Manchuria and the pressure she could wield in Peking. He did not propose an alliance but thought that an agreement might be advisable.[39]

Hayashi saw Lansdowne on 14 August and the foreign secretary defined the objects of an agreement as the preservation of the open door in China and the defence of Japanese interests in Korea. There was, however, no sense of urgency in London. Salisbury informed King Edward VII on 16 August that the feasibility of reaching an alliance would be pursued further but it was only on 6 November that Britain gave Japan the first draft of the alliance.[40] In both countries the respective foreign ministries and cabinets had to reflect on the implications of agreements and ensure that what was decided was compatible with the nation's policy. In Japan a new government had been formed by General Katsura Taro, a member of the Choshu clique and protege of Yamagata. Katsura believed that Britain offered a more reliable partner than Russia. Prince Ito Hirobumi, the distinguished *genro* and former prime minister, hankered after an agreement with Russia while appreciating that it would be more difficult to attain; Ito was departing in September 1901 for a visit to Russia via the United States. Both avenues were being explored but it was far more likely that an agreement would be concluded with Britain for the simple reason that British and Japanese interests broadly coincided, while those of Russia and Japan diverged. The new Japanese foreign minister, Komura Jutaro, supported making an agreement with Britain.[41]

Discussions in London developed between Lord Lansdowne and Count Hayashi. Hayashi thought the alliance should only become operative in the event of one ally being attacked by two or more powers. This was acceptable to Lansdowne, who in turn proposed that neither power should reach separate understandings with another country concerning China or Korea. Hayashi showed interest in including Germany in an alliance but Lansdowne felt this would complicate the task of completing the negotiations. The British cabinet considered a draft treaty in November 1901, which was approved and forwarded to Japan; the draft provided for full discussion of mutual problems and for neither power concluding agreements without prior exchanges. The Admiralty wished to include a clause dealing with naval co-operation, for there was growing concern over the expanding demand on Britain's limited resources. The War Office and the India Office wanted to insert a reference to Britain's interests on the borders of India, so as to meet the contingency of Russian pressure in this area; the cabinet preferred this to be pursued orally.[42] Tokyo decided not to assume responsibilities extending outside East Asia.

Japanese leaders contemplated their response to the British draft in November–December 1901. Discussion in Tokyo was complicated by the necessity of consulting Ito, who was by this time in Paris. Ito still wished to visit Russia notwithstanding the advanced state of Anglo–Japanese negotiations. He found the draft to be acceptable but he regretted the omission of German adherence and was not happy with the clauses concerning Korea.[43] Hayashi was irate at Ito's response and feared that it could stimulate doubts in London as to Japan's true intentions. The Japanese cabinet decided at the end of November definitely to sign an alliance with Britain. Komura notified Sir Claude MacDonald on 28 November; it was further decided that a member of the Japanese legation in London should go to St Petersburg, which Ito had reached, to obtain the carefully considered response of the *genro*. Lansdowne was unhappy about Ito's presence in the Russian capital and inquired of MacDonald whether this could account for the current delay in finalising arrangements. MacDonald replied that it was not in his view significant.[44] Ito was already intending to visit London and this was confirmed, thus partially allaying the doubts entertained in London. The *genro* as a group were consulted and gave meticulous consideration to one of the most important steps Japan had taken since the Meiji restoration. Marquis Inoue Kaoru had some reservations arising from his feeling that Japan might become embroiled in conflict with the European powers, which would impose too great a strain on her. Inoue, however, was a friend of Ito and was perhaps influenced by the latter's views and his current mission to Russia. Ito held that matters were proceeding too rapidly and tried to reduce progress but it was too late. The *genro* and the cabinet were in agreement and it remained only for the emperor to confirm his assent. This was accomplished once the emperor was satisfied that Ito's views had been borne in mind.[45]

Within the British cabinet, Balfour felt that Britain should have made more strenuous efforts to secure a Japanese promise of help with regard to Indian defence. Hicks Beach, the chancellor of the exchequer, Joseph Chamberlain, and C. T. Ritchie criticised the failure to gain more concrete promises from Japan. Salisbury took the view that Britain could be committed too readily to intervention if Japan became embroiled with Russia.[46] However, these were all points of reservation rather than fundamental opposition to the proposed treaty as such and the final discussions were rounded off successfully in January 1902. Lansdowne determined to complete the formalities as quickly as possible, perhaps being influenced by the deteriorating situation in Manchuria, where Russia was reluctant to withdraw from the regions occupied at the time of her intervention against the Boxers. Japanese leaders had finished their deliberations and the first Anglo–Japanese alliance was duly signed by Lansdowne and Hayashi on 30 January 1902. The preamble referred to the common interests of both countries in the maintenance of the *status quo* and peace 'in the extreme East, especially where the independence and territorial integrity of China and Korea were involved'. The first article read:

The High Contracting Parties, having mutually recognised the independence of China and Korea, declare themselves to be entirely uninfluenced by any aggressive tendencies in either country. Having in view, however, their special interests, of which those of Great Britain relate principally to China, while Japan, in addition to the interests which she possesses in China, is interested in a peculiar degree politically as well as commercially and industrially in Korea. The High Contracting Parties recognise that it will be admissible for either of them to take such measures as may be indispensable in order to safeguard those interests if threatened either by the aggressive action of any other Power or by disturbances arising in China or Korea, and necessitating the intervention of either of the High Contracting Parties for the protection of the lives or property of its subjects.[47]

The remaining five articles stipulated the neutrality of the other partner should Britain or Japan be involved in war with another power; for intervention in such a conflict should another power or powers intervene against the ally; that neither signatory would enter into separate arrangements contrary to the objects of the alliance; that the signatories would consult frankly when the aims of the agreement were threatened; and for the alliance to remain in force for five years.

The balance of power in the Far East was decisively affected by the making of the Anglo–Japanese alliance. The dual alliance of Russia and France, reflected in the region by the expansion of Russian power and by France's role in Indo-China, had to reckon with the contingency of British intervention in the event of war breaking out in the Far East. Certainly Japan could not be bullied into retreat by threats from the dual alliance. The principal problem facing Britain and Japan was the Russian presence in Manchuria and the difficulty of assessing the role that Russia intended to play in the future. This was naturally a far more vital issue for Japan than it was for Britain: Manchuria bordered Korea and an extension of Russian power would involve the menace of Russian domination of Korea; this would be wholly unacceptable to Japanese opinion. To Britain, on the other hand, Manchuria was remote and was not an area where Britain had particular political or economic interests. Manchuria was important to Britain as a symbol of Russian strength and as a potential threat to British interests in northern China. Japan was entirely conscious of the magnitude of a war against Russia and had no wish to embark upon this course except as a last resort. There was indeed still a faction headed by Ito which advocated a Russo–Japanese agreement. It was decided, in June 1903, at an imperial conference held in Tokyo that Japan should approach Russia to ascertain if Russia would agree to recognise the independence and integrity of China and Korea and further to recognise mutual rights in Korea and Manchuria.[48] Britain was notified the following month of Japanese intentions and invited to comment. Lansdowne and the Foreign Office officials felt that a policy of, in effect, allowing Russia to act as she wished in Manchuria would be dangerous and incompatible with the alliance. The Japanese were asked, in July

1903, to ensure that the talks with Russia 'should not be conducted in a manner which might suggest that the Anglo–Japanese Agreement has been in any way impaired'.[49]

Russia agreed to talks, which she suggested should be held in Tokyo as this would be more convenient for Admiral Alexeyev, the viceroy of the far eastern provinces, who was now established at Port Arthur. Russia offered to recognise Japan's ascendancy in south Korea on condition that north Korea was accepted as a neutral zone and that Manchuria was outside Japan's sphere of interest.[50] This was unsatisfactory to Japan, since the Russian position in Manchuria remained vague and there was no indication of when Russia would withdraw. Britain was faced with having to determine her response; great care had to be exercised if Britain were to avoid involvement in war with Russia and conceivably with France. Lansdowne deemed the Russian counter-proposal to Japan to be clearly unsatisfactory and in December 1903 he proposed to his cabinet colleagues that Britain should try to obtain assurances from Russia over Manchuria. Equally 'we should tell the Japanese distinctly that they must be content with the best bargain they can get as to Korea – the Korean clauses, barring that as to the neutral zone, are on the whole not unsatisfactory'.[51] Balfour thought that Japan should be left to handle the situation with Britain being careful not to intrude too far: there was the danger of Japan blaming Britain if advice was tendered and it did not achieve the desired results. It was realised that talks between Russia and Japan could not be protracted, for time would permit Russia to despatch naval reinforcements from European waters to the Far East. It was difficult for British ministers to determine the likely outcome of a Russo–Japanese conflict. There was no overwhelming feeling that Japan would prove victorious; it was anticipated that the struggle would be evenly balanced and that the odds might shift in favour of Russia the longer it lasted. A calm and cool policy was called for on Britain's part and decisions must depend on how the vital interests of Great Britain were affected by the day-to-day developments.

Between December 1903 and January 1904 preparations were made in Japan with increased urgency for war. The Katsura cabinet aimed to restrict the strife to Russia and Japan and to keep China neutral; much of the fighting was undeniably bound to occur in Manchuria, which was part of the Chinese empire. On 6 January 1904 Russia submitted new proposals to Japan. An imperial council in Tokyo rejected them and it was decided to send an ultimatum to Russia as a final move before Japan resorted to war.[52] When France approached Britain with a suggestion for mediation, it was politely declined. Britain had no intention of compelling Japan to accept mediation: matters must be allowed to take their course.

No reply was sent to the Japanese ultimatum and on 6 February 1904 Japan terminated diplomatic relations with Russia. As in 1894 and again in 1941, there was no formal declaration of war by Japan. It was at once announced in London that Britain would adopt an attitude of neutrality.

This was acceptable to Japan unless the circumstances provided for in the text of the alliance occurred, in which case Japan would be entitled to British aid. In April 1904 Britain reached agreement with France; this embraced causes of Anglo–French friction ranging from Egypt and Morocco to Siam and the New Hebrides. While it would be erroneous to exaggerate the significance of the agreement, it was important in exemplifying Britain's wish to improve relations with France at a time when these relations were encountering peculiar strain because of events in the Far East.[53] However, the Anglo–French exchanges originated in the common wish to settle a number of outstanding disputes, some major but most minor, in the hope of attaining a smoother relationship. Of the diplomatic ramifications precipitated by the war the most serious incident in Anglo–Russian relations took place in October 1904, when the Russian Baltic fleet, in transit to the Far East, fired upon British trawlers in the bizarre impression that they were Japanese torpedo boats. The attack led to an upsurge of bitter protest in Britain. Britain prepared to use the Royal Navy to halt the advance of the Russian fleet but a Russian apology and acceptance of a commission of inquiry removed the necessity for such drastic action. More difficulties were caused when the Baltic fleet reached French Indo-China and anchored in Kamranh Bay. This action angered Japan, who interpreted it as a violation of French assurances of neutrality. Lansdowne warned France of the danger of the situation being exacerbated; France undertook to persuade the Russians to withdraw the fleet as soon as possible.[54]

The Russo–Japanese war was a long-drawn-out struggle waged with considerable tenacity on both sides.[55] Japanese forces demonstrated much zeal and enthusiasm; in the main their armies were capably led and handled in the savage land fighting in Manchuria. The Japanese gradually defeated their foes, taking Liaoyang on 4 September 1904, Port Arthur on 1 January 1905, and Mukden on 9 March 1905. Mukden fell after a prolonged siege which exhibited many of the characteristics of the warfare to be witnessed in Europe in 1914 and after. The war at sea culminated in Admiral Togo's devastating victory in the battle of Tsushima Straits, which saw the rout of the Baltic fleet in May 1905. The lead in offering mediation was taken by President Theodore Roosevelt. Lansdowne welcomed Roosevelt's suggestion of mediation in January 1905 and thought it should be pursued. Britain agreed to 'second his efforts to the best of their ability, although they would, of course, be unable to bring pressure to bear on Japan with a view to her abating demands which are considered reasonable'.[56] Japan reacted cautiously to Roosevelt's mediation bid initially but the growing stresses being experienced by the Japanese economy rendered it extremely desirable to bring the war to an end on acceptable terms. The Japanese government indicated its terms for peace on 21 April 1905; after the result of the naval battle at Tsushima was known on 1 June 1905, Japan officially requested the American president to employ his good offices. The British role in peace-making was one of encouraging the parties primarily involved to compromise, from a position on the sidelines.[57] After a lengthy and somewhat tedious series of meetings in Portsmouth, New Hampshire, peace was concluded in September 1905 on terms that underlined the scale of Japanese success. Russia surrendered any voice in Korea and recognised that it was in the Japanese sphere of interest. She similarly gave up her stake in southern Manchuria and transferred to Japan the southern half of the Chinese Eastern Railway, south of Changchun. Japan had made astonishing progress and had fared far better than had been generally anticipated when the war began, yet the outcome disappointed much Japanese opinion, which had been led by official propaganda to expect the annexation of Russian territory and the expulsion of Russia from eastern Siberia. The disappointment gave rise to large-scale demonstrations in Tokyo; widespread violence occurred with brutal encounters between police and demonstrators. The foreign minister, Komura Jutaro, who led the peace delegation to the United States, became a scapegoat for popular wrath. The *genro*, practising 'curtain government' (power exercised from behind the scenes) began to realise the defects of fostering popular nationalism – it could reach the stage where it was hard to contain.[58]

Before the Russo–Japanese war was brought to an end, Britain and Japan had concluded a new alliance to replace that of 1902. The existing agreement was not due for renewal until 1907 but the war stimulated a common desire to bring the terms up to date. In December 1904 Sir Claude MacDonald reported that Katsura and Komura believed that 'if Japan was successful in war, she would seek for a closer alliance with England'.[59] The parliamentary under-secretary at the Foreign Office, Lord Percy, proposed that Britain should negotiate a new agreement to last for five years.[60] The Unionist government was tottering amidst the acrid debates over tariff reform, which were tearing it asunder. An additional argument for making a new alliance was that it would enforce the stable bases of British policy before the relatively inexperienced Liberals returned to office, a development which appeared almost certain in the spring of 1905. At an official dinner in Tokyo held on 12 February 1905, Komura expressed the hope in his speech that 'the alliance might be extended for a further and longer period and that its provisions might be given a larger and wider scope'.[61] When detailed talks began between Lansdowne and Hayashi, Komura warned the minister to be cautious and not to commit Japan rashly to new undertakings. In the British cabinet and in the House of Commons more attention was being paid to the importance of India and of inducing Japan to assist in its defence if necessary.[62] The Japanese cabinet discussed matters on 8 April 1905, and decided that it would favour an agreement on terms similar to those approved in 1902; the only change would occur in reference to the status of Korea.[63] Japan would wish to omit the existing allusion to Korean independence and would prefer the new agreement to run for seven years.

In London the recently formed committee of imperial defence considered the subject. It was felt that if Japan could be persuaded to accept a commitment to send troops to India in defined circumstances to assist

Britain, this would be a tangible advance. In addition, other aspects of the present alliance needed rethinking so as to reassure friendly powers, such as France and the United States, and to extend the scope of the alliance if either signatory was attacked by a third power. The Admiralty strongly supported renewal. Detailed exchanges between London and Tokyo followed, as the negotiations gathered momentum. Japan now showed more willingness to press ahead rapidly and made concessions to Britain. Japan accepted the inclusion of India in return for British acceptance of a new article on Korea. Japan also agreed to the British suggestion that the alliance should become an 'offensive-defensive' one[64] since she was anxious to advance and placate Great Britain so as to retain her sympathy during the task of peace-making and as part of her long-term reinsurance against the danger of a subsequent clash with Russia. The climax to the Anglo–Japanese discussions came in June and July 1905: the principle of striking a bargain with respective concessions over India and Korea was accepted but much debate occurred over the precise terminology to be used in drawing up the relevant clauses. Japan did not wish to become involved in disputes resulting from problems encountered in any of the states on the borders of India, otherwise a treaty largely dealing with the Far East would be extended to the Middle East, and she desired a stronger wording of the clause dealing with Korea so as to give her a free hand. The text of the new alliance was finally approved in July and formally signed on 12 August 1905. The preamble defined the objects of the alliance as:

(a) The consolidation and maintenance of general peace in the regions of Eastern Asia and India;

(b) The preservation of the common interests of all Powers in China by insuring the independence and integrity of the Chinese Empire and the principle of equal opportunities for the commerce and industry of all nations in China;

(c) The maintenance of the territorial rights of the High Contracting Parties in the regions of Eastern Asia and of India, and the defence of their special interests in the said regions.[65]

There were eight articles in the agreement. These provided for full communication whenever the interests of either power were threatened; if either signatory became involved in war in defence of its interests, the other signatory would come to its aid; British recognition of Japan's right to take such action in Korea as she deemed necessary to defend her interests; Japanese recognition of Britain's right to act in defence of the Indian frontier; neither power would enter into arrangements with another power contrary to the aims of the agreement; with regard to the continuing Russo–Japanese war, Britain would maintain 'strict neutrality' unless another power or powers intervened in the war, in which case Britain would assist Japan; the military and naval authorities of the two countries were to consult on defence problems; and the agreement would remain in force for ten years.

Thus Great Britain and Japan accepted the necessity for a new alliance. From Britain's viewpoint, the merit of the alliance had been clearly established as sustaining British interests successfully against the menace of Russia without committing Britain to war. The importance of the alliance in defence terms was demonstrated in the references to India. The probability of Japanese troops actually descending on the Indian frontier was remote and might well have been unwelcome to the civilian authorities in India had it ever transpired. Japan's success in the Russo–Japanese war was a potent source of inspiration to Asian nationalists, including India. Nationalism was in its infancy in South-East Asia and India but the Japanese victory was a decisive step in encouraging agitation against occidental hegemony, as was to be eloquently recognised by many nationalist leaders in the intoxicating days of 1942. The alliance was shortly to assume even more importance in the naval sphere once the naval race with Germany developed.

For Japan the alliance was the most valuable single buttress of Japanese foreign policy. Japan had achieved great success in the war against Russia, whatever militant Japanese nationalists might think about the peace settlement, but still needed the friendship and support of another power in order to be able to cope successfully with the challenge of the new era. China did not enthuse at the news of the alliance; neither had she rejoiced at the conclusion of the original agreement in 1902. China felt that although the alliance stood ostensibly for safeguarding her own integrity, in reality it would connote her exploitation; and the Japanese could prove as rapacious as the European powers had been.

Chapter 5

The Chinese revolution and the aftermath, 1905–1914

Intense interest in investment in China, particularly in railway projects, developed after 1901 and continued until 1914. It accentuated rivalry among the powers and, as will be seen, led to a serious Anglo–Japanese clash in 1913–14 involving a dispute over the centre of the Yangtze valley. The most controversial region before the outbreak of the Chinese revolution in 1911–12 concerned Manchuria. This huge area, the size of France and Germany combined, was experiencing a boom in the 1900s. Japanese investment, which predated the Russo–Japanese war, substantially increased after 1905 and the Japanese–owned South Manchuria Railway Company (the southern half of the former Chinese Eastern Railway) became the focus of Japanese activities while Russia dominated the northern half of Manchuria. China viewed these developments with distaste. Manchuria was constitutionally part of China, the ancestral home of the Ch'ing dynasty, and to witness the area being effectively controlled by foreign nations was obnoxious. Spheres of interest existed for Great Britain, France and Germany elsewhere in China, and these, too, were becoming far more offensive to Chinese public opinion in the era after 1900. However, the activities of these powers were not quite as blatant. The United States regarded herself as the chief protector of Chinese integrity since John Hay had circulated his 'open door' notes in 1899 and 1900. William Howard Taft succeeded Theodore Roosevelt as president in 1909 and he and his secretary of state, Philander C. Knox, embarked upon what was known as 'dollar diplomacy' – intervention in Latin America and the Far East to advance United States objectives by financial means. Taft and Knox disliked the trend of developments in Manchuria and on 6 November 1909 the United States proposed that the railway system in Manchuria should be neutralised or taken over on an international basis.[1] Britain did not welcome the American initiative; the proposal was certain to alienate Japan and Russia. The foreign secretary, Sir Edward Grey, had already reached the conclusion that Japan was entitled to expand somewhere. The United States and the British dominions were opposed to oriental immigration and a number of embarrassing clashes between Japan, on the one hand, and the United States, Canada and Australia, on the other hand, were occurring between 1905 and 1914.[2] Britain did not wish Japan to expand into China proper, which left only

Manchuria. This did not mean that Britain would readily acquiesce in Japan doing whatever she wished in Manchuria but it did connote that Japan's fundamental presence in Manchuria would be viewed with understanding. The Japanese and Russian response was exactly as foreseen in London. Both countries opposed neutralisation and China was advised not to proceed with the project for constructing a railway between Chinchow and Aigun, which had been advocated by the United States also.[3]

Relations between Russia and Japan had improved noticeably by 1910. Japan signed agreements with France and Russia in 1907.[4] The treaty with France granted Japan most-favoured nation treatment in French Indo-China and jointly confirmed their interest in the integrity of China. A secret exchange of notes accomplished mutual recognition of each country's sphere of interest in the Far East.[5] The Russo–Japanese agreement of July 1907 included secret clauses defining respective spheres of interest in Manchuria and reciprocal recognition of effective dominance of Mongolia and Korea respectively.[6] In March 1910 Japan decided to seek a new agreement with Russia, confirming that of 1907. Russia welcomed the approach and the agreement was swiftly concluded. It again comprised public and secret clauses, referring solely to Manchuria. Britain supported the Russo–Japanese *rapprochement*, subject to desiring assurances that there would be no departure from the open door in China.[7] In 1910 Japan took the significant step of carrying her rule of Korea to its logical conclusion by annexing the peninsula to the Japanese empire. Korea had been ruled by a Japanese governor-general since 1905 but a pretence of Korean autonomy still existed. In October 1909 Prince Ito Hirobumi was assassinated by a Korean nationalist while visiting Harbin. This act incensed the Japanese and stimulated determination to consolidate Japanese rule in Korea and eliminate the unrest that existed there.[8] The Japanese government advanced warily, appreciating the necessity of preparing the way and of securing foreign acquiescence. The subject was officially broached with Britain in May 1910. The British Foreign Office felt that Britain had no choice other than to condone Japanese annexation. Grey requested assurances that the existing tariff would be upheld, as guaranteed by treaty. Japan responded with a promise to maintain the Korean tariff for a period of ten years.[9]

Within Britain a more critical attitude to Japan was developing. Japan was no longer regarded as the valiant underdog, anxious to assist Britain in combating the Russian threat. Instead Japan was considered by much of British public opinion as having become too powerful and somewhat impudent. Japan was seeking to limit the actions of British firms in parts of East Asia and this was considered, in that most English of phrases, to be 'not cricket'. *The Times* correspondent in China, Dr G. E. Morrison, formerly highly sympathetic to Japan, was extremely hostile by 1910, to such an extent that some of his reports had to be amended when they reached London. The youthful Earl Stanhope castigated Japanese policy in a speech delivered in the House of Lords, following a visit he made to the Far East.[10] The animosity of British commercial circles was accentuated by the introduction of a new statutory tariff in 1910–11 to mark Japan's decisive move away from the final dying grip of the 'unequal treaties' foisted upon her fifty years earlier. Negotiations were held in London in 1910–11 for a new Anglo-Japanese commercial treaty to succeed the treaty of 1894, which would hopefully cushion the impact of the tariff. When the treaty was agreed, there were reductions for certain British exports but the rates were distinctly higher than before. The China Association, which represented traders in Japan as well as China, sent a letter of protest to the Foreign Office warning that the new tariff would 'pave the way to that Japanese hegemony of the Far East which would certainly not to be the advantage of British merchants'.[11] Sir Edward Grey welcomed the new agreement, however, and discounted the chorus of ire. The signing of the Anglo–Japanese commercial treaty was shortly to be followed by the revision and renewal of the Anglo-Japanese alliance in 1911: although a new agreement was not required in 1911, since the existing treaty was due to run for ten years, it is true that it was to some extent out of date, owing to developments that had occurred since 1905, notably the reconciliation between Russia and Japan. The revision of the alliance resulted primarily, however, not from any wish on the part of Britain or Japan to modernise the alliance but instead from another approach from the United States, which had important repercussions on Britain's attitude. President Taft suggested that Britain and the United States should negotiate an arbitration treaty, as a symbol of the desire of both nations to eradicate causes of controversy and improve relations. Grey welcomed the proposal, for he was anxious to promote better Anglo–American relations, but an arbitration treaty would mean that the alliance with Japan would require modification. Japan was not happy to hear of the American proposal, yet realised that in practice Britain could not be expected to go to war with Japan against the United States should conflict between Japan and the United States arise, so decided that it would be sensible to revise and extend the alliance. The alliance was of far less importance to Japan than when the two previous treaties were signed, yet it still offered a guarantee of stability and support. There was no certainty about Russian policy, which was liable to sudden tergiversations, and a close relationship with Britain would allow Japan to develop her resources and would perhaps ameliorate relations with the United States in the event of a quarrel developing.

The committee of imperial defence produced several reports in 1910–11 in which the powerful contribution made by the Anglo–Japanese alliance to Britain's overall strategy was emphasised. The reports were drawn up to assist in the forthcoming discussions at the imperial conference, to be held in May 1911. It was wise, therefore, to consider making a new alliance. The British embassy in Japan was becoming more dubious of Japanese policy; the ambassador, Sir Claude MacDonald, and the counsellor, Horace Rumbold, believed that Japan was revealing more aggressive tendencies and that a more cautious attitude was advisable.[12] The defect with this view was that it looked at the alliance simply in terms of the situation in the Far East and of looming Japanese ambitions in China. It did not appreciate that the principal argument from the British side for extending the alliance was in terms of imperial defence and of meeting a decisive challenge from Germany. In addition, Grey and the Foreign Office believed that more was to be gained through the influence that Britain could exert upon Japan through the alliance than would be the case if the alliance no longer existed.[13] Detailed negotiations took place in London between May and July 1911. Grey handled the talks personally with Baron Kato Takaaki, the Japanese ambassador. Japan wanted to eliminate the defunct article of the 1905 treaty referring to Korea and the Russo–Japanese war and to replace the former with a new clause giving Japan the same rights with regard to the Korean frontier as Britain enjoyed on the Indian frontier. As regards a clause dealing with the arbitration issue, Japan understandably aimed to secure wording which was as weak as possible. Britain intended to arrive at an unequivocal wording which would completely remove an obligation to assist Japan in the event of conflict with the United States.[14]

Before the new agreement could be signed, Grey had the important duty of addressing the imperial conference on the subject and of persuading the assembled representatives fully to endorse the British government's decision to extend the alliance. This was the first occasion on which the dominions were closely consulted upon such an important topic, vitally affecting the conduct of foreign policy. The emphasis lies on *consultation*, however; there was no thought of the dominions becoming a final court of appeal displacing the authority of the British cabinet. Asquith and Grey had taken the decision to consult the dominions, not only as a recognition of the growing autonomy of the dominions but, in addition, in the belief that it would have a valuable educative effect. The dominions had sometimes displayed irresponsible attitudes in the past and resentment of oriental peoples existed to some extent in each of the dominions. Grey's speech was skilfully contrived and cogently expounded. In a key passage he stated:

A paper had been circulated explaining what the strategical situation would be if the Japanese Alliance came to an end. If it came to an end owing to our giving notice to terminate the alliance, it cannot be doubted that not only would the strategical situation be altered immediately by our having to count the Japanese fleet as it now exists as possible enemies, but Japan would at once set to work to build a fleet more powerful than she would if the alliance did not exist. We, on the other hand, instead of keeping the modest squadron in Chinese waters which we do at the present time, would have to keep – if we are to secure the sea communications between the Far East and Europe, and also between the Far East and Australia and New Zealand – a separate fleet in Chinese waters which would be at least equal to a two-Power standard in those waters, including in that two-Power standard counted possibly against us not only the Japanese fleet as it is at the present time, but the fleet which Japan would certainly build if we put an end to the alliance.[15]

The warm welcome given by the representatives to Grey's address pleased him greatly and he at once proposed to the Japanese ambassador that the agreement should be signed as soon as possible, if necessary before the arbitration treaty with the United States. Further exchanges took place over the wording of the treaty. Grey indicated that Britain would prefer to omit the article referring to the Indian frontier, adding that an article such as the Japanese envisaged, dealing with Korea, might suggest ulterior designs on Manchuria and attract undesirable controversy. Japan agreed, rather surprisingly, to omit the proposed article dealing with the Korean frontier and assented to a more positive wording of the article concerning the arbitration treaty than was provided for in the wording first suggested by her.[16] The new alliance was signed by Grey and Kato on 13 July 1911. The preamble stated that the signatories had taken into account the major changes which had materialised since 1905 and then proceeded to cite the familiar concern with the 'maintenance of general peace in the regions of Eastern Asia and of India' and reiterated interest in preserving the 'independence and integrity of the Chinese Empire'. There were six articles respectively referring to consultation between the signatories; to assistance being given to one of the powers by the other should she become involved in war; to not entering into separate agreements prejudicial to the objects of the treaty; to either party not being bound to go to war against a power with whom she had reached a treaty of arbitration; to consultation between the appropriate military and naval authorities for the implementation of the defence clauses, and to the duration of the alliance and the circumstances in which the alliance might be terminated after a period of ten years. The treaty was to apply for a period of ten years.

Developments in China between 1911 and 1914 faced Britain with a number of challenges and awkward issues to resolve. These resulted from the outbreak of revolution in China in October 1911, which led four months later to the abdication of the Ch'ing dynasty and to the proclamation of a republic. The revolution inaugurated a period of progressive disintegration in China, which lasted until the triumph of the communists in 1949–50 reintroduced strong centralised authority. There was no real surprise among foreigners at the start of the revolution in 1911. After the dowager empress's death in 1908 there was no one capable of exercising leadership among the incompetent and divided Ch'ing court. The ambitious and devious Yuan Shih-k'ai retired to the background to bide his time.[17] Chinese society was rapidly transforming itself under the impact of modernisation and the widening popularity of western ideas.[18] A generation gap was opening among educated Chinese between the older adherents of traditional Confucian principles and the younger westernised people. All classes were affected by nationalism, including the peasantry. A new self-confidence could be discerned. The first act of the revolution manifested itself in the 'double tenth' (10 October 1911), the date normally taken as marking the start of the revolution. The provincial gentry of the western province of Szechwan revolted in September 1911 against the policy of railway nationalisation being enforced by the central government. On 10 October the revolt began in Wuchang, in the heart of the Yangtze valley. The revolt spread rapidly and half the provinces of China were in a state of insurrection by the end of the month. Britain was anxious for the safety of British residents and the protection of property in the disaffected areas, predominantly in central and southern China. The rebel commander, General Li Yuan-hung, promised that foreign rights would be upheld. The British minister, Sir John Jordan, instructed consuls to restrict dealings with the rebels to what was absolutely essential. Sir Edward Grey concurred, 'We must do what is in our power to protect British life and property when in danger, but any action we take should be strictly limited to this purpose.'[19] Britain believed that a cautious and watchful policy was advisable and doubted whether loan advances could be made to the Peking government until the situation was clarified.

The frightened Ch'ing government was so worried at the worsening situation that it reluctantly recalled Yuan Shih-k'ai to office at the end of October. Yuan initially feigned unwillingness to return so as to secure as much freedom as possible. He received the additional powers he desired and, at the beginning of November 1911, he became prime minister. The Ch'ing dynasty had sealed its fate: Yuan posed as a loyal adherent of the dynasty but was determined to exploit matters for his own ends. China was divided into the northern provinces, which were predominantly loyal to the Peking government, and the central and southern provinces, which were controlled by an ill-assorted variety of republicans. The third element in the equation, and the vital one, was Yuan Shih-k'ai,[20] with whom Sir John Jordan was on friendly terms and who was held to be sympathetic to British interests. Britain was satisfied at the news of Yuan's return to office. In London it was considered that China required a 'strong man' to keep her together and that Yuan fitted the role admirably.[21] Britain and Japan did not consult each other regularly in the early stages of the revolution despite the provisions for such discussion in the recently renewed alliance. The revolution shocked Japan profoundly and divergent reactions to the trend of events in China could be seen. The older, more conservative and bureaucratic circles were hostile to the Chinese republicans, viewing them as an unknown quantity and fearing that a republican victory might inspire similar sentiments in Japan. The more vociferous party politicians and younger Japanese sympathised with the republicans; the man who was regarded as the father of Chinese republicanism, Dr Sun Yat-sen, had intimate links with certain Japanese circles, notably those associated with militant nationalists, including the societies of ronin (adventurers).[22] The Ch'ing government asked Japan for arms in mid-October 1911 and Japan agreed to meet the request. The Japanese general staff preferred aiding the revolutionaries, since it was thought that they were weaker and thus assistance to them could lead to a stalemate which Japan could exploit. The Japanese cabinet determined to follow a cautious policy and to expand Japanese influence in China and Manchuria.[23] Japan decided to employ troops to defend the section of the

Peking to Mukden railway line extending from Shanhaikuan to Mukden, which could be threatened by the growing unrest visible in north-east China and in Manchuria. Grey recognised Japan's right to act if absolutely necessary but stressed that Japan should keep in mind that action by one power could encourage intervention by other countries.[24] This was a clear allusion to the possibility of Russian intervention.

In the middle of November 1911 Sun Yat-sen arrived in London. He had, perhaps fittingly, been in Denver, Colorado, engaged in fund-raising activities among overseas Chinese, when the revolution broke out. Sun had achieved fame because of his long struggle against the Ch'ing dynasty and the publicity that his activities had sometimes given rise to. He remains a curiously vacuous figure in whom there seems to be comparatively little solid substance behind the charismatic facade.[25] Sun was willing to promise any concession to anyone or any power that would undertake to assist him. He requested official approval for a loan of £1 million pounds and offered to grant concessions to Britain and the United States in return. Grey informed him that Britain had no intention of intervening in the Chinese revolution and spoke favourably of Yuan Shih-k'ai. A Foreign Office official contemptuously dismissed Sun Yat-sen as 'an armchair politician and windbag'.[26]

The situation in China in late November 1911 had deteriorated, with savage fighting occurring at Hankow. Yuan had secretly established contact with the republicans but he had to proceed stealthily until his balancing act had given him sufficient strength to administer the *coup de grâce* to the Ch'ing dynasty. Sir John Jordan agreed that the British consul-general in Hankow could deliver messages to the revolutionary commander, Li Yuan-hung. On 1 December a three-day armistice was agreed. Britain had acted without consulting her ally, Japan, and Japan similarly moved without prior discussion. Japanese leaders distrusted Yuan but had to deal with him, for Yuan was the indispensable man to whom all had to turn at this juncture. The *genro*, particularly Prince Yamagata Aritomo, were deeply perturbed at the chaos in China and feared that it could engulf Japan in time unless resolute steps were taken. They held that Japanese policy had been vacillating and should now become more decisive; it was to Japan's advantage to co-operate with Britain in attempting to restore order in China. Japan urged Britain on 1 December to agree upon terms for joint diplomatic intervention to secure a constitutional monarchy under the Ch'ing.[27] Britain agreed on the objective of a constitutional monarchy but regarded the Japanese proposal as inherently dangerous. Diplomatic intervention could easily lead to armed intervention, for the question obviously arose as to what would be done if the sides in China declined to submit to Anglo–Japanese advice. Britain definitely did not wish to become entangled in military action in China. She did not have the forces to put into China; to do so would be contrary to the logic that had governed British policy since the opening-up of China – that Britain could not commit herself to large-scale military action in China. When it came to armed action, only Japan and Russia could readily summon the necessary forces. Intervention in China could become the thin end of a singularly dangerous wedge. Britain proposed that the British and Japanese ministers in Peking should endeavour to secure the abdication of the reactionary Manchu prince regent, who was a stumbling-block to compromise in China.

Unofficial secret contacts between Yuan Shih-k'ai and the republicans had existed for some time. It was formally agreed by the two sides to hold a peace conference in Shanghai starting on 18 December 1911; this continued, with some interruptions, until 2 January 1912. More important was the fact that a private conference met on the first day of the official session, attended by representatives of Yuan and of the republicans; here it was agreed that a republic would be established and that whoever per-suaded the Ch'ing court to abdicate should become the first president of the republic. Yuan was behaving with deep cunning, posing in public as a loyal servant of the dynasty while in truth preparing to jettison the court and exchange the office of prime minister for that of president. Britain on balance thought that a monarchy would be more in harmony with peace-ful evolution but did not feel strongly on the matter; the British minister in Peking considered it to be imperative to resolve the situation expediti-ously so as to avert foreign intervention.[28] Japan was thrown into turmoil by developments in December 1911; the majority of *genro* and ministers firmly preferred a constitutional monarchy but were disconcerted by the manner in which British policy was moving and by the manoeuvrings of Yuan Shih-k'ai.[29] The trenchant British advice against intervening in China had successfully dissuaded the Japanese from intervention. Grey confirmed the lines upon which British policy should proceed in a minute written on 25 December 1911:

...we should be careful not to be drawn into any attempt to force upon the Revolutionaries or upon Yuan Shih-k'ai a solution that either of them is not pre-pared to accept. We should confine our action to mediation as hitherto, making it clear that we desired to see a united and strong China etc...otherwise the Powers will get into opposite camps and there will be all sorts of trouble between Chinese and Foreigners. Indeed, this is a grave risk to be considered before any preference is expressed or anything like pressure exerted by all the Powers in concert.[30]

Sun Yat-sen at last reached China at the end of December 1911. Not all the revolutionaries were adherents of Sun but he was indisputably the best known republican leader. On 1 January 1912 he was proclaimed first president of the Chinese republic. Sun informed Yuan that he would re-sign when Pu-yi, the boy emperor, abdicated and Yuan could then become president. Yuan was irate, interpreting Sun's assumption of office as a violation of the secret agreement of 19 December 1911. Yuan broke off the official peace talks and China was now divided between the northern provinces, which were loyal to the Peking government, and the central and southern provinces, which recognised the republican regime at Nan-king. Britain did not relish the prospect of the divisions becoming perma-nent. It was now clear that the Ch'ing court would abdicate before long, as soon as satisfactory assurances had been received on a financial settlement: trouble could be caused by reactionary Manchus in the interim period, however. Yuan offered a judicious blend of cajolery and threats to hasten the process of abdication. The final imperial edict of the Ch'ing dynasty, promulgated on 12 February 1912, announced the abdication and instructed Yuan to handle the transition to the republic. Sun Yat-sen resigned as provisional president and soon afterwards accepted the office of director of the Chinese railway system, a post that offered suitable scope for his visionary planning. Sun distrusted Yuan, however, and relations between them were soon to be strained and were to culminate in a rebellion in the summer of 1913. The Anglo–Japanese alliance had allowed Britain to influence Japanese policy in the sense of restraining Japan from acting unilaterally: this marked a change in character in the alliance with a new trend towards becoming a restraining influence on Japanese policy.

Loans to China became more significant after the revolution and required fuller co-operation among the powers. A loan consortium comprising Britain, France, Germany, and the United States was formed in 1910; Japan and Russia joined in 1912. The United States withdrew shortly after Woodrow Wilson became president in 1913 with the parting thrust that the consortium was undemocratic in its procedures. In April 1911 a loan of 60 million taels was made for currency reform and to assist industrial enterprises in Manchuria. Japan and Russia were not surprisingly annoyed at the latter reference and it stimulated their desire to enter the consortium and prevent unpalatable developments.[31] The British government used the Hong Kong and Shanghai Banking Corporation as its agent, which provoked jealousy among the other British banks and encouraged more vocal criticism of British loan policy in London. In December 1912 the membership of the British loan group was widened, but not sufficiently to satisfy all of the banks involved: a number of British banks contemplated participating in loans outside the confines of the consortium. This development was sedulously fostered by the Chinese government. Yuan Shih-k'ai employed Dr G. E. Morrison, who had left *The Times* to become Yuan's political adviser, in attempts to obtain loans on more favourable terms than could be attained from the consortium. Morrison in turn encouraged the activities of a London financier, C. Birch Crisp, who was instrumental in floating loans.[32] The consortium was not an easy body to operate, for the powers constantly bickered among themselves and Grey had to defend British policy from mordant criticism. *The Economist* was a frequent critic, maintaining that the consortium handicapped British financial acumen. Of one aspect of the implementation of the reorganisation loan, signed in April 1913, *The Economist* not inaptly observed that 'it reminds us of a scene in "Charley's Aunt"'.[33] Loans caused many headaches for Sir Edward Grey but he adhered to the opinion that it was preferable to maintain the consortium rather than abolish it. He was, however, compelled to concede in a debate in the House of Commons in May 1913 that, 'I do not regard monopolies as desirable institutions at all.'[34]

Yuan Shih-k'ai gradually consolidated his authority in 1912–13. He was provisional president pending the election of a national assembly which would be charged with the duty of electing the full president. Numerous political parties were founded and corruption abounded. Yuan possessed the levers of power and used them vigorously. He soon became involved in a power struggle with the southern republicans. Yuan disliked parliamentary institutions and aimed to become a dictator; as with his behaviour in 1911–12, timing was of the essence and he could not advance with unseemly haste.[35] For Britain and the powers the immediate issue, in February 1912, revolved around official recognition of the Chinese republic. Japan took the initiative in urging the powers not to grant recognition before achieving confirmation of treaty rights and privileges.[36] Recognition was complicated for Britain by the fact that border problems involving India and Burma were relevant. The India Office held that China should settle outstanding border differences before recognition was accorded. The Foreign Office did not like this proposal because British insistence on prior fulfilment of defined conditions would be emulated by other powers. The India Office modified its position somewhat, stressing that the most urgent aim should be to secure a Chinese promise not to disturb the *status quo* in Tibet. Grey instructed Sir John Jordan to see Yuan, who denied any wish to reassert Chinese authority over Tibet.[37] The powers were in general agreement that the situation in China was so unsatisfactory that it was wiser to wait and observe how matters evolved. The United States chafed at the decision, for the Taft administration was encountering criticism in Congress for its failure to lend tangible support to the sister republic across the Pacific. In March 1913 Sung Chiao-jen, parliamentary leader of Sun Yat-sen's newly formed Kuomintang party, was assassinated at Shanghai railway station. The murder had been engineered by Yuan. This act incensed Sun's followers.[38] Sun was already in Japan, in February–March 1913, where he sought the assistance of Japanese financiers, militarists and adventurers for a rebellion designed to overthrow Yuan and replace him himself.[39] Britain was prepared to recognise the republic regardless on condition that Yuan expressly recognised existing treaty commitments.[40] The desultory exchanges on recognition were overtaken by the outbreak of rebellion in China in July 1913.

The insurrection commenced in Kiangsi province and soon spread to Kiangsu, Kwangtung and Fukien. The British chargé d'affaires in Peking, Beilby Alston, reported on 17 July 1913 that Japan was thought in Peking to be supporting the rebellion, perhaps with the intention of establishing Japanese interests in the Yangtze valley.[41] Japanese capitalists had given assistance to the rebels; some Japanese soldiers and individual adventurers from the Pan-Asiatic societies were also involved. The Japanese government was not itself extending aid and officially adopted a policy of neutrality. However, Yuan Shih-k'ai had antagonised Japan and was rightly regarded as hostile to the Japanese role in China. Britain warmly supported Yuan, whose continued presence was felt to be essential. Alston wrote that Yuan should ruthlessly crush the rebellion and 'make an example of the leaders . . . He will never be able to consolidate his position unless he exercises the mail fist regime . . .'[42] Grey told the Japanese ambassador that 'our policy must be to wait to see the outcome of the struggle and then to decide what our attitude towards that outcome should be'.[43] The rebellion swiftly disintegrated once the momentum was dissipated and by September Yuan was completely victorious. Alston reflected on the role of Japan in August and sent a stern warning to London on the sinister implications of Japanese policy.[44]

The Foreign Office gave careful consideration to Alston's views. It was believed that a basic change in direction in Japanese policy might be in progress; Britain must observe the position and reiterate to Japan, at the appropriate moment, that she expected frank exchanges on all matters dealing with China. The British ambassador in Tokyo, Sir Conyngham Greene, commented that while individual Japanese had participated in the fighting, there was no evidence pointing to the involvement of the Japanese government.[45] The final stages of suppression of the insurrection produced an incident in which Japanese nationalists and property were attacked, causing a further serious crisis.[46] The troops of the reactionary General Chang Hsun captured Nanking on 1 September 1913 and promptly indulged in extensive pillage. In the words of the British consul, 'Wanton murder, looting, rape and incendiarism have been the unchecked amusements of the victorious soldiery . . . Up to last night hell unrestrained has reigned in the city . . .'[47] During the orgy of destruction, three Japanese civilians were killed and Japanese property looted. Other incidents occurred in Hankow and Yen Chou, including attacks on Japanese soldiers; the Japanese War Ministry demanded a firm stand and punishment of the guilty. Emotional demonstrations of protest were held in Tokyo and bitter criticism levelled at the government. The British ambassador reported on 9 September 1913 that troops might be sent to protect Japanese interests. The Japanese government sent a detailed list of demands to Peking. Alston warned the Foreign Office that Japan could be about to embark on the use of force. It was then decided by the Foreign Office to send a strong rebuke to Japan with a warning against going too far. Britain expected to be consulted, under the terms of the Anglo–Japanese alliance, upon any action Japan might contemplate taking. It was stressed that Japan should show appreciation of the disturbed state of China and should not make demands upon the Peking government which it could not reasonably fulfil. The strength of the British protest shocked the Japanese foreign minister, Baron Makino Nobuaki, who replied that matters were less grave than Britain contended.[48]

Greene told the Foreign Office that Japan had not, in his opinion, behaved contrary to the alliance. It was a matter on which some Japanese individuals felt strongly and arms had certainly reached the Chinese rebels; Greene aptly remarked that both Lord Salisbury and Asquith had experienced difficulties in preventing arms shipments to South Africa and Ulster in the 1890s and 1912–13 respectively.[49] China duly apologised for the attacks made on Japanese in recent weeks and Japan accepted the apology. Yuan Shih-k'ai was elected president by the national assembly in October 1913; the assembly was effectively controlled by Yuan as a consequence of the purge of his opponents and of the shrewd dispensation of patronage. Yuan was on the road to become president for life, which was approved by the assembly in 1914; he was to overreach himself, however, when he launched the monarchist movement in 1915. Britain and the other major powers formally recognised Yuan as president immediately following his election on 6 October 1913; in return Yuan confirmed recognition of treaty rights. The chief contribution of the rebellion of 1913 to the development of British policy in the Far East was to underline the suspicion of Japan, which had begun during the revolution of 1911–12 and which was accentuated by the growing Japanese interest in the Yangtze and by the presence of Japanese agents (whether or not they were official representatives) in Tibet.

The emerging clash between Britain and Japan over the Yangtze came to a climax in 1913–14. This is extremely important for sharply revealing the tensions within the alliance that were now coming to the surface. Britain had been the first power to exploit the riches of the Yangtze area and British trade was dominant there in 1913. The provinces of Kiangsi, Hupei, Anhwei and Kiangsu comprised the centre of British activities. It was a wealthy region, agriculturally and industrially, and it is scarcely surprising that the other powers cast covetous eyes and pondered the best methods of undermining British predominance. France had begun to penetrate the Yangtze valley after 1900 and French firms competed for railway concessions. Japan embarked on a similar programme, particularly after the revolution of 1911–12, although Japanese activity dated from the seizure of Formosa during the war of 1894–5; this was an admirable base for penetration of the Chinese mainland.[50] Anglo–Japanese talks on the Yangtze were originally started to exchange views on railway projects. The talks were held in January 1913 between S. F. Mayers, representing the British and Chinese Corporation, and Odagiri Manosuke, representing the Yokohama Specie Bank. The British government was not notified of the commencement of the exchanges at this time. Odagiri suggested co-operation in a line extending from Wuhu to Nanchang which would ultimately continue to Changsha. Odagiri explained that he was pursuing negotiations with the Chinese for a line running from Nanchang to Pinghsiang, which would be an extension of the Kiukiang-Nanchang line currently in Japanese possession. Japan would accept the status of junior partner in any co-operation, which would be unavoidable since most of the capital would have to be raised on the London loan market.[51] Odagiri thought that Japan might admit British interests to south Manchuria if Japanese interests were permitted to enter the Yangtze. The latter appears an improbable contingency and indeed the Japanese government ruled it out when further talks took place. The initial reaction of the Foreign Office was that there might be scope for some co-operation with Japan but more information was required. When the Japanese minister in Peking mentioned the possibility to Sir John Jordan, the British minister's reaction was negative. Jordan cited the traditional British predominance of the Yangtze, which was viewed as highly significant by British public opinion.[52]

Further intermittent exchanges between British and Japanese representatives occurred during the summer of 1913 but the first formal approach came on 20 August 1913. The Japanese ambassador left a memorandum at the Foreign Office referring to a new project for a railway extending from Nanking to Hsiangtan (Siangtan) in Hunan province. Japan proposed opening negotiations with China and hoped that no objection would be voiced by the British government or by the British and Chinese Corporation. Britain considered the Japanese approach to cut across the existing obligations resulting from membership of the consortium. It had been decided to separate so-called 'industrial loans' from those possessing a more overt political character. The project under reference would come under the former description but the separation had not yet been enforced.[53] Japan was informed that Britain could not approve the suggestion.[54] J. D. Gregory, the able Foreign Office official largely responsible for advising Sir Edward Grey on the matter, recommended that the best policy was to maintain Britain's existing supremacy in the Yangtze region.[55] To present the subject more diplomatically to Japan, it would be sensible to inquire what proportion of capital Japan would contribute as her share; as Japan had few resources for investment, this would be suitably embarrassing. Britain should also press for admission to south Manchuria in the event of Japan being allowed into the Yangtze. Therefore, Britain should not reject the Japanese proposal outright but should attack it on another flank by stipulating conditions which Japan was most unlikely to fulfil. Grey entirely concurred and a note drawn up in these terms was communicated to Japan on 11 October 1913.[56]

Japan was given much to reflect upon in the note and no reply was received until 26 November 1913. By this time China was urging that negotiations should begin for the Nanking–Hsiangtan project. In the Japanese note it was stated that Japan would wish to provide the funds for constructing the section from Nanchang to Pinghsiang. On south Manchuria, Japan did not give a definite answer to the points raised but merely observed that Japanese rights there resulted from political and geographical contiguity. Thus Japan sought partially to meet the British counter-arguments. Sir John Jordan had now returned to Peking from leave in Europe and vigorously opposed any acceptance of Japan's right to control the Nanchang–Pinghsiang section.[57] Grey wrote that the Yangtze was such a vast area that it became rather difficult to exclude all other powers, apart from which Britain's special relationship with Japan had to be considered. France, for example, had obtained contracts to build a bridge at Hankow and a harbour works at Pukow.[58] When Grey's thoughts were communicated to Jordan, the British minister replied by repeating his strong preference for mutual British and Japanese acceptance of each other's spheres in the Yangtze and in south Manchuria. Jordan felt that there was no political necessity to placate the Japanese because Japan was worried about the growing Russian domination of Outer Mongolia, which had virtually separated itself from loyalty to the Peking government after the revolution of 1911–12. Japan had interests in Inner Mongolia and could be expected to react with hostility to further Russian intrusion in Mongolian affairs.[59] Sir Conyngham Greene, the ambassador in Tokyo, endorsed Jordan's analysis and believed the less Britain and Japan intervened in each other's spheres the better.

The Foreign Office decided to adopt a more determined response to Japan and France. Britain's relations with both powers in the Far East became more contentious in the months preceding the outbreak of war in Europe in July–August 1914. Japan was informed on 31 December 1913 that Britain could not co-operate over railway projects in the Yangtze while Britain was excluded from the Japanese sphere. However, the Japanese government was thinking along grandiose lines and was contemplating large-scale schemes of economic co-operation with Britain, which would amount to creating an Anglo–Japanese economic alliance alongside the political alliance. Koike Chozo, head of the political division of the *Gaimusho* and previously counsellor at the Japanese embassy in London, talked informally to E. F. Crowe, commercial attaché at the British embassy in Tokyo on 23 December 1913. Koike stated that both Britain and Japan would stand to gain from closer economic alignment in China. He suggested the possibility of alliance between individual firms: shipping and commerce offered opportunities with the possibility of securing co-operation between the Nippon Yusen Kaisha and the Japan–China line, on the one side, with Jardine, Matheson and Butterfield and Swire on the other side with the aim of controlling the China Merchants Steam Navigation Company, which had been declining for some years.[60] Greene counselled against pursuing the Japanese approach further for the reasons that he and Jordan had put forward earlier – it would not be in Britain's true interests.[61] The Foreign Office fully agreed. The permanent under-secretary, Sir Arthur Nicolson, commented, 'The Japanese are endeavouring to exploit the Alliance by methods which are not likely to be to our advantage.' Sir Edward Grey added, 'I entirely agree.'[62] No reply was sent regarding the matters referred to in Koike's unofficial exchange with Crowe; Japanese diplomats did not speak of them again. However, the topic was referred to by the new Japanese prime minister, Count Okuma Shigenobu, in an interview given to *The Times* in the spring of 1914. Okuma spoke warmly of the Anglo–Japanese alliance and wondered whether it could be extended into an economic partnership.[63] The Foreign Office believed the general tone of Okuma's approach to be satisfactory but Britain did not want to embark upon economic discussions.

Exchanges on railway questions with Japan continued in the early months of 1914. Grey agreed that the final signature for a railway line from Nanking to Changsha, to be constructed by the British and Chinese Corporation, should take place. Grey saw the Japanese ambassador on 2 February and firmly defended the policy he had adopted on railways:

With regard to the railway question, I said that my position in Parliament would be impossible if I recognised spheres of interest in China for other countries without having any British sphere recognised by them. I was ready to recognise the Japanese sphere of interest in Manchuria and to decline to support British railway enterprises there; but I could not defend a refusal to support these enterprises if the Japanese were participating in a railway in a district in China which was already as far as railways were concerned a British district.[64]

Grey was consistent in his policy. In 1908–10 he had discouraged British participation in the Hsinmintun–Fakumen and Chinchow–Aigun projects in south Manchuria. In late January 1914 the British and Chinese Corporation wrote to the Foreign Office for support in the proposed construction of a railway from Peking to Jehol, bordering the Japanese sphere of influence. Grey was unwilling to support the project unless Japan first admitted Britain to south Manchuria.

In the middle of February 1914 Japan sent a considered statement on the railway projects in the Yangtze, dismissing the analogy between the Yangtze and south Manchuria because Japan's position rested on treaty rights in the latter area. The claim to participation in the Nanking–Hsiangtan railway was withdrawn but the hope was expressed that Britain would reveal a more encouraging attitude to future Japanese activities in the Yangtze. Two examples of Japanese interest were cited: that Britain would facilitate a connection between the Nanking–Hsiangtan and Nanking–Kiukiang railways and that Britain would come to a special understanding when the Nanking–Hsiangtan line was built. Reference was made to a Japanese application for a railway to be built from Foochow to Hankow.[65] The Foreign Office believed that if the project for the line from Foochow to Nanchang went forward, then Britain should construct the section from Nanchang to Hankow.[66] The British reply to Japan was sent on 21 February 1914. It started with an emphatic confirmation of Britain's faith in the Anglo–Japanese alliance and with the wish that there be improved relations between the allies in China. As Japan adhered to the defence of her sphere of interest in south Manchuria, so Britain would maintain her rights in the Yangtze: 'His Majesty's Government therefore feel bound to claim for themselves a privileged position in that part of the Yangtze Valley where their interests are predominant, and they are resolved to assert their claims against all powers whose nationals may apply for concessions in that region.'[67] The note ended with a statement that if Japanese concerns obtained a concession for a line running from the Fukien coast to Nanchang this would be acceptable to Britain on condition that British interests constructed the section from Nanchang to Hankow. British firms engaged in Chinese enterprises were encountering some problems in raising sufficient capital owing to doubts as to the stability of the political situation in China. The Foreign Office persuaded the Hong Kong and Shanghai Bank to extend additional funds to the British and Chinese Corporation to ensure the viability of the Nanking–Hsiangtan project. On the whole Britain had emerged success-fully from the contest for concessions in 1913–14 and there was general satisfaction with the outcome in the Foreign Office: British firms control-led the projected line from Canton to Ningpo and a large cluster of lines radiating from Shanghai, and Sir John Jordan was planning further con-cessions in the Yangtze.

Japan pressed forward with schemes to enhance her economic role in the Yangtze. The Japanese and Chinese Development Company was transformed into a vast syndicate for industrial competition in China, with Kiangsi province as the base. The Japanese directors came mostly from the Mitsui, Mitsubishi and Okura companies, all of which had helped to promote the abortive rebellion in China in 1913. In March 1914 the gov-ernment headed by Admiral Yamamoto Gombei resigned as a conse-quence of the crisis over naval scandals.[68] The new Okuma government had as its strong man Baron Kato Takaaki, the former ambassador in London and now leader of the Doshikai party. Kato was extremely capable, if somewhat arrogant, and was a firm believer in the need for an assertive foreign policy.[69] He was linked by marriage to the Mitsubishi interests, which may well have stimulated his desire to advance Japan's economic position. Kato was a fervent advocate of the Anglo–Japanese alliance but this did not mean that he was prepared to pursue a submissive policy towards London on economic questions. On 10 June 1914 he gave a note to the British ambassador deploring the British refusal to accept Japanese construction of the full length of the line from Foochow to Hankow: Japan demanded the right to construct the section from Nanchang to Han-kow. Kato followed this note by privately complaining about Britain's unhelpful attitude over the Yangtze; the foreign minister stated that he did not understand the reasoning behind British policy.[70] Grey decided to pursue an unyielding response and flatly rejected Kato's protests. Jordan was disturbed at the expansionist traits of Japanese policy in China. He sent a dispatch to London on 4 July 1914, enclosing a memorandum by the military attache on the strategic implications of Japanese-acquired railway concessions, including those secured in south Manchuria. The military attache believed that the Japanese general staff had almost cer-tainly been prominent in urging the Japanese interest in railways,[71] and recommended both that Britain should resist Japanese infiltration outside Fukien province and that British ascendancy in the heart of the Yangtze must be defended.[72] His report stiffened the resolve of the Foreign Office. There was probably some justification for the fears of military motives accounting for Japanese policy but not to the extent claimed by the attache. Political and economic factors were most likely more influen-tial in Kato's decision-making. Britain and Japan were still engaged in sharp exchanges over the Yangtze when the European crisis over-shadowed everything in July and August 1914. Had it not been for the transformation effected by the coming of the First World War, it is probable that the Anglo–Japanese argument would have become more acrimonious and led to a direct confrontation.

The controversy over the Yangtze shows the pressure that Britain was facing in preserving the Yangtze region as her sphere of interest. Japan and France were threatening Britain's position. British trade in China was experiencing intensified competition from Japanese, French, German, and American firms. The dominance established in the middle of the nineteenth century was declining: the sun was beginning to set on British supremacy in China. This decline was to be much accelerated by the repercussions of the First World War in the Far East. Japan was presented with opportunities undreamed of before 1914, but she was not to exploit them as successfully as might have been expected.

Chapter 6

The impact of the First World War in East Asia, 1914–1919

The first sounds of the guns firing on the two European fronts, in August 1914, signalled the end of the era in the Far East that had lasted since the opening-up of China and Japan in the middle of the nineteenth century. The days of establishing and consolidating the western presence in China were over; from 1914 onwards the occidental powers were executing a gradual retreat. For Japan, 1914 did not mark a decline in her position in China; rather it witnessed an impetus to her presence. Japanese political and economic interests steadily expanded in China until Japan eventually became engaged in full-scale war and occupation of much of China between 1937 and 1945. Britain in the First World War was heavily dependent on Japan remaining on the allied side and providing significant naval assistance in the Far East and Pacific: she could no longer defend her interests with the tenacity displayed before August 1914, but she did not abdicate. During the crisis provoked by the Japanese 'twenty-one demands' in 1915 she asserted herself with more vigour than might have been anticipated. The making of the original Anglo–Japanese alliance in 1902 had been an admission of British weakness in the Far East. This was even more true of the making of the second and third alliances in 1905 and 1911; the naval aspect assumed greater importance as time went by. Without the alliance in 1914 Britain would have found herself in a position not dissimilar to that which arose in 1939–41 with consequences that were all too evident in 1941–42. Fundamentally this explains why Britain had no choice but to seek Japanese assistance in August 1914, in order to assure adequate protection to British trade, troop convoys, and the Pacific dominions. A German naval squadron headed by Admiral von Spee was not notably inferior to the British China squadron; however, the addition of the British East Indies squadron and the Australian fleet ensured British predominance. The threat from the German squadron showed the price that had to be paid for concentrating British naval resources in the North Sea and the Atlantic; it was an early manifestation of the challenge of war. The problem was that Spee's squadron escaped into the Pacific at the outbreak of hostilities in Europe and could not be located. The squadron, together with individual German raiders, could clearly wreak havoc until found and eliminated. To achieve this objective, Japanese aid was essential. Apart from the naval question in itself, there were wider implications of retaining Japanese friendship through involving her positively in the war. A certain amount of muddle and mishandling was involved in British discussions with Japan in August 1914, which cast a shadow over Anglo–Japanese relations.

The rapidity with which the European crisis broke and reached its climax unavoidably meant that little attention could be paid to the role and function of the Anglo–Japanese alliance. Sir Edward Grey saw the Japanese ambassador on 1 August 1914 and indicated that it was unlikely that the alliance would be invoked.[1] When the Foreign Office investigated the situation soon afterwards, the conclusion was reached that the alliance would become operative in the event of a German attack on Hong Kong or Weihaiwei. Japan was then informed that if either of these contingencies materialised, Britain would expect Japanese aid.[2] Kato Takaaki, the Japanese foreign minister, told the British ambassador in Tokyo that if Germany attacked British possessions in East Asia, Japan would help. He stated that the Japanese navy was making preparations for action in case this proved necessary. Grey expressed gratitude for the information but added, citing the Russo-Japanese war as a precedent, that he hoped it would be feasible for Japan to remain neutral. When the Foreign Office and the Admiralty looked into the implications of the strategic position, it was decided that Britain would have to seek Japanese assistance. However, it was felt that there must be restrictions on the scope of Japanese activities; it was not desirable to give Japan a free hand in China and an attack on the German concession of Kiaochow, in Shantung province, should be avoided if possible. Grey personally wrote out, on 6 August, a telegram to the Tokyo embassy requesting Japanese naval assistance:

As our warships will require some time to locate and destroy the German warships in Chinese waters it is essential that the Japanese should hunt out and destroy the German armed merchant cruisers who are attacking our commerce now. If the Japanese Gov[ernmen]t would employ some of their warships in this way it would be of the greatest assistance to us. It means of course an act of war against Germany but we do not see how this is to be avoided.[3]

Kato Takaaki was an Anglophile and a personal friend of Sir Edward Grey. He made up his mind strongly to support Japanese action, not for sentimental reasons but because he grasped the splendid opportunity that fate had handed Japan for enhancing her role in the Far East. He was determined that there should be no delay. Opinion in Japan was divided but the consensus was in favour of adhering to the alliance and supporting Britain. The *genro* and the navy were broadly sympathetic to Britain. The army, which had been trained on Prussian principles, was largely pro-German and believed Germany would win the war. While powerful, the army did not possess the dominance it would reach in the 1930s; decisions would be reached by the cabinet and *genro*. A cabinet meeting was held on 7 August 1914 and Kato prevailed upon his colleagues to agree to

Japanese intervention; however, Japan would first issue an ultimatum to Germany and it was agreed that Japan could not accept limitations upon her actions.[4]

Britain was confronted with an awkward diplomatic problem over Japanese intervention. There was already apprehension in the United States and British dominions over Japanese ambitions in China and in the Pacific and it was most desirable to see that additional encouragement was not given to such fears. On 10 August Japan sent a note to Britain clearly explaining Japan's intentions: she was willing to give naval assistance to Britain but this would involve a declaration of war on Germany. Japan believed this to be wholly compatible with the terms of the Anglo–Japanese alliance.[5] Grey unwisely decided to try to prevent Japan from advancing formally under the terms of the alliance and to indicate limits within which Japanese action should take place. He personally drafted an *aide-mémoire* for the Japanese ambassador on 10 August reading:

To avoid internal trouble and disturbances of trade in China we are anxious to limit acts of war to operations at sea, and more particularly protection of British merchant vessels . . .

I understand from Baron Kato's communication that if Japan declared war upon Germany she could not restrict warlike operations to the sea alone.

I understand this view, but for the present His Majesty's Government believe that acts of war in the Far East will be restricted as described, and they think it very desirable to maintain this attitude as long as possible. His Majesty's Government will therefore for the present refrain from invoking action under the treaty. But should further developments of a serious character occur, such as attack upon Hongkong, His Majesty's Government would reconsider their decision.[6]

Grey told the ambassador that as Japan reasonably felt that she could not accept limitations on her action, he preferred no action to be taken by the Japanese government. Grey was motivated by the wish to quieten suspicions of Japan lurking in the United States and the dominions. The lack of trust implicit in Grey's move alienated the Japanese government to some extent and not least Kato, who had taken a forthright stance in the cabinet in support of Britain. Kato replied that Japan would definitely declare war on Germany but he was prepared to give an assurance that Japan's action would be restricted to 'measures which are absolutely indispensable'.[7]

Grey recognised that the neutralisation of the Pacific could not be secured and informed the United States. He persisted in efforts to prescribe limits to Japan's activities:

I agree . . . to a statement that the two Governments, having been in communication with each other, are of opinion that it is necessary for each to take action to protect the general interests contemplated by the Anglo–Japanese Alliance. It should also be stated that the action of Japan will not extend beyond Asiatic waters westward of the China Seas, or to any foreign territory except territory in German occupation on the continent in Eastern Asia. This is important to prevent unfounded misapprehension abroad.[8]

Kato at once stated that Japan could not accept the geographical limitations on freedom of action envisaged by Grey and instead suggested formal assurances to the powers with possessions in the Pacific that Japan would respect their positions. Japan intended to launch operations against the German fortress of Tsingtao in Shantung; Chinese neutrality would be respected except that it would be necessary to cross a small area of Chinese territory near Tsingtao. Grey believed that it was imperative for reasons of prestige, to give some influence over Japanese action, that British forces should participate in the operations against Tsingtao.

On 15 August Japan sent an ultimatum to Germany demanding the withdrawal of German armed vessels from Japanese and Chinese waters and the surrender, within one month, of the leased territory of Kiaochow; if no reply arrived by 23 August, Japan would be at war. The British embassy in Washington warned that German-American circles would use Japanese intervention to whip up feelings against Britain. Senator Cabot Lodge, then in London, warned Grey that Japan should not take German Samoa because this would assist those in the United States hostile to Britain.[9] Grey then approved the issuing of a statement by the Press Bureau in London, which stated 'that the action of Japan will not extend to the Pacific Ocean beyond the China Seas, except in so far as it may be necessary to protect Japanese shipping lines in the Pacific, not beyond Asiatic waters westward of the China Seas or to any foreign territory except territory in German occupation on the continent of Eastern Asia'.[10] The statement had been issued without prior consultation with Japan and Kato objected when he heard of it. Grey lamely replied that something had to be said and it did not claim to be an exact definition.

On 23 August Japan declared war on Germany. China was alarmed to hear the news, appreciating her vulnerability with the European powers locked in combat. Yuan Shih-k'ai knew that the Japanese had old scores to settle with him; he would require all his not inconsiderable store of deviousness to avert the deadly embrace. Immediately it was clear that fighting would take place on Chinese territory once the siege of the German fortress of Tsingtao commenced. Japanese forces landed at Lungkow, in Shantung, on 2 September 1914, and the first clash of arms with the Germans occurred twelve days later. The British contingent comprised the second battalion of the South Wales Borderers plus half a battalion of Indian troops with Brigadier-General Barnardiston in command. The British were under the Japanese supreme command. The German fortress was strongly built and defended by 3,500 regular troops reinforced by 2,500 reservists. The German resistance was futile, since there was no possibility of relief forces arriving. The siege lasted from 22 October to 7 November, when the Germans surrendered. The British contribution to the siege was minor and the co-operation with the Japanese troops was not particularly amicable. Critical reports on the Anglo–Japanese operation were submitted by two British consuls; J. T. Pratt, the consul at Tsinanfu, described the operation as 'a fiasco'.[11] Given the

limited number of British troops available for the action, it was inevitable
that it should be dominated by the Japanese.

In the naval sphere, Japan similarly took the initiative to expand her
power and made up her mind to occupy the German island possessions in
the Pacific. This created the danger of a clash with Australia and New
Zealand, who were preparing expeditions to take the German islands. The
islands concerned were New Guinea, Samoa, Rabaul, and the Caroline,
Marshall, Mariana and Palau groups. German New Guinea and Samoa
were captured by Australian expeditions at an early stage but a more
leisurely approach was adopted towards the other islands. Japan was certain to be more interested in the fate of the islands north of the equator,
which were closer to Japan. This subject was discussed by Britain and
Japan between October and December 1914. The Foreign Office was not
happy at the thought of Japan occupying Pacific islands because of the
repercussions on the United States and the dominions. However, the
Japanese navy was assisting the Royal Navy in the search for Spee's
squadron and for the individual German raiders at large in the Pacific and
Far East.[12] Winston Churchill, the first lord of the Admiralty, deplored
the suspicions of Japan: 'The Admiralty would strongly deprecate any
action towards Japan which would appear suspicious or ungracious. We
are deriving benefit from their powerful and generous aid. They have inti-
mated that their occupation is purely military and devoid of political
significance and there I trust we may leave the matter for the present.'[13]
Japan occupied all German islands north of the equator by the middle of
October 1914 and on 1 December Kato informed the British ambassador
that Japan would seek to retain them. Grey pointed out that this was
contrary to Japan's initial assurances at the beginning of the war but that
he was prepared to accept the situation until the ultimate peace settlement.[14] Spee's squadron was defeated at the battle of the Falkland Islands
at the beginning of December 1914, having first routed a British squadron
at Coronel, off the Chilean coast, a short time before.[15] Individual German raiders were still at liberty and continued to prey on shipping.

Between January and May 1915 Britain was concerned with the crisis
provoked by the twenty-one demands delivered to Yuan Shih-k'ai by the
Japanese minister, Hioki Eki, on 18 January 1915. The origins of the
demands are obscure; it is likely that they reflected the aims and wishes
of diverse pressure groups in Japan, including the cabinet, the *genro*, the
army, and the nationalist adventurers of the *Kokuryukai* ('Black Dragon
Society').[16] The demands were formulated in Tokyo between August and
December 1914; they were a direct consequence of Japan's entry into the
First World War and in effect constituted Japan's desire for prompt payment of what was due as a reward for services rendered. The demands
were divided into five groups, of which the first four were specific in
character and the fifth, and most notorious, was vague. The first group
comprised four articles dealing with Shantung province and required
Chinese acceptance of Japanese ascendancy in the former German sphere
of interest. The second group consisted of seven articles concerning south

Manchuria and eastern Inner Mongolia. Japan aimed to consolidate her presence in this region, principally through securing the extension of leases on crucial railway lines for an additional period of ninety-nine years after the existing leases expired in 1923. The third group involved the Hanyehping Iron and Coal Company, an important enterprise in the heart of the Yangtze valley, which Japanese interests had been seeking to control for some time; China was required to accept Japanese direction of the company. The fourth group comprised a declaration that China would not grant harbours or ports as concessions to another power; this was intended to obviate United States interest in possibly acquiring a naval base in Fukien province. The fifth group called upon China to appoint numerous Japanese advisers in the political, financial and military spheres; to permit Japanese to own land and to provide for Sino-Japanese control of the police; China was to purchase arms supplies from Japan and establish an arsenal under joint control; Japan was to be given the right to construct railways between Nanchang and Hangchow and between Nanchang and Chaochow; Japan was to be consulted on any investment projects in Fukien; and Japanese subjects were to be given the right to preach in the interior of China.

If implemented fully, the fifth group would have erected a Japanese protectorate in China. It is probable that the first and third groups were drawn up largely to satisfy two of the *genro*, Prince Yamagata Aritomo and Marquis Inoue Kaoru, who had urged the government to extend Japan's position in Shantung and in the Yangtze. The second group dealt with aspects with which the foreign minister, Kato Takaaki, was particularly interested: just before he left London, in January 1913, at the end of his term as ambassador, he had told Sir Edward Grey that he wished to consolidate Japan's authority in south Manchuria when the moment was opportune. Grey commented that he understood this ambition but he could not commit a future British government to automatic approval of actions taken by Japan.[17] It was, however, obvious that Grey personally was sympathetic to Kato's aim. The Japanese army was also anxious to make Japan's position in south Manchuria more secure. The reasons for including the fifth group are more difficult to explain. Kato described the fifth group, after his resignation from the *Gaimusho*, as 'concessions made to internal politics'.[18] Kato did not expound further on his meaning. The most convincing explanation is that the fifth group was inserted to satisfy the militarists and extreme nationalists in the secret societies. The army was becoming more vocal and many within its ranks were less willing to accept the cautious leadership of Yamagata. The bellicose nationalists of the *Kokuryukai*, led by the sinister Uchida Ryohei, had an appreciable nuisance value in stirring up popular unrest on controversial national issues and the Okuma government was in a somewhat weak parliamentary position in 1914–15.[19] Kato was endeavouring to mollify various elements, therefore, and hoped to retain effective conduct of the diplomacy of the demands in his own hands.

Kato intended to force Yuan Shih-k'ai to accept rapidly the first four groups of the demands. Kato drew a distinction between the first four groups and the fifth group; the latter was regarded as less imperative than the former, although the Japanese minister was instructed to press them with vigour. The demands were handed to Yuan on 18 January 1915. Hioki, the Japanese minister, emphasised that Japan wanted the matter resolved speedily and that if China did not respond positively, Japan might be compelled to assist Sun Yat-sen, then living in exile in Japan. Yuan was perturbed yet, at the same time, confident that he could, with good fortune, outmanoeuvre the Japanese. Kato did not communicate the demands to Britain beforehand. He sent a short summary, with one omission, of the first four groups to London; no reference was made to the fifth group. This version was supplied to the Foreign Office by the Japanese ambassador on 22 January 1915. Grey told the ambassador that he understood the reason for some of the demands, especially those concerned with south Manchuria. However, he was worried lest Japan should 'get into bad relations with China'.[20] The consensus in the British Foreign Office was that the subject was likely to cause difficulties, since China would be unwilling to comply, and the position was also delicate owing to American interest.[21]

The first indications that the Japanese demands were more extensive than suggested was reported to London on 29 January 1915, when Sir John Jordan passed on information conveyed by the Russian minister. Additional confirmation was soon forthcoming from Petrograd and from Peking. On 10 February 1915 Kato gave a confidential interview to the Peking correspondent of *The Times* and admitted that he was pursuing certain 'wishes' apart from 'demands' in Peking. The news was reported by the correspondent to Sir Conyngham Greene, the British ambassador, who at once visited the foreign minister. Kato behaved arrogantly and implied that he was uninterested in what Britain thought.[22] A summary of group five of the demands was given to Grey by the Russian ambassador on 16 February; two days later Jordan sent the full text of the Japanese demands, including the 'wishes'. Jordan warned that Japan was clearly seeking to obtain railway concessions already promised to Britain. The Foreign Office was alarmed and Grey helped to draft a telegram to Tokyo in which he refrained from detailed comment but reiterated that Britain would expect free discussion on matters affecting British interests and that care should be taken not to affect adversely the independence or integrity of China.[23] Grey's courteous rebuke, together with advice from the Japanese embassy in London that a more amenable approach should be adopted, caused Kato to become more helpful. He informed the British ambassador on 22 February 1915 that he would always be willing to listen to Grey's views and would consult on matters involving British interests.

The negotiations in Peking proceeded slowly. Yuan deliberately worked to spin out the talks over as long a period as possible, thus allowing time for the powers to bring some pressure to bear on Tokyo and for internal dissent to manifest itself in Japan. If necessary Yuan was prepared to concede the less odious of the demands if no alternative was left. Britain was faced with an embarrassing and potentially dangerous situation. The war was not going well in Europe and it was vital to retain American goodwill; the United States was already highly suspicious of Japanese policy. Britain would have to do what she could to ameliorate matters but without going too far. On the whole, Grey blended the two aspects successfully. Within Japan Kato came under increasing criticism because of the protracted talks. The army and the nationalist adventurers felt he was not being tough enough and thought that an ultimatum should be delivered to Yuan. The *genro* were kept in ignorance of the detailed progress of the talks, for Kato did not believe in allowing them to influence policy formulation excessively; indeed he treated them with what amounted to contempt and this was to be another factor in his discomfiture in April–May 1915.[24]

In April 1915 matters came to a head. Kato wanted the talks concluded but Yuan was still procrastinating. In a desperate bid to achieve a diplomatic settlement, Kato put forward on 26 April a modified version of the demands that had not been resolved. This version was less intimidating, especially where the fifth group was concerned. The amended proposals were communicated to Britain on 28 April with a statement that Japan would make no further concessions and her patience would then be exhausted.[25] The permanent under-secretary in the Foreign Office commented: 'The situation between Japan and China is becoming serious and the question of our Alliance threatens to become also a debatable point. The question altogether is of such seriousness especially in regard to its possible developments that it emerges from being a departmental one.'[26] Grey brought the matter before the cabinet and it was decided that he should inform Japan that Britain would deplore conflict between Japan and China arising from an attempt to compel China to accept conditions contrary to the objects of the Anglo–Japanese alliance. Grey personally drafted an important telegram for Tokyo, emphasising that the future of the alliance was threatened.[27] A political crisis was developing in Tokyo, where the *genro* had descended on the capital and were demanding full discussion with the cabinet on the handling of the talks in Peking. Bitter criticism was expressed of Kato and the representations from London accentuated the concern of the *genro*. After prolonged and acrimonious debates, it was jointly agreed by cabinet and *genro* that an ultimatum should be sent to China based on the first four groups of the demands, omitting the fifth group. If China did not comply, war would ensue. Kato frankly admitted to the British ambassador that an ultimatum could hardly be reconciled with the terms of the alliance.[28] Realising the gravity of the crisis, Sir John Jordan urged Yuan Shih-k'ai to compromise. Grey spoke in similar terms to the Chinese minister in London, Alfred Sze, and warned that the occidental powers were so immersed in the European war that they could not intervene directly in the Sino–Japanese dispute.[29] Yuan knew that the time had come to accept qualified defeat, which was the best he could hope for. On 8 May he decided to accept the Japanese ultimatum. The final phase of the twenty-one demands crisis witnessed diplomatic intervention by the United States, deeply alarmed at the menace of war in the Far East when she was simultaneously alarmed at German intentions in the Atlantic. Britain stressed that all possible steps had been taken to avert a Sino–Japanese conflict. Despite being heavily involved in Europe, Britain had acted more vigorously over the crisis than might have been expected. The United States had vacillated, partly owing to disagreements between President Wilson and the secretary of state, William Jennings Bryan; Wilson inclined towards a more resolute policy and Bryan towards a temporizing one.[30]

The crisis was virtually at an end. Treaties incorporating the first four groups of the demands were signed at Peking on 25 May 1915. Japan had eventually gained much of what she wanted but emerged bruised and somewhat discredited from the encounter. Kato's high reputation had been dented; a few months afterwards he resigned as foreign minister when Okuma reconstituted his administration. It was to take Kato longer than he had expected to secure the office of prime minister (until 1924); this in part resulted from his mishandling of the demands and from the increased animosity between Yamagata and himself. Yuan Shih-k'ai's tactics had been skilful, except that he had alienated Japan utterly with consequences that soon became evident. The twenty-one demands showed the growth of Japanese ambitions in China, an ominous pointer to developments two decades later. For Britain the crisis demonstrated how the allies were drifting apart: Britain wished to conserve what she possessed and Japan aimed to expand.

The personal circles surrounding Yuan Shih-k'ai, notably his son, Yuan K'e-ting, made the disastrous mistake, in the summer of 1915, of launching a monarchical movement designed to install Yuan as the first emperor of the new dynasty.[31] China was in an extremely unstable condition following the repeated upheavals of the preceding five years. The basis of Yuan's power came from the loyalty of his military commanders, most of whom had been associated with him in the years when he had built up the Peiyang army. This loyalty was strained once Yuan began to regard himself as a future emperor. In addition, the central and southern provinces were in a state of latent disaffection. Japan was implacably opposed to Yuan and was determined to bring him down when the opportunity presented itself; the monarchical movement provided the opportunity. Japanese army men, financiers and adventurers became involved in the plotting against Yuan; Japanese officials encouraged the revolt, which began in the south-western provinces of Yunnan and Kwangtung in January 1916. Yuan was declared emperor on 12 December 1915. Britain was uneasy at the development of the monarchical movement, discerning the enhanced opportunities for Japan to exploit the situation.[32] The prolongation of the European war meant that care had to be exercised in executing policy. At first Britain favoured recognising Yuan's elevated status but Japan's opposition prevented Britain, France and Russia from so acting.[33] In January 1916 the rebellion in south-western China commenced and spread rapidly. Too late Yuan awoke to the perils of his predicament. He tried to cancel the monarchical movement and revert to being the president of the republic. He had overplayed his hand, however, and antagonised too many people. Japan had attained her objective. Yuan's power was at an end and he died on 6 June 1916, a broken figure. His death ushered in the classic warlord era in which all pretence of centralised authority in China vanished. Instead, numerous warlords of varying power and importance competed ceaselessly for supremacy; an endless game of musical chairs was played. Warlordism involved less actual fighting and bloodshed than might have been anticipated. 'Silver bullets' (bribery) were far more relevant to the switching of alliances and ever-shifting coalitions. The ordinary people suffered, as always; while not all the warlords were brutal and negative in their policies, the majority revealed these characteristics and possessed an amazing ingenuity in levying taxes on about every conceivable object.[34] Japan became involved in financing the Anfu clique of warlords, led by Tuan Chi-jui, which controlled the nominal government in Peking from 1916 to 1919; loans were channelled by the government of Field Marshal Terauchi Masatake through the agency of Nishihara Kamezo. Japan was not, however, to gain suitable rewards for the sums of money expended.

The possibility of China joining the allies and breaking with Germany had been under consideration in London since 1915. The German community in China facilitated intrigues and plots against allied interests. It was not easy to combat the plotting while China maintained diplomatic relations with Germany and Austria–Hungary. Chinese entry into the war would render it more awkward for Japan to pursue her ulterior aims in China. This explains why Britain supported the case for Chinese intervention in 1915 and why Japan expressed reservations. After Yuan's death there were two governments in China, one based at Peking and one in Canton. The Peking regime was headed nominally by Li Yuan-hung but was dominated by the Anfu warlords, notably Tuan Chi-jui and Feng Kuo-chang. In southern China, Sun Yat-sen's supporters now found it easier to re-emerge and contrived to co-operate with the southern military governors.[35] In October 1916 the Okuma government was replaced by the more conservative administration of Terauchi. The new prime minister was one of the leading men in the army, a member of the Choshu clique and a protégé of Yamagata. The new foreign minister was Baron Motono Ichiro, previously ambassador in Petrograd. The new government's relations with Britain were better than had been the case with the Okuma government. The Terauchi government aimed to protect Japan's special interests in south Manchuria, Inner Mongolia and Fukien but did not wish to continue the more grandiose designs put forward by Kato. Motono told the British ambassador that he was opposed to the previous Japanese policy and desired close co-operation with Britain.[36] There now appeared to be a definite chance of persuading Japan to accept China's adherence to the allied side. The United States was moving rapidly towards the final confrontation with Germany, culminating in her declaration of war in April 1917. The American minister in Peking, Paul S. Reinsch, advocated securing China's entry. The Peking regime was prepared to consider entry but desired full membership of the peace conference at the end of the war and financial assistance from the United States in equipping her forces. Reinsch encouraged the Anfu leaders to believe that they would gain much from participation in the war.[37]

Britain supported the plan. The new British foreign secretary, A. J. Balfour, informed the Chinese minister on 8 February 1917 that Japan must be properly consulted on this vital issue.[38] Japan supported the proposal and Motono notified the allied ministers accordingly. It was made clear that Japan expected Britain, France and Russia entirely to recognise Japanese claims at the ultimate peace conference. Once this aspect had been clarified, Japan was willing to encourage China to declare war on Germany within the near future. Tuan Chi-jui wished to declare war but faced opposition from the president, Li Yuan-hung, and from Feng Kuo-chang. After argument in Peking in February and early March 1917, the differences within the ruling circle were settled; on 14 March 1917, China formally broke off diplomatic relations with Germany and Austria–Hungary. However, China did not advance to the final step and declare war on Germany. The opponents of a declaration of war included those who feared a separate peace between Germany and Russia, following the March revolution in Russia; the merchants desirous of peace to foster trade; and the supporters of Sun Yat-sen, who maintained that China had suffered enough from the allied powers since 1914. As usual, Sun Yat-sen was giving contradictory assurances to different people. In public he was more critical of Japan but in private he maintained his close links with the nationalist societies.[39] A political battle ensued in Peking between Li Yuan-hung and Tuan Chi-jui in which violence and corruption were applied by both sides; the position was extremely unstable, with rumours of a Ch'ing restoration. The United States was afraid that the unity of China, already severely strained, might deteriorate and Robert Lansing, the secretary of state, adopted the view that it was preferable for China to preserve as much unity as she could rather than degenerate into civil war over the question of declaring war on Germany.[40] Britain and France did not agree. Britain considered Chinese entry into the war to be a topic of major importance but, at the same time, recognised that the divisions over the matter in China required cautious action. Japan disliked the American action but did not complain officially.[41] On 1 July 1917 General Chang Hsun took temporary control of Peking and declared the restoration of the last Ch'ing emperor, Pu-yi. This action forced the retirement of Li Yuan-hung and was at once followed by an advance by Tuan Chi-jui's troops, who entered Peking and defeated Chang Hsun. Tuan was now strong enough to introduce the declaration of war for which he had pressed formerly. On 14 August 1917, China delared war on Germany.[42]

China's participation in the First World War was purely nominal. There were approximately 200,000 Chinese labourers assisting the allied war effort already but this had no connection with China's formal involvement. Tuan Chi-jui stated in April 1917 that China would be willing to supply the allies with fighting men for the European front. The United States and France showed enthusiasm for the suggestion but Britain regarded it as absurd, one official commenting, 'It is impossible to imagine a greater waste of time, trouble, equipment, money and tonnage.'[43] Balfour termed it 'idiotic' and 'insane'.[44]

Relations between Britain and Japan were strained in 1915 after the crisis over the twenty-one demands and took some time to improve. There were rumours that Japan was reconsidering her role in the war and that she might even change sides and join Germany. Many leading men in the army were sympathetic to Germany, as were a number of leading scientists, professors and journalists.[45] Peace feelers were inspired from Berlin and purely unofficial exchanges took place through the German minister in Peking, Admiral Paul von Hintze, in 1915 and again in January 1916. Talks were held also in Stockholm in 1915–16 between the Japanese minister, Uchida Sadazuchi, and German emissaries. Germany was prepared to accept the retention by Japan of the former German colonies occupied by her.[46] From the Japanese viewpoint the exchanges were useful as a way of gently reminding Britain of Japan's importance and that her presence should not be taken too much for granted. There was no intention on the part of the Okuma or Terauchi governments between 1915 and 1918 of reversing alliances; information on the talks with the Germans was communicated to the British government. The Foreign Office in London was fully aware of the dangers of a Japanese–German *rapprochement*. Grey observed in February 1916:

... I do not wish to make offers to Japan at the expense of China but in my opinion if we had not made it clear that we should not bar Japan's expansion of interests in the Far East [undertakings Grey had given that if China entered the war and German interests were taken over Japan could have the former German concessions] it would have been clearly to Japan's advantage to throw in her lot with Germany. Japan is barred from every other part of the world except the Far East and the Anglo–Japanese Alliance cannot be maintained if she is to be barred from expansion there also and if we are to claim the German concessions in China as well as taking German colonies in Africa and elsewhere.[47]

Hintze made an approach to the Japanese consul-general in Tientsin in 1917 before he left Peking but this, too, was abortive. Japan remained loyal to the alliance with Britain because most of her leaders believed, despite the doubts voiced in military and academic circles, that Britain would be on the winning side.

At the beginning of the First World War Japan had emphasised that her contribution to the war effort would be restricted almost entirely to the Far East. Japan had no intention of dispatching her troops to become cannon fodder on the European fronts. Her navy would assist Britain in far eastern waters, in the Pacific, and in the Indian Ocean but not beyond these seas. This attitude, while disappointing to some in the allied countries, was realistic and wise. Japan was still in the comparatively early stages of developing her might – not yet predominantly an industrial power – and it would be foolish to dissipate her resources in the struggle that was tearing Europe apart and fast reducing European ascendancy. Britain had accepted the facts of the situation and had not pressed Japan for additional aid after the early period of the war.

Feelings changed in London at the beginning of 1917. Asquith had fallen from office, discredited by a number of reverses and particularly undermined by his failure to radiate confidence in the future. He had been replaced by Lloyd George, who possessed immense vigour and dynamism. The state of the war was not encouraging. There was no sign of a breakthrough in Europe and British naval supremacy in the Atlantic was threatened by the ravages of German submarine warfare. Huge quantities of British merchant shipping were being sunk and no remedy was in sight; in fact, a remedy was at hand in the convoy system but the conservative admirals were reluctant to adopt it and it was only implemented from April 1917 as a result of Lloyd George's determination to shake up the Admiralty. Admiral Jellicoe felt, in December 1916, that Britain should ask Japan to provide more assistance in the naval sphere.[48] Destroyers were required in the Mediterranean and light cruisers in the south Atlantic. The Admiralty wished two Japanese light cruisers switched from Singapore to the Cape of Good Hope to contend with German raiders and a flotilla of destroyers placed at Malta to assist with submarines and defend trade. This request was submitted to Japan on 11 January 1917.[49] The Terauchi government was in the process of reappraising policy independent of the British approach. It had been the aim of Baron Motono, upon taking charge of the *Gaimusho*, to put Japan's relations with her allies on a more harmonious footing. He believed in warmer collaboration with Britain and he succeeded in removing much of the acrimony that had obtained in 1915–16. Motono saw the British ambassador on 26 January 1917: he handed Greene a note stating that Japan would welcome formal recognition by Britain of Japan's right to retain the former German possessions in Shantung and in the Pacific. Japan was not asking for additional concessions but for reiteration of informal undertakings made by Sir Edward Grey.[50]

The naval assistance was promised by Japan on 2 February 1917. It was not made contingent on Britain's fulfilment of political concessions but this could be regarded as implicit. Japanese vessels would be sent to the Cape of Good Hope and to the Mediterranean. The ships would cooperate with the Royal Navy but would not come under British command.[51] On the same day the Japanese ambassador visited the Foreign Office and left two memoranda concerning the fate of the former German island possessions in the Pacific. Japan desired confirmation of Grey's recognition that Japan should negotiate with China on the position in Shantung; with regard to the Pacific islands, Japan wished Britain to accept that they would be retained in Japanese occupation.[52] The matter was considered by the war cabinet and referred to Australia and New Zealand for their observations. It was agreed to give Japan the assurances she sought; this was achieved when Greene, the ambassador, visited the *Gaimusho* on 14 February.[53] A telegram, sent to Greene for his own information, stated:

HM Government are quietly resisting attempts to allow the Japanese to get a footing in industrial undertakings in China in provinces bordering India and Thibet, and in the Yangtze valley . . . It is doubtful whether, in the present condition of British political and financial helplessness in the Far East, HM Government are secure enough to maintain the existing state of things against any pressure that may suddenly arise. Moreover, it must be realised that, should it be necessary at any time to ask for military and even largely increased naval favours from the Japanese, the price that would have to be paid could only be . . . at the expense of British interests in China.[54]

Britain then requested that Japan should recognise that the British Empire would have the right to dispose of the Pacific islands south of the equator. Japan immediately gave the undertaking. The exchange of notes was a necessary consequence of Britain's reliance upon Japan's continued friendship in the perilous situation of the European conflict in 1917. As the war at sea continued to preoccupy the policy-makers in London, further requests for Japanese aid were made. In April 1917 Britain inquired whether destroyers could be sent to European waters to assist in patrol and convoy duties; Japan declined but agreed subsequently to send four ships to the Mediterranean. Japanese vessels also helped with the protection of transports between Aden and Colombo.[55] While the allied naval dilemma was improved by the entry of the United States into the war, Britain periodically raised the topic of further Japanese help later in 1917 and early in 1918, but to no avail. A Japanese squadron remained in the Mediterranean until the end of the war but beyond this Japan understandably would not go.[56]

Developments in Russia produced new problems for Britain and Japan; a chapter of perplexity and muddle was opened that was only ended in 1921–22 and then with consequences that were to have enduring impact on relations between Britain, Japan and Russia. The euphoria discernible in the immediate aftermath of the March revolution in Russia gradually collapsed when it became clear that Russia was not going to be a powerful bastion of liberal democracy. Instead Russia was subsiding into a future that was hard to predict, except that it was not likely to assist the allied war effort. In November 1917 the Bolshevik *coup* took place in Petrograd and Lenin and his followers succeeded to the inheritance of the tsars. Russia was dissolving into chaos with the Bolsheviks endeavouring to consolidate their tenuous authority and numerous anti-communist forces of different political persuasions materialising. The new situation was profoundly alarming to both Britain and Japan, if for divergent reasons.

Britain wanted to keep Russia in the war and hopefully to regalvanize the Russian war effort. The Bolsheviks were committed to a policy of withdrawing Russia from the war and of making peace with the central powers; apart from ideological aspects, Britain was not prejudiced in favour of the Bolsheviks. For Japan the pressing issue was the fate of the Russian empire in the Far East: what was to happen to the vast frozen wastes of Siberia? There were conflicting views within Japan and divided opinions as to whether Japan should intervene by force in Siberia.[57] The subject of allied involvement in Siberia arose in November–December 1917. Britain and the United States were contemplating dispatching forces to guard allied stores at Vladivostok and sought Japanese views, emphasising that the powers must act with cohesion.[58] Within the British war cabinet, Lord Milner was a staunch advocate of Japanese action. He believed that Britain should have adopted a more positive attitude to Japan during the war and that she was partially responsible for the coolness which had affected Anglo–Japanese relations. He wrote to Balfour in February 1918: 'I know there is a very strong prejudice against Japan among the Entente Powers, a feeling that she is playing entirely for her own hand etc. I think myself that a good case could be made on the other side on *general grounds*, and that if Japan has not done much for the Alliance, she has, on the other hand, not been very tactfully handled by it.'[59] Milner advocated Japanese intervention:

[Siberia] is a case where she is in a far better position to act than any of the rest of us, and where she quite evidently would like to act, *if action become necessary*... Why should we not encourage her at least to the extent of suggesting that, if allied intervention is necessary, it is Japan who should take action on behalf of the Allies? At the worst, this is making a virtue of necessity. If Bolshevism becomes too rampant in that quarter, Japan certainly will intervene whether the Allies like it or not... The objection to her doing so is twofold (1) that Russia might resent it (2) that Japan would seize the opportunity to take undue advantage of her allies... I think too there is a certain advantage in getting Japan more deeply committed than she actually is in the world-struggle against Germany and German influences...[60]

Balfour observed that there were more complications surrounding the issue than Milner had realised. The impact of a Japanese expedition on Red or White Russians had to be remembered, as had the repercussions on the United States. The Foreign Office favoured, in January 1918, Japanese action to assume control of the entire length of the Trans-Siberian railway in Asia. This was drastic intervention and exceeded domination of eastern Siberia. The war cabinet approved the recommendations of the Foreign Office and the proposal was forwarded to Washington for consideration. Woodrow Wilson opposed it, since he was deeply suspicious of Japanese aims in any event.[61] Britain and France still proceeded to ask Japan to take over the eastern section of the Trans-Siberian railway. Opinion in Japan was divided. The foreign minister, Baron Motono, and the army general staff supported intervention but the prime minister, Marshal Terauchi, and the principal *genro*, Prince Yamagata, were hostile; Yamagata believed that Japan should act only if the United States supported such action.[62] The majority in the cabinet and *genro* leaned in the latter direction and Motono resigned in protest on 10 April

1918. He was succeeded by Baron Goto Shimpei, a choice not approved of in London, since Goto was held to be sympathetic to Germany and a difficult man to co-operate with.[63] For the moment Japan would not participate in intervention.

In March 1918 Germany compelled the Bolshevik government to sign the extremely harsh treaty of Brest–Litovsk. Trotsky's attempted compromise of 'neither peace nor war' had failed to satisfy the German generals, who insisted on Russian acceptance of their terms. The British legation in Peking was sceptical at the time of the prospects of the assorted White Russians in Siberia, an impression accentuated by the defeats experienced by Semenov, the Cossack leader who soon became a Japanese puppet.[64] Matters became more serious in the spring and summer of 1918, leading to large-scale allied armed intervention in Siberia. The occasion was provided by the spontaneous action of the Czechoslovak forces, who seized control of the Trans-Siberian railway when clashes occurred between the Czechs and the Bolsheviks. The Czechoslovaks were Austro–Hungarian prisoners of war who were hoping to return to Europe via the Far East and the United States to fight for the freedom of their homeland on the western front. Their dangerous predicament aroused much sympathy in the United States and caused President Wilson's opinion to change. On 7 June 1918 the allied war council asked Japan to support a joint expedition to rescue the Czech forces. Japanese leaders were consulted and adhered to the view they had adopted in March 1918: the United States must wholeheartedly support the venture.[65] On 6 July 1918 Wilson indicated that American support would materialise. There were divisions between those favouring and opposing intervention in Tokyo. Baron Goto now favoured intervention but the Seiyukai party leader, Hara Takashi, was hostile. Eventually agreement was reached that Japan would intervene but that she could not submit to American pressure to restrict intervention to the Vladivostok area or, for that matter, to eastern Siberia. Britain concurred with the Japanese feeling that it was not feasible to define in advance the limits of an unpredictable operation.[66]

On 2 August 1918 final agreement was arrived at in Tokyo in favour of intervention and it was stated that Japan would send troops to act in conjunction with an American expeditionary force. Shortly afterwards a Japanese division landed at Vladivostok. Britain welcomed Japan's decision and was critical of the United States for her tergiversations.[67] Japan was to put approximately 75,000 men into Siberia and her forces were not finally to be withdrawn until 1922. Britain, Japan and the United States had been drawn into an enterprise of a highly speculative nature which was easier to start than to terminate. Britain hoped that intervention would give greater credibility and strength to the White Russian forces, so that what Winston Churchill termed 'the foul baboonery of Bolshevism' could be eradicated.[68] With the advent of Admiral Kolchak in January 1919 as the leader of a supposedly united White Russian force in Siberia, it appeared that such hopes stood some chance of success.[69]

After initial spectacular success, Kolchak's offensive experienced even more spectacular defeat. Intervention in Russia failed and it required Lloyd George's not inconsiderable store of ingenuity to extricate Britain from the untenable position that she occupied.[70] Britain disliked the communist government and deemed it a threat to the stability of the Far East and to her rule in India but realities had to be recognised. Japan's ideological detestation of the new government in Moscow was, if possible, greater than Britain's yet she, too, had to accept the inevitable and come to terms with the communists.

In the autumn of 1918 the German front crumbled dramatically and the long-awaited allied breakthrough had arrived. On 11 November 1918 came the armistice and the end of the First World War. Despite a few errors, Sir Edward Grey and A. J. Balfour had pursued a realistic and effective policy. The exigencies of her involvement in Europe meant that Britain had little choice but to accept a substantial increase in Japan's influence. All powers involved in the First World War expected to secure some spoils as compensation for the lives and money expended. Japan was no exception and the compensation for her was bound to lie in China. However, Britain did not give Japan a free hand in China and attempted to protect British interests from being completely undermined. Relations between Britain and Japan were strained and unavoidably so. The divergencies between the allies visible before 1914 had grown. Britain was more dependent on the United States and American–Japanese relations were far cooler than Anglo–Japanese relations. Britain would soon have to determine her future relations with both powers: the outcome would deeply affect her role in the Far East.

Chapter 7

The end of the Anglo–Japanese Alliance and revival in China, 1919–1931

As peace slowly returned to a shattered world in 1919, so Britain had to assess the evolution of her policy and interests in the Far East. Major question marks hung over her relationship with both China and Japan. Both were to make great demands on her statesmen, diplomats and defence planners in the period extending to the outbreak of the Pacific war in 1941. In China the new spirit visible in the 1900s was stirring with far more vigour. There was no genuine centralised government and the chaos of warlordism persisted, yet among every section of Chinese opinion a new mood was emerging, a mood that voiced frustration at China's political weakness and at the contemptuous ways in which the foreign powers acted towards her. The period between 1919 and 1925 was distinguished by the development of organised campaigns against foreign nations and their activities in China. The boycott was refined into a more potent weapon than it had been under the Irish nationalists, who had originally given meaning to the term. British interests were slowly declining *vis-à-vis* those of other powers but Britain continued to be the country with the greatest single economic stake in China. As such, Britain became the chief target for the vocal animosity of Chinese nationalists and was the recipient of numerous demonstrations in the treaty ports. British firms and traders in China appreciated that Britain was facing dangerous competition from other foreign interests and tended to come together in a more exclusive form. There was, for instance, a trend towards the formation of chambers of commerce for which only British nationals were eligible; during and after the First World War such chambers of commerce were formed in Shanghai, Canton, Tientsin, Hankow, Foochow, Chefoo, Amoy, Chinkiang, Swatow, and Newchwang.[1] It was felt that British firms needed improved organisation and leadership if they were to defend themselves against French, American, Japanese, and doubtless a revived German commercial impetus. On 5 November 1919, a general conference of representatives of every British chamber of commerce in China was convened at Shanghai, resulting in the formation of the Association of British Chambers of Commerce in China and Hong Kong with a permanent headquarters in Shanghai and its own journal. The new body was not designed to replace the China Association but to reinforce the efforts of the China Association, which were primarily concentrated in London.[2] The long-established British firms, Jardine, Matheson, Butterfield and Swire, and the Hong Kong and Shanghai Banking Corporation were well to the fore. New firms were appearing, an important one being the Asiatic Petroleum Company, which was an offshoot of Shell. Sir John Jordan, who was about to retire after a lifetime spent in the Far East, warmly welcomed the new spirit.[3] The commercial initiative was a belated recognition of the challenge that British firms had encountered in China for at least a generation. There was little understanding or sympathy with the rise of Chinese nationalism. A few more astute observers comprehended the mood of many Chinese, especially younger Chinese, but the majority did not. Most British traders lived mentally in the Victorian era and regarded the Chinese with innate superiority; all that was needed was to produce the big stick and keep the insolent Chinese in order. Friction therefore arose between the British government and the British commercial community in China when opinion in Whitehall came down in favour of a more conciliatory approach to Chinese nationalism in 1926–27.

In 1919 China came under discussion at the Paris peace conference in connection with the disposal of former German interests and possessions. One of the motives for Chinese entry into the World War had originally been to give her a voice in the peace-making. However, China had entered the conflict at too late a stage and her contribution had been slight. The peace conference was dominated by Britain, France, the United States, Italy and Japan. Japan was not particularly interested in the interminable wrangles over European questions that preoccupied the other victors but she was determined to secure her objectives on far eastern issues. She received the former German islands in the Pacific as C-class mandates under the notional supervision of the League of Nations, which meant that the islands could be treated as 'integral portions' of Japan's territorial possessions; owing to the reference to the authority of the League, the implication was that the islands could not be fortified.[4] The islands south of the equator were retained by the British Empire as C-class mandates.[5] Japan firmly urged the insertion of a racial equality clause in the covenant of the League. The proposal did not commend itself to the United States or to the British dominions (as distinct from Britain herself), which had been involved in acrimonious disputes over oriental immigration in the past. Woodrow Wilson successfully opposed adoption of the clause. This deeply offended the Japanese and was indeed a patent insult to the world inhabited by those not possessing white skins. Through the attitude shown by the dominions, Britain was involved in the controversy and the position did not augur well for the future of Anglo–Japanese relations.[6] As far as China was concerned, Japan insisted that she should receive without qualification the former German possessions in Shantung. Britain was bound through wartime agreements to endorse the Japanese view. It was made clear that if Japan did not obtain what she desired she would refuse to sign the covenant of the League.[7] The Council of Three requested A. J. Balfour to discuss the subject with the Japan-

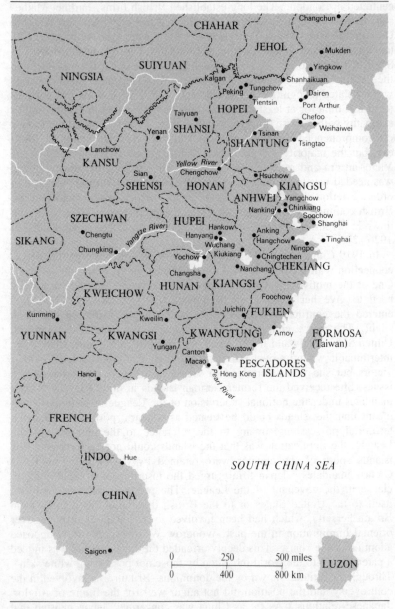

Map 6. Twentieth-century China

ese delegates and report back on the terms under which Tsingtao would ultimately be returned to China.[8] After due consideration, Japan agreed 'to hand back the Shantung Peninsula in full sovereignty of China, retaining only the economic privileges granted to Germany and the right to establish settlement under the usual conditions at Tsingtao'.[9] The council of prime ministers in Paris then discussed the topic and it was decided, on 29 and 30 April 1919, that German rights should be transmitted to Japan and not to China. Japan secured much but not everything she desired. The treaties of 1915 and 1918 had not been accepted unambiguously; neither did the powers accept the Chinese position and rule the treaties to be invalid. On balance, Japan gained more because there was no time limit governing the return of the rights in Shantung.[10] Balfour maintained that the formula accepted by Japan was to the advantage of China, – 'by the efforts of Japan and her allies without the expenditure of a single shilling or the loss of a single life China had restored to her rights which she could never have recovered for herself'.[11] Balfour's optimism rested on the belief that China would regain Shantung soon but there was no guarantee that this would be so.

The basis upon which Japan would return Kiaochow to China was incorporated in a note conveyed to the Chinese delegation in Paris by the Council of Four. The Japanese promise was satisfactory but Japan was not willing for it to be published. Lloyd George's private secretary, Philip Kerr, wrote in a memorandum that the Japanese undertakings were encouraging 'if properly and promptly executed [but] the question is how far the Japanese will prove true to their word and here experience of the past regarding Japanese policy in Manchuria makes it difficult not to feel some suspicions as to their real intentions in Shantung'.[12] Lord Curzon, who was administering the Foreign Office during Balfour's absence in Paris, attempted to press Japan into rapidly publishing a statement on Shantung. On 2 August the Japanese foreign minister, Uchida Yasuya, announced in Tokyo that Japan would return Shantung peninsula to China, keeping only the economic privileges previously held by Germany; when an agreement was signed between Japan and China, Japanese troops would be withdrawn from Shantung.[13]

Chinese public opinion was outraged by Japan's behaviour and by the seeming condonation of Japan's conduct by the western powers. It accentuated the disillusionment with the west already prevalent among intellectuals and young Chinese; a bitter reaction set in and led to the famous May Fourth movement. The term 'May Fourth movement' is used to describe the political, social, literary and cultural manifestations that gathered momentum in 1919; the movement amounted to a vociferous expression of fundamental dissatisfaction with the humiliating treatment accorded China by the western world and Japan and a determination to secure a new spirit in China, connoting the spiritual and political revival of the Chinese people.[14] The overt political side was sparked off by news of the decisions in Japan's favour over Shantung at Paris. The nominal warlord government in Peking was willing to accept the outcome. Many Chinese, notably intellectuals and students, were antagonised thereby and monster demonstrations of protest were organised in Peking. A new spirit was certainly at work in China and was to contribute enormously to the growth both of the Kuomintang and the communists during the 1920s. Despite the personal leanings of some members of the warlord-controlled government in Peking, it was impossible, in the light of the vehement public opinion in China, for Sino–Japanese negotiations over Shantung to be held in 1919–20. The thorny issue was resolved later, after the Washington conference.

The principal subject to be settled in British far eastern policy at the end of the First World War was the fate of the Anglo–Japanese alliance. The alliance had been renewed for ten years in 1911 and was due for renewal or termination in or before 1921. The questions to be assessed and answered by the British government were whether the alliance should be renewed or not and, in the latter eventuality, what, if anything, should replace the alliance. In 1919 the British Foreign Office was distinctly less enthusiastic over the alliance than had been the case before 1914 and public opinion was generally critical of it. It was anticipated that the dominions would either oppose it or be highly critical of continuing it. The United States had disliked the alliance for a long time and American influence was far more significant in 1919 than before the war. It was going to be a delicate matter and would require meticulous handling. Japan was aware of the coolness with which she was widely regarded in 1919; she wished to continue the alliance, which had advantages in the sense of fostering a more stable foreign policy. However, Japan realised that matters had changed considerably as a result of the war and that she was not as valuable a partner for Britain as she had been when the alliance was last renewed in 1911. Apart from the obvious political aspects of the alliance, an extremely important consideration was naval rivalry between Britain, Japan and the United States. The Anglo–Japanese alliance constituted a naval partnership which was complementary in character. If the alliance did not exist, Britain and Japan would have to react accordingly and could in time become locked in dangerous and expensive rivalry. The United States had embarked upon a major building programme during the war and possessed immense resources if these were fully realised. Therefore, the seeds were present of a formidable naval rivalry. Furthermore, the position of China could not be ignored in any decisions reached.

The role of the dominions in the formulation of British foreign policy was more significant in 1920–21 than it had been a decade earlier. Dominion nationalism had grown in the wartime atmosphere of struggle and strife: while the dominions were closely attached to London in the defence context, they were starting to develop their own foreign policies and could no longer be treated in the paternalistic manner characteristic of the prewar era. A conference of dominion prime ministers was due to be held in 1920 or 1921 and it was essential to prepare the ground thoroughly. Discussions took place between government departments in Whitehall and exchanges occurred with the *Gaimusho* in Tokyo and with the American State Department. The consensus among British diplomats pointed towards some form of triple agreement comprising Britain, the United States and Japan, if it could be obtained.[15] A new ambassador to Tokyo, Sir Charles Eliot, was appointed in December 1919 to succeed Greene; Eliot had enjoyed an unconventional career, having been in the diplomatic service as a young man and then having left it to pursue an academic career, including holding office as vice-chancellor at the universities of Sheffield and Hong Kong. Eliot was sent to Tokyo early in 1920 to prepare a report on the future of the Anglo–Japanese alliance which he submitted in July 1920: he believed that Japan wanted to retain the alliance and thought himself that this would the best course for Britain to adopt. The alliance would permit Britain to influence Japanese policy in a positive direction; to end the alliance could antagonise Japan and produce a threat to British interests in East and South-East Asia and India. The dominions would gain from the extension of the alliance and any aggressive Japanese tendencies in China could be moderated by British persuasion. Eliot skilfully expounded the argument for retaining an alliance.[16] Victor Wellesley, head of the far eastern department at the Foreign Office, suggested to Lord Curzon, the foreign secretary, in September 1920, that a small departmental committee should be set up to consider every aspect of the alliance question: Curzon approved the idea and a committee comprising Wellesley, Sir William Tyrrell, Sir Conyngham Greene and Sir John Jordan was established. It was probably unwise to form the committee exclusively from within the Foreign Office, since this reduced the likelihood of broader issues concerning defence and the dominions receiving adequate attention. The committee worked diligently and requested the views of the ambassadors in Tokyo and Washington. Eliot supported renewal of the alliance. Sir Auckland Geddes, the ambassador in Washington, also favoured renewal but thought it should be restricted to four years and that a similar treaty should be concluded with the United States. The committee submitted its report on 21 January 1921. It recommended that the alliance should be terminated and replaced with 'a Tripartite *Entente* between the United States, Japan, and Great Britain, consisting in a declaration of general principles which can be subscribed to by all parties without the risk of embarrassing commitments'.[17] If the United States refused to adhere, an agreement should be reached with Japan flexible enough to permit American signature at a later date. Curzon regarded the report as unsatisfactory and it had no serious effect on his policy. It was impossible for Britain to advance further until the imperial conference met and considered its attitude. Similarly the new Republican administration of Warren G. Harding was assuming office in Washington in March 1921, with the distinguished Charles Evans Hughes as secretary of state. Some time would have to elapse before the new American policy became clear.

The British cabinet discussed relations with Japan at length at a special cabinet meeting held on 30 May 1921. Lord Curzon fairly summarised the arguments for and against continuing the alliance. He found the former more convincing than the latter. The alliance had lasted for almost twenty years and Britain had to keep in mind the danger of being opposed in the future by a combination of the two powers at whom the alliance had been historically directed, Russia and Germany. There were powerful arguments on defence grounds for retaining an alliance. The problem about a triple agreement including the United States was uncertainty as to whether the obdurate American senate would tolerate it and whether the United States would adhere to it in subsequent years.[18] Winston Churchill, the colonial secretary, warned of Canadian antagonism to renewal. Lloyd George spoke in typical vein. He thought that Curzon's conclusions were cogent. Lloyd George: 'liked the Japanese. The reasons they gave very often for doing things were quite unintelligible and they might have no conscience but they did stand by those who stood by them and they had given unfailing support to their Allies at the International Conferences.'[19] The cabinet resolved to support President Harding's proposal to convene a conference of the Pacific powers but only when it had been made clear to Japan that Britain would not end the alliance; the period of renewal should be shorter than the existing term of ten years and the alliance should be consistent with Britain's obligations to the League of Nations. Views should be exchanged with the United States and China before renewal.[20] The ambassadors in Tokyo and Washington were asked if their attitudes had altered since they were last consulted. Eliot confirmed his previous conclusions. Geddes recommended a tripartite agreement including the United States, since there were now indications that the Harding administration would support a triple agreement, contrary to the anticipation of the British cabinet.[21]

The imperial conference began on 20 June 1921. Lloyd George delivered an introductory speech and emphasised the valuable contribution the alliance had made in past years.[22] Each of the dominion prime ministers spoke fully, as did Lloyd George and Curzon. The two extreme approaches were represented by Canada and Australia. The positions of these two countries had been effectively reversed since the 1911 imperial conference; at that time, Canada had warmly supported renewal and Australia had shown some scepticism. Canada vehemently opposed renewal in 1921 and Australia favoured renewal. New Zealand supported Australia and South Africa adopted a middle position which was nearer to the Canadian outlook. W. M. 'Billy' Hughes, the redoubtable Australian prime minister, stated at the beginning: 'Australia is very strongly in favour of the renewal of the Treaty . . . We will do well for the world's peace – we will do well for China – we will do well for the Commonwealth of British nations to renew this Treaty. We want peace.'[23] General Smuts talked in visionary terms, stressing the move away from the old diplomacy of pre-1914 days and urging those present to think of the future: 'We wish to see a real Society of Nations away from the old ideas and practices of national domination or Imperial domination, which were the real root of the great war. No, not in alliances, but in a new spirit of amity and co-operation do we seek the solution of the problems of the future...'[24] When the conference advanced to detailed consideration of the issues, Lord Curzon put forward the views of the British government. It might well be argued that the alliance was obsolete or undesirable given the attitude of the United States towards it. However, the alliance connoted stability in the Far East and Japan had rendered important assistance in the past. The Foreign Office maintained that renewal on an amended basis in consultation with the United States, China and the League of Nations offered the most satisfactory solution. The attack on Japan was led by the Canadian prime minister, Arthur Meighen, who trenchantly expressed his opposition to an extension of the alliance: 'I would regret to see the Treaty continued in any form at all... Japan has far exceeded her rights and progressively violated her covenant.'[25] Hughes counter-attacked. He had listened 'as well as I am able' to Meighen's remarks:

It is quite obvious that his views, as the views of all men, are coloured like the dyer's hands, by what they work in. We all naturally reflect our environment... Now let me speak plainly to Mr Meighen on behalf of Australia. I for one will vote against any renewal of the Anglo–Japanese Alliance upon one condition and one only and that is that America gives us the assurance of safety which our circumstances absolutely demand.[26]

Without an American commitment, Australia had to regard the alliance as her best means of defence. Smuts commented on the difficult nature of the problem before the conference: 'I do not remember in the twelve years that I have taken part in the Empire debates a greater or more difficult or far reaching issue being raised for the Empire as a whole than this one. It is not just a question merely of the continuance of the Japanese Alliance. The question is much bigger...'[27] Smuts emphasised the importance of trying to reconcile friendship with the United States and Japan: the problems of the Pacific required regular consideration by conferences of those powers involved in the region.

The Indian representative, the Maharao of Cutch, advocated extension of the alliance but with the reference to India omitted; it was unwise to perpetuate the impression that Britain relied on Japan to defend her empire and some Japanese had been taking too intimate an interest in Indian affairs in recent years, which included links with subversive elements.[28] Lloyd George reiterated his belief in the case for renewal and quoted part of Grey's address to the 1911 conference. In his view Japan should not be dropped merely to placate the Americans. Britain should recall Japan's aid in the past – 'I think the British Empire must behave like a gentleman.'[29] Eventually the conference agreed that Curzon would approach the relevant powers and propose that a conference be summoned to discuss the problems of the Pacific. Curzon suggested that if all else failed the alliance should be continued but Smuts contended that an agreement embracing Japan and the United States was imperative. On 11 July Lloyd George informed the conference of President Harding's intention to hold a conference on disarmament to be preceded by a conference on Pacific problems. Lloyd George commented that Harding's decision resulted from the initiative taken by the British Empire.[30] The idea of holding another conference to pursue defence matters and the alliance appealed to the whole imperial conference.

Japan was unhappy at the proposal to hold a conference in Washington to determine the future of the alliance and of naval questions. Japanese leaders could see the likelihood of a coalition between the United States and Britain with Japan being pressured into accepting whatever was decided. Japan resented the frequent exchanges occurring between London and Washington with information reaching Tokyo only belatedly. In addition, Britain had consulted China unilaterally which, given the bitter state of Sino–Japanese relations, was certain to offend Japan.[31]

The Washington conference assembled in November 1921 and lasted until February 1922. It met to deal with three subjects: the fate of the Anglo–Japanese alliance, naval competition, and stability in China. Britain and Japan were anxious lest the United States endeavour to place the alliance before the plenary session of the conference; Britain informed the United States in August 1921 that she could not debate the alliance 'or any matters of Pacific policy affecting the safety of the Pacific dominions and India' at plenary sessions.[32] The British delegation was led by A. J. Balfour, now old and deaf, but an appropriate choice given the fact that Lloyd George was preoccupied with the delicate state of the Irish negotiations in London. Balfour was immensely experienced in foreign affairs and defence and had lived closely with the Anglo–Japanese alliance throughout its history. He was supported by the first lord of the Admiralty, Lord Lee of Fareham, and by Sir Auckland Geddes, the ambassador in Washington. The Japanese delegation was headed nominally by Prince Tokugawa Iesato and in reality by Admiral Kato Tomosaburo, an able naval bureaucrat of broader intellectual horizons than most naval and certainly military men in Japan. Kato was assisted by Baron Shidehara Kijuro, the capable and shrewd ambassador in Washington. The British delegates were given more freedom to act than their Japanese counterparts. In the defence sphere, the prevailing opinion was that the alliance should be extended to help Britain to cope with the burden of defending far eastern and Pacific waters. As regards the wider political matters, it was decided that Britain should work for a tripartite agreement covering Britain, the United States and Japan and for a naval treaty relating to the Pacific. Britain wished 'to secure the largest possible limitation of armaments consistent with the safety of the British Empire'.[33] The Japanese delegates were given detailed instructions. Japan wanted a naval treaty with Britain and the United States and ideally would like to have kept the existing alliance, but was willing to accept a tripartite agreement. Upon other topics on the conference agenda Japan was determined to adopt a tougher line, such as Tsingtao, Siberia and Yap.[34]

The Washington conference proved a more amicable and less argumentative international gathering than many in London and Tokyo had feared beforehand. Balfour aimed to achieve a strong compromise between the attitudes of the United States and Japan in the form of a tripartite agreement of a flexible character which would permit the making of a defensive alliance with Japan should Germany or Russia pose a threat again in the Far East.[35] Balfour decided that the reference to China in the present Anglo–Japanese alliance should be transferred to a separate agreement to be signed by all the powers attending the conference. Balfour began exchanging views with Charles Evans Hughes without simultaneously involving Japan, and handed Hughes a copy of the draft treaty he had drawn up. He had, however, talked to Prince Tokugawa and mentioned the matter to him; Tokugawa, who was in essence a figurehead, did not convey Balfour's remarks to Shidehara. Shidehara was mollified when informed, but at this point was taken seriously ill and was to be largely immobilised for the bulk of the conference. Kato accordingly had to handle the more overt political matters, apart from naval issues. The Japanese deemed Balfour's draft too potent for American tastes, and from his sick-bed Shidehara prepared an alternative version envisaging a consultative pact rather than a military agreement,[36] which Balfour agreed to support, as did Hughes. The American secretary of state proposed that Shidehara's reference to summoning conferences whenever disputes arose in the Pacific should be extended to include France. Britain and Japan were not enthusiastic at this suggestion but accepted it on condition that no other powers were added. After further discussion among the prospective signatories, the quadruple agreement was signed on 13 December 1921. The treaty referred to the common interest of the four powers in the Pacific area; each recognised the rights of the others and if any controversy likely to threaten co-operation occurred 'they [the signatories] shall invite the other high contracting parties to a joint conference to which the whole subject will be referred for consideration and adjustment'. The powers would consult in the event of another nation threatening their positions. The treaty would be valid for ten years and would remain operative after that date unless specifically denounced.[37] In one sense it was a considerable achievement to have reached agreement on the treaty but, when examined more closely in the light of the tests to which the agreement was subjected a decade later over Manchuria and Shanghai, it is seen that the achievement was a strictly qualified one. Japan was not happy at the trend away from the old alliance but had tolerated it and, in the shape of Shidehara's action, perhaps even encouraged it at the conference. The explanation is that Japan realised that she had little option but to acquiesce in the development. However, Japan did not regard the treaty highly and the consultative mechanisms provided for were not used.

On the naval side, the Washington conference opened with a ringing appeal by Hughes for a drastic solution to the dangers of expensive rivalry. He advocated a limitation on the number of capital ships and a ten-year naval holiday. The proposal necessitated careful investigation by each power; a great deal would depend on the precise application of the American proposal with reference to the type of construction to be permitted and the role to be played by submarines, destroyers and torpedo-boats. The United States wanted equality with Great Britain; the British delegation had to determine whether this would be worked out according to the number of vessels or total tonnage. Clearly the nature of ships and their age would have to be borne in mind.[38] Britain would have to be allowed to replace some of her ships or the British fleet would become obsolete. Apart from the position of the powers primarily concerned with the Pacific, France had to be considered. Britain's relations with France had cooled appreciably after the war and doubts were entertained as to French ambitions; the French air force was powerful and the role of the French navy in European waters had to be assessed. Britain required safeguards in the treaty over the number of submarines to be possessed by each power.[39] France, therefore, had to be added to the list of prospective naval signatories. Italy was prestige-conscious and clamoured for inclusion; this was reluctantly conceded and five countries were thus participants in the naval debates. Balfour skilfully promoted reconciliation in the detailed exchanges. The five-power naval treaty was signed on 6 February 1922. This laid down the naval ratio of 5:5:3:1.75:1.75 for construction of capital ships. Japan had wanted a 10:10:7 ratio for the principal powers but eventually consented to modify her attitude. Admiral Kato Tomosaburo did not believe that the defence of Japan had been jeopardised by the concessions made but there was a division of opinion on the subject within the Japanese navy. The majority of opinion supported the Washington naval settlement but a vocal minority was opposed. One of the leading figures in the latter group, Admiral Kato Kanji, was later to maintain that the road to the Pacific war began with the ratio agreed at the Washington conference.[40]

The third important agreement signed at Washington, in February 1922, was the nine-power treaty relating to China. The objective of the powers was to secure a more stable situation within China by minimising intervention in China's internal affairs. The signatories undertook:

To respect the sovereignty, the independence and the territorial and administrative integrity of China.
To provide the fullest and most unembarrassed opportunity in China to develop and maintain herself as an effective and stable government. To use their influence for the purpose of equal opportunity for the commerce and industry of all nations through the territory of China.
To refrain from taking advantage of conditions in China in order to seek special rights or privileges which could abridge the rights of subjects or citizens of friendly states, and from countenancing action inimical to the security of such states.[41]

The United States, in particular, attached great importance to the nine-power treaty as the foundation of a new era of international co-operation in the Far East. Subsequent American administrations regarded it as sacrosanct and during the troubled 1930s there were to be numerous American protests that Japan was violating the commitments into which she had freely entered. The nine-power treaty was designed by the United States to assist China but came to be seen by growing numbers of Japanese as a means whereby the western powers could limit Japanese expansion at a time when they were erecting tariff barriers against Japan from 1930 onwards. By the standards of the day it was an achievement to have secured the Washington settlement. However, the defect with it was that it produced paper formulas which were not capable of standing up to great pressure. The Washington conference tried to promote stability by freezing the *status quo*. Japan was a dynamic nation and could not be held down in this way.

British politicians and officials, however, were satisfied with the results of the Washington conference. Britain had to determine future defence policy for the Far East following the termination of the alliance. It had been decided in 1921 that a naval base would be constructed at Singapore, which was the most satisfactory site. The non-fortification provisions of the five-power naval treaty prevented the use by Britain or the United States of bases east of Singapore or west of Hawaii. Thus began the unhappy and controversial saga of the Singapore base.[42] Plans for constructing the base were devised but the history of its construction was erratic in the extreme. This was attributable to political and economic reasons. The Labour party, which formed two minority governments in 1924 and 1929–31, was strongly oriented towards restricting armaments expenditure as far as possible and halted work on construction.[43] The Conservative government of 1924–29 was committed to completing the base but did not believe that there was real urgency. The National governments of 1931 and after were preoccupied with the economic depression and did not proceed more rapidly until the mid-1930s. The governments of the interwar years were generally inclined towards limiting expenditure as far as they could and to maintaining balanced budgets. Bitter arguments surrounded the strategy of the Singapore base, particularly between the navy and the air force. The navy considered British defence policy in the Far East to be a matter primarily for them; it followed that in their eyes the navy would control the base and play the key role in its defence. The air force, whose views were propounded with much vigour by Sir Hugh Trenchard, emphasised the potential importance of air power. In the early 1920s it was perhaps understandable that the significance of air power was not yet fully grasped but the admirals remained stubbornly convinced of the superiority of capital ships until the outbreak of the Second World War.[44] The Royal Navy was not unique in this respect, for the same was true of other navies.[45] The reasoning behind the Singapore base strategy was that Britain would send a fleet to East Asia should the need arise and this fleet would be based on Singapore. However, this rested on the assumption that the situation in Europe and the Mediterranean would be sufficiently peaceful to allow the dispatch of a fleet. While defence planners could not be expected to foresee the full combination of horrors that the middle and later 1930s had in store, it was sanguine in the extreme to function in the hope that there would be no serious difficulties in Europe. Equally important was an aspect not properly appreciated in London until 1940 and, in some respects, until the disasters of 1941–42. Singapore was not and could not be a fortress in its own right: Singapore was only defensible if the Malayan peninsula itself was defended and held, which would be essential in order to combat a land invasion from Thailand or a sea invasion from French Indo-China. The army and the air force would have much to contribute in such circumstances but these problems and complexities were not resolved before the Japanese invasion in December 1941. It is sufficient for the moment to comprehend the defence dilemma precipitated by the end of the Anglo–Japanese alliance and the unceasing effort to square the circle.[46]

Between 1922 and 1931 British policy in the Far East was dominated by the strident challenge of Chinese nationalism and the attacks, physical and verbal, made upon British interests in China. The internal state of China was chaotic in the 1920s, if with a slow trend towards more cohesion. The Kuomintang was revitalised and became a powerful force. The Chinese communists, following the policy decreed by the Comintern, co-operated with the Kuomintang and stimulated its organisational prowess; it was too soon to attempt the socialist revolution and communists had to support bourgeois nationalism in liquidating the remnants of feudalism.[47] The Kuomintang itself comprised a strange amalgam of liberal intellectuals, treaty port bankers, generals, and rural landlords. Under the charismatic leadership of Sun Yat-sen, the Kuomintang was held together and stood for a vague social reformism. Sun taught his revamped San Min Chu I ('Three Principles of the People') connoting the restoration of national unity, the eventual introduction of a constitutional method of government after a long period of military rule, and an imprecise formula for land reform and agrarian harmony. Sun's ideas were so vague that they could appeal simultaneously to people who were radical and conservative, Sun's personality temporarily surmounting the inherent contradictions. In May 1925 Sun Yat-sen died and a power struggle began within the Kuomintang between Hu Han-min, Wang Ching-wei and Chiang Kai-shek from which Chiang emerged as the victor in 1927.[48] Under Chiang the Kuomintang moved swiftly away from any genuine interest in social reform and became a reactionary party dominated by militarists and Chiang's cronies. The Kuomintang was active in the early and mid-1920s in castigating the foreign presence in China and, in particular, assailing Great Britain. Boycotts of British goods were organised and large-scale demonstrations occurred. The crucial phase of confrontation came between 1925 and 1927. This brief period witnessed popular fervour attaining great heights and the might of the Kuomintang and the communists expanded. In July 1926 the Kuomintang launched the march north, aimed at eliminating regional warlords and making China a unified country once more: the march ultimately triumphed in December 1928, when the Manchurian warlord, Chang Hsueh-liang, accepted the authority of the new Kuomintang government based at Nanking.

British nationals and interests were involved in a number of difficult and sometimes violent clashes. One of the worst conflicts arose in Shanghai on 30 May 1925 and was exacerbated by incompetent police handling of demonstrations. The incident was occasioned by the murder of a Chinese labourer working in a Japanese cotton mill in the international settlement at Shanghai. The municipal police arrested three students for making provocative speeches: a crowd assembled and hurled abuse at the police, who were British-officered. A British inspector, Edward W. Everson, directed the crowd to leave and when they instead advanced on the police station, Everson ordered his men to open fire. The shooting resulted in seven deaths and a large number of wounded.[49] British officials defended the action of the police as consistent with the powers of the police force to employ arms as a last resort and refuted communist allegations that the police had fired on peaceful students.[50] The British minister, Sir Ronald Macleay, wrote that, 'the action of the police was fully justified by the events with which they had to deal...'[51] The attitude of the British government and British officials was that while they did not like violence and wished to avoid it, they would, if the situation warranted it, resort to force again. A huge demonstration was held on 23 June 1925 with the aim of taking over the Shameen concession in Canton in protest at the arrogant and harsh conduct of the British police in Shanghai. Shots were fired from the Chinese side and the forces guarding the British and French concessions fired back. More than fifty Chinese were killed and more than double that number were wounded.[52] The consul-general had no doubts that the Chinese were responsible for starting the shooting; he blamed the Comintern advisers for inspiring the riot. A widespread boycott movement was organised throughout southern China, affecting all major ports, and the crown colony of Hong Kong. The effects were quickly visible in strikes that prevented trade and the unloading and departure of ships. It was reported by a correspondent in Swatow that:

British activity in the port has been attacked by the Chinese with amazing ferocity. Trade ceased entirely... Chinese in the employ of British subjects, in whatsoever capacity, were forced to strike. British property was destroyed and residences, offices and clubs were burgled and looted...

No reason has been given for this atrocious treatment except the vague cry of 'British Imperialism'. The game still goes on... Both strike and boycott are pursued with unabated vigour and intensity. Loyal and friendly Chinese have been imprisoned, tortured and even murdered.

The continued strain has broken up nearly every British home in the place. All this is the work of agitators, Bolshevik-trained and taught in Moscow and Canton. These people have a 'Red' military Government behind them. They are the people with the guns and therefore have the power...[53]

The British Foreign Office contemplated the use of force, blockade, aid to the elements opposing the communists, protests to the Soviet Union, and conciliation. It was by now clear that the Chinese could not be subdued by force, as in bygone years; force would worsen matters, not improve them. Blockade was deemed impracticable. Anti-communist elements lacked cohesion and leadership (the Kuomintang and the communists continued to co-operate until April 1927). Complaints to Moscow would achieve nothing. If pursued in the correct manner, conciliation offered possibilities.[54]

The position in China remained deeply unsettled as Chiang Kai-shek began his march north in the spring of 1926. Chiang's relations with the communists were encountering strain but Chiang did not wish to break with them as yet and the Comintern's policy was to preserve the alliance with the Kuomintang for some years ahead. The communists and left wing of the Kuomintang, which was collaborating closely with the communists in 1925–27, believed in continuing the pressure on foreign interests. On 3 January 1927 a Chinese mob attacked the British concession at Hankow, which was defended by British marines. Force was not used by the marines; when the demonstrations persisted on the next two days, the decision was taken to leave the concession. This action, although appearing to be weak, was wise and averted widespread bloodshed. British nationals were permitted to re-enter the concession several days later but the Kuomintang was faced with the responsibility of having to provide for stable government in Hankow.[55] The government in London was alarmed at the trend, fearing that serious clashes might occur in Shanghai. The chiefs of staff reported on 11 January 1927:

In the last few months the situation has very much deteriorated . . . The Nationalist Government, working to a considerable extent under Bolshevist influence, has obtained control of the greater part of China south of the Yangtse.

We recognise that the magnitude of our interests at Shanghai and the reaction of a disaster there on our interests and prestige in other parts of China and of the whole East may be such as to compel us to an active defence. We admit the possibility also that by showing a bold front at Shanghai we may stop the rot. But we feel bound to point out that our attitude may lead to a war, the consequences and magnitude of which cannot be foreseen.[56]

The government sent 12,000 troops to defend British interests in China. Chiang Kai-shek deplored the British move: 'The attitude adopted by Great Britain towards China up to the present is exactly as if she were dealing with her own Colonies, and proves that she does not understand China.'[57]

On 24 March 1927 in Nanking rioting Chinese soldiers attacked foreign nationals and property. Three British subjects perished and the consul-general was injured. The situation was so menacing that British and American naval vessels on the Yangtze were summoned to assist. The city was promptly bombarded by destroyers and foreigners were evacuated. The initiative in the Chinese action had been taken by Chiang's opponents, anxious to embarrass him and thrust him into conflict with the powers. Chiang decided that the time had arrived to strike ruthlessly at his foes; in April 1927 a drastic and bloody purge was implemented, which had the effect of castrating the labour movement in the cities and ports of China. The streets literally ran with the blood of butchered comrades.

Chiang's purge bolstered his position in the short term but it may be argued that in the long term he had helped the communists, by compelling them to concentrate on establishing themselves in the rural areas that constituted most of China: the internal debate among the communists as to whether their future lay in urban or rural areas was solved for them. Until July 1927 the communists maintained a tenuous partnership with the left wing of the Kuomintang led by Wang Ching-wei. In July 1927 Wang broke with the communists, too, and started to move back to the mainstream of the Kuomintang. Britain welcomed the upheavals and the emergence of Chiang Kai-shek as the new strong man of China; the foreign secretary, Sir Austen Chamberlain, described the events as encouraging: the communists and their Russian friends had been routed. Britain became far more sympathetic to the Kuomintang than formerly. It was a reciprocal process but essentially a marriage of convenience: from the British viewpoint the Kuomintang were infinitely preferable to the communists; Chiang Kai-shek disliked all foreigners, for he was basically xenophobic, but he needed support in order to build up his domestic authority.

The belief that China could in the future become a source of immense importance for British trade was as tenaciously held in the 1920s as it had been in the 1830s and 1850s. S. P. Waterlow, a member of the far eastern department of the Foreign Office, wrote in May 1925 that:

In the whole range of international politics there is no problem of which a settlement would be of greater or more rapid material benefit to this country. We are dealing with a quarter of mankind, not rivals in industry but producers of raw material. By incredible toil the Chinese contrive to make good the ravages of civil war and bandit raids, to meet every kind of exaction for the upkeep of useless armaments and hordes of armed coolies, and yet to have something over to exchange for our manufactures.[58]

As part of the overall assessment of British policy in China, it was recognised that compromises would have to be made over tariffs because of the Chinese wish to regain tariff autonomy. It was imperative to secure built-in safeguards for British trade in whatever changes were decided upon. When the tariff conference met in September 1925, Britain desired the abolition of likin in exchange for the surtaxes of 2.5 per cent on ordinary dutiable articles and 5 per cent on luxuries approved at the Washington conference. The termination of likin was an essential preliminary to consideration of tariff autonomy and debt consolidation. The conference agreed to recommend to the powers represented that China should recover tariff autonomy as from 1 January 1929 and that a pledge of the abolition of likin from the Chinese government should be accepted. Sir Ronald Macleay recommended approval but the Foreign Office entertained doubts, feeling that more was required by way of concessions from China.[59] The tariff conference met intermittently until April 1926 and then closed without achieving anything tangible. In the ensuing recriminations Britain was blamed by the United States and Japan for the failure on the grounds that she wished to perpetuate a privileged position. The attitude of the Foreign Office was that the failure was the fault of the Americans and the Japanese, who were motivated by the ambition of obtaining payment of unsecured debts through the impounding of customs revenues by the inspector-general of the Maritime Customs.[60]

The head of the Foreign Office far eastern department, Sir Victor Wellesley, reflected on the future evolution of British policy in August 1926. British policy had recently been criticised for vacillations and weakness. The commercial community in China and the China Association in London maintained that Britain had been indecisive in discussions over tariffs and that the Chinese had not surprisingly taken advantage of this. Wellesley contended that Britain would gain from a bolder policy of treating China more generously.[61] He urged that Britain should come out unequivocally in favour of abolishing the unequal treaties: 'We cannot maintain the "unequal treaties" indefinitely ... Our policy in China must be one of treaty revision; the question is how and when such revision must come, and what course it is to take.'[62]

Wellesley's proposed strategy was approved by the foreign secretary, Chamberlain. In a public statement, issued on 25 December 1926, Great Britain promised to restore tariff autonomy, to liberate all revenues from foreign control, and to apply the recommendations of an international committee dealing with extraterritoriality. Despite the disappointment engendered by the clashes in which Britain and China were involved early in 1927, the new policy was forward looking and was to be vindicated by events. The new British minister to China, Sir Miles Lampson, was initially sceptical of the policy but he subsequently supported it and extended it. The policy did not commend itself to the British community in China, most of whom viewed it with distaste as another sign of the lethargy and weakness characterising Britain's approach to world problems. Lampson favoured a flexible policy of conciliation and firmness – to be too forthcoming in the early stages of negotiations would simply encourage the Chinese to demand more[63] – and was fundamentally an advocate of a distinctly tougher line than the Foreign Office. He was critical of the consul-general and naval commander in Hankow for surrendering the concession before obtaining something in return. Lampson advised leaving the Chinese in occupation of Hankow but refused to recognise the action pending negotiations. Chamberlain and the Foreign Office overruled him and supported making an immediate agreement. On 19 February 1927 this agreement was signed by Owen O'Malley, counsellor of the legation, and by Eugene Chen of the Hankow Kuomintang government.[64] The agreement gave China control over the concession at Hankow. Lampson censured it as 'a complete surrender to Chinese extremist demands and ... has shaken the whole British position in China'.[65] He believed that Britain must retain a foothold in the concessions because they were axiomatic to the functioning of commerce and banking: the concessions continued to afford law and order to facilitate trade, conditions that did not obtain elsewhere in China. Developments showed that the Foreign Office was more perceptive than Lampson. Reasonable order was maintained in Hankow by the Chinese authorities and trade soon recovered. The Foreign Office expressed satisfaction at the outcome, '. . . it seems a fair statement of the case to say that the Hankow Agreement has placed us in a position of moral and tactical advantage'.[66]

In January 1927 Britain proposed a comprehensive list of measures under the heading of treaty revision. The items included recognition of Chinese law in British courts, eligibility of British subjects to pay Chinese taxes and a reduction in concession privileges. The aim was to secure a propaganda victory over the Chinese and in part to bring the Chinese to appreciate that it might be to their advantage to keep some aspects of the treaty port structure. Detailed talks began between Britain and China in 1928. Britain wished to persuade China by a process of mutual bargaining and concession to recognise the importance to Britain of the port of Shanghai and to extend guarantees on British interests there. Put simply, Britain was prepared to sacrifice interests elsewhere in China in order better to protect her stake in Shanghai. The emphasis on Shanghai is wholly understandable in that approximately three-quarters of British investment in China was concentrated there. The principal British traders, firms, and banks in China were based in Shanghai – Butterfield and Swire, Jardine, Matheson and Company, the Hong Kong and Shanghai Banking Corporation, and the Chartered Bank of India, Australia and China. British interests also controlled the Shanghai Waterworks Company and the Shanghai Gas Company. Most foreigners in China lived in Shanghai and within the hybrid context of east and west it had a strong British flavour to its life and work. Britain was proud of Shanghai and of what she had contributed to its phenomenal growth. The British residents of Shanghai were generally conservative and disinclined to contemplate change. In the discussions with China and in convincing the British residents of Shanghai to accept if not to welcome change, Sir Miles Lampson played a most important role.[67] The membership of the municipal council in Shanghai was reformed so as to allow equal British and Chinese representation. Lampson took the lead for Britain in the detailed negotiations over extraterritoriality ending in the draft extraterritoriality treaty of June 1931. The talks were extremely complex and embraced the full gamut of British commercial relations in China and the legal framework governing them. Lampson pursued adroit negotiating tactics by dealing with the less controversial issues first and holding back the chief topics for subsequent agreement. Defence of British interests at Shanghai was the key to his strategy: Lampson wished to stave off the termination of extraterritoriality in Shanghai for a longer period than in the other treaty ports. The discussions were frequently tedious and repetitious; eventually Britain and China agreed that extraterritoriality would last for a maximum of ten years in Shanghai and for five years in Tientsin.

The treaty was not actually signed and the negotiations were halted when the Manchurian crisis broke in September 1931; China entered an era in which she was completely occupied with the grave challenge posed by Japanese imperialism and by the internal conflict between the Kuomintang and the communists. The treaty port system lived on until eliminated by Japan following the outbreak of the Pacific war. Indeed, as the 1930s progressed Chiang Kai-shek wished the powers to remain in the treaty ports as a buffer against the ravages of Japan. The British in Shanghai then had to turn their attention to outwitting the aggressive Japanese in place of combating the resurgent Chinese. British diplomacy had operated effectively between 1927 and 1930 in conducting the first stages of imperial retreat. Despite the skill with which Lampson on occasions endeavoured to conceal it, Britain was negotiating the return of the privileges that she had first obtained almost a century before on the China coast. It was understood that the treaty port system would change but it was hoped and expected that the foreign presence would endure. China would need western investment, technology and education. There would still be a place for the merchant, banker, teacher, and missionary in the new China. Sir Miles Lampson, a forceful, masterful, and dynamic personality, was broadly satisfied with his achievement. To begin with, he had been rather negative when it came to implementing the new British policy towards China promulgated in December 1926, but from the latter part of 1927 onwards he had demonstrated a deeper understanding and had laboured effectively. He was soon to be involved in problems of a different character as Japanese ambitions in Manchuria cast an ominous shadow over the Far East.

As Britain contemplated the end of extraterritoriality in the not too distant future, it is appropriate to reflect on Britain's economic position in China around 1930. In 1880 the British accounted for more than 50 per cent of foreign nationals in China; by 1899 this had fallen to 32 per cent and by 1913 to only 5 per cent. The latter figure is less dramatic than it might at first seem, since it reveals the influx of Russians and Japanese into Manchuria.[68] By 1930 the British comprised only a little over 3 per cent. In 1913 the British population of the treaty ports was 8,966 as against 5,562 in 1899. In 1930 the total British population in China was 13,015; the British in the international settlement in Shanghai totalled 6,321.[69] British investment in China in 1931 amounted, according to the estimate of C. F. Remer, to approximately £244 m.; business investments were £198 m. and government obligations £46 m.[70]. The British share of shipping was still appreciable; in 1930 the British controlled about 37 per cent compared to 41 per cent in 1913. The share of coastal shipping was over 50 per cent.[71] As regards direct trade with China, Britain's share was less than 8 per cent as against more than 11 per cent in 1913. Hong Kong's share was 30 per cent in 1913; by 1930 this had fallen to 17 per cent (in 1926, after the boycott, it was 11 per cent).[72] In 1930 the British Empire accounted for under one-third of China's trade; in the later 1870s the proportion had been 85 per cent.[73] British exports to China declined from £57 m. in 1920 to £13 m. in 1930; the cotton piece-goods trade suffered notably with a fall in the quantity exported from 452 m. square yards in 1920 to only 61 m. square yards in 1930.

The decline in monetary terms was from £34 m. in 1920 to under £2 m. in 1930.[74] Chinese imports of machinery for the developing textile industries in the vicinity of the treaty ports were growing in the early 1920s; the demand for machinery, boilers and turbines and for electrical goods and chemicals was expanding.[75] Overall Britain's economic position was worsening in China. In the words of C. F. Remer, 'The outstanding fact was the decline in the relative importance of Great Britain over the whole period.'[76]

In the naval sphere an important five-power conference was held in London in October 1930. The Washington conference had not tackled the aspects of cruisers, destroyers and submarines. Competition in cruisers developed in the aftermath of the Washington conference for which reason the United States called a conference in Geneva in 1927. The latter failed when the United States rejected a compromise proposal on cruiser strength put forward by Britain and Japan.[77] It was expected that difficulties would arise from Japan's desire to obtain a more generous deal than the one achieved at Washington. Opinion was becoming more militant in the Japanese navy and there was a demand for a 70 per cent ratio in heavy cruisers and in the total tonnage of auxiliary vessels; the Japanese wanted 70,000 tons in submarines in order to sustain the existing strength.[78]

Agreement was eventually reached that Japan would have 69.75 per cent of American tonnage; in large cruisers Japan would have 60.02 per cent and Japan could build up to 70 per cent before the next scheduled naval conference in 1935; in submarines there would be equality fixed at 51,700 tons. A bitter dispute raged in Japanese political and naval circles as to whether the agreement reached was acceptable. Fierce opposition was voiced by militants in the navy headed by Admiral Kato Kanji. The navy minister, Admiral Takarabe Takeshi, supported the agreement, as did the prime minister, Hamaguchi Yuko.[79] Eventually the formula was approved but it was a Pyrrhic victory: within a few years the anti-treaty faction had triumphed and Japan moved decisively away from co-operation with the powers. Britain was satisfied with the outcome: the second Labour government attached importance to containing armaments expenditure. Ramsay MacDonald was particularly interested in securing close working relations with the United States, which he had sought to attain in his meeting with President Hoover in 1929.[80] MacDonald, the foreign secretary, Arthur Henderson, and the first lord of the Admiralty, A. V. Alexander, were happy that agreement had been reached, if also weary from the tedium and argument entailed.[81] Japan's willingness to compromise ensured the signing of a three-power agreement and compensated for the intransigence of France and Italy in the broader directions in which the conference had been concerned.

Chapter 8

The Manchurian crisis and after, 1931–1937

On 18 September 1931 officers of the Japanese Kwantung army staged an incident in which a small section of railway line near Mukden was allegedly blown up. The Kwantung army held disorderly Chinese elements to be responsible and because of the apparent threat to the stability of south Manchuria, the army rapidly took control of neighbouring areas adjacent to the railway zone in which Japan was permitted to retain troops.[1] It was a fateful development, marking the beginning of extensive Japanese expansion in the ensuing decade and a half: in some ways it can be considered as the first move in the chain of events culminating in the Second World War.[2] The Mukden incident was the product of a number of diverse trends and episodes. Japan had consolidated her position in south Manchuria since the Russo–Japanese war of 1904–05. Investment had been poured into the vast region with the government-owned South Manchuria Railway Company as the vehicle for the fostering of industries, factories and mines in south Manchuria. The basis was being prepared for the take-off under Japanese rule after 1931 into one of the principal industrial areas on the continent of East Asia. Japan attached deep significance to her stake in south Manchuria for a mixture of political, economic, strategic, and sentimental reasons. The Japanese presence in Manchuria was required to act as additional protection for the Japanese empire in Korea; it was a barrier against the Soviet Union, which retained the northern half of the main railway network, the Chinese Eastern Railway; it was complementary to Japan's economic offensive in China; and it could never be forgotten that Japan's position in south Manchuria was secured amidst the heroism and valour of the war against Russia. Most Japanese believed in the validity of Japan's presence in Manchuria and were not willing to see this position undermined. This was the attitude of Japan's distinguished foreign minister for much of the 1920s, Baron Shidehara Kijuro. Shidehara believed in international co-operation and favoured the peaceful resolution of conflicts between nations if possible but he was tenacious in defending Japanese interests. Shidehara was regarded as weak and ineffectual by the bellicose nationalists and by many army officers.[3] The resurgence of nationalism in China in the 1920s presented a growing threat to Japan, particularly in the later 1920s. After the revolution of 1911–12 in China, Manchuria was largely dominated by a colourful former bandit, Chang Tso-lin. Chang was originally supported by the Japanese military but the younger elements in the Kwantung army turned against him when Chang showed increasing independence.[4] He was assassinated in 1928 when his train was blown up as he was returning from a visit to Peking; the murder was masterminded by younger Japanese army officers. Chang's son, Chang Hsueh-liang, succeeded his father and soon revealed his intention of associating more closely with the new Kuomintang government of Chiang Kai-shek based at Nanking. Arguments and conflicts grew between Chang Hsueh-liang and the Japanese, many of a minor character but some of a more weighty nature. In September 1931 there were over three hundred unsettled disputes in south Manchuria.[5]

Plotting developed in the Kwantung army. The policy of the Tokyo government was viewed with contempt and anger for its alleged cowardice; the ire of many of the younger army officers was accentuated by the profound economic and social distress affecting rural Japan. The depression in Japanese agriculture had existed since the First World War and was exacerbated by the world economic depression from 1929. The sad state of the Japanese nation was blamed on the corrupt and incompetent party politicians.[6] Japan needed new leadership, a Showa restoration, referring to the reign of the young emperor Hirohito, who had ascended the throne in 1926.[7] It was in this atmosphere of an assertive military, in which older officers deferred more frequently to the pressures of their younger subordinates, and of a government whose grip was visibly declining in 1931, that the Mukden incident occurred.

The new crisis in the Far East occurred when Britain and the United States were grappling with the dire effects of economic depression.[8] In August 1931 the second Labour government of Ramsay MacDonald was finally overwhelmed by the problems facing it. MacDonald formed the National government with the Conservative and Liberal parties; it was at first intended to be a brief emergency administration but MacDonald was to remain prime minister until 1935 and the label 'National' government survived as an inaccurate and shabby description until 1940, when the term took on a genuine meaning again. Britain was concentrating on trying to save the gold standard in August–September 1931 and then, when this objective failed, in coping with the aftermath of departure from the gold standard, and was thus not in a state to worry excessively over an obscure clash in East Asia in September 1931. The United States was in a similar, in fact worse, position. The full magnitude of the depression was hitting the United States savagely; an embittered and bewildered President Hoover was vainly endeavouring to restore stability and confidence domestically. By force of circumstances he largely left the conduct of foreign policy to his ebullient and excitable secretary of state, Henry L. Stimson. Stimson was to leave his mark on the Manchurian crisis but not in an especially constructive way.

When news of the Mukden incident reached London and Washington, the immediate response was to urge both sides to keep calm and refrain

from action liable to exacerbate matters. It took some time for the gravity
of the situation to be appreciated. China immediately appealed to the
League of Nations for assistance and the League was soon involved in
attempting to settle a dispute of a peculiarly complex and difficult nature,
rendered more awkward because the League was overwhelmingly a
European organisation set up to deal with European problems. The
involvement of the League was an important aspect in the formulation of
British and French policies, owing to the implications for European stability of decisions taken in the Far East. The League passed its first resolution on 30 September 1931, appealing to both parties to resolve their
differences peacefully. Fighting between the forces of Chang Hsueh-liang
and the Japanese continued sporadically; while there were a few bitter
and hard-fought exchanges, the overall picture was of a numerically
superior Chinese army steadily disintegrating against the infinitely better
trained and led troops of the Kwantung army. The Foreign Office in London first became aware of the deteriorating situation when the city of
Chinchow was bombed by Japanese aircraft in early October 1931. The
caretaker foreign secretary, the Marquis of Reading, at once sent a
sharply worded telegram to Tokyo urging restraint.[9] Shidehara was
deeply embarrassed by the events in Manchuria and was trying to restore
a measure of control over the initiatives taken by the Kwantung army
independently of the Wakatsuki government. Reassuring statements came
from the *Gaimusho*, confirmed by Japan's delegate to the League of
Nations, Yoshizawa. The feeling in the British Foreign Office was that
there was little that Britain could do beyond counselling the two sides to
co-operate and not to take measures that would worsen the situation.[10]
The bombing of Chinchow antagonised the United States and Stimson
agreed to authorise an American representative to sit in on the deliberations of the League Council in Geneva in mid-October.[11] Lord Reading
was concerned that the authority of the League should be sustained and
determined to visit Geneva himself. He decided that the League should
adopt a more resolute policy even if this involved a dangerous element of
bluff. He wrote to the permanent under-secretary, Sir Robert Vansittart,
on 21 October 1931 that 'a failure by the League to find some way round
the difficulty would be nothing short of a calamity . . . and might imperil
any hopes we may have of making progress in the more immediate field
of Europe . . .'[12] Reading supported a draft resolution prepared by Aris-
tide Briand, the president of the League Council, stipulating a deadline
for Japanese withdrawal from the areas occupied outside the railway
zone. The resolution, approved on 24 October 1931, called for Japanese
withdrawal before the next meeting of the League's Council in a month's
time. It was a calculated and unwise gamble. Naturally the League
wished to exert decisive influence in a crisis of deepening proportions but
this had to be tempered by recognition of what could reasonably be
accomplished. The sad fact was that the League had overreached itself.
The Kwantung army was not going to be coerced by verbal threats from a
far-off body of which it knew little and cared less. The only method of

stopping the Japanese army was through the use of force, which could not be brought to bear.

Stimson believed the League resolution to be mistaken and he was also wary at the attempts in Geneva to draw the United States into the crisis so as to place more responsibility for solving it on American shoulders. He accordingly followed a more cautious policy for the next few months, as regards co-operation with Geneva. The failure of the efforts to settle the dispute under article 11 of the League covenant led to speculation about possible resort to economic sanctions, as provided for in article 16. British policy-makers remained in agreement throughout the crisis of 1931–33 that whatever happened, Britain and the League should not embark upon sanctions against Japan.[13] Apart from fundamental British doubts as to whether Japan's action in Manchuria merited the use of sanctions, the burden of enforcing them would fall mainly on Great Britain or, to be more explicit, upon the Royal Navy. Britain's defences were in a precarious state, as the Shanghai crisis was shortly to demonstrate.[14] The United States would not become involved in the use of sanctions. The deduction was that conciliation remained the sole avenue to pursue and it would be necessary to follow this road to its logical conclusion – the employment of every means of producing a settlement stopping short of sanctions or armed force.

In November 1931 the Kwantung army extended the range of its operations against the retreating forces of Chang Hsueh-liang, almost as if in insolent defiance of the appeals from Geneva. The League Council had to retrace its steps and accept that an erroneous decision had been made in the resolution of 24 October. The most obvious requirement was to achieve some diminution in tension and to allow time to elapse during which an impartial investigation of the issues could be undertaken. In the early stages of the crisis Japan had resisted the idea of an inquiry but her attitude changed in late November 1931. The Wakatsuki government was tottering amidst internal criticism of its lack of resolution in not standing up more vigorously to foreign pressure and of international criticism of its failure to curb the autonomous zeal of the Kwantung army. It was felt in the *Gaimusho* that it could be in Japan's interests to accept a commission of inquiry, because much of the responsibility for the origins of the crisis could be laid at the door of China: the absence of effective centralised government in China and the provocative actions of Chang Hsueh-liang's regime in Manchuria would surely be appreciated. The British government warmly supported the concept of an official inquiry. It would provide a valuable breathing-space and hopefully the commission would locate some means of reconciling Japan and China. Sir John Simon had now succeeded Lord Reading as foreign secretary after the National government's massive victory in the general election of October 1931 and the consequent cabinet reshuffle. Simon was the leader of the Liberal Nationals, who had seceded from the Liberal party to work closely with the Conservatives. He possessed one of the most acute legal minds of his generation but it was combined with a certain coolness and irresolution

which prevented him from being either popular or outstandingly successful as a politician.[15] Simon was new to foreign affairs but was before
long to become all too familiar with the dreary character of the Manchurian crisis. He warned the cabinet on 23 November 1931 that Japan
was possibly aiming to create a puppet government in Manchuria and to
detach the area from any political connection with Nanking.[16] Simon's
view, based on consultations with his advisers, was that Japan had just
grievances in Manchuria but had adopted the wrong method of rectifying
them.[17] Following discussions between the various delegates to the
League Council, Japan and China accepted the proposal to establish a
commission of inquiry. The resolution was approved unanimously by the
League Council on 10 December 1931 and the commission was appointed
soon afterwards, comprising the Earl of Lytton as chairman (British),
General Henri Claudel (French), Dr Heinrich von Schnee (German),
Count Luigi Aldrovandi (Italian), and General Frank McCoy (American).
The commission departed for the Far East in February 1932 and eventually reported back to Geneva in September 1932. Further consideration of
the commission will be deferred for the moment while other developments in Manchuria and Shanghai are discussed.

Stimson welcomed the establishment of the Lytton commission as an
encouraging sign. He was, however, feeling irate at the truculent
behaviour of the Japanese army and concluded that a firm moral statement of the American position was required. Influenced by the precedent
of William Jennings Bryan's action during the crisis over the Japanese
twenty-one demands in 1915, he determined to issue a statement bluntly
refusing to recognise the validity of changes in the territorial *status quo*
brought about by force, contrary to the Kellogg–Briand anti-war pact of
1928. Stimson wanted Britain to join in his action but Simon thought it
wiser not to do so: the foreign secretary believed that conciliation stood
some chance of success in early and mid-January 1932. Simon did, however, seek assurances from Japan that British interests in Manchuria
would be protected and the assurances were given.[18] Stimson was most
disappointed at the British reaction and the lack of positive response
became the ostensible justification for the later protests of Stimson and
other Americans that, at a crucial stage of the Manchurian crisis, he had
proposed forthright action which had been opposed by Britain. The truth
was that Stimson had suggested a statement of moral disapproval which
had little effect on Japanese policy: British adherence would not have
produced a different reaction. The final stages of the mopping-up operations by Japanese troops took place in Manchuria in January–February
1932. The Kwantung army pressed ahead with plans to declare Manchuria independent as the state of Manchukuo with the previous emperor
of China, Pu-yi, as nominal head of state. There was a new, more
nationalistic government in Tokyo, headed by Inukai Tsuyoshi, which
was better disposed than its predecessor to the actions of the army in
Manchuria. At the same time Inukai was hoping to reach a compromise
with China and opened confidential contacts with friendly Chinese he had

known from the days when he had been a personal friend of Sun Yat-sen.[19] When these contacts came to light, they led to Inukai's assassination, in May 1932, by enraged young naval officers. In March 1932 Manchukuo was proclaimed as an independent state by the Kwantung army.

In late January 1932 a serious crisis erupted in Shanghai. This was distinct from the Manchurian events, yet was clearly linked to Manchuria. The crisis was caused by the action of a Japanese officer in organising an incident in which five Japanese, including two Buddhist priests, were beaten up by Chinese factory workers. The intention was seemingly to create an incident in Shanghai to distract attention from the final moves to establish Manchukuo. In retaliation for the insult, a Japanese mob attacked the factory and a Chinese police post. The situation quickly escalated with a Japanese demand for an apology from the local Chinese authorities, reinforced by a threat from the local Japanese naval commander to take 'appropriate steps to protect the rights and interests of the Japanese Empire'.[20] The matter could have been settled expeditiously had it not been for the determination of Rear-Admiral Shiozawa Koichi to seize his opportunity to advance the prestige of the navy by occupying the Chinese suburb of Chapei.[21] Japanese marines were landed and clashed with the Chinese (Cantonese) nineteenth route army. This constituted the first phase of the relatively short but severely fought battle at Shanghai.

The news from Shanghai caused great alarm in London. It is instructive to compare the British response to events in Shanghai to those in Manchuria. In the latter case Britain felt full sympathy for Japan, since Manchuria had been in the Japanese sphere of interest for nearly thirty years and, as Sir Edward Grey had concluded before 1914, the Japanese had to expand somewhere. It was wrong for Japan to have used military force to the extent that she had but there was understanding of the dilemma the Japanese found themselves in. Shanghai was a totally different matter. Here was the mighty metropolis of the Far East, largely created by British brain and investment. For the Japanese to intervene in Shanghai and attempt to create a new sphere of interest was intolerable. It was imperative to restrain Japan from making the situation still worse and to assess what Britain could do if the fighting became sufficiently serious to require evacuation of British nationals and defence of British interests. On 28 January 1932 Simon saw the counsellor of the Japanese embassy and emphasised the danger of allowing the position to deteriorate further. Sir John Pratt, who had been at first rather slow to discern the menace, drafted a memorandum in which he warned that Japan could be embarking on a policy of aggrandisement, which would not be compatible with the maintenance of British interests.[22] The permanent under-secretary, Vansittart, drafted a succinct and accurate minute stating that Japan was likely to challenge Britain's role in East and South-East Asia and in India; Japan would ultimately be stopped only by the United States.[23]

The Shanghai crisis jolted the Foreign Office and the chiefs of staff into a realisation of the vulnerability of Britain in the Far East and of the paucity of the resources to hand in the event of armed conflict with Japan. According to the Admiralty, the outlook was dire: at Shanghai and Tientsin five battalions of infantry were surrounded by stronger Japanese forces; at Shanghai three cruisers were heavily outnumbered; in the Yangtze one cruiser, two sloops and twelve gunboats were isolated; Hong Kong was almost defenceless; the base at Singapore was only partially built and its defences were extremely inadequate; Trincomalee, the naval base in Ceylon, was without defences.[24] Stanley Baldwin, the lord president of the Council and chairman of the committee of imperial defence, termed the Shanghai crisis 'a nightmare; I daren't express my feelings on what is happening as it might be dangerous'.[25] Britain's policy was governed by weakness in defence. This did not stop the dispatch of diplomatic protests in Tokyo but care was exercised to ensure that Britain was not led into taking dangerous action. Britain co-operated with the United States in February 1932 to achieve a ceasefire but was careful not to be drawn into intemperate outbursts on the initiative of Stimson, who was fulminating at Japan's conduct.[26] Stimson was again dissatisfied with the response in London. He believed that disapproval of Japan should be expressed in unmistakable terms so as to convey support for China and to reiterate the moral principles for which the United States stood. He therefore drafted his open letter to Senator William E. Borah of Idaho, chairman of the Senate foreign relations committee, which was sent on 23 February 1932. In the letter Stimson underlined the basic importance to the United States of the Washington treaties of 1921–22. The treaties were interdependent and a strong hint was given to Japan that if she undermined the nine-power treaty, the United States might consider the non-fortification provisions of the five-power treaty no longer binding.[27] Stimson intended the letter to be an implicit rebuke to Britain. The feeling in London was that Stimson's action was misguided, because he was resorting to empty threats; there was no likelihood of the United States suddenly adopting an interventionist policy and implementing a major rearmament policy. Sir Francis Lindley, the British ambassador in Tokyo, had consistently warned of the volatile state of Japanese government and of the undesirability of uttering provocative remarks. Lindley sometimes lost sight of the necessity of steering a course that would not diminish the prestige of the League of Nations but he was correct to indicate that verbal threats couched in militant language, unaccompanied by a willingness or ability to take resolute action, were foolish. Perhaps Simon should have explained Britain's attitude more lucidly to Stimson. Simon's tendency to avoid being too blunt in his comments in a trans-Atlantic telephone conversation with Stimson conceivably led Stimson to believe that Britain would adopt a more positive approach than was the case.[28] Stimson felt that Britain had 'let America down' and told the counsellor of the American embassy in London that this could be communicated to the Foreign Office.[29]

Sir Miles Lampson, the minister to China, and Admiral Sir Howard Kelly, commander of the China squadron, were doing their best to secure a truce in Shanghai. The flamboyant Kelly believed that the British voice must be heard more prominently at the beginning of February 1932. He objected to Japanese planes flying over his ships and informed the Japanese admiral that if this continued, he would shoot the planes down.[30] The Foreign Office and the Admiralty were alarmed and warned Kelly to be more cautious. The Japanese government did not want the Shanghai crisis to be extended; it had caused much embarrassment in Tokyo when Japan was coping with the ramifications of the Manchurian dispute. After bitter fighting in March, a truce was signed by Japanese and Chinese representatives in May 1932; Shanghai experienced no further conflict until August 1937, following the start of the Undeclared war.

Soon after the beginning of the Shanghai crisis, in January 1932, China asked that the dispute with Japan be handled under articles 10 and 15 of the covenant instead of under article 11 and that it should be in the hands of the League Assembly and not, as hitherto, the League Council. Since China desired more decisive action, it was a sensible move; the Assembly comprised all members of the League and was less easily dominated by the great powers. For the same reason the development was less palatable to Britain and France but they had to accept it. After the experiences at Shanghai, Simon felt the League had to make a further pronouncement in order to emphasise the League role and give reassurance to the small nations. It was decided to follow the line adopted by Stimson in January–February 1932 and to refuse to recognise changes brought about by force. Simon spoke at the League in support of the motion, which was approved and became League policy on 11 March 1932. This was the last major act by the League prior to publication of the Lytton report.

The summer of 1932 was peaceful in comparison to the preceding nine months. It was, however, an ominous calm akin to the lull before the storm. Britain was soon to be faced with producing a suitable response to the Lytton commission's report. Whatever was recommended by the commission could confidently be expected to be unacceptable to either Japan or China, most probably the former. Britain and the other members of the League would have to reach a decision that could lead to a rupture between the League and Japan. As for the United States, Stimson was happy at the thought of the League following in the path he had started. Stimson was careful not to draw too close to the League, however: American public opinion was still extremely suspicious of the League and a presidential campaign was about to commence. The members of the Lytton commission worked industriously and rapidly, given the fact that they had to visit China, Japan and Manchuria and compile their report. Despite being affected by ill-health for much of the commission's work, the chairman, Lord Lytton, provided a sense of purpose and leadership. He was determined that the commission would produce a clear, cogent, and readable report. There were inevitably differences among the members of the commission, notably between Lytton and Claudel, but the commission concluded its business by submitting a unanimous report. It was signed in Peiping (as Peking had been renamed) on 4 September 1932 and published by the League a month later. Divided into chapters examining the origins of the conflict in Manchuria; the course of events between September 1931 and the summer of 1932; the Shanghai crisis of 1932; and recommendations as to how the Manchurian crisis might be solved, given a willingness to compromise, the report dealt fairly with the origins in depicting the growth of Japanese interests and the problems that had arisen in Manchuria before 1931. The narrative of events was judicious, with scrupulous attention being devoted to the evidence presented by both sides. While not exonerating China, the commission maintained that Japan was primarily responsible for the course that events had followed. The commission produced a detailed set of recommendations envisaging a special autonomous form of government for Manchuria with interlocking treaties to be signed by Japan and China; the interests of the Soviet Union would be safeguarded.[31]

The report was a document of admirable clarity but with the best will in the world the Lytton commission could not achieve terms acceptable to Japan. The reason was that virtually all opinion in Japan had rallied behind the army's action in assuming control of Manchuria and creating the puppet state of Manchukuo. The Japanese government itself had officially recognised the 'independence' of Manchukuo before the publication of the Lytton report but when the attitude of the members of the commission was known. The government was now headed by a retired naval bureaucrat, Admiral Saito Makoto, following the assassination of Inukai in May 1932. Matsuoka Yosuke was dispatched to Geneva to expound Japan's case as convincingly as he could; Matsuoka hoped that Japan could remain within the League if possible and was less intransigent than has sometimes been contended.[32]

The Lytton report was favourably received in Britain. The Foreign Office thought it to be an able document; there were no illusions as to its likely reception in Tokyo. Sir John Simon looked at the recommendations of the report with the practised eye of a barrister: while the report was critical primarily of Japan, there were various criticisms of China, too. It would only be fair to give some weight to the latter when he addressed the League Assembly. Simon spoke to the Assembly on 7 December 1932. In a speech meticulously drafted to include balancing comments on Japan and China with the accent on conciliation, Japan was censured for having 'not employed the methods of the League' but equally China was responsible for the chaotic conditions that existed in Manchuria and China itself.[33] Simon's speech was offensive to China, was disliked by the smaller powers, and incurred the disapproval of the United States. When Simon met the Japanese and Chinese delegates to the League, however, he made clear his dislike of Japan's actions and stated that in his view a breach of the covenant had occurred.[34] He was determined not to advance beyond this point and embark upon a debate as to whether article 16 of the covenant, dealing with sanctions, was applicable. The committee of nineteen, set up in March 1932 by the League Assembly, considered the whole position further before submitting a final report with recommendations to the Assembly. Anthony Eden, the rising younger member of the government responsible for League affairs, represented Britain on the committee of nineteen. Japan pursued an obstructive attitude, objecting to the participation of the United States and the Soviet Union in the renewed attempt at conciliation, and would not compromise on the existence of Manchukuo. The committee could achieve no more and on 15 February 1933 decided to wind up their deliberations and submit a final report. The report accepted most of the conclusions of the Lytton commission, yet refrained from stating expressly that Japan had violated the covenant. Recourse to article 16 was therefore sidestepped.[35]

The Assembly met to discuss the report against a background of renewed fighting on the border between north-east China and Manchukuo. The struggle arose from the threatened advance of Japanese troops into Jehol, which the Japanese wished to incorporate within Manchukuo. The danger of Japan moving in the future from Manchukuo into China was manifest. The new outburst of fighting continued until the Tangku truce was concluded on 31 May 1933. The extension of the conflict stiffened the resolve of the League to reach a definite conclusion to the prolonged discussion of the dispute. The Assembly gathered on 24 February 1933. China warmly endorsed the report of the committee of nineteen and approved the recommendations. The Japanese delegate, Matsuoka, defended Japan's record of international co-operation over the years and urged that the report should not be accepted. Britain was determined to support the report. Throughout the Manchurian crisis, Britain had been handicapped in endeavouring to reconcile the protection of British interests in the Far East with loyalty to the League and the principles it represented. It was impossible for Britain to become involved in armed conflict with Japan; Britain did not believe Manchuria justified war and had some sympathy with Japan's original grievances against China. Fundamentally Britain was far too weak in defence terms to risk war with Japan but could not simply wash her hands of the problem, however; as one of the two leading members of the League she had to preserve its authority, at least in moral terms. The League must be seen to have done all it could in the moral context to restrain Japan. The League approved the report by a massive majority: Japan voted against and Siam abstained, the latter being attributable more to the nationalistic spirit felt in Siam after the 1932 revolution rather than to strong sympathy with Japan. As soon as the vote was announced, Matsuoka led his delegation out of the Assembly; Matsuoka viewed the decision to leave as sadly inevitable.[36]

The crises over Manchuria and Shanghai posed profound questions for the future of Britain's role in the Far East. It was not certain by any means that Britain and Japan were bound to clash militarily in the future but it was essential to devote greater attention to Britain's world defence commitments. The period from the close of the Manchurian crisis to the outbreak of the Undeclared war in China (March 1933 to July 1937) is fascinating in the evolution of British policy for the exploration of various possibilities in the realm of accommodation with Japan, all of which petered out. The most striking feature of policy formulation was the inner competition that developed between the Foreign Office and the Treasury, in which the latter for a time usurped some of the traditional rights of the Foreign Office. This strange situation was caused by political and economic developments and was affected by the principal personalities involved. The most ambitious senior member of Ramsay MacDonald's National government was the chancellor of the exchequer, Neville Chamberlain,[37] who was determined to be prime minister and knew that it was probable that he could attain his ambition within the near future. The exigencies of the political and economic crisis in which Britain was immersed gave the Treasury more power than before in a number of areas of policy-making. Chamberlain was alarmed at the trends in Europe and the Far East with the steady deterioration of the international situation. Increases in the defence budget were inescapable; Chamberlain had introduced the lowest defence estimates of the inter-war years in 1932 and did not relish the prospect of a large increase in defence expenditure, which would be contrary to his faith in the balanced budget and would jeopardise his plans for gradual economic recovery. The chiefs of staff produced their annual review in October 1933. The report emphasised the defence problems in the Far East and the urgent need to find solutions,[38] and stressed naval weakness as the most significant element. Chamberlain made up his mind to resist pressure to construct a larger fleet, believing that it should be feasible to restore Anglo–Japanese relations to a more amicable footing and he urged this course upon the Foreign Office.[39]

A cabinet committee investigated British defence commitments in 1933. There were indications that the anxieties induced by the crises over Manchuria and Shanghai were subsiding and the committee came to more sanguine conclusions on the future of Anglo–Japanese relations. It was accepted that the chiefs of staff were correct in identifying the Far East as the source of immediate concern. Britain should strive to improve relations with Japan but as a prerequisite it was necessary, in the curious phrase employed, for Britain to 'show a tooth' in East Asia, that is to demonstrate an ability to bring some force to bear if required. The committee commented starkly on Britain's chronic weakness: 'We cannot overlook the danger created by our total inability to defend our interests in the Far East. Japan is fully armed both in the material and moral sense. This is not our position.'[40] The Foreign Office maintained that while Britain wished to improve relations, it was delusory to think that it could be achieved overnight. When the report of the defence requirements committee was debated in cabinet, Chamberlain criticised the inner contradictions of the report with its call for qualified rearmament and friendship with Japan and advocated a vigorous attempt to secure *rapprochement* with Japan. He suggested a bilateral pact of non-aggression with Japan and thought that Britain should disentangle herself from the United States: Anglo–Japanese relations had suffered from the way in which Britain had deferred to the Americans while obtaining little in return.[41]

Sir John Simon showed sympathy for Chamberlain's remarks and undertook to conduct a reappraisal of relations with Japan. A paper was drawn
up by the Foreign Office which reviewed the case for and against a pact
with Japan. In favour of a pact would be the conveying of British sympathy but against it would be the repercussions within the League of
Nations and on relations with China and the Soviet Union. Simon leaned
against rather than in favour of the proposal.[42] However, he felt that the
idea could be kept in reserve until the next phase of naval negotiations
when it could be brought into play. Naval matters were assuming more
urgency in 1934 because of impending decisions on the Washington and
London naval treaties. Britain desired to retain naval agreement with
Japan if possible but Japan was moving rapidly in the opposite direction.
The first lord of the Admiralty, Sir Bolton Eyres Monsell, and the first
sea lord, Admiral Sir Ernle Chatfield, believed that the navy had been
inflicted with excessive cuts in expenditure in the previous decade or so
and that this unhealthy and potentially disastrous trend must be reversed.
They wanted to see a navy powerful enough to protect Britain's world-
wide imperial interests and able to resist Japanese aggression.[43] Chamberlain was adamantly opposed to such expansion, which Britain could not,
in his judgement, afford.

The Japanese navy had become largely disenchanted with naval ratios,
which were felt by many Japanese naval officers to be against the true
interests of Japan. The ratios were considered to be a means of holding
back Japanese strength whilst bolstering that of Britain and the United
States.[44] The British Foreign Office aimed to keep co-operation among
the powers concerned in the naval sphere if this could be achieved; it was
appreciated that it would be a challenging task. Chamberlain reiterated his
views in favour of a political agreement with Japan in a new cabinet
committee, established to prepare the guidelines for the naval conference
in London in 1935. So far as he could perceive, China was the obstacle to
rapprochement. Chamberlain was cynically willing to contemplate an
Anglo–Japanese deal at the expense of China, contrary to what had been
established as British policy at least since 1918.[45] The remaining members of the naval committee were less extreme than Chamberlain, while
understanding the need to improve relations. Chamberlain and the permanent under-secretary at the Treasury, Sir Warren Fisher, continued to
argue the case for an agreement with Japan as the most efficacious means
of protecting the British possessions and investments.[46] The Foreign
Office differed from the Treasury, holding that the Treasury was too naive
and did not possess adequate knowledge of the background to be able to
arrive at a valid assessment. Sir Robert Vansittart, the permanent under-
secretary at the Foreign Office, emphasised the importance of not
antagonising the United States, despite the frustrations inseparable from
dealings with Washington.[47] The defect with the Foreign Office's
approach was that it looked suspiciously like a policy of drift and
appeared flaccid in comparison with the vigorous line urged by Chamberlain and Fisher.[48]

On 18 April 1934 what became known as the 'Amau statement' was issued in Tokyo. The statement was made by Amau Eiji, spokesman for the *Gaimusho*, and stressed that Japan regarded East Asia as her sphere of interest and did not favour foreign intervention in China. In effect, the statement connoted the proclamation of a Japanese Monroe doctrine for East Asia. There was nothing surprising in the gist of the communication, for it represented the essence of Japanese policy as it had evolved since 1931. The tone was crude, however, and unaccompanied with the anodyne remarks that usually distinguished statements from *Gaimusho* spokesmen. C. W. Orde, head of the far eastern department, minuted: 'The whole tenor of the statement is highly objectionable for it obviously amounts to warning other powers off action which may be entirely proper and to reserve liberty of such action to Japan though she is pledged to the principle of equal rights for all powers in China.'[49] Questions were asked in parliament and it was decided that Japan's attention should be drawn to the nine-power treaty of 1922. The representations were a response to pressure from MPs, particularly those from the Midlands and Lanca-shire.[50] British textile interests, especially, were alarmed by Japanese competition and were disturbed at an apparent attempt to restrict or close access to the China market. The American ambassador, Robert Bingham, approached Simon for his reactions and understood the foreign secretary to support 'close Anglo–American consultation and co-operation' over the subject. This indicated a much stronger reaction from Britain than Simon had intended to give. The view in the Foreign Office was that it was preferable not to become too closely involved with the United States for fear of unduly alienating Japan.[51]

Discussions on defence were resumed in the summer of 1934; it was important to take decisions on future defence planning and priorities with reasonable speed.[52] The two personalities at the front of the debate were Neville Chamberlain and Sir Maurice Hankey, secretary to the cabinet. Hankey possessed immense knowledge of defence issues from his twenty years' experience of the cabinet secretariat and of the committee of imperial defence. He had an imperial outlook in that he was always conscious of Britain's world role and commitments and not least her obligations to the dominions.[53] Chamberlain considered the threat to Brit-tain's safety to be greatest in Europe; he urged a substantial expansion of the Royal Air Force while cutting expenditure on the army and navy.[54] Hankey stressed the gravity of the Japanese challenge and deprecated Chamberlain's brushing aside of Japan. If Britain were to be capable of defending successfully her territorial, political and economic interests in the Far East and Pacific, she must possess a strong navy. The alternative would be to let down the dominions and admit openly that Britain could not defend her empire.[55] The ministerial committee was not convinced by Chamberlain and supported the view that the perils in the Far East must be considered; the Treasury and the Admiralty were instructed to consult on the naval programme, which would be approved following the naval conference.[56] It was a compromise reflecting uncertainty as to exactly what should be done: the hard decisions were postponed, which was entirely characteristic of the erratic nature of British defence policy in general and of defence policy on the Far East in particular. Again typically, the government did not inform the dominions of the discussions in London. In one respect this could be deemed understandable, since defence policy was in a muddle and it would be embarrassing to have to admit it openly. It was, however, a repeated failing of British governments in this period to show reluctance to spell out the harsh facts of life to the dominions. The decision was taken on this occasion that Hankey should undertake a mission to the dominion prime ministers to acquaint them with the outcome of the ministerial committee's investigation.

In August 1934 Chamberlain drafted a memorandum in which he once more advocated an agreement with Japan. Chamberlain thought, in the light of information on political and naval issues emanating from Tokyo, that a positive response from Britain would encounter a similar reaction from Japan and that the results would be beneficial to both countries. He suggested that a non-aggression pact should be concluded with Japan to which should be attached a 'gentlemen's agreement' on naval issues. The latter would define qualitative limits within which each power would be free to build and to facilitate subsequent co-operation; the essential features of each country's naval programme would be given to the other.[57] The Foreign Office disliked Chamberlain's ideas; in their view, a non-aggression pact might lead Japan to attack the Soviet Union with resulting effects on Germany and British policy in Europe. The position of China was important and it appeared impossible to induce Japan to refrain from developing her position in China.[58] In cabinet Chamberlain conceded that Britain would require assurances from Japan that she would not commit acts of aggression against China or the Netherlands East Indies. The cabinet agreed, on 25 September 1934, that the British ambassador in Tokyo should ascertain if Japan would be interested in a pact. The ambassador, Sir Robert Clive, saw the Japanese foreign minister, Hirota Koki, shortly afterwards and asked Hirota what he had had in mind when he first mentioned a pact in July 1934. Hirota explained that he had wanted to underline his wish for friendly relations with Britain in the event of the naval talks breaking down. Hirota thus demonstrated that he and Chamberlain were at cross-purposes in their mutual interest in a naval pact: to Chamberlain it would help to secure naval co-operation, while to Hirota it would smooth over the end of the naval agreements. The Foreign Office reflected further upon the concept of a non-aggression pact and concluded that it could only proceed on the understanding that it would not adversely affect the nine-power treaty. The Foreign Office viewed the proposal with profound doubt.[59] The scepticism was muffled in a paper submitted to the cabinet on 16 October 1934, which bore the hallmark of Chamberlain's thinking. The projected pact was described in generally favourable terms. The cabinet deferred a decision until there was further news on the naval discussions.

The Japanese delegates to the naval talks in London assembled in

October 1934; the delegation was led by the ambassador in London, Matsudaira Tsuneo, and Admiral Yamamoto Isoroku. Yamamoto was probably the most brilliant man in the imperial navy, with highly original ideas and an interest in air power. The Japanese wanted a flexible system of a common upper limit of tonnage based on the needs of the power requiring the biggest navy. Britain was opposed to the proposal, since it would handicap the power with interests ranging over the globe. Japan was adamant that existing naval ratios should be ended, as they were bitterly resented by most elements in the country. There seemed to be room for manoeuvre, however, and Britain hoped that it would be feasible to arrive at a 'gentlemen's agreement' incorporating a declaration of equal status.[60] The American delegation, headed by Norman Davis, was notified of the progress of the exchanges with the Japanese. Britain was anxious to act impartially and not to let the Japanese think there was an Anglo–American attempt to pressure them. Japan decided not to accept the British proposal and gave notice of intention to terminate the existing treaty. For Britain it was a serious, if not unexpected, outcome; the last remnants of the Washington settlement created in 1921–22 were disappearing: any possibility of securing a political agreement with Japan within the immediate future had vanished. On a personal level, the talks had gone successfully and British representatives were impressed with Admiral Yamamoto, who was indeed not unsympathetic to Britain and the United States whilst also wishing to see the expansion of the Japanese navy.[61]

The Foreign Office, the Treasury, and the Board of Trade were involved in much discussion in 1934 over the future of British trade in China. British firms in China and the China Association had urged a more active commercial policy, so as to defend Britain's existing stake and to utilise opportunities for enhancing Britain's role. Neville Chamberlain was impressed with the arguments put forward. Chamberlain was contemptuous of the Foreign Office, which he felt to be too lethargic and negative in its entire approach. He was reinforced in his opinions (or prejudices) by the eccentric Warren Fisher. Chamberlain tended to reflect the belief in the long-standing myth of the China market and what could be accomplished if suitable energy was only displayed. China was in the process of reforming her currency in the 1930s with the aim of transferring from an economy based on a silver standard to one based on paper currency and required assistance from the powers in implementing this policy. Chamberlain decided that a British official should be sent to the Far East to advance British interests, advise the Chinese, and if possible to achieve reconciliation between China and Japan. The decision marked the climax to the bureaucratic struggle between the Treasury and the Foreign Office. The Treasury was assuming some of the functions of the Foreign Office and without full consultation and agreement: 'dual diplomacy' had been born. The man chosen by the Treasury to undertake this mission, containing so many challenges, was the government's chief economic adviser, Sir Frederick Leith Ross. In the words of a startled

Foreign Office official, he was a 'big gun'.[62] Leith Ross was an able and tough financial expert but was not a diplomat and lacked sufficient knowledge of the problems with which he was confronted. He was accompanied by Edmund Hall Patch of the Treasury, who had worked in Siam, and by Cyril Rogers from the Bank of England. The Leith Ross mission was an important development in British policy, an ambitious, calculated gamble carried out at the instigation of Neville Chamberlain, who hoped the mission would strengthen Britain's authority in the Far East and produce a sense of partnership between Britain, Japan, and China. In reality the mission antagonised Japan and led only to short-term gains in Britain's relations with China.

Leith Ross was the recipient of a great deal of advice from commercial and financial quarters in Britain. The China Association, the Manchester Chamber of Commerce and the principal British firms trading in China emphasised the need for a vigorous policy; Leith Ross must establish rapport with Chiang Kai-shek if anything was to be achieved.[63] It was decided that Leith Ross should visit Japan before going to China and that, since it would be useful to hear what the United States thought, he should travel via America. However, the American secretary of the Treasury, Henry Morgenthau, did not wish to meet Leith Ross, so he travelled via Canada instead. Leith Ross was not handed written instructions but it was decided that China should be advised to issue notes payable in foreign currency, notably sterling, in place of silver and that Britain would be willing to assist with China's foreign exchange reserves. It might be possible to approve a loan for China using Manchukuo revenues as security provided that an overall deal on Manchukuo, approved by Japan, could be reached. The Foreign Office rightly doubted the viability of the project but Chamberlain was insistent; a change in government posts brought Sir Samuel Hoare to the Foreign Office in place of Simon and Hoare called upon his officials to show a more positive attitude towards the Treasury[64] Leith Ross conceived of his mission as designed to secure a new foundation of stability in the Far East. A treaty would be signed by Japan, Manchukuo and China which would include mutual commitments to refrain from intervening in political matters affecting each other's interests; China would recognise the independence of Manchukuo and Manchukuo would pay a thirty-year annuity to China; Japan would release her share of the Boxer indemnity and would renounce future indemnity payments. Japan would agree to work with Chiang Kai-shek; Britain would recognise Manchukuo. Leith Ross did not discuss the plan with the Foreign Office and it was not pursued due to the absence of enthusiasm in Japan.[65]

Leith Ross met Japanese officials when he reached Tokyo in September 1935. He talked mainly to Tsushima Juichi, the vice-minister of finance, whom he had met on a number of occasions in the past and raised with him the possibility of a loan based on Manchukuo. Tsushima felt that if China recognised Manchukuo, progress could be made but he doubted whether China would take the first step. Leith Ross explained other British aims to the Japanese; these comprised satisfactory security, the continued appointment by China of a British national to head the Maritime Customs, ensurance of proper use of loans, reforms of the Chinese financial administration, and settlement of railway debts.[66] Leith Ross next proceeded to China, where he held discussions with T. V. Soong, H. H. Kung, and Wang Ching-wei. The Chinese were anxious to obtain loans but ruled out recognition of Manchukuo, since it would not be acceptable to public opinion. China was advancing with the project for currency stabilisation and desired a loan of £10 million from Britain. Leith Ross believed the request should be met, although he was conscious of the 'corruption, nepotism and inefficiency' that constantly hampered progress in China.[67] The Foreign Office thought Leith Ross was losing his critical judgement in being willing to support the loan without adequate prior assurances. Growing differences in attitude occurred between the Foreign Office and the Treasury with the latter keen for Leith Ross to go as far as he could to record some positive achievements for his mission.[68] The British ambassador to China, Sir Alexander Cadogan, reluctantly supported Leith Ross's advocacy of the loan. Cadogan found it difficult to oppose Leith Ross on a financial matter of which Leith Ross had expert knowledge; furthermore, Cadogan was exposed to propaganda from British firms in favour of a more active policy.[69] The Foreign Office then deferred to the Treasury and agreed to the loan. The Japanese reaction had to be considered, however, and Sir Robert Clive warned from Tokyo that Japan should be given full information. The Treasury wished to proceed regardless and the Foreign Office was alarmed at the 'rare mess' that threatened to ensue.[70]

China announced on 1 November 1935 that silver would be nationalised and a prohibitive export tax on silver levied. Holders of silver must exchange it for government notes. T. V. Soong requested Leith Ross to ensure the co-operation of British banks. The latter were prepared to comply, subject to a guarantee that depositors would not be forced to hand over silver. It was agreed in London to issue a King's Regulation to satisfy China's request. Japan was extremely suspicious of the currency reform and of Leith Ross's role in events. The Japanese banks in China declined to exchange their silver for paper on the grounds that it should be purchased at world prices or they should be able to export it. Other foreign banks shared this attitude. The Treasury wished to proceed regardless but the Foreign Office objected: it would be unwise and possibly humiliating to take action when other countries refused.[71] It was eventually agreed to wait to see how far the Chinese themselves were complying with the new law before moving. As regards the loan, Leith Ross and Cadogan firmly supported advancing with it. Rather surprisingly, Sir Robert Clive agreed from Tokyo that the loan should be extended. The Foreign Office believed that Britain must extricate herself from the loan and the tactics to adopt should be to demand evidence of progress in China in such matters as reform of the running of the railways and payments to bondholders where default was involved. The object of so doing would be to gain time and thus stave off action indefinitely.[72]

At this point Japan began a forward policy designed to infiltrate the north-eastern areas of China bordering Manchukuo, a policy urged by the army and accepted by the *Gaimusho*. It was reported from Tokyo in September 1935 that agreement had been reached between the *Gaimusho*, the army and the navy upon pressing for political and economic co-operation between Japan, China and Manchukuo, with particular reference to north China for defence against communism, and for the suppression of movements hostile to Japan.[73] The news from Nanking of the currency reform and associated measures alienated the Japanese military and new demands were presented to China envisaging considerable economic concessions to Japan in the north-eastern provinces of China.[74] The new pressure upon China was undoubtedly inspired by the chain of events unleashed by the Leith Ross mission, the fate of which was discussed by the Treasury and the Foreign Office in November 1935. Chamberlain recognised that time was needed to allow the tension to cool down but he adhered to the view that a loan should ultimately be made. Leith Ross was instructed to remain in China for the present but not to continue with further aspects of a loan. He had become, in the phrase of a Foreign Office mandarin, 'this gallant hero of a lost cause'.[75] Sir Victor Wellesley, deputy under-secretary in the Foreign Office, wrote in January 1936:

All this is the result of allowing our far eastern policy to drift into the hands of the Treasury. It is very dangerous. I have always sympathised with Sir F. Leith Ross for being sent out on a wild goose chase. It is high time he came home for as long as this bull remains in the China shop there is no knowing how much political crockery may be broken.[76]

After lingering in China for some months, Leith Ross returned to Japan. He reached Tokyo in June 1936; the atmosphere was more friendly than on his previous visit. He talked to the foreign minister, Arita Hachiro, and the vice-minister, Horinouchi Kensuke. Various topics were pursued including Japanese policy in northern China, the future of the Maritime Customs and market sharing and textile competition in China. The Japanese were agreeable but little that was tangible developed from the visit.[77] Leith Ross returned briefly to China to see Chiang Kai-shek and sailed for Britain on 23 June 1936. His mission was over and its results clearly vindicated the Foreign Office rather than the Treasury: it had given encouragement to China but had also raised false expectations of what the western powers might be willing to do to assist her. Despite Japan's more congenial attitude at the mission's close, Japan was hostile to Leith Ross's presence in China and the mission accentuated the developing policy of Japanese aggrandisement in China.

The new Japanese ambassador in London, Yoshida Shigeru, urged that a special effort should be made to improve Anglo–Japanese relations. Yoshida was the son-in-law of Count Makino Nobuaki, lord keeper of the privy seal, and thus had contacts extending to the imperial court. He was out of favour with the more bellicose nationalists and distrusted by the army. It would appear that Yoshida acted on his own initiative in his talks with the Foreign Office, when he put forward diverse proposals amounting to a plan for a world-wide Anglo–Japanese agreement: the proposal included economic and political assistance to China; advice to China on halting the menace of communism; discussions on economic matters between Britain and Japan; and a closer alignment in general between British and Japanese policies in East Asia.[78] The Foreign Office regarded both Yoshida and his proposals with scepticism but it was decided to pursue the talks further. The exchanges continued on a desultory basis until overtaken by the outbreak of the Undeclared war in July 1937. The Yoshida–Eden talks are significant simply for revealing yet again the periodic desire to improve Anglo–Japanese relations, witnessed in approaches from both sides. In this case the initiative was a distinctly personal one and there was no likelihood of the talks achieving anything even had the situation in China not taken an ominous turn for the worse.

After the annexation of Burma in 1886, the government of India assumed responsibility for the running of the annexed country. This decision was unfortunate, since it meant that Burma's problems would inevitably be subordinated to those of India and that Burma would be treated as a backwater.[79] Britain was faced with serious unrest in the years after annexation and it took some time and appreciable military effort to restore order. British rule was tolerated but British influence was never more than superficial, while the revival of Burmese nationalism was stimulated by developments in the Indian Congress movement and by developments in Ireland with the rise of Sinn Fein. The new attitude was revealed in the potent reaction to the decision to reserve Burma's case rather than to treat Burma on the same basis as India following the Montagu–Chelmsford report.[80] Much of the agitation was inspired by younger Buddhist monks; university students in Rangoon and school pupils were prominent in demonstrations. The British government decided to extend the system of dyarchy from India to Burma. The legislative council now had 103 members, including 79 elected on a liberal franchise. The governor was assisted by an executive council to deal with reserved areas, which largely involved defence, the law and financial aspects.[81] The vote was given to householders who had reached the age of eighteen and there was no discrimination by sex. Burma was to be represented in the new Indian legislature in New Delhi and the number of local bodies was increased substantially.

The General Council of Burmese Associations assumed greater significance in the early 1920s and pursued extreme policies under the leadership of U Chit Hlaing; it opposed the holding of new elections under the new constitution. This provoked a split with the emergence of the Peoples' Party led by U Ba Pe. The new party was prepared to co-operate on the understanding that Britain would proceed rapidly to the implementation of self-government. The Peoples' Party secured the largest number of seats at the first election: however, a mere seven per cent of the electorate voted. The proportion reached sixteen per cent at subsequent elections. In 1928 the Simon Commission recommended that Burma should be separated from India, which was a logical deduction from the difficulties that had been experienced. It was, however, regarded with deep suspicion by advanced nationalist opinion in Burma, partly because the establishment was prominently identified with the advocacy of separation. A fervent campaign against separation was waged in which Dr Ba Maw, an ambitious lawyer educated in England and France, was in the forefront. The Anti-Separation League favoured adhering to the Indian federation with provision for secession and triumphed in the general election of November 1932. The movement against separation was essentially tactical in motivation and the British authorities called their bluff by making it clear that separation would be permanent and not temporary if applied. Opinion was reversed and separation was provided for under the terms of the Government of India Act of 1935. Separation formally took place as from 1 April 1937.[82] The governor possessed control over foreign matters, defence, and various financial or monetary aspects. A cabinet headed by a prime minister was set up; the legislature comprised two houses – the Senate and the House of Representatives. The latter consisted of 132 members; approximately two-thirds represented geographical areas and the rest represented particular interests, including education, commerce and labour. Numerous political parties developed and personal rivalries became intense. The progress towards increased self-government was overshadowed by the worsening crisis in China; the Burma road was becoming more important for the sustaining of the Chinese war effort. Inexorably Burma was being dragged into the struggle between Japan and the western powers.

It will be recalled that Malaya was divided, at the beginning of the twentieth century, into the Federated Malay States, the Unfederated Malay States, and the Straits Settlements. The term 'federation' was misleading. Provision was made for meetings of the four rulers in the Federated Malay States but the conferences could not exercise legislative powers. Under the system created by Sir Frank Swettenham in 1896, a resident-general was appointed to oversee the functioning of the four states and to pursue necessary representations through the residents appointed in each state. The resident-general was under the authority of the governor of the Straits Settlements, who held the post of high commissioner. A federal civil service was created; each of the four state councils had to approve legislation and the rights of the rulers within states were supposedly retained. The conference of rulers achieved little and policy was effectively implemented by officials in Kuala Lumpur.[83] The resident-general became an extremely powerful official: prominent Malays and representatives of western capitalistic enterprise felt that their views should be adequately considered. The high commissioner, Sir John Anderson, took the lead in setting up the Federal Council in 1909; the high commissioner was president, the other members being the four rulers, the resident-general, and the four residents with four members nominated by the high commissioner.[84] The Federal Council met annually and considered a budget for each state: all vital decisions were made in the Federal Council. The Unfederated Malay States and Johore did not wish to join the new arrangement, since they possessed more autonomy as they were. Pressure for more freedom in the Federated Malay States developed. In 1927 Sir Laurence Guillemard, the Straits governor, introduced changes whereby the number of unofficial nominated members of the Federal Council and of official members were both increased. More heads of departments were added to the Council but the sultans no longer participated. The high commissioner and chief secretary saw the sultans regularly; the latter discussed impending business with the residents. Subsequently the chief secretary's title was changed to federal secretary and he was essentially responsible for co-ordinating the work of the residents. State councils became more significant again and resumed the power of making legislation;[85] contemplated budgets were submitted to the Federal Council. The system of government and administration in Malaya was haphazard and inefficient; it reflected the somewhat strange manner in which the presence of the British in Malaya had developed and the compromises rendered necessary by the attitudes of the various interests involved.[86] The colonial administration at Singapore was responsible for the administration of Penang (with Province Wellesley), Malacca, the Cocos islands, Christmas Island, and Labuan.

The Malayan economy continued to thrive with rubber and tin dominating Malayan exports. In 1926 approximately 391,000 tons of rubber worth 711,302 Malayan dollars were exported, comprising 56 per cent of Malayan exports.[87] Competition was encountered from rubber produced in the Netherlands East Indies, which cut across attempts to limit production in Malaya with the aim of stabilising the market. With the onset of the world economic depression the price of rubber fell: in 1932 478,000 tons of rubber were exported from Malaya and were worth only 77,805 Malayan dollars, comprising 21 per cent of Malayan exports.[88] Tin exports amounted to 99,000 tons in 1928, which was worth 191,279 Malayan dollars; this constituted 22 per cent of Malayan exports.[89] In 1932 the tin trade had slumped to the point where only 48,000 tons were exported, which was worth 55,687 Malayan dollars; this comprised 15 per cent of Malayan exports.[90] It is interesting to note that Japan's trade with South-East Asia was expanding rapidly in the 1930s. The Japanese share of Malayan imports of manufactured goods was growing: the proportion doubled from 6 per cent to 13 per cent between 1924 and 1933. During the same period the British share dropped from 30 per cent to 20 per cent.[91] Some Japanese investment in the rubber estates and tin mines was developing during the 1930s. The widening nature of the war in China was shortly to affect Malaya directly and with more profound repercussions than anybody in Malaya could have anticipated in the leisurely atmosphere prevailing. The catastrophic developments in Europe and China transformed the entire situation.

Chapter 9

The Sino-Japanese War and the approach of the Pacific conflict, 1937–1941

Between 1937 and 1941 the situation foreshadowed to some extent before 1937 developed to a climax that had been feared by Britain in 1932. Japan embarked upon a large-scale expansion in China which was to lead her on, in 1940–41, into expansion in South-East Asia. Relations between Britain and Japan worsened greatly and consistently, apart from occasional limited periods when there seemed to be a possibility that the deterioration could be halted, if not reversed. The crisis in the Far East coincided with an even more rapid exacerbation of the European situation. Germany, under Hitler's leadership, was pursuing a far more militant policy in central and eastern Europe, the chief examples of which were the Anschluss with Austria in March 1938, the Czechoslovak crisis of May–September 1938 culminating in the Munich agreement, and the onslaught on Poland in September 1939 that precipitated war in Europe. The Mediterranean had become a focal point of tension since the Ethiopian crisis of 1935–36; the bitterly fought civil war in Spain (1936–39) accentuated the alarm in London and the strain on Britain's defence resources. Serious rearmament was just beginning to attain significant proportions in 1938–39 and it was extremely difficult to see how Britain could fight a war against Japan while she was so heavily committed in Europe. Diplomacy had to be employed with as much skill as could be mustered in an attempt to defend British interests in the Far East, while simultaneously playing for time. It was not a particularly impressive policy but it was the best that could be achieved. Fundamentally it was a question of awaiting the moment when the United States would commit herself to a decisive role in East Asia and the Pacific.

The Undeclared war began with a minor clash between local Japanese and Chinese troops at the Lukouchiao bridge, near Peiping, on 7 July 1937. The clash resulted from Japanese penetration of the area and from concomitant Chinese resentment at the Japanese incursions. Neither side set out to create a major conflict but each miscalculated the policy of the opposing country. The Japanese prime minister, Prince Konoe Fumimaro, wished to assert Japanese power and force concessions from China; the Japanese war ministry and field army wanted to expand but the general staff did not. As for China, Chiang Kai-shek could not risk the accusation of weakness and had to resist a Japanese attempt to force him to make concessions; Chiang had been criticised in the past and he was now, on paper at least, allied with the Chinese communists, following the Sian incident (December 1936), in a strong national policy.[1] The importance of the incident at the Lukouchiao bridge was not at first appreciated by Britain. Neville Chamberlain, the prime minister, and Anthony Eden, the foreign secretary, were concerned with developments in Europe and the newly appointed ambassador to Tokyo, Sir Robert Craigie, had not arrived in Japan. In the early days of the Undeclared war, Britain restricted her activities to urging restraint on both sides and to consultations with the United States. Sir Alexander Cadogan, the deputy undersecretary and former ambassador to China, was disturbed at the parallels with September 1931.[2] Cadogan's fears were justified, for matters worsened with attitudes in Japan and China hardening against compromise and with reports being received of Japanese air raids. The Foreign Office was divided as to the consequences of a Sino–Japanese war. Eden was interested primarily in Europe but was becoming worried at the possibility of a prolonged struggle in China. The most positive aspect of Eden's approach was his desire to promote close co-operation with the United States. The members of the far eastern department were less concerned and were critical of the Chinese; the head of the department, C. W. Orde, described the Chinese as 'such inveterate wrigglers and self-deceivers'.[3]

The Undeclared war moved into its first really serious phase in August 1937 with the development of sustained fighting in Shanghai. Britain was deeply alarmed for the same reasons as in January–March 1932; Shanghai was the most important centre of western enterprise in China with many foreign interests to be safeguarded. There were 50,000 foreigners in Shanghai, including 9,000 British residents, and a military operation of some magnitude would become necessary to evacuate them. There were few British troops and resources available in Shanghai. Britain and the United States appealed for a cessation of fighting but the appeal was in vain. The consensus within the Foreign Office was that Britain must exert what diplomatic influence she could but that her defence weakness dictated a policy which would not embroil Britain in conflict with Japan.[4] The pursuance of this policy was rendered more difficult by the truculence of the Japanese army and navy. In late August a car carrying the British ambassador to China, Sir Hughe Knatchbull–Hugessen, was machine-gunned from the air and the ambassador was seriously wounded. Japanese ships started intercepting British vessels off the China coast with growing frequency.[5] Sir Robert Craigie, having begun to acclimatise himself to Tokyo, advised at the end of September 1937, that Britain should endeavour to mediate; there were risks in mediating but even greater risks in allowing the war to become a lengthy struggle.[6] Eden was willing to employ Britain's good offices if this was wanted. However, it would be imprudent to advance without indications that Japan and China desired British help. On 5 October 1937 President Roosevelt made a major speech on foreign affairs at Chicago, in which he warned the American people that they could not hope to insulate themselves against the ever-widening aggression in the world. Roosevelt suggested, in a singularly opaque phrase, that the law-abiding states might have to organise a 'quarantine' of aggressor states. The speech was impressive as an oration and courageous, given the vocal extent of isolationism in the United States. It was unclear, however, as to what exactly Roosevelt meant and, more important, what (if anything) he intended to do.[7]

Chamberlain and Eden diverged in their anticipation of the value to be attached to a more active American policy but both agreed that Britain could not contemplate economic sanctions unless the signatories of the nine-power treaty of 1922 were willing to act together. In November 1937 the Brussels conference gathered to see if anything constructive could be done to alleviate the strife in China; the conference was attended by the signatories of the nine-power treaty with the addition of the Soviet Union, Norway and Denmark. The conference stood no chance of success, for Japan refused to attend and regarded it with thinly disguised hostility and no country represented at Brussels was prepared to consider economic sanctions, let alone force. The policy laid down by the British cabinet towards the conference was one of innate caution; all Britain could contribute was assistance in mediation.[8]

Between late November 1937 and the middle of January 1938 consultation took place between Britain and the United States over possible action in the naval sphere. The initiative was taken by Britain; after the Japanese air attacks on the British and American ships, HMS *Ladybird* and the *Panay*, President Roosevelt authorised the holding of naval talks. Roosevelt was pondering the possibility of organising an economic blockade and quarantine of Japan with the aim of severing supplies of raw materials to Japan; it could take eighteen months for the blockade to achieve its purpose and Roosevelt did not believe that war would be likely. Roosevelt told the British ambassador on 17 December 1937 that he would send Captain Royal E. Ingersoll of the American navy to London immediately for naval talks.[9] Full exchanges of view occurred when Ingersoll was in London in early January 1938. The Ingersoll mission improved mutual understanding but was simply the first stage in Anglo–American defence co-operation. Roosevelt indicated to the British ambassador at the beginning of January 1938 that he would be prepared to alert the American Pacific fleet if Britain announced definite arrangements to send a fleet to the Far East within the near future. Anthony Eden was on holiday when Roosevelt's message was received and Eden's relations with Neville Chamberlain were deteriorating because of Chamberlain's growing intervention in foreign affairs and because of his desire to restore relations with Italy; Eden resigned from the government in February 1938. Chamberlain was opposed to mobilising the fleet owing to the gravity of events in Europe and because of his doubts as to how much the United States would contribute.[10]

The first significant act of appeasement by Britain in the Far East arose over the Maritime Customs in the spring of 1938. The extension of the war in China caused friction over the functioning of the customs administration. Britain wanted to persuade Japan to co-operate through agreeing to place the customs revenues in a neutral bank; Japan would not agree and Britain then assented, on 3 May 1938, to a settlement on terms favourable to Japan. Customs revenues from ports under Japanese control were to be paid in to the Yokohama Specie Bank, which would facilitate meeting foreign obligations. The agreement was denounced by China, which correctly interpreted it as a sacrifice of China's rights to assist British trade.[11] As if to balance out concessions to Japan, the Foreign Office endeavoured to induce the Treasury to support British economic aid for China. In response to China's appeals to the League of Nations, Britain had pledged moral support but had not advanced beyond it. The new foreign secretary, Lord Halifax, urged that economic assistance be extended to China.[12] The subject was discussed in cabinet meetings between May and July 1938 to no avail. The Treasury opposed making a loan to China because of the risks of becoming more overtly embroiled in the Sino–Japanese war. Chamberlain was hostile to a loan owing to the worsening situation in Europe, where the Czechoslovak crisis was causing major headaches; in addition, Italy was behaving unpredictably.[13] It was decided not to proceed with the loan.

In the summer of 1938 there appeared to be grounds for believing that some at least of the obstacles created by Japanese military activities in China to the conduct of British trade might be removed through a series of discussions between the new Japanese foreign minister, General Ugaki Kazushige, and Sir Robert Craigie. Ugaki was a liberal by the standards of the Japanese army and was believed by Craigie to be better disposed towards Britain. The encouraging note on which the Craigie–Ugaki talks began was not, however, to lead to concrete progress: the threat of war in Europe over Czechoslovakia and a more bellicose approach within the Japanese army doomed prospects for success in Anglo–Japanese exchanges.[14] Ugaki resigned office at the end of September 1938, owing to internal dissension within the government over control of policy in China. The Munich settlement did nothing to boost British prestige. In October 1938 the Japanese army embarked upon new offensives directed at the Wuhan region of the Yangtze valley and at Canton, advances which brought them into centres of British investment and trade. The offensives were completely successful; Canton was captured on 21 October and the temporary Kuomintang capital of Hankow shortly afterwards. Japanese leaders were intoxicated at their victories. An air of supreme self-confidence, of profound faith in Japan's 'holy war' in China and of her mission to carry it further, characterised pronouncements made in November–December 1938. Japan proclaimed her intention of securing a new order in East Asia.[15] The Foreign Office gloomily concluded that, given the state of her defences and developments in Europe, Britain could do little other than employ her diplomacy as skilfully as she could to resist Japan. It would, however, be advisable for tactical reasons to let the Japanese understand that Britain was not averse to treaties being modified provided that this was secured by discussion and mutual agreement and not by unilateral action. A note to this effect was sent to Tokyo on 5 January 1939.[16] The debate in London as to how to combat Japanese expansion in China continued in 1938–39. Assuming a positive policy was to be pursued, Britain had the choice between enforcing economic retaliation against Japan or supplying economic aid to China.

Economic retaliation had been discussed by a cabinet committee in the autumn of 1937 and it had been concluded that it would be difficult to ensure success owing to the problem of gaining adequate co-operation from other countries and because of the danger of Japan resorting to armed resistance if the retaliatory measures were sufficiently rigorous. The Foreign Office consulted other government departments in June and July 1938 but there was no enthusiasm for implementing retaliation.[17] An inter-departmental committee was set up in July 1938 under the chairmanship of Knatchbull–Hugessen. This reported that there were considerable obstacles to the enforcement of sanctions.[18] The Foreign Office showed more enthusiasm for retaliation than other departments, yet was reluctantly compelled to recognise that it could not advance when faced with such negative views. The alternative possiblity of extending economic aid to China was considered again. Chiang Kai-shek was having to rely more heavily on the Soviet Union for aid, since Germany had withdrawn the military mission led by Falkenhausen in May 1938. The British ambassador to China, Sir Archibald Clark Kerr, met Chiang in early November 1938. The generalissimo professed astonishment at Britain's failure to act more effectively against Japanese aggression.[19] Lord Halifax met the Chinese ambassador, Quo Tai-chi, on 18 November 1938, and drew attention to Britain's help for China, as exemplified in the approaching completion of the construction of the Burma road to improve communications between China and Burma and facilitate transport of supplies to assist Chiang Kai-shek; further financial assistance would be given for the purchase of lorries for use on the road.[20] Halifax decided to renew the debate with the Treasury for broader aid to China and urged that a loan of £3 m. be made to the Chinese currency stabilisation fund. Sir John Simon expressed scepticism of the purposes to which the Chinese would put the loan; Neville Chamberlain vacillated, initially inclining towards the proposal and then commenting that the risks were too great.[21] The United States revealed interest in aiding China in December 1938 and this stimulated the cabinet into approving a scheme for a British contribution of £3 m. to the stabilisation fund. The Japanese occupation of the island of Hainan, in February 1939, speeded up the rather complex procedures. Simon believed that a total sum of £10 m. was necessary and that the fund should be managed by a committee in the form of a banking operation. The loan was announced publicly on 8 March 1939. The fund of £10 m. was to be provided by four banks (two Chinese and two British, the latter being the Hong Kong and Shanghai Bank and the Chartered Bank); the British contribution would be guaranteed by the Treasury.[22]

Early in 1939 a review of Britain's defence commitments in Europe was undertaken, which had serious implications for the Far East. The report was submitted by the chiefs of staff to a meeting of the committee of imperial defence (CID) held on 24 February 1939; it included a statement that the size of the fleet to be sent to Singapore would depend on the extent of British commitments and on the situation in Europe. The Admiralty was alarmed at the Royal Navy having to withdraw from the Mediterranean in the event of a fleet having to be dispatched to Singapore and felt that one or two capital ships might constitute a sufficient threat to discourage Japan from rash adventures. Chamberlain and Lord Chatfield, now minister for the co-ordination of defence, drew attention to repeated British promises to the dominions that if a grave crisis occurred, a fleet would be sent to the Far East. This delicate subject was referred to the strategical appreciation sub-committee for further investigation.[23] The sub-committee's report demonstrated the enhanced significance being attached to the Mediterranean, resulting from the bellicosity of Germany and Italy and the change in British policy towards giving guarantees of assistance to Greece, Rumania and Turkey. The sub-committee endorsed the view of the Admiralty that it was not feasible to state how soon after Japanese intervention in a European crisis a fleet could be sent to the Far East.[24] The CID accepted the report of the sub-committee; Britain could not commit herself to dispatching a fleet to the Far East by a definite date and neither could the size of the fleet be determined. The fact was that the European scene was so dangerous that Britain would be unable to send a fleet to the Far East in the foreseeable future. This was extremely embarrassing in the context of relations with the dominions, particularly Australia.[25] How awkward Britain's position was in reality came to be demonstrated with stark brutality when the crisis over Tientsin exploded in June 1939.

The north-eastern treaty port of Tientsin was an important centre of British commerce in China. Tientsin was situated geographically in an area that had been exposed to Japanese infiltration since 1933 and which had been effectively under Japanese domination since the first few months of the Undeclared war. The foreign concessions in Tientsin were anathema to the Japanese army. The concessions were lonely citadels of resistance to the new order, harbouring Chinese guerrillas, silver deposits of the Chinese government placed in British and French banks, and offering encouragement to the circulation of the Chinese fapi (currency), which the Japanese were trying to undermine by circulating their own federal reserve board currency. It could be predicted with reasonable certainty that a crisis would occur at Tientsin before long. The Foreign Office found it a curiously intangible matter to deal with. It was hard for the overworked and harassed officials in London to grasp the precise situation in Tientsin and they were not helped by differences of view between the ambassador to China, Clark Kerr, and the consul-general at Tientsin, E. G. Jamieson. Clark Kerr was opposed to making concessions to the Japanese unless absolutely necessary, whereas Jamieson believed in compromising at an early stage so as to avert a major confrontation. Tension had been gradually building up in Tientsin during the winter of 1938–39 and Sir Robert Craigie expressed apprehension in January and March 1939 about the worsening atmosphere.[26]

The crisis was set off by the assassination of a Chinese puppet official in the British concession at Tientsin on 10 April 1939. This was the last straw for the incensed Japanese military, who demanded that Britain should suppress anti-Japanese movements and expel Chinese engaged in subversion. The Foreign Office decided to hand over Chinese against whom there was evidence of involvement in assassination and that Chinese guilty of lesser offences should be expelled. The British and Japanese authorities in Tientsin consulted during the hunt for the assassins of the puppet official and the British police arrested four men on suspicion of complicity. Two men admitted responsibility but later maintained that they had done so after being tortured by the Japanese. Jamieson, the consul-general, believed the men nevertheless to be guilty and thought they should be handed over for trial. He gave an assurance to this effect to the local Japanese officials but for some reason did not inform the Foreign Office; the latter heard of it only six weeks later, by which time matters had taken a substantial turn for the worse.[27] Clark Kerr was opposed to the men being handed over and said that his conscience could not condone handing suspects over to the Japanese to a certain death.[28] Craigie recommended that the four men should be transferred quickly. The Foreign Office decided to keep the men in Tientsin pending further investigation and to authorise the consul-general to hand over future cases where he was satisfied of participation in terrorist activities. The Japanese military authorities in Tientsin were exasperated at the failure to give them the four men and prepared to operate a rigorous blockade of the British concession.[29] The blockade commenced in 14 June 1939 and was conducted with extreme thoroughness. Everybody entering the concession was stopped and searched; there were a number of cases of people being stripped in the course of the searches. Public opinion in Britain reacted bitterly. The crisis had escalated to a point where it necessitated urgent consideration by the cabinet and the chiefs of staff.[30]

The chiefs of staff submitted a report to the cabinet foreign policy committee on 19 June. They were opposed to retaliatory action against Japan because of the dangers involved; it would be impossible to send more than two capital ships to reinforce the China squadron unless ships were withdrawn from the Mediterranean. The heightening tension in Europe had caused a reassessment of British strategy: Britain could not rely on Italy keeping out of a European war and she was accordingly faced with the threat of a struggle against Germany, Italy and Japan. The aim of British strategy should be to avoid war with Japan and to defeat the weakest opponent – Italy – first. Some criticisms of the report were voiced by Lord Chatfield, who felt that the chiefs of staff had adopted an excessively pessimistic line. At the same time Chatfield did not quarrel with the conclusion of the chiefs of staff that Britain should avert conflict in the Far East if possible.[31] Sir Robert Craigie urged that he be permitted to see the Japanese foreign minister, so that he could ascertain if negotiations could begin to secure a settlement. Lord Halifax, the foreign secretary, doubted if a satisfactory arrangement could be reached but Chamberlain thought it offered the only solution. The key aspect was the attitude of the United States; if the Americans showed anxiety and a willingness to intervene, the position would be improved. Chatfield emphasised the apprehension within the Admiralty and that, if the fleet were sent, the reaponsibility would be that of the cabinet.[32] Chamberlain opted for a diplomatic solution.[33] The cabinet decided to follow Craigie's advice and seek a negotiated escape from confrontation, entrusting Craigie with the onerous task of handling the negotiations.

Japan was willing to open talks; responsible Japanese leaders did not wish the crisis to worsen lest the United States intervene. However, they were determined to utilise Britain's predicament to maximum advantage and hoped to compel Britain to retreat from her policy of lending moral support to Chiang Kai-shek's government. Japan exaggerated the support Britain was giving China and thought that, if Britain would only moderate her policy in Japan's favour, Chiang could be induced to compromise. Craigie's aim was to achieve an agreed statement that would, hopefully, allow a comprehensive solution to the issues involved in Tientsin. Craigie held discussions with the foreign minister, Arita Hachiro, and signed a statement with Arita on 22 July, containing British recognition of the Japanese need to take special measures in pursuance of their military operations; Britain undertook not to countenance any act or measure prejudicial to attainment by Japan of her objective of maintaining security and order in the areas controlled by Japanese forces.[34] It was humiliating for Britain to have to assent to the statement but it was undoubtedly all that could be done in the circumstances. Craigie had achieved a significant diminution in tension. British public opinion, China, and the United States all criticised the agreement but the Tientsin crisis propelled the Americans into taking the first positive, if limited, step against Japan in the economic sphere. Notice was given to Japan on 26 July 1939 of the American intention to terminate the American–Japanese trade treaty of 1911 at the end of the statutory six months' notice. This action was taken without consultation with Britain. President Roosevelt told a member of the British embassy that he had decided to act 'in order that the dictators should not imagine that they could get away with it'.[35] Roosevelt's action may have been influenced, too, by secret Anglo–American naval exchanges which had taken place in Washington in June 1939 on the initiative of the Admiralty with the intention of acquainting the Americans with recent modifications in British naval strategy. The Admiralty was represented by Commander T. C. Hampton, who explained the change in thinking brought about by the European crisis. It was now far more difficult for Britain to contemplate sending a fleet to the Far East. Sympathetic understanding was revealed in the response of the American admirals Leahy and Ghormley, but it was not politically feasible to indicate in detail what the United States would do if she became involved in war as an ally of Britain.[36]

The worst of the Tientsin crisis was over, despite the fact that the Anglo–Japanese talks on detailed issues involved in Tientsin broke down later in August 1939. Japan sought to coerce Britain into compromising over the Chinese silver deposits in British and French banks and over the circulation of Chinese currency. Britain believed she could adopt a firmer policy on these matters because they also involved the United States and France and declined to compromise further, so the talks were adjourned on 20 August 1939, to be resumed after the outbreak of the European war. Anglo–Japanese relations unexpectedly improved in late August 1939 in the aftermath of the astonishing news of the Nazi–Soviet pact, signed in Moscow on 22 August 1939 and contrary to the Anti-Comintern pact signed by Germany and Japan in November 1936.[37] The news shocked Japan, which regarded the Soviet Union with a mixture of fear and hatred, and caused political turmoil, leading to the resignation of the Hiranuma government; a caretaker administration was formed by General Abe Nobuyuki. Japan's relations with Germany were cold and distant, while a warmer attitude towards Britain could be discerned in Tokyo. It was certain that Japan would not involve herself in European affairs within the near future. On 1 September 1939 Germany attacked Poland; on 3 September Britain and France declared war. British policy in the Far East would function amidst the numerous complications and problems engendered by war in Europe.

There seemed, in September 1939, to be a possibility of reaching a *rapprochement* between Britain and Japan. However, the obstacles to achieving a fundamental improvement in Anglo–Japanese relations were considerable. Britain could not make too many concessions for fear of undermining Chinese morale in her continuing struggle with Japan and because the effects on American policy would be detrimental. The role of the United States was far more important, given the outbreak of the European war, and Britain could not offend her. Japan was still bent on a policy of expansion and Japanese leaders had no intention of retreating. The principal problem was China; Japan was committed to the fulfilment of her holy war in China and basic divergences over China remained the chief cause of friction until the beginning of the Pacific war. The same was true of the United States, indeed the American sense of obligation to assist China and eschew a Munich-style agreement over China was stronger than the British. There were, however, advocates of a far-reaching attempt to secure agreement with Japan. One of the most prominent in high circles was R. A. Butler, parliamentary under-secretary at the Foreign Office.

Russia and Japan are bound to remain enemies and with our position in India and the East it would pay us to make a return to the Anglo–Japanese alliance possible. It does not appear that there are the makings of a war between America and Japan; the American interests in the Far East are insufficient to justify a major war. I do not believe it will in the end pay us to keep Japan at arm's length and distrust everything she does for the sake of American opinion. I have never been happy since the Japanese Treaty was allowed to lapse. I believe it is still possible to obtain American interest on our side in fighting dictators in the West, while improving relations with Japan.

I am fortified in wishing to draw nearer to the Japanese by the lack of fighting skill, and indeed fighting at all, shown by the Chinese . . .[38]

Butler advocated a settlement of the issues at Tientsin; withdrawal of British garrisons from China; the conclusion of barter agreements whereby Britain supplied Japan with raw materials in exchange for war material; and the promotion by Britain of a Sino–Japanese peace settlement. The prevailing view of the permanent officials in the far eastern department was that it would be dangerous to proceed too rapidly. Talks were held with Shigemitsu Mamoru, the Japanese ambassador, and his staff to see if an improvement in relations could be effected in the economic sphere, but little came of them. A settlement of the Tientsin question was attained in June 1940, after lengthy talks which were patiently and effectively conducted by Sir Robert Craigie. Chiang Kai-shek expressed serious doubts as to the scope of the Anglo–Japanese discussions but the British government was determined to reach a settlement. The European situation had worsened catastrophically in April–June 1940 with the string of astonishing successes recorded by Hitler. An agreement on Tientsin would dispose of this long-running difficulty and might minimise the dangers of a new clash with Japan. The agreement was signed in Tokyo on 12 June 1940. Britain agreed to work with Japan to maintain law and order in Tientsin. The silver coin and bullion were to be sealed until further decisions were taken, except for the allocation of the sum of £100,000 to be employed for relief purposes in Tientsin, following the grave floods which had hit the city in the autumn of 1939. It was agreed that Britain would not hamper the circulation of federal reserve board currency.[39]

Germany's huge successes in Europe had prompt repercussions in Japan. Doubts as to the reliability of Germany persisted but it was felt that Japan must seize her opportunity; in the phrase of the moment, Japan must not 'miss the bus'. British support for China, epitomised in the role played by the Burma road, was the immediate target for Japanese demands as the road, completed in 1939, assumed greater importance as a means of conveying supplies to China in 1940. The alternative routes were the railway from French Indo–China to southern China and the long overland road from Soviet Central Asia. The French route was highly vulnerable to Japanese pressure and the French administration at first reduced and then halted supplies to China. The Burma road was not in a particularly satisfactory state, because of the mountainous terrain, wet weather, and because of the reluctance of the government of Burma to spend sufficient money on its development. The government of Burma was also influenced by a long-standing argument with China over the ill-defined border between Burma and China. However, the Burma road was making a growing contribution to China's war effort. According to statistics provided by the Burma Office in June 1940, the total value of arms and ammunition imported into Rangoon for re-export to China was 262.83 lakhs of rupees (£2,022,000): of these 100.32 lakhs (£771,000) or about 38 per cent were of Russian origin. The corresponding figures for April to October 1939 were 401 lakhs (£3,085,000), of which 15 lakhs (£108,000) were of United States origin and 76.5 lakhs (£588,000) were of Russian origin. Prior to September 1939 the bulk of arms shipments came from Germany, Czechoslovakia (under German domination from October 1938), France and Belgium. Britain did not contribute a great deal to the arms supplies; out of a total of £7,028,362 worth of munitions imported into Rangoon for outward transit to China between March 1939 and March 1940, only about £239,000 or 3.4 per cent originated in the British Empire.[40] In the middle of June 1940 the British military attaché in Tokyo was told by the director of military operations in the War Ministry that Britain must close the Burma road and the Hong Kong frontier if war with Japan was to be averted. The same advice was tendered, if more courteously, by the vice-minister of the *Gaimusho* to Craigie.[41] Initially Craigie did not believe Japan would attack British possessions but that a blockade of Hong Kong or a bombing offensive against the Burma road was possible. In the light of European events, Craigie recommended that Britain should submit rather than to take risks when she was ill-equipped to cope with the consequences.

The situation, like that at Tientsin a year before, required consideration by the cabinet and the chiefs of staff. The response of the chiefs of staff was entirely predictable: no risks should be taken with Japan, the Burma road should be closed, and an attempt made to secure a general peace settlement in East Asia.[42] Craigie suggested closure at the beginning of July but the Foreign Office believed closure to be too drastic and humiliating a step; they thought of limited concessions falling short of closure. The war cabinet was divided with the majority leaning against closure. Craigie warned on 1 July 1940 that the atmosphere was becoming more tense in Tokyo, with rumours of increased bellicosity among younger army officers.[43] The chiefs of staff reiterated that a settlement should be reached. The war cabinet discussed the position further on 5 July and decided that the risks were too great to resist. The prime minister, Winston Churchill, stated with reluctance that there was no alternative to closing the road. The burden of facing Japan should be assumed by the United States: 'In the present state of affairs he did not think that we ought to incur Japanese hostility for reasons mainly of prestige.'[44]

The British ambassador in Washington, Lord Lothian, saw the secretary of state, Cordell Hull, on 5 July 1940 and explained Britain's predicament. Hull was sympathetic but thought that the Burma road should be kept open. It was clear that with the United States about to begin a presidential campaign, it was extremely improbable that America would become involved in the Burma road question. The dominions supported closure. Lord Halifax was inclined to see if Japan would be satisfied by a reduction in supplies to China as against closure but the war cabinet decided that the road would have to be closed unless Craigie could somehow persuade Japan to accept less. Craigie was instructed to obtain the best arrangement he could and to assent to closure if Japan could be satisfied in no other way. In Tokyo the Yonai government was experiencing intense opposition from the army and in a final effort to sustain itself was disinclined to consider a compromise with Britain: it was made clear to Craigie that Britain must submit or face the consequences. Craigie reported back to London, suggesting that it might be possible to obtain closure of the road for three months on the understanding that Japan would make serious efforts to reach a general peace settlement with China. The war cabinet was conscious of Australian anxiety at the danger of war. Information from Washington indicated that Britain's dilemma was understood and that closure would be condoned. The war cabinet decided, on 11 July, to seek a settlement on the basis proposed by Craigie.[45] The ambassador saw Arita and agreement was reached that the Burma road would be closed for three months from 18 July to the transport of arms, ammunition, petrol, trucks, and railway material. During the period of closure a special effort would be made to secure peace in China. Closure was criticised by the United States and China, particularly by the latter.[46]

Japan made no attempt to conclude peace with Chiang Kai-shek in the summer of 1940. Instead Japan pressed ahead with final plans ·for the inauguration of the 'Purified Kuomintang' government at Nanking, headed by Wang Ching-wei. Wang had been one of the most prominent leaders of the Kuomintang in the 1920s and 1930s but had broken with Chiang Kai-shek in the late 1930s and advocated co-operation with Japan. He did not intend to become a Japanese puppet and wanted a substantial measure of autonomy. The Japanese army would not agree to his receiving such freedom. Wang was in effect a prisoner of the Japanese: he had gone too far to retreat and could only continue, hoping that he could render the Nanking regime attractive to the Chinese people. He failed, since he was indelibly associated with the evils of Japanese militarism.[47] The British Foreign Office thought in late 1939 that there was a chance that Wang could establish himself as a credible figure but as 1940 progressed, they rightly discounted the idea. Between July and September 1940 the various departments of the British government pondered the shape of a far eastern peace settlement; it was not believed that a settlement was likely but it was deemed helpful to explore the problems involved. The Foreign Office regarded recognition by Japan of the integrity and independence of China to be axiomatic. Japan would have to be coaxed into acceptance through economic inducements, chiefly in supplying raw materials and financial assistance, and would also be expected to recognise the integrity of European colonial possessions in East Asia, South-East Asia, and in the Pacific. Extraterritoriality would be ended in China. The Foreign Office anticipated great difficulty in persuading Japan and China to talk to each other; strenuous efforts would have to be made by the powers acting as mediators.[48] The other government departments consulted did not believe that any progress could be made and doubts were expressed as to whether it was in Britain's interests for the Sino–Japanese war to end; large numbers of Japanese troops were tied down in China who could be deployed elsewhere if the war terminated.[49]

In mid-July 1940 the Yonai government resigned and was succeeded by an administration led by Prince Konoe Fumimaro with Matsuoka Yosuke as foreign minister. During Konoe's term of office (to October 1941) fateful decisions were taken that committed Japan to the European Axis and to confrontation with the United States and Konoe and Matsuoka deeply regretted the climax in December 1941 to the process they had set in motion.[50] In September 1940 Japan signed the tripartite pact with Germany and Italy which Japanese leaders hoped would deter the United States from adopting an interventionist policy towards either the Pacific crisis or the European war. In fact the pact profoundly antagonised the United States and pushed her into becoming more active in the Far East. In addition, in September 1940 Japan forced the Vichy administration in Indo–China to accept a Japanese military presence in the northern part of the colony. Britain believed that the Burma road should be re-opened in October 1940, when the three month agreement expired. Japan had flagrantly ignored the British request that she should seek a peace settlement with China and this could accordingly be cited as the reason for Britain's decision. Britain had just survived the Battle of Britain in August–September 1940 and the victory strengthened morale. The United States wished to see the Burma road re-opened and was pursuing a more forthright policy towards the European war, exemplified in the destroyers-bases deal announced at the beginning of September 1940.[51]

The sharp deterioration in relations with Japan brought about a reappraisal of British defences in East Asia. It was the first thorough report produced by the chiefs of staff for three years referring explicitly to the Far East. The chiefs of staff assumed that the demand on defence resources caused by the wars in Europe and the Middle East would not lessen and that it would be a question of managing as best Britain could. Malaya was directly threatened by land, air, and sea as a result of Japan's having established effective domination of the coast of China and of her looming threat to intervene in South-East Asia. Britain had to be prepared to hold the Malayan peninsula against a Japanese invasion by sea and by land from Thailand. The reality of Britain's dilemma was contained in the following plaintive paragraph:

In the absence of a Fleet our policy should be to rely primarily on air power. The air forces required to implement that policy, however, cannot be provided for some time to come. Until they can be made available we shall require substantial additional land forces in Malaya, which cannot in present circumstances be found from British or Indian resources.[52]

The chiefs of staff believed that war with Japan should be averted if possible and that every effort should be made to obtain a general peace settlement in the Far East. The report was correct in stressing the importance of defending the whole of Malaya but Singapore was still overvalued as a base and Japanese prowess in the air was seriously underestimated. As regards British air strength, it was believed that a total of 336 aircraft was required, approximately four times the existing air strength.[53] The prime minister was unimpressed with the report. Churchill was interested in the 'real wars' in Europe and the Middle East and dismissed the Japanese threat as remote and unlikely to materialise. He did not understand Japan and was not personally concerned at assessing the repercussions of war in the Far East. To some extent this was comprehensible: the challenges confronting Churchill in the summer of 1940 and after were daunting by any criterion and the defence of the British Isles was bound to be uppermost in his mind. This did not contribute, however, to the formulation of a cohesive British policy towards Japanese expansion.

Steps were taken to improve co-ordination of defences through the appointment of a commander-in-chief, Far East, with authority over the army and air force commands based in Singapore; the navy continued under a separate command. Air Chief Marshal Sir Robert Brooke-Popham took on the appointment as commander-in-chief, Far East, in October 1940. Brooke-Popham came out of retirement to assume the post; he possessed considerable shrewdness in weighing up men and situations but was rather too old for such a demanding and difficult post, although he did achieve some improvement in the defence administration and co-operation within it, partly through changes in personnel.[54] Whatever was achieved in streamlining the defence establishment and in securing co-operation between the military and the civil authorities, nothing could compensate for the chronic weakness in material resources. Brooke-Popham was having largely to maintain a facade of optimism and confidence in public as to the chances of withstanding a Japanese offensive, while possessing grave doubts in private as to what would happen.

The most significant development in defence terms in 1940–41 was the extension of consultation with the United States. Defence talks were held in Washington in January–March 1941: full and frank exchanges on the complexities of defence policy occurred. The talks were intended to survey global defence strategy and to ascertain the extent to which harmony prevailed in Anglo–American thinking. Churchill emphasised that, in the naval sphere, Britain should defer to the wishes of the United States 'in the matters concerning the Pacific theatre of war'.[55] The talks were, in broad terms, successful in leading both sides to a closer understanding of the views held by the other. However, appreciable differences existed over future strategy in the Far East and Pacific in the event of war. Britain attached fundamental importance to the role of Singapore as the principal base which must be held; Singapore was a symbol of British might and exerted a potent influence on the dominions and the dependent colonial empire.[56] The United States could not commit herself to entering a war against Japan in hypothetical circumstances. President Roosevelt warned the American defence chiefs that they must not trespass on delicate political territory. Roosevelt himself was uncertain, at the beginning of 1941, as to what the United States would do if Japan attacked British or Dutch colonial territories but did not attack American possessions. He probably thought that America would act but he was adamant that he could give no commitment. He eventually gave the elusive promise of help at the beginning of December 1941, when it was obvious from intercepted Japanese codes that war was imminent. The American defence chiefs agreed that the Malay barrier must be retained and that a counter-offensive against Japan should be launched at the earliest opportunity, but the Americans did not regard the retention of Singapore as absolutely crucial to the allied position. Clearly its loss would be a major setback but 'the United States Staff Committee holds the view that the loss need not have a decisive effect upon the issue of the war'.[57] The United States agreed with Britain that the battle in the Atlantic came first and that it would be unwise to transfer ships to the Pacific. It was clear from the talks that the Americans were wary of the accusation that they were willing to intervene to defend the colonial possessions of the British and the Dutch; the anti-imperial tradition of the United States had to be borne in mind.

From the autumn of 1940 Britain debated what could be done to increase aid to China and to put a brake on Japan through discreet economic pressure. Chiang Kai-shek uttered vocal appeals for substantially increased assistance, combined with a dark warning that China might have to withdraw from the war unless such aid was forthcoming. Chiang told the British ambassador that China must not be regarded as 'semi-colonial' and that she should be accorded equality of status with Britain.[58] The British Foreign Office sympathised with Chiang but did not see how Britain could respond effectively. The Chinese army was weak, contrary to Chiang's remarks, and Britain was so hard pressed herself that it was out of the question for large-scale economic assistance to be given to China. It was held that something could be achieved in the military sphere by way of talks on a British contribution to Chinese guerrillas and on contingency planning for Britain becoming involved in war against Japan. Limited economic aid would be feasible in the form of a loan for currency stabilisation or export credits.[59] In November 1940 Britain determined to send a military mission to Chungking; the mission could assess the competence of the Chinese army. The War Office described China's assistance against Japan as 'of immense value'.[60] The Foreign Office ruled out a possible alliance with China; it would be impossible to obtain American adherence and an Anglo–Chinese alliance would incense Japan. The Foreign Office had heard indirectly that China might be prepared to supply ten divisions for service in Burma. The rumour met with a mixed reaction but the prevailing opinion was that the troops would be of dubious calibre and that any formal proposal should be treated cautiously.[61] On 10 December 1940 Britain granted £5 m. to the China stabilisation fund, together with additional export credits of £5 m. It was not a large sum but it was all that the Treasury regarded as possible.[62] The military mission reached China at the beginning of 1941 and was headed by General L. E. Dennys. A number of meetings were held with Chiang Kai-shek and his military advisers between February and April 1941. The topics pursued included co-operation following the outbreak of war with Japan. General Dennys stated that Britain would like six aerodromes for use against Japanese air forces in the Hong Kong–Canton area and hoped that China could improve the functioning of the Burma road, so that supplies could be moved more swiftly.[63] Britain would have liked to do more to assist; it was thought that, given the extreme pressure Britain was under, more should be done by the United States.

Matters concerning China and Japan were examined in London by a newly-formed committee, the far eastern committee. This body was set up in October 1940 under the chairmanship of R. A. Butler, who remained in the chair until June 1941 when he was succeeded by Richard Law, and consisted of representatives of every government department dealing with the Far East; issues of general interest were discussed with the aim of improving co-ordination. The committee was primarily concerned with relations with Japan involving economic questions[64] and implemented restrictions on trade with Japan so as to prevent Japan from assisting Britain's enemies and building up significant stocks. Machinery was erected throughout the British Commonwealth to apply a licensing system with the aim of restricting exports to Japan to normal figures in respect of all goods deemed to be German, Italian or Japanese deficiencies. The aim was to tighten the economic screw on Japan and to make Japan aware of the impact but without introducing measures sufficiently stringent to raise the danger of war. The United States was also applying economic measures against Japan but in a different manner from that employed in Britain.[65]

Relations between Britain and Japan were tense from the autumn of 1940 onwards. Suspicion and hostility were accentuated by the behaviour and bizarre pronouncements of the Japanese foreign minister, Matsuoka, who was garrulous and not infrequently self-contradictory in his statements. A constant theme was the need for Japan to extend the benefits of the new order into what was now referred to as the 'Greater East Asia Co-Prosperity Sphere'. Matsuoka emphasised that a new era had dawned for Asia, one that would help the suffering peoples in colonial territories to obtain independence (under Japanese guidance) and which would see the end of western domination. The British Foreign Office resented Matsuoka's allusions to parts of the British Empire. In January–February 1941 it was feared that Japan might be preparing to attack British territories, an apprehension stimulated by a bellicose speech made by Matsuoka in the Diet and by intelligence reports that an attack could be imminent. Churchill and Anthony Eden, who was foreign secretary again, determined on a tough stance. Japan was told that Britain could not accept that Japan could make claims involving British possessions and that Matsuoka's language was firmly disapproved of.[66] Churchill sent a personal message to Roosevelt on 15 February 1941, stating that a Japanese attack was possible.[67] The tension gradually subsided in the latter part of February 1941 amidst a mass of diplomatic verbiage. Mat-suoka vehemently denied that his foreign policy was extreme and con-tended that Britain and the United States bore much responsibility for the way that the situation had evolved. [68]

The catalyst in the far eastern crisis in 1941 was the Japanese decision to occupy bases in southern French Indo-China in July 1941. Japanese influence in Indo-China had grown steadily since September 1940, when the first bases in the northern half of the colony had been occupied, and the Japanese advance into southern Indo-China meant a further step for-ward towards Malaya and the Netherlands East Indies. This was an act taken in defiance of the United States, which was now playing a far more active role in the Pacific crisis. Roosevelt acted firmly and introduced economic sanctions against Japan, which were seen to be of a drastic nature when the full dimensions of American policy became clear in Sep-tember 1941, although initially considerable muddle and obscurity sur-rounded the introduction of the measures because Roosevelt had, very typically, not given lucid instructions to the bureaucracy for applying them. [69] The feeling in the British government in July 1941, prior to the Japanese advance in Indo-China, was that it was necessary to move with some care and not to introduce measures that might drive Japan to attack. [70] There was no Anglo–American consultation before the Ameri-can action was announced in Washington. Eden informed his colleagues in the war cabinet on 31 July that the United States intended to freeze Japanese assets, subject all Japanese imports to licence, and restrict pet-roleum exports. He proposed delaying a statement of British policy until the scope of the American measures had been clarified. He indicated that Britain should then denounce the Anglo–Japanese commercial treaty of 1911 and freeze Japanese assets. It was agreed that Britain must follow a resolute line whatever the Americans did. There were certainly reserva-tions in London as to whether full-scale economic sanctions were wise, but once the United States had stated that strong action would be taken it was advisable to adhere to that policy and not appear to vacillate. [71] By the beginning of 1941 the range of the British action was clear. Mag-nesium was the only indispensable import from Japan; no new licences were being granted in Britain. All exports from Britain, India, Burma, and the colonies were subject to licence. [72] The combined economic sanc-tions operated by Britain, the United States and the Netherlands East Indies confronted Japan with the choice of retreating and compromising or of advancing to war within a short period. Differing views were held in London: it was thought possible that Japan might moderate her policies but equally that war might well materialise. However, Britain had to fol-low in the footsteps of the United States and accept the consequences.

Churchill was delighted with the positive initiatives in Washington. He believed that Japan should be warned, in explicit terms, against further expansion, so as to leave no room for doubt in Japanese minds. Churchill had an obstinate faith in the value of stern warnings and was still urging Roosevelt to issue a warning at the beginning of December 1941. In

August 1941 Churchill crossed the Atlantic and met Roosevelt at Placentia Bay, Newfoundland, for a candid exchange on world problems. The prime minister trenchantly put the case for a warning in unmistakable terms and Roosevelt agreed to send the warning on his return to Washington. He was dissuaded by Cordell Hull on his return, for Hull believed a warning would be counter-productive and would not assist the talks he was currently conducting with the Japanese ambassador in Washington, Admiral Nomura Kichisaburo.[73] Instead Roosevelt gave the ambassador a mild and vague warning.[74] Hull was important in dissuading Roosevelt from another act a month later. The Japanese prime minister, Prince Konoe, suggested that a personal summit conference should take place between Roosevelt and himself in a bid to avert the danger of war. Konoe was alarmed at the gravity of the Pacific crisis and was gambling on his ability to persuade Roosevelt to make concessions and, in addition, on his power to gain the emperor's support in overruling the army and militant nationalist opinion on the concessions Japan would have to make.[75] Roosevelt liked the proposal, as he always enjoyed personal meetings, but Hull was resolutely opposed, maintaining that agreement was necessary before Roosevelt and Konoe met and there was no sign of preliminary agreement that would justify a summit conference. British policymakers were suspicious of the suggested meeting, fearing that it could lead to appeasement of Japan and thus undermine the recent trend towards a more tenacious policy. The ghost of Munich continued to haunt statesmen and officials.

The principal feature of the Pacific crisis in the final approach to war was the continuation of the protracted talks in Washington between Hull and Nomura. The discussion lasted from April to December 1941, with brief adjournments. Britain was not a party to the talks and was largely in ignorance of what was said in them, a situation which arose because Cordell Hull consistently maintained that he was pursuing exploratory exchanges in order to ascertain if sufficient agreement could be reached to place matters on the level of formal negotiations. He promised to consult Britain, the Netherlands government in exile, and China when the latter stage was reached. Britain had tried to give advice to Hull in May 1941 but the subject had been mishandled by the British ambassador, Lord Halifax; Hull became irate and stated that he did not want to receive lectures from the British government.[76] The Foreign Office then wisely decided that a policy of effacement was indicated and left Hull to keep Britain informed. In fact, little information was forthcoming from Hull and British officials were left to speculate on their course.[77] Slowly Hull provided more information in September and October 1941 but he did not become expansive until November, when it was clear that the crisis was approaching its climax.

The attitude of the British leaders to the Washington talks was mixed. Churchill was not too perturbed, since he believed that the United States should cope with Pacific issues, but Eden and his officials were less contented. The Foreign Office feared that Japan might outmanoeuvre the

United States and that a settlement from which Japan could gain substantially might occur. In the second half of November, in a final attempt to achieve at least a temporary solution, Japan proposed a *modus vivendi* based on the withdrawal of troops from southern Indo-China in exchange for lifting sanctions. Hull was not satisfied with this as presented but consulted Britain, the Netherlands and China about possibly putting forward an alternative *modus vivendi*.[78] The Foreign Office, after showing some interest in a possible compromise, decided firmly against it when more information was available, one of the principal reasons being British concern over China's ability to sustain her war effort against Japan as the news from China was hardly encouraging and Chiang Kai-shek had been loudly appealing for assistance. Churchill was conscious of China's situation. Chiang's reaction was extremely bitter when he heard of the Japanese offer and the Netherlands was not enthusiastic. Hull, weary of the tedious talks and in ill-health for much of the time, decided to wash his hands of the situation. It was obvious from intercepted Japanese codes that Japan was about to attack, although it was not clear who would be attacked or where.

Roosevelt intervened decisively in the last days of peace. He held several meetings with Lord Halifax and reviewed American and British policies in a somewhat discursive manner. Britain wished to gain American approval for her strategy for dealing with a Japanese invasion of Malaya, once it was definitely known that a Japanese invasion fleet had set sail for Malaya. The chiefs of staff and the commander-in-chief, Far East, had for some months discussed a British operation to move into the narrow Kra isthmus of Thailand so as to forestall Japanese seizure. It was a delicate operation to contemplate, because it would mean invading Thai territory. The position of Thailand was equivocal : Thai leaders were divided between a pro-British and a pro-Japanese camp and the British minister in Bangkok, Sir Josiah Crosby, believed that there was a chance of persuading Thailand to support Britain if the matter was handled carefully. Roosevelt approved of an operation to take the Kra isthmus but thought it required skilful diplomacy.[79] Roosevelt was concerned with the impact of developments on American public opinion. It was vital, if he was to be able to deal successfully with the political complexities in Washington, that Japanese moves should be seen as patently aggressive acts and that the aggression should be new and not an extension of former aggression. For this reason, Roosevelt felt it would be difficult for him to take a tough line over a Japanese attack on the Burma road. Roosevelt gave, in the manner of an aside, the promise of support for Britain if her territories were attacked, which had been sought by Churchill for so long. Roosevelt agreed with Churchill that a final warning should be given, the scope of which would embrace a Japanese attack on Thailand, Malaya, or the Netherlands East Indies:

> He [Roosevelt] thinks that if the warning is given by the United States, ourselves and the Dutch, we should act independently all within 24 hours using different language to mean the same thing ... He would prefer the United States

to get in first. On account of political considerations here, it was important that their action should be based on independent necessities of United States defence and not appear to follow on ourselves . . . [80]

Roosevelt decided to make an appeal to Emperor Hirohito, not in the belief that it was likely to effect a dramatic change in the situation but so that it 'would strengthen his general case if things went wrong'.[81] The message was held up in Tokyo and did not reach Hirohito.[82]

On the eve of the Pacific war, Britain knew that the United States would be fighting alongside her. Britain then gave the same undertaking of support to the Netherlands East Indies as had been given to her by the United States. The Netherlands had sought the promise of support for a considerable period, but it had not been extended previously because of the opposition of Churchill and the Admiralty, who contended that Britain did not have the resources to implement the promise unless Britain, in turn, was assured of American support. Down to the summer of 1941 Britain had borne the brunt of facing Japan, a burden which she was not capable of carrying when so heavily involved elsewhere. That burden had now been assumed by the United States.

Chapter 10

The war in the Far East, 1941–1945

The Japanese used the term 'Greater East Asia War' to describe the huge conflict in which they were engaged from December 1941 to August 1945. In the United States and Britain, especially the former, the term 'Pacific war' has been widely used. Perhaps neither phrase is ideal to describe a massive struggle that was fought out from the borders of India to New Guinea and countless Pacific islands.[1] The war began with the brilliantly audacious, if not wholly successful, attack on Pearl Harbor and the Japanese offensive against Malaya; the first Japanese landings in Malaya preceded the attack on Pearl Harbor by an hour. The first phase of the war down to the battles of the Coral Sea (off the eastern coast of Australia) and Midway was astonishingly successful for Japan: a string of unbroken victories, mostly secured with considerable rapidity and distinguished by exceptional tenacity and ingenuity, was recorded in Malaya, Burma, the Netherlands East Indies, the Philippines, and various Pacific islands. The victories exceeded all but the wildest expectations of the most fanatical Japanese nationalists. The problem for Japan was that she had conquered a vast physical area while simultaneously having to retain a large army in China – it would be a formidable task to defend the area once the United States had recovered from the shock of Pearl Harbor and mobilised sufficient resources to launch a powerful counter-attack. Japan's hope of retaining dominance of the regions she had occupied lay in the progress of the European war: if Germany could defeat Russia and turn her attention to Britain, the United States might accept a compromise peace which would allow Japan to control East Asia and the western Pacific. Japanese leaders had not carefully assessed their prospects of winning the war they had launched; they had advanced to war in a mood of fatalism, feeling that the unyielding attitude of the United States and Britain left no option but to proceed.[2] Japan's crucial weaknesses for waging such a gigantic struggle were her lack of sufficient industrial strength and raw materials and shortages of shipping; the shipping aspect progressively crippled the Japanese war effort from 1943 onwards.

For Britain, the Japanese onslaught meant the addition of another major struggle to those in which she was so heavily engaged in Europe and the Middle East. At the beginning of the war it was believed in London that Japan could be held on the Malayan peninsula for a long enough period to enable the British, Americans and Dutch to formulate a cohesive and effective strategy to contain and ultimately defeat Japan. The prewar illusion generally held by British and American politicians and military men that Japan could be so held was rudely shattered from the first hours of the war: Japan had seized the initiative and was to keep it throughout the first phase of the war. Britain started the war in Malaya badly and, despite occasional rallies, the story of superior Japanese strategy, tactics, and morale was maintained throughout the Malayan campaign.[3] Brooke-Popham, the commander-in-chief, Far East, did not implement Operation *Matador* to take the Kra isthmus, hesitating to authorise the operation until it was absolutely certain that Japanese forces were about to invade, owing to the importance of not antagonising Thailand. Japanese troops landed without difficulty and without encountering much significant resistance on the Malayan coast. Thailand submitted to Japanese pressure and allowed Japanese troops to pass through. Britain suffered a profound blow to prestige and morale when the *Prince of Wales* and the *Repulse* were swiftly sunk by Japanese aircraft on 10 December, thus indisputably demonstrating the vulnerability of capital ships to concentrated air attack. The ships had been sent to the Far East on the insistence of Winston Churchill and contrary to the advice of the Admiralty,[4] lacking air support and adequate backing from destroyers. Admiral Sir Tom Phillips had left Singapore in a bid to prevent Japanese landings on the Malayan coast; it was a courageous if unwise act. Phillips had subscribed to the prevalent naval view that the menace from the air should not be exaggerated; he went down with his ship. The disastrous news deeply shocked the British forces and civilians in the Far East. The British Commonwealth forces in Malaya were in no sense a unified force, comprising as they did a mixture of British, Australians and Indians. Many of them were raw soldiers with little training, ill-equipped for war against the well-trained Japanese.[5] The command was headed by Brooke-Popham for the first fortnight of the war but he had received notice of recall before the war began. His replacement, Lt.-General Sir Henry Pownall, arrived in Singapore on 23 December 1941. The army in Malaya was headed by Lt.-General A. E. Percival, an intelligent and courageous man but without the inspirational qualities necessary for successful war leadership.

The Malayan campaign was wholly disastrous. Grave errors were made in prematurely evacuating aerodromes and defensive positions and in allowing valuable supplies of oil and food to fall into Japanese hands. In some places an atmosphere of panic prevailed. Brooke-Popham, dismayed at the position, drafted a statement for all RAF units, calling attention to the need for greater efficiency and reminding units of service traditions.[6] Defences were extremely rudimentary or non-existent because of the importance of maintaining the Malayan economy at full strength with its crucial production of rubber and tin and because of prejudice against erecting defences owing to the effect on morale.[7] The Japanese consistently possessed the initiative and demonstrated skill and ingenuity in their rapid progress down the Malayan peninsula. From the beginning of the fighting, Japan possessed air superiority over the obsolescent and numerically inadequate British planes; at sea there was no significant British presence after the sinking of the *Prince of Wales* and the *Repulse*.

Immediately after the attack on Pearl Harbor, Churchill believed that he must meet Roosevelt as soon as possible to discuss world strategy. The advent of the Pacific war, quickly followed by Hitler's foolish declaration of war on the United States, forged the most remarkable partnership seen between two leaders, Winston Churchill and Franklin Roosevelt. Correspondence between them began when Churchill returned to the Admiralty in September 1939 and continued until Roosevelt's death in April 1945.[8] The two men respected each other with the recognition due to such supreme political masters and operators. They shared an appreciation of the profound challenge to liberal values implicit in Nazi Germany and, to a lesser extent, in Japan and were determined to eradicate this threat no matter how great the burden. The extremely important positive side of the relationship must be kept in mind, especially when seen in the light of the strains that developed in the middle and later stages of the war. As personalities they were very different, the chief resemblance being their enjoyment of conversation or, to be more accurate, monologues. In the political sphere, divisions between them were always present over colonial issues. Roosevelt shared the hostility to western colonial empires inbred in most citizens of the United States. Colonialism was abhorrent and Roosevelt hoped to see a world at the end of the war in which colonial empires would have dissolved, at least in South-East Asia where the Japanese were in the process of liquidating them. He communicated his views to Churchill at times with reference to India and Hong Kong in particular. Churchill's reactions were so bitter that the president usually refrained from direct reference to the subject thereafter. Churchill was passionately committed to the perpetuation of the British Empire/Commonwealth: he was determined to see Britain's colonial territories regained in South-East Asia so as to avenge the humiliation of the loss of Singapore and Burma. More fundamentally, the Second World War exemplified the fast-changing relationship between Britain and the United States. Britain was carrying enormous burdens which were to rob her of much of her strength and resilience. The United States was rapidly developing to become a superpower, intent on exploiting the opportunities this connoted in the political and economic spheres. It is not surprising that there was often tension and recrimination between British and American officials and service personnel. It is perhaps more a matter for comment that Britain and the United States worked together as successfully as they did during the war in the Far East and the Pacific.[9]

Churchill proceeded to Washington in late December 1941 accompanied by the chiefs of staff. Before he left London Lord Halifax, the ambassador in Washington, warned that care was required in that the American public was still adjusting to the novel idea of being a leading participant in the war. It was agreed at the Washington talks that the war in Europe, the Atlantic and the Middle East would take precedence over the war in the Pacific, a view adhered to by Roosevelt throughout the war, despite pressure from certain generals (notably MacArthur) and some Republican politicians for concentrating primarily on the defeat of Japan. The Americans advocated a large area of command against the Japanese extending from Burma to New Guinea with a British general at the head. Churchill was not convinced of the merits of the plan but deferred to American pressure. General Sir Archibald Wavell received the dubious honour of appointment to the ABDA (American-British-Dutch-Australian) command. It was an impossible assignment for one man to fulfil successfully. Wavell was faced with disparate forces fighting desperate rearguard actions and there was no time for cohesion to be achieved. Wavell did his best to prop up ABDA but it was a doomed concept which ended in March 1942 when the Japanese had captured Malaya, most of Burma, the Netherlands East Indies, and the Philippines.

Churchill's meeting with Roosevelt was valuable in that it constituted the first of the series of encounters in time of war and effective rapport was established between them. This was of vital importance for the successful waging of the Second World War. Despite the strains inevitably present in the relationship, Churchill and Roosevelt enjoyed close co-operation and friendship. Each respected the other, although there was more warmth on Churchill's side than on Roosevelt's. Both were powerful charismatic leaders who had done much to revive confidence in their respective countries, Roosevelt through the impetus provided by the New Deal and Churchill through his war leadership since attaining the premiership. Churchill possessed vigour, stamina and potent qualities of inspiration as a war leader. He was too obstinate, however, in pressing his own often unsound strategic ideas and talked too much at war cabinet meetings, as his long-suffering colleagues were to protest. Roosevelt was more enigmatic than Churchill. A master politician, he was curiously bizarre or vacuous in many of his remarks, a poor administrator and presided over muddle and competing agencies within his administration. To Churchill the war in the Far East was far less significant than the struggles in Europe and the Middle East; his interest in the war against Japan was largely connected with its impact on American opinion with the concomitant danger of the diversion of resources away from Europe to the Pacific. Roosevelt had to make due allowance for such pressure from American opinion; throughout the period of direct American participation in the Second World War approximately fifty per cent of American resources were devoted to the war against Japan.

The war in Malaya ended swiftly and against the orders of Churchill and Wavell that resistance on Singapore island should continue to the end. On 15 February 1942 the bankruptcy of the prewar Singapore strategy was blatantly revealed with the formal surrender of the island. In total about 130,000 British Commonwealth forces surrendered to General Yamashita Tomoyuki's army of approximately 30,000. General Pownall wrote in his diary two days before the surrender:

I fear that we were frankly out-generalled and outfought. It is a great disaster for the British arms, one of the worst in history, and a great blow to the honour and prestige of the army. From the beginning to the end of this campaign we have been outmatched by better soldiers. A very painful admission, but it is an inescapable fact.[10]

Japanese troops enjoyed sweeping successes in Burma, too; concentration upon developments in Malaya meant that nothing was done to strengthen British troops there. The Japanese advanced rapidly and British forces were compelled to retreat rapidly, as were Chinese forces which had crossed into Burma to assist the British.[11] Similar victories were achieved in the Philippines and the East Indies, so that Japan thus controlled virtually all the colonial territories in East and South-East Asia and in the western Pacific. The repercussions for the lands occupied by the Japanese were profound.[12] The occidental empires had liked to depict themselves to their subject peoples as invariably superior and invincible. Western dominance of colonial areas rested basically on bluff rather than force. Now the bluff had been called and with devastating consequences for any aspirations of restoring the *status quo ante* that were harboured in the western countries.[13] Japan was imbued with a fervent belief in her mission to liberate the peoples of Asia and the Pacific from occidental exploitation – the seeds of this sense of mission had been sown in the circumstances of the Meiji restoration of 1868, with its inherent determination to throw off the shackles of western authority and secure complete independence, and had been fostered in the late nineteenth and early twentieth centuries by the Pan-Asiatic nationalist societies which had created contacts with some of the spokesmen of emerging nationalism in India, Burma, the East Indies and the Philippines, apart from China. In the 1930s, belief in identification of interests between Japan and the peoples of the colonial empires was trumpeted in official propaganda and was a fundamental constituent of the new order and the Greater East Asia Co-Prosperity Sphere.

The message spread by Japanese propaganda as their forces advanced and took over in the vacuum left by the abrupt collapse of western colonial authority was that Japan would free peoples suffering from exploitation and degradation inflicted upon them by their late colonial masters. Japan wished to help peoples in adjusting to freedom; Japanese troops would remain in the conquered territories until the western powers had been completely defeated. What would happen thereafter was unclear; little thought had been given to the practical problems of ruling the areas taken over.[14] The ultimate purpose of the Co-Prosperity Sphere and the nature of the Japanese relationship with the peoples of South-East Asia was obscure. The emphasis in propaganda was placed on the need for genuine partnership. Appreciable differences in attitude and behaviour between different Japanese officials occurred in the conquered lands, because official policy as laid down in Tokyo was strong on cloudy rhetoric and weak in precise direction. The importance of consolidating and later bolstering Japan's war effort inevitably took precedence; the ideal of common brotherhood with the newly liberated peoples of South-East Asia was stressed. It was difficult to reconcile the two in the midst of the war when Japan was bound to be preoccupied with the military campaigns. However, many Japanese army officers had no intention of even making the attempt. The average Japanese army officer had received a narrow, somewhat brutal education and thought only of giving orders to inferiors; swift punishment would follow failure to comply. Some army and navy officers did reveal sympathy and understanding for the peoples among whom they found themselves; they were a minority, however. The response of political leaders in South-East Asia towards the Japanese varied: some were extremely enthusiastic and naive, others more watchful and critical. The masses themselves were in general resigned or apathetic.

In Burma the conquerors were warmly welcomed by the most prominent of Burmese political figures, Dr Ba Maw.[15] Ba Maw had risen fast in Burmese politics in the 1930s and had held the office of prime minister from 1937 to 1939. He was intensely ambitious, capable but vain; he was bitterly hostile to British colonial rule and objected to Burma's involvement in the European war in September 1939,[16] having conducted a campaign against British policy, asserting the primacy of Burmese interests; not surprisingly he had been arrested in consequence. The prime minister in 1940–41 was U Saw, who had trimmed his sails to co-operate with the British authorities. He visited London in November 1941; he was subsequently discovered to be in contact with enemy agents and was interned in Uganda for the duration of the war. In 1940 the Japanese had recruited the 'thirty comrades' including the future leaders, Aung San and Ne Win; the comrades were young, intensely nationalistic Burmese, filled with determination to shake off British dominance and with admiration for Japan's achievements in recent years. They had been trained on the island of Hainan with the aim of equipping them for leading positions in a Japanese-run Burma.[17] The Japanese army wished to control Burma as effectively as possible after the defeat of the British and to permit the minimum of freedom to the Burmese leaders with whom they co-operated.

The British military position in Burma disintegrated rapidly in February–March 1942. The governor, Sir Reginald Dorman-Smith, and his officials retreated to Simla to form the Burmese administration-in-exile. Dorman-Smith had taken over as governor in 1941: he had been a minister in Chamberlain's government and had revealed no outstanding gifts in that role. He believed firmly in pursuing the policy of securing full self-government in Burma once the Japanese were expelled; he revealed courage in standing up to Churchill on this question in the debates on the future of Burma that took place in the middle and latter stages of the war.[18]

In the immediate aftermath of the collapse of British rule in Burma chaos existed in much of the country. Old scores were settled and the

Burmese officials supporting the Japanese proved unable to contain the situation. The Japanese generals in Burma realised that they needed the services of an outstanding political figure and decided to install Ba Maw, who had escaped from imprisonment soon after the outbreak of war in the Far East. He accepted office under the Japanese in August 1942 and indulged in lavish praise of the Japanese and of the benefits that Japanese rule would bring to the inhabitants of Burma and of other parts of South-East Asia. Yet Ba Maw's attitude towards the Japanese was ambivalent: while he admired the remarkable achievements of Japan's modernisation and expansion, yet he was very conscious of the brutality and repression that represented the reality of Japanese rule as opposed to the ideal. Ba Maw found some Japanese to be amiable and anxious to remove causes of friction; others were obstructive and almost openly contemptuous of the Burmese.[19] Some Japanese were even involved in a plot to assassinate him on one occasion.[20] Ba Maw attributed Japanese recalcitrance to the ignorance and callousness not infrequently displayed by Japanese officers and to a failure to ensure that the guidelines on policy, decreed by General Tojo Hideki in Tokyo, were sincerely implemented. In 1943 the Japanese government decided that it was time to foster more enthusiasm for the war in Burma and to give some credibility to the Japanese claim to be liberators. The independence of Burma was proclaimed with effect from 1 August 1943; Ba Maw became the head of state but real power remained in the hands of the Japanese military. Ba Maw firmly believed that he was following the best course from the viewpoint of the peoples of Burma; he could hope to defend the inhabitants from the worst excesses of the military and take Burma closer to true independence, and he remained loyal to the Japanese to the end. The economy of Burma was devastated as a result of the fighting and exploitation by the Japanese. In the closing stages of the war, in 1944–45, bitter fighting occurred as the Japanese were gradually pushed back. Within the Burmese army discontent developed and General Aung San opened discreet contacts with the British in the autumn of 1944. In April 1945 Aung San led the army and the recently formed Anti-Fascist Peoples Freedom League (AFPFL) over to the British side and in so doing strengthened his claims for leadership of the new Burma after the war.[21]

In Malaya reactions were complicated by the racial divisions between Malays, Chinese and Indians. Malay nationalism was slowly developing before 1941 but was certainly far behind the Burmese position. In general the Malays were astonished by the speed of the British collapse and regarded the Japanese with indifference. Some Malay intellectuals were captivated by Japanese propaganda and became enthusiastic advocates of the Japanese cause. Others were covertly hostile to the Japanese. From the Japanese viewpoint it was obviously desirable to favour the Malays and the Indians. As regards the Malays it was hoped to stimulate Malay nationalism in the former Netherlands East Indies and Malaya; for this reason Sumatra was joined for administrative purposes to Singapore from 1942 to 1944. The Japanese enjoyed some success in this policy, although less than they had hoped, but were more successful in influencing the Indians; Indian officers from the British Indian army captured in the Malayan campaign were persuaded to change sides and to urge Indians to unite against the British. They met with considerable support. The Chinese community in Malaya could not be seduced; the ·Chinese, whether they supported the Kuomintang or the communists, were appalled at Japan's treatment of China since 1937 and supported the British in the defence of Malaya. The Japanese wreaked their revenge after the fall of Singapore when numerous atrocities were committed against the Chinese populace. The Chinese became active in the resistance movement in Malaya and the roots of the enduring activities of communist guerrillas in the period of the emergency date from this time.[22] Malaya was regarded by the Japanese as being in a similar position to the East Indies: both areas were of crucial significance to Japan because of the valuable raw materials procurable there, notably rubber and tin in Malaya and oil, bauxite and rubber in the East Indies. In the eyes of the Japanese, Malaya and the East Indies were less advanced politically and, in the case of the East Indies, too important strategically to be permitted the limited measure of autonomy accorded to Burma and the Philippines. While the British position in Malaya was undoubtedly seriously weakened as a result of Japanese rule and an impetus was given to the growth of Malay nationalism, there was much less opposition to Britain than there was in Burma. At the same time, Malay nationalism was about to flourish to an extent that most British officials would have deemed unlikely in 1941.

The overall effect of the Japanese occupation of South-East Asia was to discredit the former colonial powers decisively and to speed up the process of change. It was Japan's deliberate aim to undermine western rule utterly. The revenge of the present for the contemptuous western treatment of colonial peoples was visited in the cruel treatment of western prisoners of war and the savage punishments often inflicted on them. This is not to say that the most responsible Japanese leaders in Tokyo were aware of the full extent of the sadism often shown by officers and guards (the latter were sometimes Koreans) in prison camps. Discipline had deteriorated in the Japanese army for at least a decade before the start of the Pacific war and the behaviour revealed during the war was a lamentable decline from the chivalric heroism witnessed in the Russo-Japanese war of 1904–05. However, Japan's aim was to ensure that even if the unthinkable happened and Japan lost the war, then the white powers would not be able to put the clock back to the conditions obtaining in 1941. In this respect, Japan was wholly successful in all the areas she occupied. The importance of the war in the Far East in transforming the situation in the contiguous colonial empires can scarcely be exaggerated. The consequences came fully to be appreciated after 1945.

In the military campaigns against Japan, Britain was primarily concerned with plans to carry through an offensive aimed at defeating the Japanese in Burma and at driving towards Singapore. Churchill was anxious to erase the sad memories left by the rout in Malaya and Burma,

while at the same time his deep concern with the wars nearer London in-
hibited the efforts he put into contemplating the Far East. The formulation
of strategy was rendered more complex by the interrelationship between
Britain, India, the United States, and China. Britain considered Burma to
be undoubtedly a sphere in which British decision-making should be
paramount, just as the United States occupied the main role in the Pacific.
The political situation in India was tense and difficult with Gandhi and
Nehru clamouring for a British decision to grant India independence with
the launching of the 'Quit India' campaign in the summer of 1942. The
leading figures in Congress were on the whole suspicious of Japanese
attitudes and displayed a more critical attitude towards Japan than their
equivalents in the colonial territories of South-East Asia. Nehru, for
example, was shocked by Japanese behaviour in China and was a trenchant opponent of European fascism.[23] The threat posed by the Japanese
military successes early in 1942 led Churchill to dispatch Sir Stafford
Cripps, the lord privy seal and a prominent left-winger expelled from the
Labour party in 1939, to see if he could secure a compromise whereby
the Indian leaders would fully support the war effort.[24] Cripps held lengthy
discussions with Indian representatives but his mission foundered on
the obduracy of the viceroy, Lord Linlithgow, who disapproved of further
concessions and was confident that Britain could control the situation in
India. Events proved Linlithgow right in the sense that the 'Quit India'
campaign was a fiasco and there was no serious internal threat to British
authority in India during the war. However, in the context of developments in the Indian sub-continent over the following five years, the failure to reach an understanding in 1942 was extremely regrettable. In January 1942 Chiang Kai-shek visited India with his wife in a bid to engender
enthusiasm for the struggle against Japan. Chiang was openly critical of
British rule and of the British failure to act in a more conciliatory manner
towards Congress, and antagonised the viceroy with certain of his
remarks. Chiang communicated his views to the Americans and
Roosevelt conveyed his concern. Churchill resented American pressure
and regarded Chiang with scorn.

   Chiang Kai-shek had been recognised as the supreme commander of
the China theatre by Roosevelt and Churchill in January 1942. Roosevelt
thought well of Chiang at this time and anticipated that, with American
encouragement, China could make a vigorous contribution to the defeat
of Japan. Britain and the United States diverged in their attitude to
China.[25] Churchill could not consider China as remotely equal to Britain
and the United States and regarded the American championing of China
as rather ludicrous. The Foreign Office was less influenced by the Victorian prejudices of the prime minister and was more disturbed by the
accumulating evidence of incompetence, corruption and lethargy emanating from Chungking: it was depressingly evident that China was unlikely
to play a prominent part in defeating Japan despite Chiang Kai-shek's
promises of all he could achieve if only given more aid. Roosevelt, on
the other hand, professed deep faith in China and what could be accom-

plished if China was treated with respect and encouragement. Roosevelt had a better understanding than Churchill of the trend in world affairs and that China would become more important in the future than she had been in the past. He was wrong to elevate Chiang Kai-shek, however. The Chinese communists at Yenan, in the process of being reorganised under Mao Tse-tung's leadership on new, efficient, and dynamic lines, offered the best guide to the future.[26] Few in London or Washington grasped the importance of the communists; they were viewed frequently as mere agrarian reformers. Chiang Kai-shek expected to be properly consulted on allied strategy in the Far East; his chief American adviser, General Joseph Stilwell, was an able if eccentric soldier of Anglophobe inclinations. It did not take Stilwell long to discover that the 'Peanut', as he referred to Chiang, had a limited interest in assisting the defeat of Japan and was more concerned with building up his reserves for an eventual confrontation with the Chinese communists. Chiang was remote, rigid in his opinions, and petulant, but from the allied viewpoint he had a definite nuisance value when it came to raising complaints with Roosevelt and Churchill.[27]

In April 1942 Churchill ordered the chiefs of staff 'to frame plans for a counter-offensive on the Eastern Front in the summer or autumn'.[28] General Wavell, now commander-in-chief, India, gave instructions to his staff to start preparing a campaign in Burma. The campaign would obviously be extremely demanding: it would entail crossing mountainous country noted for malaria and the monsoon connoted torrential rain from May to October. The forces at Wavell's disposal were inadequate and there was little prospect of them being increased in the near future. Defence planners believed that sea operations would be vital in the Burma campaign: to facilitate such operations, it would be imperative to gain control of the Bay of Bengal.[29] Churchill did not comprehend all these difficulties involved in a campaign and tended to issue sweeping instructions which were not capable of swift fulfilment. Wavell tried patiently to explain the problems and the importance of meticulous planning but neither Churchill nor Stilwell sympathised. Stilwell was immersed in matters on the Chinese side and considered a joint Anglo–Chinese offensive in Burma the only way of galvanizing China into action through re-opening the Burma road. Stilwell was always critical of the British for allegedly putting insufficient effort into the war in Burma, and indeed in the whole theatre of war against Japan, and was not reticent in expressing his views in private or in public. Wavell convinced Churchill at last that more time was required to complete planning. Churchill indicated, in one of his famous minutes, the character of Operation *Anakim*:

. . . In principle the Operation should comprise three parts. First, the engagement of the enemy front in Assam through our increasing pressure and also, if possible, by guerrilla diversions in the Chin Hills. Secondly, the seizure of Akyab at a moment convenient to the growth of our air power in the Bay of Bengal and the rest of the plan. Thirdly, the attack upon Rangoon and Moulmein with the ultimate object of an advance towards Bangkok by an overseas expedition from India.[30]

Developments in other theatres, particularly in Russia and North Africa, made it necessary to postpone *Anakim* to 1943; this was clear by the end of July 1942. Unrest in India also contributed to the postponement.

Consultations between Britain and the United States over strategy in their respective spheres of the Pacific war were unsatisfactory in the first year of the conflict. This was fundamentally the product of adjustment to the conditions in waging world war as allies: it was accentuated by difficulties in securing harmonious relations between different services in one nation, apart from the problems of achieving a cohesive policy between nations.[31] Gradually improvements in co-ordination were obtained with Field Marshal Sir John Dill smoothing over troubled waters in discussions with the American chief of staff, General George Marshall, in Washington. Wavell and Stilwell began to talk to each other more meaningfully but Stilwell continued to feel that the British lacked a sense of urgency and wanted the United States to win the war for them; there was only one British general for whom Stilwell had respect and this was Slim. Chiang Kai-shek demanded, as prior conditions for Chinese participation in a Burmese campaign, a British attack on Rangoon and sufficient naval forces to secure control of the China and Java seas, apart from the Bay of Bengal. Wavell made it clear to Stilwell that it would not be feasible to provide forces on this level[32] and concluded that American and Chinese co-operation in the campaign to recapture Burma would be essential.[33] Chiang Kai-shek caused difficulty, since he was not satisfied with the efforts Britain was making and was not willing to allow Chinese troops to come under British command. Further substantial delays were made necessary by problems of gathering personnel and resources to implement the combined land and sea operations. The combined staff planners in Washington investigated the position and concluded, in October 1942, 'that it is not possible to collect the necessary forces, especially landing-craft and troops trained in amphibious operations, in time for the operation to be mounted prior to the next monsoon season. This means that the execution of the operation is impractical before the fall of 1943.'[34]

In January 1943 Roosevelt and Churchill met at the Casablanca conference to review strategy. The United States defence chiefs were under the impression that the British chiefs of staff did not attach sufficient importance to the war in the Pacific. The Americans were committed to Europe being first in the scale of priorities but the struggle in the Pacific was proving tough and savage and there was no sign of Japan being defeated for a long time to come.[35] Indeed Japan reached the furthest extent of her advances in New Guinea in January 1943. Churchill and his advisers had to reassure the Americans that Britain was fully committed to the war against Japan and that, as soon as Germany had been defeated, Britain would bring all the resources she could muster to bear in securing the attainment of this objective. Churchill confirmed this emphatically, even suggesting that a formal treaty to this effect be concluded to allay American fears.[36] The British agreed that the United States should begin offensives in the Solomon islands and in New Guinea while Britain should undertake operations in Burma to recapture Akyab, to establish bridgeheads in the Chindwin valley, and to build a road from Ledo via Myitkyina to Lungling.[37] The combined chiefs of staff agreed that preparations for Operation *Anakim* should go ahead and that a definite decision on the timing of the operation would be taken by the combined staffs in the summer of 1943. The British and American defence chiefs agreed on their aims of threatening enemy communications with the East Indies, the Philippines and the South China Sea; opening communication with China via Burma; arrangements to assist the Soviet Union should Japan attack her; and action by land, sea and air to 'continue and intensify attrition of enemy strength'.[38] Britain envisaged beginning *Anakim* on 15 November 1943 but a final decision would be deferred until July 1943. Criticisms were expressed by Roosevelt, who felt that not enough was being done directly to help China. He leaned towards starting a major offensive against Japan from China, which he thought preferable to a Burma campaign or a campaign of jumping over Pacific islands. In deference to the president it was decided to give more emphasis to China, but the priorities remained in the Pacific and Burma.[39]

At the close of the Casablanca conference Roosevelt and Churchill announced that the allies intended to secure the unconditional surrender of Germany, Italy and Japan. The statement had not been given any appreciable consideration beforehand but Churchill had given it some prior thought, contrary to his later recollections.[40] The decision was an illustration of the intense sense of commitment in both Britain and the United States to complete victory, for the war was regarded as being of an unprecedently barbarous nature. While undestandable enough, the pledge to unconditional surrender was a mistake and was, in particular, to handicap the eventual task of making peace with Japan.

Debate continued on the chances of embarking upon *Anakim*. Wavell was extremely pessimistic as to the likelihood of being able to undertake it; he was receiving wholly inadequate supplies and could not see how an ambitious offensive could be pursued.[41] He wrote to his planning staff:

It is obvious that the natural difficulties are such that, even if the Japanese forces in Burma are not increased, we may have to look elsewhere for a speedy and effective blow against the Japanese lines . . . the objective I have in mind for such a blow is the control of the Sunda Straits between Sumatra and Java. This would threaten Singapore and the whole Japanese position in the Netherlands East Indies. If we could at the same time seize a base in Northern Sumatra from which to control the Malacca Straits we should have gone far towards the defeat of Japan.[42]

This scheme was subsequently to appeal to Churchill. It demonstrates the divergence in thinking between Wavell and his American and Chinese partners. American policy was vacillating, too, as a result of Roosevelt's reservations about Stilwell.[43] The defence planners in London examined *Anakim* and, reaching the conclusion that it presented too many difficulties to succeed, they considered an operation in north Sumatra to be preferable. The current military action in Burma failed. The Arakan operation, which had begun in September 1942 and lasted until February 1943, had failed to achieve its objective; by May 1943 the British had been compelled to retreat.[44]

Roosevelt was becoming alarmed at the deteriorating political and economic situation in China and was receptive to the vociferous pleas of General Claire L. Chennault for a large increase in air resources in China and to put more emphasis on this as opposed to a military campaign in Burma; Chennault was vehemently opposed to Stilwell and claimed that the Japanese could be defeated from air bases in China, provided sufficient resources were put into this theatre.[45] It was felt in London that an operation aimed at north Sumatra, to be followed by a landing in Malaya, was desirable but impracticable. Instead attention was focused on the possibility of cutting Japan's maritime communications and depriving her of oil, which could perhaps be accomplished by building up naval strength in the Pacific and the American air forces in China.[46] Activities in Burma would be restricted to those needed to protect air communications and to hold down the Japanese. Churchill inclined towards a campaign in Sumatra; Wavell was sympathetic but the chiefs of staff were not. General Brooke maintained firmly that while Britain was so heavily committed against Germany it was impossible to commence a major offensive in the Far East.[47] At the second Washington conference, in May 1943, Roosevelt amended his views on the paramountcy of air power in China and supported a proposal by Stilwell for limited operations north of Lashio to open a road from Ledo to Yunnan.[48] The joint planners then urged that land operations should be started comprising an Anglo–Chinese offensive in November–December 1943 to open the Burma road which would include initiatives by the long range penetration groups; operations to obtain air bases on the Arakan coast; and a bid to capture Rangoon.[49] The British chiefs of staff regarded the proposals critically, doubting if they were capable of fulfilment. After quite lengthy discussions, it was decided that the capacity of the air route to China must be improved; that vigorous operations should be launched from Assam into Burma via Ledo and Imphal, so as to hold down Japanese forces and to aim at reopening the Burma road; to capture Akyab and Ramree island; and to interrupt Japanese sea communications to Burma. Churchill and Roosevelt accepted the proposals, if with some reservations.

Looking ahead after the second Washington conference, British and American planners believed that Japan would follow a defensive strategy directed at maintaining and consolidating control of the areas occupied. The defeat of Japan could entail invasion and physical conquering of the country. Japan must be worn down as far as possible by bombing raids; bases necessary for an invasion would have to be secured. Bases could most satisfactorily be found in the Shanghai region, although there were alternatives. It would be imperative to take Formosa, Luzon, or Hainan as a preliminary to later operations. The defeat of Japan could not be achieved speedily; enemy forces would probably not surrender until 1948.[50] This pessimistic forecast was hardly acceptable but it was not clear what could be attained more quickly. With growing attention being concentrated on strategy for South-East Asia, a new command structure was required for the area. The existing position of the British commander-in-chief, India, handling strategy for South-East Asia was unsatisfactory and Churchill believed that Wavell was too tired for the post of commanding the Indian army. A new command for South-East Asia would be established but concrete decisions were postponed until the next Anglo–American conference at Quebec three months later.

The Quebec conference met in August 1943. One of the most important decisions for the Pacific theatre was the creation of a new Central Pacific Force, commanded by Admiral Chester W. Nimitz; this would aim to advance through the Gilbert, Marshall, and Caroline islands. General Douglas MacArthur would continue to command the other advance through the Bismarck archipelago and along the northern coast of New Guinea.[51] On Burma, the joint chiefs of staff stated that a land route to China through northern Burma should be opened and air support should be extended to China in order to obtain bases suitable for the ultimate stages of the campaign directed at Japan.[52] This meant in general terms that operations should be implemented for the capture of Upper Burma, commencing in February 1944; preparations would be continued for an amphibious campaign to capture Akyab and Ramree. The new South-East Asia Command (SEAC) was established formally to embrace South-East Asia, including Sumatra and the eastern Indian Ocean. There was considerable argument over the powers to be exercised by the SEAC commander and, in particular, whether the commander should function on the model of General MacArthur or on the North African model. The British preferred the former and the Americans the latter. The final decision was closer to the American position than the British. The combined chiefs of staff would apply 'general jurisdiction over strategy' and would determine resources to be applied to the South-East Asia theatre and to the Chinese theatre. The British chiefs of staff would supervise 'all matters pertaining to operations'.[53] Vice-Admiral Lord Louis Mountbatten, the young and dynamic naval officer who had headed combined operations, was appointed as supreme commander with General Stilwell as his deputy; Stilwell could continue with his existing responsibilities in China. Mountbatten proved a vigorous, able commander with a shrewd grasp of political dimensions; Stilwell initially liked him but then reversed his opinion, terming him 'The Glamour Boy'. Admiral Somerville thought Mountbatten was too interested in self-projection – 'He is out MacArthuring MacArthur.'[54] The experienced General Pownall was appointed as Mountbatten's chief of staff to keep him 'on the rails', since Mountbatten was thought to require someone to discourage him from excesses. The

SEAC command faced grave problems and took some time to establish itself; eventually it made a significant contribution to the defeat of Japan. Mountbatten was also later faced with the formidable problems of supervising the transition from war to peace in much of South-East Asia.

The Cairo conference opened on 26 November 1943, preceding the conference with Stalin in Teheran. Chiang Kai-shek joined Churchill and Roosevelt at Cairo for his sole appearance at a summit meeting with American and British leaders. Churchill and Roosevelt met Chiang again after their meeting with Stalin. Chiang was accompanied by Madame Chiang, who sought to complement her husband's efforts to advance China's cause. Stilwell was also present. Chiang urged that the airlift over the 'Hump' should be continued at the level of 10,000 tons a month regardless of developments in Burma; that the contemplated advance across the Chindwin should be directed at Mandalay; and that a naval operation should be launched to accompany the land offensive, as Churchill had unwisely promised him in a telegram sent in October 1943.[55] The British and American chiefs of staff emphasised to Chiang that it was unrealistic for the airlift to function at the level proposed. Mountbatten told Chiang that an advance on Mandalay could not be accomplished owing to lack of aircraft.[56] Britain did not want to promise China more than it was felt Chiang had a right to expect. However, Roosevelt gave the generalissimo an undertaking, in private conversation, that an amphibious operation would be launched across the Bay of Bengal within a few months. At Teheran Stalin promised that Russia would enter into the war against Japan when Germany had been defeated: '. . . The Soviet Forces in the Far East were more or less sufficient for defence, but they would have to be at least trebled in order to assume the offensive. The moment for their joining their friends in this theatre, would be the moment of Germany's collapse; then they would march together.'[57]

The Cairo meeting resumed afterwards; changes were made, in the light of decisions taken on European strategy at Teheran, in the provisional plans for the Far East. Stalin had been assured that a second front would be started through British and American landings in France in May 1944. This had to be the main priority and resources could not easily be spared for operations in the Far East. The combined staff planners produced a report on strategy against Japan which envisaged an advance along the New Guinea-East Indies-Philippines axis concurrently with operations aimed at capturing the mandated islands. Operations in the Central Pacific seemed likely to be most successful; it was hoped to begin a major attack in the Formosa-Luzon-China area in the spring of 1945.[58] In South-East Asia the aim should be to capture Upper Burma in the spring of 1944; to improve air and land communications with China; and to begin an amphibious operation at about the same time. The combined chiefs of staff concluded that it was simply not feasible to undertake operations in Burma on the scale envisaged at the start of the Cairo conference. Roosevelt was deeply unhappy, for it meant retreating from the promise he had given Chiang. He informed the generalissimo and requested him to proceed with an operation in northern Burma, as planned, including the commitment to keep naval control of the Bay of Bengal.[59] The British chiefs of staff had made clear their dissatisfaction with the land and amphibious aspects of plans.[60]

Meanwhile the Japanese army was reconsidering its strategy for Burma and decided to attempt a breakthrough into Assam. Japan's partnership with the Indian National Army had been cemented since the arrival by submarine from Germany of Subhas Chandra Bose. Bose was a prominent leader of the Indian independence movement but had experienced considerable differences of opinion with Gandhi and Nehru; he had become a fervent advocate of supporting the axis powers as a means of securing freedom for India.[61] The exploits of Orde Wingate's long-range penetration groups led the Japanese to realise that it was not as difficult as they had believed to launch operations over the Indian border. It would be to Japan's advantage to reach Indian soil: the advance would have salutary effects upon Japanese morale and might encourage a rising in India. Thus the campaign which was to lead to bitter fighting at Imphal and Kohima was in formation. Japanese military strength was built up to almost 200,000 and on 4 February 1944 the offensive in Arakan began. At first the Japanese were successful and threatened a breakthrough. Gradually fortunes changed and the balance swung in favour of the British. By early March Britain was gaining the upper hand and the Japanese had been defeated in several battles. By June the Japanese offensive had been defeated in one of the most important land victories of the war against Japan. The consequences in terms of morale and prestige were profound for both sides: the British had discovered that the Japanese could be routed; the Japanese correspondingly lost confidence and recriminations were bitter among the Japanese commanders. The offensive intended to restore Japanese vigour and confidence ended by having the opposite result.[62]

The war cabinet and the chiefs of staff considered the future evolution of British strategy in the Far East and Pacific in February–March 1944. A definite division of opinion existed between the chiefs of staff, who favoured a policy of concentrating largely on the Pacific and of assisting the United States in this theatre rather than beginning a major offensive in Burma, and Churchill, who advocated conducting amphibious operations against the Andaman and Nicobar islands and Sumatra.[63] The position was investigated more thoroughly by the joint planners, who produced a paper on 12 April 1944, based on the amended views of the chiefs of staff that 'the main British effort against Japan should take the form of an advance on the general axis Timor-Celebes-Borneo-Saigon'.[64] The level of opposition from Japanese forces was not expected to be large. The attack would be launched from north-west Australia avoiding Timor, where the enemy strength was uncertain, and proceed to Amboina. The advantages of this plan would be that Britain would be pursuing an active policy in the Pacific; that Borneo could be reached more swiftly; and that it would permit an attack on Malaya from east as well as west.[65] Detailed considerations extended over the summer of 1944 as to which of the various modifications to the 'middle strategy' should be implemented with Amboina as the target: dominion forces would participate with a small British fleet functioning from northern Australia and the main fleet based in the east. The operation should begin in October 1944. The chiefs of staff alluded to the politically sensitive issue of the South-West Pacific area, commanded by General MacArthur; they believed that this area should become one of joint responsibility with a separate command structure under the overall command of MacArthur.[66] It was anticipated, as Churchill observed, that MacArthur would object to a system that would reduce or hamper his authority.

Churchill, Attlee, and other members of the government believed that it was imperative for political reasons that Britain should liberate her subjugated possessions in the Far East. This was essential to restore self-confidence and to counteract the American dislike of western colonialism.[67] Decisions on the new strategy were left for final decision at the second Quebec conference in September 1944. The British and American defence chiefs agreed rapidly on instructions to Mountbatten; the aim was to recapture the whole of Burma as soon as possible. Churchill emphasised Britain's determination to secure the defeat of Japan and her willingness to devote resources to attaining this objective: 'We had every reason for doing so. Japan was as much the bitter enemy of the British Empire as of the United States. British territory had been captured in battle and grievous losses had been suffered. The offer he, the Prime Minister, now wished to make, was for the British Main Fleet to take part in the major operations against Japan under United States supreme command.'[68] Churchill stated that there was no intention of interfering with MacArthur's command. The combined chiefs of staff discussed the details and agreed that the British fleet should take part in the main operation against Japan in the Pacific and that it would be self-supporting; an indication of the extent of help Britain could give in the air would be forthcoming subsequently.[69] It was envisaged that the defeat of Japan would not be accomplished until approximately eighteen months after the end of the European war.

In the autumn of 1944 the campaign in Burma was slowly pushing the Japanese back following the failure of the Japanese attempt to invade India. The British fourteenth army in Burma was commanded by General Sir William Slim, who proved outstandingly successful in leading his troops. Slim was a highly intelligent, capable commander with a bluff manner, who had risen to prominence at a late stage in his career.[70] He had taken part in the dismal retreat in Burma in 1942 and was imbued with a detestation of the Japanese; he was determined to reverse the outcome of 1942, given the opportunity. Slim communicated his genuine interest in the troops, who gave him deep loyalty in return; he was affectionately known as 'Uncle Bill'.[71] The fourteenth army pursued a successful campaign and began, in late 1944, inexorably to drive back the Japanese. By late January 1945 the land route to China was open again and Chinese forces were co-operating with the British and Americans in the advance into Burma. The fighting was intensive but the allies now enjoyed superior morale and resolution. Imphal-Kohima had robbed the Japanese of their former resilience. Rangoon was captured at the beginning of May 1945; substantial Japanese forces remained in north and north-west Burma to be mopped up. SEAC prepared for further operations to capture Singapore and to begin the effective re-establishment of British authority in South-East Asia.[72] Arrangements had to be made for the governing of liberated areas and for the British role in assisting the Dutch and the French to establish themselves in their former colonial territories in the East Indies and Indo-China, since Churchill believed in the restoration of colonial empires and was committed to assisting the Dutch and the French. Roosevelt had always been critical of European colonialism, especially of the French: he believed they had achieved nothing during their occupation of Indo-China.[73] He was less critical of the Dutch, perhaps because of his own Dutch origins. From the British viewpoint the campaign in Burma had been protracted and for much of the time unrewarding. However, while it was less important than the fighting in the Pacific in achieving the defeat of Japan, it was nevertheless highly significant: the Burma campaign resulted in the deaths of approximately 128,000 Japanese, just over ten per cent of the estimated numbers of Japanese killed in the fighting in the Far East and the Pacific.[74] The greatest single defeat of the Japanese army was achieved in Burma.[75]

When the last of the conferences attended by the original allied leaders met at Yalta in February 1945 the end of the war in Europe was in sight. How long it would take to secure Japanese surrender was a matter for speculation. The United States and Britain would require the assistance of Russia in accordance with the pledge given by Stalin in 1943.[76] Large-scale concessions were made to the Soviet Union at Yalta, including the promise that Manchuria could be transformed into an effective Russian sphere of interest with possession of the old Russian naval base of Port Arthur, lost to Japan in the war of 1904–05. Stalin promised that Russia would fight Japan within three months of the end of the European War. Russia would receive from Japan the Kurile islands, south Sakhalin and nearby islands, and the lease of Port Arthur. The railways in Manchuria were to be jointly operated by the Soviet Union and China.[77] Between the end of 1944 and the summer of 1945 the United States devoted a great deal of attention to plans for the ultimate defeat of Japan, including the invasion of the home islands of Japan. With the allied victories recorded in impressive number throughout the Pacific and South-East Asia by June 1945, an invasion of Japan necessitated careful planning. There was a clear American wish to dominate the operation. Most of the forces to be employed would be American and a positive British role was not contemplated; it was felt that the British could contribute elsewhere. By the time the Potsdam conference met in July 1945, the Americans did not desire Russian entry into the far eastern war; President Truman was experiencing more arguments with the Russians as it was over the fate of Poland.

The heavy casualties anticipated in the event of landings on the Japanese home islands caused deep concern until allied leaders received news of the successful testing of the atomic bomb. The scientists had worked ceaselessly to perfect the new weapon. A potent stimulus originally was the fear that Germany might be ahead of the allies and might use the weapon first. The intensive work certainly pointed to the likelihood that the bomb would be used by the allies. It was uncertain, in the summer of 1945, whether Japan could be persuaded to surrender without recourse to the bomb. Japan had clearly lost the war and had been exposed to the concentrated conventional bombing of Tokyo with devastating results.[78] In fact, the peace party in Japan was gaining ground; it was appreciated that Japanese resistance could not be prolonged but there was much apprehension over the probable terms of surrender and particularly over the issue of the future of the monarchy.[79]

Controversy has surrounded the use of the atomic bomb in the context of the origins of the Cold War, where it has been argued that the American decision to drop the bombs on Hiroshima and Nagasaki was not motivated primarily by the wish to terminate the Pacific war but rather as a warning to the Soviet Union to adopt more amenable policies in Europe.[80] Under the Quebec agreement of 1943, a decision to use the atomic bomb required prior consultation with Britain and joint assent. General Marshall informed Field Marshal Wilson in April 1945 that use of the bomb was under discussion. Winston Churchill indicated that satisfactory machinery for Anglo–American consultation must be set up.[81] Churchill was in agreement with the decision to use the bomb if necessary and wished to discuss the subject further with President Truman; British approval was given in mid-June 1945 without hearing a full statement of the case for dropping the bomb.[82]

The test bomb was successfully exploded in New Mexico on 16 July 1945. Truman was then engaged in the Potsdam conference. It was obvious from Truman's discussions with Churchill that the American president had scant sympathy for Japan and was fully conscious of the burden he bore in minimising American casualties in the continuation of the war.[83] Japanese leaders were most concerned over the doctrine of unconditional surrender and its consequences for them. The allied leaders at Potsdam issued a declaration on 26 July 1945 emphasising that there was no intention of enslaving the Japanese nation; fundamental changes in Japanese government and society would occur, however, and 'stern justice' would be enforced against those responsible for committing atrocities. The unconditional surrender of Japanese armed forces was called for.[84] Japan was desperately trying to secure peace terms through approaches to the Soviet Union, of which Stalin informed Truman and Churchill. The attitude of the Japanese military was divided and there were fierce opponents of making peace, especially on terms of unconditional surrender. The government in Tokyo was moving towards surrender under its elderly prime minister, Admiral Suzuki Kantaro, but the cabinet believed that it could not accept the Potsdam declaration, pending further clarification. The failure of the Japanese to respond immediately and positively sealed their fate. It was decided to drop an atomic bomb on a Japanese city without warning. It was believed that the bomb had to be dropped on a densely populated area in order to drive home unmistakably to Japan, and particularly to the Japanese army, the dire consequences of continued resistance. Hiroshima was chosen as the site, Kyoto having been ruled out by the American secretary of war, Henry L. Stimson, on account of its ancient cultural history. The bomb was dropped on 6 August, to be followed three days later by the dropping of the second bomb on Nagasaki. On 8 August the Soviet Union notified Japan of her intention to commence war. On 14 August 1945 Japan surrendered; a section of the Imperial Guard revolted upon hearing the news. The war against Japan was at an end.

For Britain the war had always been secondary to the European conflict; British public opinion did not show the interest in developments in the Far East and the Pacific displayed by American opinion. However, British leaders did not regard the war as insignificant, as some American generals and admirals maintained. The extent of British political and economic interests in the Far East, together with a desire to punish the Japanese for the nature of the defeat inflicted on Britain in 1941–42, meant that Britain was fully committed to the cause of defeating Japan. Churchill notoriously thought of the might of the British Empire, which he wished to see resurrected in the Far East. Churchill left office in July 1945, following the overwhelming victory of the Labour party in the general election. While his successor, Clement Attlee, was infinitely more progressive in his attitude to India than Churchill, he, too, believed that the British Commonwealth would endure and that there would be a dependent colonial empire for a long time to come. Britain now had to face up to the repercussions in the Far East of Japanese occupation of Britain's colonial territories.

Chapter 11

The end of the British role in the Far East

At the end of the Second World War Britain was exhausted by the immensity of the struggles from which she was emerging. Britain had declined throughout the twentieth century; for much of this period she had attempted to fulfil commitments that were excessive in terms of her resources and responsibilities in other spheres. The general election in July 1945 brought the Labour party to power with a massive majority; the principal Labour leaders, Clement Attlee, Ernest Bevin, Herbert Morrison, Hugh Dalton, and Stafford Cripps had been prominent members of Churchill's wartime coalition and believed that Britain still had a significant part to play in world affairs. The role would inevitably diminish, however, given the wide range of problems facing Britain and the greater interest in domestic reforms preoccupying the members of the government and Labour MPs. In the Far East Britain's interests after 1945 revolved around the reform of Japan; the internal convulsions in China and relations with the new communist government; and the fate of Britain's colonial territories. In general terms British power was less assertive than formerly: the United States dominated the scene, despite initial doubts in 1945 as to the strength of the American commitment to defend Anglo–American interests in the region. Relations between the United States and Britain were erratic in character. The two powers were fundamentally devoted to the same broad values and objectives but the weight of emphasis varied appreciably. The United States was imbued with a sense of might and achievement yet was unsure of the direction in which she was heading. American leaders still regarded themselves as being hostile to European colonialism and standing for an approach that was significantly different. At the same time communism appeared as a growing menace, so that despite its initial inclinations America was in time to succeed to the position of the colonial powers, most obviously in Indo-China in 1954. Britain was frequently not consulted adequately or at all on policy formulation and conflict was experienced in handling various issues. By the middle 1970s Britain's political and strategic responsibilities had effectively ended in the Far East and the United States was reassessing her task and function following the collapse of the pro-American regimes in south Vietnam, Cambodia and Laos.

The immediate challenge in the first days of peace in 1945 concerned the form of administration in Japan. Planning for the situation had been proceeding in Washington and London in the latter part of the war but the surrender of Japan came sooner than had been anticipated; this meant that Britain did not have detailed schemes available.[1] More important was the fact that there was no unanimity within or between official circles in Britain and the United States. It was usually the case that those best acquainted with Japanese society favoured a policy of caution and of incorporating assurances that the imperial institution would not be terminated. In contrast, those who were not specialists on Japan tended to believe that reforms should include the disappearance of the monarchy and the possibility of putting Emperor Hirohito on trial as a war criminal. Winston Churchill had originally opposed a trial of enemy leaders, maintaining that it was preferable simply to take the most notorious and shoot them.[2] The United States was firmly committed to the moral justification of a trial even though there was an implicit assumption that the accused would be found guilty which was somewhat difficult to reconcile with normal standards of justice. The British government agreed to support the American decision to set up the International Military Tribunal for the Far East (IMTFE), comprising eleven judges representing the United States, Britain, Australia, Canada, New Zealand, India (which became independent during the trial), France, the Netherlands, the Soviet Union, China, and the Philippines. The allied investigators sifted through the records of numerous Japanese who had participated in government or in the armed forces during the war. Eventually twenty-eight were chosen as representative figures associated with the alleged Japanese conspiracy dating from 1928 to establish Japanese hegemony in the Far East and Pacific.[3] The IMTFE was formally set up by the supreme allied commander, General Douglas MacArthur, and he heard the appeals at the close of the trial. An Australian judge, Sir William Flood Webb, was appointed as president of the court, thus symbolising the closer relationship between the United States and Australia during the Pacific war.[4] The trial was far more protracted and conducted along less satisfactory lines than the corresponding trial at Nuremberg:[5] consistent bias was shown against the accused; certain judges absented themselves for lengthy periods; there was a pervading sense that the outcome was inevitable. Wartime atrocities inflamed emotions and affected public opinion in Britain. Most political leaders in Britain supported IMTFE or kept silent on the subject. One of the few to oppose the trial openly and vehemently was the distinguished former civil servant and minister, Lord Hankey. Hankey might at first appear an unlikely critic, for he came from a service background and was a fervent advocate of the civilising mission of the British Empire. However, Hankey was possessed of a strong sense of fairness and did not consider the Tokyo trial to be compatible with recognised judicial procedures. He was propelled into action by the inclusion of Shigemitsu Mamoru among the accused. Shigemitsu had been energetic and subtle as ambassador in London from 1938 to 1941 and Hankey, in common with others, had been impressed with the ambassador's wish to improve Anglo–Japanese relations. In reality Shigemitsu was more deeply devoted to Japanese expansion than his British friends suspected. Hankey courageously castigated the principles and functioning of IMTFE but he was a lone voice and encountered much abuse.[6] The British government's attitude was that IMTFE had to proceed to its preordained conclusion as part of the cleansing process in Japan. Britain would do nothing to interfere with it. The trial began in May 1946 and was concluded only in November 1948 when MacArthur rejected the appeals against the seven death sentences approved by a small majority of the judges. The only rapid aspect of the trial was its conclusion: the condemned men, including General Tojo, were promptly hanged, dressed in American servicemen's uniforms 'devoid of insignia of any kind'.[7]

IMTFE had in essence been an American-dominated body. This was true of the allied occupation of Japan in total. The British Foreign Office was conscious in 1945 of the need to convey British interest in Japan and to prevent the occupation being completely dominated by the United States. As had been the case at least since 1939, the wider repercussions of British decisions on the American attitude to Britain in general had to be considered: the assertion of British interest could not jeopardise the basic relationship with Washington. Britain wished to secure an economic footing in Japan in the midst of reforming the Japanese economy. It was hoped that the allied occupation of Japan would be of limited duration and that a formal peace treaty with Japan could be concluded without undue delay. Sir George Sansom observed, while visiting Japan early in 1946, that there was:

no object in maintaining an enormous Army of Occupation. It is bad for the men, who have nothing to do. Personally as a taxpayer, I resent the expenditure of public funds on our contribution to a Commonwealth force. When the main lines of occupation policy are fixed there should, in my opinion, be no reason against withdrawing practically all occupation troops and controlling Japan by indirect methods.[8]

The British wish for an effective voice in the running of Japan involved some initial sympathy for the position of the Soviet Union, at any rate until the point at which the development of the Cold War assumed more importance.[9] The framework of allied consultation in Japan was provided in the Allied Council for Japan (ACJ) and in the Far Eastern Commission. MacArthur intended to have as few restrictions as possible on his power to reshape Japan as he saw fit: he regarded any criticism or remarks as undermining his work.[10] Just before the war ended in August 1945, Britain proposed the establishment of an Allied Control Council comprising the five nations involved in the occupation. It was envisaged that the Council and an Allied Advisory Committee consisting of seven countries would issue policy instructions to MacArthur. Clearly MacArthur's scope for independent action would then have been seriously restricted.[11] American reactions to the British representations were cool and unenthusiastic. The new British foreign secretary, Ernest Bevin, wrote to James F. Byrnes, the American secretary of state, on 12 September 1945 that the administration of Japan should 'give us a voice in the control commensurate with what we have suffered from Japanese treachery, with our contribution to Japan's defeat and with our responsibility towards our own peoples for preventing any renewal of Japanese aggression'.[12] The developing acrimony between Washington and Moscow compelled Britain to modify representations, for Britain could not risk alienating the United States when greater issues were at stake.

MacArthur envisaged the occupation of Japan lasting for between three and five years with a probable period of civil control after the peace treaty was signed.[13] The supreme commander took no notice of the ACJ and resented interference with his activities. He especially disliked the vociferous Australian representative, W. MacMahon Ball, whom he suspected of communist sympathies.[14] The combative Australian minister of external affairs, Herbert Evatt, declined to recall Ball and himself loudly proclaimed Australian policy. The tension in Anglo-Australian relations was again a continuation of the situation prevailing since 1941, accentuated by the presence of the more nationalistic Labour party in office in Canberra. The British Commonwealth forces stationed in Japan were situated in the southern parts of Japan. The area of command comprised Hiroshima and the adjoining prefectures; the British pressed for the area to be extended to include Kobe and Osaka. MacArthur did not wish to see the British occupy further territory and, in any event, Britain decided in October 1946 to withdraw the British troops due to shortage of manpower.[15] The Foreign Office deprecated withdrawal but the chiefs of staff maintained that there was no alternative. In the economic sphere, Britain adopted a liberal view and Bevin urged that the only restrictions should be of a strategic nature. No attempt was made to shield vulnerable British industries from Japanese competition, with the result that MPs from the affected constituencies eventually opposed the peace treaty with Japan.[16] The remaining period of the occupation down to the peace treaty signed at San Francisco in 1951 revealed the previous mixture of friction and co-operation with the United States. In Britain deep concern over future Japanese competition manifested itself in the pronouncements of commercial circles. The Manchester Chamber of Commerce was perturbed at the future threat from Japanese textiles. The message from British industry, whether expressed overtly or implicitly, was that steps should be taken to ensure that the former enemy powers should not be in a position to threaten the trade and full employment policies of allied countries.[17] The president of the Board of Trade, Sir Stafford Cripps, made it clear in October 1946 that 'at the present stage we cannot use preventions on Japan for the purpose of protecting British trade'.[18] In contrast to the vocal alarm of the men of commerce, and the animosity to Japan not infrequently displayed, political bodies did not reflect anxiety over the development of Japan. The Labour party, the Trades Union Congress, the Conservative party and the Liberal party paid no attention to Japan in their conferences and publications. Curiously, the Union of Democratic

Control published a perceptive pamphlet on Japan in 1947, analysing the dilemma of the occupation and the consequences for American policy of the civil strife in China.[19] Interest had been expressed at times by Labour spokesmen in parliament in the fostering of the trade union movement in Japan as a means of democratising society. However, the simple fact was that the British contribution to the reorganisation of Japan during the occupation was a minor one; the United States determined what happened and Britain had to accept the situation.

With the end of the allied occupation of Japan, the Japanese resumed control of their destinies. Officially Japan was forbidden to possess armed forces but in practice the United States encouraged the growth of the self-defence forces in the light of the onset of the Cold War. Japanese leaders had no inclination to pursue an active foreign policy; they were content to shelter under the American umbrella for defence purposes and wisely to concentrate upon economic recovery and economic expansion.[20] Thus Japan's quiescence in political terms plus Britain's decline as a power meant that Anglo–Japanese relations were less close and less acrimonious than they had been in the years prior to 1941: there was no imperative reason for Anglo–Japanese co-operation, as between 1902 and 1921, nor cause for mutual antipathy, as between 1937 and 1941. Difficulties were to be experienced during the 1970s as a consequence of the remarkable success of the Japanese economy dating from the later 1950s. Japanese exports formed an increasingly important aspect of trade between the two countries, the balance of which swung decisively in favour of Japan. Japanese competition was most noticeable with electrical goods, especially television and hi-fi equipment, and with motor cars. The competition was felt more keenly owing to the combination of stagnation and inflation affecting the British economy in the same decade. Protests at the supposedly unfair nature of Japanese competition were once more to be heard, as in the 1930s. Manufacturers, trade unionists and MPs demanded protectionist measures. The Japanese government showed sensitiveness in understanding the clamour and appreciated the repercussions of adopting a negative attitude. Japan voluntarily undertook to limit exports in the most contentious areas and not to press competition too far. Japanese firms revealed interest in investing in Britain, therefore reversing the old Anglo–Japanese relationship. Opportunities existed in Japan for British firms possessing the requisite commercial acumen and linguistic expertise, although foreign firms were hampered by various administrative devices deployed by Japan in an effort to prevent or delay foreign encroachment on the Japanese domestic market. It appears unlikely that the trade balance between Britain and Japan will be reversed in the foreseeable future. What is perhaps more likely is that Japan herself will be overtaken by intensified competition from South Korea, Taiwan, and other fast developing, cheap centres of production in the Third World.

With regard to China, the British Foreign Office had harboured fears during the Pacific war that Chiang Kai-shek might lead a bellicose

Kuomintang government into adventurous initiatives in South-East Asia, partly at Britain's expense.[21] There were indeed ambitious designs entertained in Chungking as to the policy China could follow after the defeat of Japan, which included exerting more influence in Indo-China and Burma. However, the developing hostility between the Kuomintang and the communists ruled out this possibility other than the part played by the Kuomintang troops in Tongking before the restoration of French authority. The British quickly restored their power in Hong Kong and removed any impression that they were willing to contemplate returning the crown colony to China, as President Roosevelt had suggested during the war.[22] The aim was to build up the commercial importance of Hong Kong and, so far as possible, to resume the prewar life and methods of operating. The same was true in Shanghai, Tientsin, and the other former treaty ports. Extraterritoriality itself had been abolished in 1943 by agreement between Roosevelt, Churchill and Chiang Kai-shek; however, foreign firms and nationals often expected to revert to their former mode of existence and Shanghai did enjoy some of its old dominance before the communist victory in the civil war. British officials had few illusions about the Kuomintang by 1945. The pervading mixture of corruption, brutality and decay was realised. At the same time there was no penetrating grasp of the communists and what they had to offer. Most British officials lacked sufficient information on the evolution of the communists in Yenan: whilst the vigour and tenacity of the communists was recognised, their fundamental dedication to radical revolution was not comprehended. The communists were too often regarded, as in the United States, as 'agrarian radicals'.[23] It was believed that when the decisive struggle occurred in China in 1945–46, the Kuomintang forces were likely to triumph because of their superior numbers. Britain was bound to play an inferior part to the United States in China by virtue of the American involvement in the China theatre since the beginning of the Pacific war. As G.F. Hudson, then employed in Whitehall, wrote in December 1943:

Apart from the advantages accruing to the USA in China from the circumstances of the war, there seem two fundamental reasons for expecting a predominance of American, as opposed to British, influence in post-war China: (1) the fact that the USA will be in a position to grant loans and credits on far more favourable terms than we can and (2) the absence of territorial or quasi-territorial issues between China and the USA in contrast to the Sino–British disputes over Hong Kong and Tibet . . . and those which are likely to arrive later over Malaya.[24]

Britain experienced profound disagreement with the Truman administration over far eastern policy with application to China and Korea, anticipating the further arguments that were to arise over Indo-China under the Eisenhower administration.[25]

In 1945 the United States hoped for the restoration of unity in China and worked to this end until 1947. Those American officials who went to Yenan or encountered communist representatives were distinctly impressed by their determination, enterprise, and resilience: it offered a stark contrast to the double-dealing and black-marketeering characteristic of Chungking.[26] The Truman administration was occupied principally with Europe between 1945 and 1949 and with the worsening of relations with the Soviet Union accompanying the appearance of the Cold War, so that Truman and his leading advisers spent inadequate time in assessing developments in the Far East. They believed that the most dangerous threat to the interests of America and the free world was located in Europe where, as Churchill said in his famous address at Fulton, Missouri, in 1946 an 'iron curtain' was descending. Truman sent General George Marshall to China on a mission of mediation which lasted from December 1945 to January 1947. The American attitude to the communists was not unfriendly and the communists responded in similar manner. Neither side in China would compromise, since each was confident of victory and wished the decisive confrontation to take place before long.[27] In 1946 full-scale civil war began and continued until the communist victory was accomplished on mainland China in 1949. There was considerable sympathy for the communists within Britain, where they were frequently regarded as sincere patriots interested in agrarian reform, perhaps occupying a position somewhat to the left of the British Labour party. Politicians in the Labour and Liberal parties expressed respect and admiration for communist achievement but no real comprehension of Mao Tse-tung's ideas and of his complete overhaul of the Communist party during the Yenan period (1935–45). Politicians in the Conservative party in Britain were less enthusiastic but the Chinese communists were nevertheless felt to be different from the Russian variety and fundamentally less dangerous.[28] During the Korean war Conservative attitudes veered sharply in the direction of believing the Chinese communists to be far more menacing. This remained true until the 1970s when Conservative politicians moved towards a more amicable view in the process of devising a counterweight to the threat posed by the Soviet Union. The British Foreign Office seems to have thought, between 1945 and 1948, that the most likely eventuality would be a communist victory in northern China with the Kuomintang retaining dominance in southern China. In a memorandum transmitted to the American State Department in January 1949 the Foreign Office recognised the ideological driving force of Mao's ideas: it was accepted that a communist victory would connote economic hardship for foreign interests and intervention in the functioning of firms, most likely leading to expropriation. However, British trade in China would continue for as long as was feasible.[29] The swift disintegration of the Kuomintang armies stimulated urgent discussion of the question of recognising the communist government. British policy was approved by the Attlee cabinet in August 1949, when it was decided that it would be futile to attempt to prevent a communist victory; that it was essential not to push the Chinese communists towards dependence on the Soviet Union; that the Chinese communists must be encouraged to appreciate the economic benefits to be gained from co-operating with the western powers; and that it was imperative to prevent communism succeeding in

South-East Asia.[30] With the proclamation of the Peoples Republic by Mao in Peking on 1 October 1949, the issue of recognition had to be resolved.

The traditional attitude to recognition in Britain was that it should be accorded when a government was demonstrably in control of a country. Recognition did not necessarily connote approval of the character of a regime; it was realistic recognition of a situation. Within Britain most leaders held the opinion that the new Chinese order should be recognised. Churchill stated in the House of Commons on 17 November 1949 that:

Recognizing a person is not necessarily an act of approval... One has to recognize lots of things and people in this world of sin and woe that one does not like. The reason for having diplomatic relations is not to confer a compliment but to secure a convenience...

Now the question has arisen also of what our attitude should be towards the Chinese Communists who have gained control over so large a part of China. Ought we to recognize them or not?...

When a large and powerful mass of people are organized together and are masters of an immense area and of great populations, it may be necessary to have relations with them. One may say that when relations are most difficult that is the time when diplomacy is most needed.[31]

The members of the Labour government and prominent figures in the Liberal party believed that recognition should be extended: it would be absurd not to do so. In addition, men like Lord Stansgate and Lord Samuel had sympathy for a movement which clearly represented the aspirations of a large number of Chinese.[32] British assets in China totalled approximately £200 m.; the China Association and British firms in general advocated recognition as the most effective method of endeavouring to defend British interests.[33] The evidence contained in public opinion polls is that a majority of the electorate was opposed to granting recognition in November 1949. This is possibly explained by the incidents earlier in 1949 involving clashes between British warships and communist forces on the Yangtze: the best known of these had involved the frigate *Amethyst*, which escaped to the sea after being detained by the communists.[34] Conservative MPs on the whole were reluctant to contemplate recognition, despite the view expressed by their leader.[35] The Attlee government exchanged views with fellow members of NATO and with the Commonwealth. In addition, a conference of experts on South-East Asia was held at Singapore. The conference recommended recognition accompanied by a more vigorous campaign against communism in South-East Asia. On 15 December the British cabinet approved recognition, which was formally announced on 6 January 1950.[36] The British approach diverged from that of the United States. America deemed recognition to denote moral approval and was disinclined to consider this move at a time when the Truman administration was striving to contain the communist menace in Europe. Truman, Acheson and their colleagues were, however, disgusted at the ineptitude and corruption of the Kuomintang and in effect washed their hands of Chiang Kai-shek. Truman was not prepared to consider recognition in 1949–50, faced as he was by a bitterly critical Republican party. As D. C. Watt has remarked, it is perhaps fortunate that Anglo–American differences did not develop further before the outbreak of the Korean war created a totally new situation.[37] Be that as it may, it is clear that Britain was entirely correct in extending recognition when she did. It was singularly unfortunate that the United States was not to take the same step until virtually a generation afterwards.[38]

On 25 June 1950 the war in Korea began. Much argument continues to rage over the distant and immediate origins of the conflict. Did it result from the aggression of North Korea, believing that a cheap victory could be secured in unifying the Korean peninsula under a communist regime? Or did South Korea provoke or even invade North Korea in the hope of obtaining full American support, which had eluded it previously? What roles were played by the Soviet Union and China? It is impossible to provide a categorical answer to these questions in the absence of reliable information concerning Russia, China and North Korea. It appears most probable that while there may have been provocation from South Korea, North Korea launched the invasion in the belief that the United States would not intervene militarily in Korea. Since American leaders had indicated that the United States would not intervene in the past, this was a reasonable supposition. It might have suited the Soviet Union to see the United States embroiled outside Europe; however, the North Koreans were entirely capable of acting themselves. The United States reacted vigorously and decided to marshal opinion in the United Nations; this was easier to accomplish while the Soviet Union was absenting itself from the Security Council, ostensibly because of the failure to seat the new communist government in place of Chiang Kai-shek's remnants, which had withdrawn to Taiwan. Britain fully supported resistance to the North Korean aggression. It was such a flagrant case of aggression, contrary to the UN Charter, that all except fellow travellers or pacifists endorsed the decision of the Security Council.[39] *Tribune*, the organ of the Labour left, stated that '. . . the United States Government has, in our view, taken the correct and inevitable course'.[40] In the first stage of fighting in Korea, the UN forces under General MacArthur had been compelled to retreat but later in September 1950 the tables were turned and a decisive defeat was inflicted on the North Korean forces. MacArthur advanced over the 38th parallel, which had marked the territorial division in Korea. In Britain opinion in the Labour and Liberal parties pointed towards a negotiated settlement while Conservative opinion supported a solution reached by military means.[41]

In November 1950 China intervened to prop up the disintegrating North Koreans. Veiled warnings of China's intention of acting unless MacArthur's offensive was halted had been ignored by the United States. The war had taken on a new sombre character with the threat of escalation to a third world war. Widespread alarm was expressed in the House of Commons, particularly at the possible use of the atomic weapon, and Attlee flew to Washington for a meeting with President Truman. The president emphasised that he would proceed with caution. The outcome of Attlee's mission was welcomed in Britain but doubts were raised as to the sagacity of MacArthur: it was feared that he could embark on rash action that could enlarge the conflict. Truman's courageous dismissal of MacArthur, following the growing differences between the two men, was supported in Britain.[42] Officially the United Nations was controlling the operations in Korea; the American contribution, however, constituted the overwhelming majority. British troops were dispatched and were promptly engaged in operations. Total British casualties during the Korean war amounted to 4,500 in comparison with the 140,000 suffered by the United States.[43] In reply to American criticisms of continued British trade with China, the Labour government gradually imposed more restrictions. Churchill pressed for the termination of rubber exports from Malaya; some Labour MPs considered trade to be salutary, however, and to be contributing to the reduction of tension.[44] There was justification for Churchill's criticism: rubber exports from British territories to China amounted to 70,700 tons in the second half of 1950 compared with a figure of 15,881 tons in the corresponding period of 1949. The trade in rubber was subsequently stopped by administrative action in May 1951. Trade in non-strategic commodities was continued by the Attlee and Churchill governments.[45] When Churchill resumed the premiership after the general election of October 1951, he attached importance to preserving a reasonably close identification with Washington if possible. The leaders of the Labour party, now in opposition, had to pay more attention to internal party politics and therefore adopted a somewhat more critical attitude to Conservative policies.[46] In the American presidential election of 1952 General Dwight Eisenhower was nominated as Republican candidate, to the relief of British leaders; Eisenhower was popular in Britain, was a former commander of NATO, and was infinitely preferable to General MacArthur or Senator Robert A. Taft. Eisenhower promised to visit Korea if elected and to work for a peace settlement. In the election in November 1952 he easily defeated Governor Adlai Stevenson, his Democratic opponent. Eisenhower redeemed his promise, went to Korea, and provided impetus for the armistice concluded on 27 July 1953.

The Korean war was over but its legacy lived on. In the far eastern context the importance of the war was to be found in the globalisation of the Cold War. Most Americans thought of the Chinese as working hand in glove with the Russians, a hysterical atmosphere which engendered maximum tension in the United States. American foreign policy was imprisoned within a straitjacket from which it was only to emerge some twenty years afterwards and then, ironically enough, under the aegis of a president originally renowned for his Cold War rhetoric, Richard Nixon. The majority of British leaders believed in the reality of the Cold War and of the menace of communism: this was true of Churchill, Attlee, Morrison, Gaitskell, Clement Davies and of trade union stalwarts such as Tom Williamson, Will Lawther and Arthur Deakin. However, the degree of moral fervour and excitement in the United States was disturbing and hindered the pursuance of flexible and realistic policies that most British governments had traditionally sought to pursue. This was illustrated in the problems experienced by Churchill and his foreign secretary, Anthony Eden, in trying to obtain a diplomatic settlement of the struggle in Indo-China.[47] France had stubbornly attempted to reimpose control of her possessions after 1945 and had become involved in a bitter struggle with the Vietminh. The latter was effectively dominated by the communists, led by Ho Chi Minh and Vo Nguyen Giap.[48] The French position steadily worsened, despite evanescent bids, such as that by General Lattre de Tassigny, to reverse the tide. Churchill and Eden wished to achieve a negotiated settlement which would extricate France and lead to a diminution of tension in the Cold War. Eden worked with infinite patience to foster negotiations,[49] but was hampered by the brusque and frequently churlish attitude of the American secretary of state, John Foster Dulles. Eisenhower largely delegated the formulation of foreign policy to Dulles, who was a fanatical believer in the Cold War, and Eden's personal relations with Dulles were poor. Eden thought of Britain and Russia co-operating and persuading both sides to compromise in Indo-China. Molotov, the Soviet foreign minister, had urged the convening of a five-power conference, including Communist China, to discuss the situation in Indo-China. Dulles viewed the participation of China with extreme distaste.[50] In March–April 1954, just before the Geneva conference was due to meet, Dulles urged that the western powers should put pressure on China to cease encouraging the Vietminh. He further proposed Anglo-American action to aid France and prevent the fall of Dien Bien Phu.[51] The British government declined to comply. The Labour party was vehemently opposed to any British military commitment in Indo-China; much the same was true of the Conservative party, if for more pragmatic reasons than those motivating the national executive of the Labour party.[52] Dulles next suggested the establishment of a new grouping of powers with interests in South-East Asia to block communist expansion. Britain reacted more positively in this case, since communism was viewed as a serious threat in the region and because Britain resented her exclusion from the ANZUS pact.[53] Hugh Gaitskell, a fast rising figure in the Labour hierarchy, supported the proposal and maintained that SEATO could equal NATO in significance. Understandably these sentiments did not commend themselves to his colleagues on the left of the party. Aneurin Bevan censured Eden for not standing up more resolutely to American dictates and demonstrated his penchant for resignation by departing from the shadow cabinet.[54] The government confirmed that the deliberations at Geneva took precedence over the creation of SEATO; the new organisation was ultimately set up in September 1954 with eight members (the United States, Britain, France, Australia, New Zealand, Pakistan, the Philippines, and Thailand).

The Geneva conference was a vindication of Eden's persistent efforts and a reward for British action even if the kudos for Eden was soon to be overtaken by the catastrophe of Suez in 1956. Eden's aim was to bring all those vitally concerned to the conference table and to secure an agreement that would not mean communist supremacy in Vietnam. All gained from the conference. France was able to withdraw and pass her responsibilities on to the shoulders of the United States. The United States helped to prevent the imminent growth of communism in South Vietnam. North Vietnam obtained western recognition of communist dominance in the north. Provision was made for free elections to be held throughout Vietnam as a prelude to reunification. However, the anti-communist regime in the south, with American encouragement, prevented the holding of elections. Vietnam was only reunited in April 1975 with the fall of Saigon following the American withdrawal.

Britain's relations with Communist China were cool and distant from the 1950s to the 1970s.[55] The British charge d'affaires in Peking occupied a lonely post with little immediate prospect of Anglo–Chinese relations becoming closer. The Chinese government concentrated upon internal developments in the consolidation and extension of the revolution. Mao Tse-tung expounded his visionary message and propounded the view in 1958 that China could, via 'the great leap forward', catch up with the advanced western economies within a short period. The disputes between the idealists and the realists resulting from the failure of Mao's bold statement caused considerable acrimony and led, in the middle and later 1960s, to the upheavals of the 'great proletarian cultural revolution'. Mao encouraged his radical supporters to struggle against the established bureaucrats in the party elite.[56] The domestic cultural revolution was accompanied by its foreign manifestations: a stridently revolutionary policy was adopted, identifying Peking with revolutionary movements in the Third World, notably in Africa and Latin America. By this time relations between China and the Soviet Union had rapidly worsened; the Sino-Soviet split, which had become overt following Kruschev's withdrawal of Russian advisers and termination of Russian aid in 1960, widened into a chasm.[57] Mao was intent equally upon preventing China following the capitalist road, symbolised by Washington, and the revisionist road, symbolised by Moscow. Britain was regarded with contempt and ire by the radicals and the British embassy in Peking was one of the targets of the huge demonstrations that took place. Physical attacks were made on embassy staff. In London members of the Chinese embassy were engaged in a fierce incident in which axes were used in the London streets adjoining the embassy. Clearly all the British government could do was to deplore the excesses and wait for a calmer climate to appear in Peking. This at last materialised in the early and mid-1970s, as the cultural revolution subsided and as the pragmatic moderates led by the durable Chou En-lai cautiously asserted themselves.

Britain was naturally always overshadowed by the United States; Britain's relations with China could not improve significantly until Sino–American relations were on a happier footing. President Nixon and his national security adviser and afterwards secretary of state, Henry Kissinger, worked for *rapprochement* with China in the light of the gradual American disengagement from Vietnam. In April 1972 Nixon made his historic visit to Peking and China's relations with the western powers began to improve.[58] There were numerous problems to be surmounted on both sides: the influence of the more deeply committed anti-communists in the American political parties, the activities of the Taiwan lobby, and the difficulties inherent in the United States withdrawing a commitment to Taiwan which had existed since the Korean war. It was only in 1979 that President Carter extended full American recognition of the communist government, although he combined this with limited undertakings to Taiwan for the near future. Chinese leaders showed a growing desire for economic and cultural contacts with Britain. Delegations from each country visited the other. British political leaders visited China, including prominent figures in the Conservative party. Edward Heath was warmly welcomed in Peking, as was his successor as leader, Margaret Thatcher. Since Conservative leaders were usually to the fore in warning of the Russian menace, they were more congenial to the Chinese leaders than Labour party luminaries. Delegations of British businessmen toured China and returned with not unfamiliar descriptions of the size of the potential Chinese market. The Chinese revealed particular interest in purchasing British aeroplanes and in obtaining British guidance in organising their antiquated car assembly methods, and also wished to encourage educational contacts with British universities and to send science and technology students to various institutions in Britain. The volume of British trade with China increased substantially in 1978–79. In 1978 British exports to China were worth £91 million and in the first nine months of 1979 were almost double that amount.[59]

Hong Kong had proved a focal point of tension during the cultural revolution when serious riots occurred in the colony. The Chinese government derived tangible economic benefits from the functioning of Hong Kong and an amicable relationship was secured in the 1970s. China had no intention of disrupting the life of Hong Kong; harmony was promoted by the astute British governor in the 1970s, Sir Murray Maclehose. In 1979 he paid the first official visit to Peking since the communists came to power. The chief difficulties facing the British administration in Hong Kong followed from the rapid population growth, accentuated by the numbers of Chinese wanting to enter Hong Kong from neighbouring provinces. Previously China had either prevented or discouraged emigration but this changed after the mid-1970s; the influx reached proportions that alarmed the British officials and the subject was discussed with Peking. The real question mark with Hong Kong concerned the future of the colony in 1997 when the New Territories, acquired a century earlier, were scheduled to revert to China. Hong Kong would not be viable without the New Territories. However, Britain and China were content to leave this thorny matter to be resolved at a future date.[60]

In the wider colonial setting at the end of the Second World War in

1945, Britain had to determine policy for her colonial territories, notably for Burma and Malaya. In the case of Burma there was a clash of attitudes between South-East Asia Command (SEAC) and the 'old Burma hands' associated with the exiled administration at Simla. Mountbatten and Slim were impressed with the strength of Burmese nationalism and maintained that it was in Britain's interests to co-operate with Aung San, the charismatic leader of the Anti-Fascist Peoples Freedom League (AFPFL).[61] The advisers of the British governor of Burma, Sir Reginald Dorman-Smith, were mostly conservative, if not reactionary, and did not grasp the extent to which Burma had changed as a consequence of the Japanese occupation. Old-style officials and their Burmese friends thought of restoring the *status quo ante* and regarded Burmese who had participated in the Japanese-supported government as traitors. This attitude was encouraged by the spokesmen of British firms and by those members of the landowning Burmese élite who had worked most closely with the British down to 1942 and, in some instances, at Simla subsequently. Mountbatten favoured a progressive policy of co-operating with advanced Burmese nationalists; however, Mountbatten became preoccupied with the numerous other pressing problems of SEAC in South-East Asia. In addition, it was decided in London that Dorman-Smith should take over again. The British government had not devised other than a holding policy for Burma in 1945–46. The intention was to restore law and order and gradually to prepare the way for the introduction of new constitutional arrangements as a prelude to ultimate full self-government. Dorman-Smith and his ministers worked to secure acceptance of British authority once more and suppressed elements that they deemed to be unreliable. Aung San himself was regarded with hostility and his arrest was envisaged in 1945–46 by some members of the administration on a charge of murder connected with an episode during the war. Thus opportunities for reaching accord with the rising forces of mass nationalism in Burma were lost; it was too late afterwards to recover the ground, at least to the point where Burmese leaders could be convinced of the desirability of remaining within the British Commonwealth.[62] The Attlee government was so busy with other domestic and foreign business that it was some time before the deterioration in Burma was understood. Debates in the House of Commons demonstrated that the Labour backbench critics of the government, briefed by Burmese leaders, were more perceptive in their remarks than the official spokesmen or the Conservative opposition.[63] After reviewing matters, it was decided to withdraw Dorman-Smith and replace him by General Sir Hubert Rance, formerly in charge of part of SEAC policy relating to Burma. Rance was shrewd and progressively minded; he was respected by Burmese politicians and popular with them. Rance aimed to restore the smooth functioning of the governmental machine and to advance with reasonable speed towards independence. The Attlee government had decided to press ahead with independence for India in 1947 and an analogous view was taken of Burma. Aung San had emerged as by far the most important political leader in Burma, capable of keeping the amorphous AFPFL together and of providing inspirational enthusiasm for the new Burma. Aung San was practical and warned the Burmese people that they could not expect too much of their leaders and that the road ahead would be tough.[64] He went to London in January 1947 and met Attlee: from their discussions came the Aung San-Attlee agreement, stipulating a swift advance to independence; Burma would have a Westminster-type parliamentary constitution with safeguards for the minority peoples on whom the British had often relied for support in the past.[65] Aung San was appointed prime minister; he co-operated closely with Rance. Then tragedy struck: U Saw, the former prime minister interned by the British in Uganda during the war, engineered the assassination of Aung San together with most of his cabinet. It was a savage blow and robbed Burma of ministers she could ill afford to lose. U Saw's motives had been personal jealousy and resentment of Aung San. Rance dealt coolly and effectively with the challenging crisis. He appointed Aung San's colleague, U Nu (who had luckily escaped assassination) as the new prime minister. U Nu was a capable politician but lacked the charisma and stimulating qualities of Aung San.

In December 1947 the documents providing for the independence of Burma were formally approved in London. In January 1948 Burma became an independent republic outside the British Commonwealth, the only part of the former empire to opt out of the Commonwealth.[66] Burma experienced chaotic and rapidly changing governments between 1948 and 1962. U Nu dominated the scene for most of this period but diminishingly in the latter stages. In 1962 General Ne Win, one of the original 'thirty comrades' recruited by the Japanese in 1940, seized power. Narrow military rule was implemented thereafter and Burma became an inward-looking country, concerned with internal issues. Politically and economically Burma was stagnant.[67] A communist rebellion, dating from the time of independence, continued with Chinese encouragement. The minorities were restless or in a state of insurrection. In the north-east, on the borders with Thailand and Laos in the so-called 'golden triangle', remnants of Chiang Kai-shek's defeated forces had crossed into Burma in 1949–50. Some were airlifted to Taiwan in the mid-1950s; the remainder became engaged in the lucrative drugs traffic. As for British influence, this had effectively disappeared soon after 1948. Major British firms like Burmah Oil were pushed out. The British presence in Burma had always possessed a highly superficial character, unlike India. It was perhaps fitting that it disappeared so quickly after 1948.

In Malaya, British policy at the close of the Pacific war contemplated a sharp reduction in the authority of the sultans, who were thought in several cases to have collaborated too warmly with the Japanese. British officials in the Colonial Office in London believed, too, that the Chinese and Indians should be treated more justly than had been the position before 1941. In 1945, therefore, the broad policy enunciated in London decreed a more centralised British policy with the sultans being subordinated rigorously to British authority. Former Malayan civil servants, including

the nonagenarian Sir Frank Swettenham, warned of the dire political consequences of the new policy of equality for the different racial communities in Malaya which was laid down. Not surprisingly the Malay
community, awakened politically by the impact of Japanese rule, showed
much alarm and, more important after the first shock, anger. At first the
sultans accepted the new position as stated by the British emissary, Sir
Harold MacMichael, but the British proclamation of the Malayan Union
met with trenchant opposition; in the face of the opposition displayed in
1945–46, it was decided to modify policy in the direction of accepting
the position of the sultans again. Political activity among the Malays
developed; the principal personality in this development was Dato Onn
bin Ja'afar, the chief minister of Johore. He founded, in March 1946, the
United Malays National Organization (UMNO). In opposition to UMNO
appeared the Malay Nationalist party led by Dr Burhanuddin; this soon
afterwards merged with other groups to constitute the People's United
Front (PUTERA).[68] In 1946–47 British officials in Malaya consulted
representatives of each section of the community in Malaya. A new federation was proclaimed in February 1948; it was decided to exclude Singapore, resembling the former plan for the Malayan Union in this respect.
The centre of administration was Kuala Lumpur. The various states possessed executive and legislative powers; each local government had a
chief minister under the sultan. The chief British representative at Kuala
Lumpur was given the title of high commissioner. The legislature
included a majority of members who were not officials, with a predominance of Malays.[69] The sultans were to meet again at regular intervals
during the year. With regard to citizenship, the regulations were modified
in a direction that was more favourable to the Malays; Malays at once
qualified for citizenship–others could become citizens depending on the
length of time they had lived in Malaya.[70] Singapore was a crown colony
with executive and legislative councils; after 1945 the latter was given a
majority of non-official members representing the different racial groups
in Singapore.[71] The island of Labuan, which had been placed for administrative purposes under Singapore in 1906, having previously been under
Sarawak, was assigned to North Borneo in 1946. The Cocos islands and
Christmas Island remained under Singapore until they were transferred
from the chartered company that had run them before the Japanese invasion
to the British crown with effect from July 1946. Brunei was returned to
British protection. Sarawak was ruled by the army in 1945–46. The
Brooke dynasty briefly took over again in April 1946; after a somewhat
contentious debate in the local legislature, transfer to the British crown
was approved to take effect on 1 July 1946. The old paternalistic direction of the Brookes was replaced by a British governor and the colonial
structure.[72]

Britain's first high commissioner in Malaya after the war was Sir
Edward Gent, who wished to achieve a more integrated community and
did not subscribe to the traditional attitudes of racial superiority typifying
many white officials and rubber planters. In order to co-ordinate policy in

South-East Asia a special commissioner for the region was appointed. The first holder of this office was Lord Killearn (formerly Sir Miles Lampson). He was succeeded by Malcolm MacDonald, a former cabinet minister and high commissioner in Canada, who was given the title of commissioner-general. MacDonald was critical of Gent's approach and it is likely that he was responsible for Gent's recall in May 1948.[73] The worsening of the security situation, with the proclamation of the emergency in 1948, accelerated Gent's fall. From 1948 to 1960 the Malay authorities, originally under Britain and from 1957 under an independent Malaya, were engaged in the fight against the insurrection waged by the Malayan Communist party (MCP).[74] The MCP had grown rapidly during the Pacific war, when it comprised the heart of the resistance movement in Malaya, and was almost entirely a Chinese movement in membership and support. The Chinese in Malaya were treated with much brutality by the Japanese. In the later stages of the Pacific war British agents and supplies from Force 136 were parachuted in to assist the resistance operations. One of the most distinguished Malayan Chinese resistance figures was Chin Peng, who was awarded the Order of the British Empire (OBE) for his efforts. He later became head of the MCP and the principal organiser of the insurrection. The leader of the MCP before, during, and for a time after the war was the bizarre Loi Tak, who had enjoyed a strange and chequered career: born in Annam, he had worked for French intelligence, moved to Malaya in the 1930s and was recruited by British intelligence. When the Japanese conquered Malaya he transferred his loyalties to them, which explains his otherwise curious ability to drive around Singapore in an open car. Near the end of the war he reverted to working for the British. Loi Tak's dual role helps to account for the muddle and failure of the MCP immediately after the Pacific war.[75] In contrast to the Vietminh in 1945, who considered themselves strong enough to form an administration, the MCP was passive and acquiesced in the restoration of British power. The MCP took the line that the objective conditions for successful revolution did not exist in 1945; the weakness of the party also resulted from the double–dealing of Loi Tak. Dissatisfaction with his leadership grew in 1947 within the MCP. Loi Tak then left Malaya and was rumoured to have been murdered, probably in Thailand.[76] The MCP required some time to adjust following his abrupt departure but by 1948 this had been accomplished. The circumstances were to some extent encouraging for an uprising. There was appreciable discontent among workers in rubber plantations at their wages and conditions of work; trade unions grew more rapidly after 1945 and members of the MCP became prominent in them; the Malayan police force was poorly paid and inefficient; the British administration in general was ill-prepared for an insurrection. On the other hand, the MCP appealed in the main to only one section of Malaya's population — the Chinese. Most Malays were not attracted by communism and the Indians were more interested in the newly-independent India and Pakistan.

The industrial situation in Malaya worsened in the first few months of

1948. This must be seen against the background of the development of the Cold War and the apprehension of communist conspiracy inspired by Moscow.[77] In mid-June 1948 three European planters were killed on rubber estates in part of Perak. These incidents led the administration, which had been anxiously surveying the situation for some weeks, to proclaim on 16 June 1948 a state of emergency, initially for areas within Perak and Johore: it was then extended two days later to the whole of Malaya. The Malayan authorities and the MCP had to some extent been shadow-boxing, with each side afraid that the other might launch a dramatic initiative. The more combative units of the MCP had acted in Perak and were poised to strike in other states and districts against the owners or managers of rubber estates. With the advent of the emergency, the MCP was committed to an all-out struggle. The emergency lasted twelve years and was at its climax between 1950 and 1955. The strength of the MCP lay in the jungles where a number of guerrilla leaders had gained valuable experience in the years of fighting the Japanese. Chinese workers on the rubber estates often aided the guerrillas through choice or coercion. The hope of the MCP was that sufficient support would be forthcoming from the workers to frighten the white managers and produce the breakdown of the Malayan economy. The MCP was closely following the teachings of Mao Tse-tung, whose texts were used word for word.[78] The rural areas would be infiltrated using the guerrilla methods so successfully initiated by Mao in China: eventually the cities would be taken and the rout of the British and their allies from the Malay establishment would have been achieved. A limited amount of progress could be made by these methods but the analogy with China was more misleading than illuminating. In Malaya the racial divisions, especially between Malays and Chinese, prevented the MCP from reaching its goal. In addition, whilst the British administration was inept in a number of respects, it was capable of reforming itself in conjunction with the leaders of the Malay community and was able to defeat the MCP.

In October 1951 the high commissioner, Sir Henry Gurney, was murdered. The assassination was not carefully planned in advance but was the outcome of a chance encounter between Gurney's car and a party of guerrillas along an isolated road.[79] Gurney had previously served in Palestine and brought a number of former police officers from Palestine with him with the aim of reorganising the police force. Gurney was a competent administrator but showed no profound grasp of counter-insurgency. He should not be censured too harshly in this respect, for the most efficacious methods of combating terrorist activities were discovered on a trial and error basis during the operations in Malaya. The British government was shocked at the news of Gurney's death and decided that a tough leader should be appointed to succeed him with the intention of grasping terrorism by the throat. The man chosen was General Sir Gerald Templer.[80] Unlike many military men, Templer had political sense and knew that a solution could not be reached in purely military terms. He held the post of high commissioner from February 1952 to July 1954, a period which saw the decisive defeat of the guerrillas with a sharp fall in the number of incidents. This was accomplished partly as a result of action instigated under Gurney now reaching fruition and partly from the vigour and tenacity engendered by Templer himself, who believed in applying a mixture of fairness and firmness. He did not condone arrogance or brutality, especially involving racial discrimination, and he soon made obvious his dislike of the attitudes of racial superiority still frequently encountered among whites. Templer maintained that in pursuing effective operations against guerrillas respect for the security forces was axiomatic. Therefore, villages suspected of supplying guerrillas would be punished. The principal methods employed by the British forces comprised cutting off food supplies through rigorous searches and curfews; physical transfer and resettlement of villages known or suspected of harbouring guerrillas; the regalvanizing of the police through improved pay, conditions, leadership, and morale; improved intelligence and greater proficiency of the army and air force in the light of experience.[81] The cohesion of the guerrillas began to be affected and more defections were recorded. Templer's term of office had seen major success and he left an infinitely more sanguine prospect for his successor than the one he had inherited.[82]

Political parties had developed in Malaya after 1945 and gained momentum. Malays and Chinese were both prominent and co-operated in the United Malays National Organisation (UMNO), the chief political party. Pressure developed for self-government and independence was ultimately granted. The legitimacy of the aim was recognised by the Attlee government and upheld by the Conservative government in 1951. The colonial secretary under Churchill, Oliver Lyttelton, reiterated this consistently and it was an additional factor strengthening the campaign against insurgency. The Malay community and the more conservative Chinese knew that Britain would be transferring power before long; it was in their interests as well as Britain's that the MCP should be defeated. In 1956–57 arrangements were completed for Malaya to become independent in 1957 as a monarchy with an elected ruler, the latter rotating among the Malay sultanates. UMNO, led by Tunku Abdul Rahman, took Malaya to independence, which was secured on 31 August 1957, although Britain retained a defence agreement with Malaya.

Singapore was proceeding more slowly to self-government; this was achieved in May 1959. The People's Action Party, led by Lee Kuan Yew, won the first election and Lee became prime minister the following month. In Malaya the emergency was officially terminated in July 1960; the scale of conflict had steadily diminished for the preceding four years. The struggle against the guerrillas in the Malayan peninsula showed what could be achieved in repelling a guerrilla campaign, given sufficient resolution and tenacity. However, the guerrillas had not been liquidated; a hard core remained in the inaccessible areas on the border with Thailand and in the middle and later 1970s the guerrillas became active again, demonstrating the potential that existed for a renewed challenge to the government should its vigilance slip. The details of those killed in the emergency are as follows:

	Terrorists killed	Security forces killed	Total no. of incidents[83]
1948	374	149	1,274
1949	619	229	1,442
1950	648	393	4,739
1951	1,078	504	6,082
1952	1,155	263	3,727
1953	959	92	1,170
1954	723	87	1,077
1955	420	79	781
1956	307	47	435
1957	240	11	190
1958	153	10	90
1959	21	1	12

In May 1961, Tunku Abdul Rahman proposed the establishment of a new state of Malaysia comprising Malaya, Singapore, Sabah (North Borneo), Sarawak, and Brunei. The plan was favourably received in London, where it was believed that the new grouping would strengthen the region against the menace of communism. It would be necessary to obtain the consent of the elements other than Malaya for which Britain carried ultimate responsibility. Complications could well arise with the Philippines and Indonesia, as proved to be the case: these two neighbours of Malaya feared the consequences of the creation of a powerful new state. Between February and April 1962 a commission headed by Lord Cobbold visited the Borneo territories to ascertain the wishes of the inhabitants regarding participation in Malaysia. The commission drew attention to the possible dangers of racial tension in the territories following British departure, but believed that about two-thirds of the inhabitants of Sarawak and Sabah either supported the concept of Malaysia or could be induced to support it given adequate safeguards.[84] The sultan of Brunei had no desire to join Malaysia, believing that such a step would reduce the freedom for manoeuvre he had acquired through his skilful policy towards the British in recent years.[85] In August 1962 it was announced that the federation of Malaysia would formally be established in one year's time. Increasing rumblings of dissatisfaction from the Philippines and Indonesia were heard in 1962–63; the Philippines laid claim to Sabah and President Sukarno of Indonesia proclaimed the advent of 'confrontation' with Malaysia in February 1963. Discussions took place between the three states directly concerned and the United Nations conducted an inquiry into the views of the Borneo territories. On 16 September 1963 Malaysia formally came into existence; Indonesia and the Philippines refused to recognise the federation. The British defence agreement with Malaya was extended to incorporate the other states of the federation.[86] British forces were soon involved in combating the guerrilla activities encouraged by

Indonesia along the border of almost 1,000 miles in Borneo. Indonesian forces took part in some of the raids together with communist opponents of Malaysia from the Borneo territories. A Malaysian Defence Council was set up to co-ordinate the response to the developing aggression. Britain, Australia and New Zealand emphasised that they would defend Malaysia; at the end of September 1963 there were about 6,000 British Commonwealth forces protecting northern Borneo.[87] The confrontation lasted for almost three years; it consisted of periodic incursions by Indonesian forces with continual verbal abuse of Malaysia and its defenders. Raids occurred on the coast of Malaya and bomb incidents took place in Singapore. Britain, Australia and New Zealand moved additional forces into Borneo in the autumn of 1964 and in the first few months of 1965.[88]

Tension between Kuala Lumpur and Singapore developed in 1964–65. Lee Kuan Yew was too vociferous and active for the likings of the Malaysian authorities. He was critical of Malay attitudes of superiority towards the Chinese and believed that much more needed to be done to ensure racial harmony within Malaysia. On 7 August 1965 Tunku Abdul Rahman and Lee Kuan Yew signed an agreement providing for the secession of Singapore from Malaysia; in reality the position was rather that Singapore was being expelled from the federation.[89] Britain was not consulted beforehand. It was agreed that Malaysia and Singapore would co-operate for economic and defence purposes after separation. Singapore became a republic and Lee Kuan Yew was determined to stimulate economic growth and racial harmony on a basis of unyielding opposition to communism. Confrontation was eventually ended after talks were held between Malaysian and Indonesian leaders from May to July 1966; an agreement to this effect was signed on 11 August 1966,[90] made possible by the changed political atmosphere in Djakarta with the reduced power of President Sukarno following the crushing of the Indonesian Communist party. The British government welcomed the end of confrontation and announced the withdrawal of 10,000 British troops. British and Indonesian casualties were reckoned at 388 and 1,583 respectively.[91]

The confrontation between Malaysia and Indonesia was the last major military action in which British forces were committed in the Far East. At the time when Britain's remaining military role in the Far East was rapidly declining, the military involvement of the United States increased dramatically with the fast escalating American commitment in Vietnam. The American involvement in Vietnam had started to develop under President Kennedy but the real take-off came under President Lyndon Johnson in 1964. Johnson believed that it was essential that communism should not triumph and carried the ringing declarations of his predecessors, Harry Truman and John F. Kennedy to their logical–or illogical–conclusion.[92] Harold Wilson assumed office as British prime minister in October 1964; he once stated, in Kiplingesque terms, with reference to relations between India and China after the border war in 1962, that Britain's frontier was 'on the Himalayas'.[93] The harsh realities of Britain's political and economic decline compelled recognition of the limits to British power. Britain had no part to play in the Vietnam war; Australia sent some troops but there was no possibility of British forces joining them. Most British political leaders felt vague sympathy with the American involvement in Vietnam to the point where the sheer size of the American commitment and the accumulating evidence of the sickening brutality of the war pushed them in the direction of constructive criticism with offers of mediation. Perhaps nothing could more sharply underline the degree of British decline than the fact that Britain played no part in the greatest conflict seen in South-East Asia since the end of the Second World War. Pressure from British public opinion arguably added to the total pressure on the United States to escape from a conflict that could not be won.

British defence commitments in the Far East were soon brought to an end in the late 1960s and early 1970s. British forces left Singapore in 1971; Britain still retained a small number of troops at Hong Kong with a nominal RAF presence there in 1979. It is difficult to avoid the feeling that the situation has turned full circle. In the nineteenth century Britain had pioneered the opening of the Far East to intensified foreign intercourse and activity. In the last quarter of the twentieth century Britain's role was largely extinguished. Britain still had sizeable investments in the region and hoped – familiar sound – to expand trade with China. Expectations of the potential for expanding trade with China were greatly stimulated by the visit of the Chinese prime minister, Hua Guofeng, in October-November 1979. However, Britain belonged to the European Community and was concerned with pressing political, economic and social difficulties at home. In essence, Britain's role in the Far East belonged to history.

References

Introduction

1. For Macartney's account of his visit to Peking, see J. Cranmer-Byng, (ed.), *An Embassy to China : Lord Macartney's Journal, 1793–1794* (Longman, 1963).
2. On Anglo-Dutch relations, see N. Tarling, *British Policy in the Malay Peninsula and Archipelago, 1824–1871*, 2nd edn (Oxford U.P., Kuala Lumpur, 1969) and *Imperial Britain in South-East Asia* (Oxford U.P., Kuala Lumpur, 1975), pp. 7–27.
3. For a lucid discussion of Japanese policy, see I. H. Nish, *Japanese Foreign Policy, 1869–1942* (Routledge & Kegan Paul, 1977), pp. 1–104.
4. See Tarling, *Imperial Britain in South-East Asia*, pp. 6, 55–6.
5. The nature of the Japanese challenge is discussed with admirable clarity and wit in R. Storry, *Japan and the Decline of the West in Asia* (Macmillan, 1979).
6. This argument was advanced by Professor Hosoya Chihiro at an Anglo–Japanese conference on the Second World War, held in London in July 1979.
7. See P. Lowe, *Great Britain and the Origins of the Pacific War* (Clarendon Press, Oxford, 1977), Ch. 7.
8. See P. Darby, *British Defence Policy East of Suez, 1947–1968* (Oxford U.P., 1973), pp. 232–8.
9. J. Gallagher and R. Robinson, 'The imperialism of free trade', *Economic History Review*, 2nd series, **6** (1953–54), 1.
10. Ibid., **6**, 3, 15.
11. Ibid., **6**, 9.
12. O. MacDonagh, 'The anti-imperialism of free trade', *Economic History Review*, 2nd series, **14** (1961–62), 489–501.
13. Ibid., **14**, 493, 495, 497.
14. Cited D. C. M. Platt, 'The imperialism of free trade : some reservations', *Economic History Review*, 2nd series, **21** (1968), 301. See also D. C. M. Platt, *Finance, Trade, and Politics : British Foreign Policy, 1815–1914* (Clarendon Press, Oxford, 1968), pp. 8–20, 262–307, and Platt, 'Further objections to an "imperialism of free trade", 1830–1860', *Economic History Review*, 2nd series, **26** (1973), 77–90.
15. See D. McLean, 'Commerce, finance, and British diplomatic support in China, 1885–6', *Economic History Review*, 2nd series, **26** (1973), 469, and P. Lowe, *Great Britain and Japan, 1911–15* (Macmillan, 1969), Ch. 3–5.

16. J. A. Hobson, *Imperialism : a Study*, 3rd edn (Allen & Unwin, 1968); V. I. Lenin, *Imperialism, the Highest Stage of Capitalism* (Foreign Languages Publishing House, Moscow, n.d.).
17. D. K. Fieldhouse, *Economics and Empire, 1830–1914* (Weidenfeld & Nicolson, 1973), pp. 39–40.
18. Cited ibid., p. 40.
19. For an interesting reassessment of Hobson, see P. Clarke, *Liberals and Social Democrats* (Cambridge U.P., 1978), passim.
20. C. F. Remer, *Foreign Investments in China* (Macmillan, New York, 1933), pp. 352–3, 360–1.
21. Ibid., p. 395.
22. E. M. Gull, *British Economic Interests in the Far East* (Oxford U.P., 1943), p. 51.
23. Ibid., p. 51.
24. Ibid., p. 84.
25. Ibid., p. 52.
26. Ibid., p. 52.
27. Ibid., pp. 53–4.
28. Remer, *Foreign Investments in China*, pp. 340, 352–3.
29. H. Feis, *Europe the World's Banker* (Yale U.P., 1930), p. 33, as cited in Fieldhouse, *Economics and Empire*, p. 55.
30. Gull, *British Economic Interests*, p. 84.
31. Ibid., p. 84.
32. Ibid., p. 86.
33. Ibid., p. 87.
34. Ibid., pp. 92–3.
35. Ibid., pp. 97–8.
36. Ibid., pp. 97–8.
37. W. D. McIntyre, *The Imperial Frontier in the Tropics, 1865–75 : a Study of British Colonial Policy in West Africa, Malaya, and the South Pacific in the Age of Gladstone and Disraeli* (Macmillan, 1967), p. 209.
38. Fieldhouse, *Economics and Empire*, p. 55.

Chapter 1

1. For a valuable wide-ranging survey of nineteenth-century China, see J. K. Fairbank (ed.), *The Cambridge History of China*, vol. 10, Pt 1, *Late Ch'ing, 1800–1911* (Cambridge U.P., Cambridge, 1978), especially pp. 1–162.
2. F. Wakeman, 'The Canton trade and the Opium War', in Fairbank (ed.), *Cambridge History of China*, vol. 10, Pt 1, p. 163.
3. For a lucid account in broader terms of the East India trade, see P. J. Marshall, *East Indian Fortunes : the British in Bengal in the Eighteenth Century* (Clarendon Press, Oxford, 1976). For a succinct assessment of trade with China, see M. Greenberg, *British Trade and the Opening of China, 1800–42* (Cambridge U.P., 1951), Ch. 1.
4. Greenberg, *British Trade and the Opening of China*, p. 3.
5. Ibid., p. 11.
6. Ibid., pp. 11–12.
7. Ibid., p. 13.
8. Ibid., pp. 13–14.

9. Wakeman in Fairbank (ed.), *Cambridge History of China*, vol. 10, Pt 1, p. 172.
10. Greenberg, *British Trade and the Opening of China*, p. 221.
11. Wakeman in Fairbank (ed.), *Cambridge History of China*, vol. 10, Pt 1, pp. 172–3. See also K. N. Chaudhuri, 'India's foreign trade and the cessation of the East India Company's trading activities, 1828–1840', *Economic History Review*, 2nd series, **19** (1966), 345–63.
12. Greenberg, *British Trade and the Opening of China*, p. 181.
13. Ibid., p. 192.
14. Wakeman in Fairbank (ed.), *Cambridge History of China*, vol. 10, Pt 1, p. 175.
15. Cited G. S. Graham, *The China Station : War and Diplomacy, 1830–1860* (Clarendon Press, Oxford, 1978), p. 62.
16. Wakeman in Fairbank (ed.), *Cambridge History of China*, vol. 10, Pt 1, p. 177.
17. Wakeman in Fairbank (ed.), *Cambridge History of China*, vol. 10, Pt 1, pp. 179–80.
18. Wakeman in Fairbank (ed.), *Cambridge History of China*, vol. 10, Pt 1, p. 187. The cohong were in any case not as prosperous as formerly: it was more onerous and expensive to be a hong merchant. See P. W. Fay, *The Opium War, 1840–1842* (University of North Carolina Press, Chapel Hill, N. C., 1975), p. 27.
19. Wakeman in Fairbank (ed.), *Cambridge History of China*, vol. 10, Pt 1, p. 187.
20. Graham, *The China Station*, p. 98.
21. Ibid., p. 98.
22. Ibid., p. 99.
23. Ibid., p. 97.
24. Cited S. Y. Teng and J. K. Fairbank, *China's Response to the West : a Documentary Survey, 1839–1923* (Harvard U.P., Cambridge, Mass., 1961), pp. 24–7.
25. Graham, *The China Station*, p. 106.
26. Wakeman in Fairbank (ed.), *Cambridge History of China*, vol. 10, Pt 1, p. 194.
27. Wakeman in Fairbank (ed.), *Cambridge History of China*, vol. 10, Pt 1, p. 194.
28. W. C. Costin, *Great Britain and China, 1833–1860* (Clarendon Press, Oxford, 1937), pp. 71–8.
29. Ibid., p. 78.
30. Cited Wakeman in Fairbank (ed.), *Cambridge History of China*, vol. 10, Pt 1, p. 195. See Fay, *The Opium War*, for the most satisfactory account of the conflict.
31. Graham, *The China Station*, p. 104.
32. Wakeman in Fairbank (ed.), *Cambridge History of China*, vol. 10, Pt 1, p. 197.
33. Wakeman in Fairbank (ed.), *Cambridge History of China*, vol. 10, Pt 1, p. 199.
34. Cited Costin, *Great Britain and China*, p. 96.
35. Graham, *The China Station*, p. 176.
36. Ibid., pp. 159–60.
37. Wakeman in Fairbank (ed.), *Cambridge History of China*, vol. 10, Pt 1, p. 206.

38. Wakeman in Fairbank (ed.), *Cambridge History of China*, Vol. 10, Pt 1, p. 209.
39. Graham, *The China Station*, pp. 233–4.
40. J. K. Fairbank, 'The creation of the treaty system' in Fairbank (ed.), *Cambridge History of China*, vol. 10, Pt 1, p. 218.
41. Fairbank in Fairbank (ed.), *Cambridge History of China*, vol. 10, Pt 1, p. 221.
42. Cited ibid., p. 223.
43. Ibid., p. 228.
44. Ibid., pp. 233–4.
45. Ibid., p. 229.
46. Ibid., p. 231.
47. Cited Graham, *The China Station*, p. 240.
48. Cited ibid., p. 242.
49. Cited ibid., p. 243.
50. Ibid., p. 245.
51. Ibid., p. 245.
52. See ibid., Ch. 11, and G. Fox, *British Admirals and Chinese Pirates, 1832–1869* (Kegan Paul, Trench, Trubner, 1940).
53. D. G. E. Hall, *A History of South-East Asia*, 3rd edn, (Macmillan, 1968), p. 489. See also C. N. Parkinson, *Trade in the Eastern Seas, 1793–1813* (Cambridge U.P., Cambridge, 1937), pp. 54–6, and N. Tarling, *Imperial Britain in South-East Asia* (Oxford U.P., Kuala Lumpur, 1975), pp. 7–27.
54. Hall, *History of South-East Asia*, p. 498.
55. Ibid., p. 479. On Raffles, see C. E. Wurtzberg, *Raffles of the Eastern Seas* (Hodder & Stoughton, 1954), and M. Collis, *Raffles* (Faber, 1966).
56. Hall, *History of South-East Asia*, p. 501.
57. Cited ibid., p. 506.
58. N. Tarling, *British Policy in the Malay Peninsula and Archipelago, 1824–1871*, 2nd edn (Oxford U.P., Kuala Lumpur, 1969), p. 17.
59. Hall, *History of South-East Asia*, p. 506.
60. C. M. Turnbull, *The Straits Settlements, 1826–67 : Indian Presidency to Crown Colony* (Athlone Press, 1972), pp. 21–2.
61. Ibid., p. 53.
62. Ibid., pp. 58–9.
63. Ibid., pp. 184–6.
64. Ibid., p. 188.
65. Ibid., p. 187.
66. Ibid., p. 24.
67. Ibid., pp. 28–9.
68. Hall, *History of South-East Asia*, p. 513. For a valuable discussion of Britain's relations with Siam from the 1820s to the 1850s, see Tarling, *Imperial Britain in South-East Asia*, pp. 89–232.
69. Hall, *History of South-East Asia*, pp. 514–15.
70. Ibid., p. 515.
71. Ibid., p. 516.
72. Ibid., p. 516. See also Tarling, *Imperial Britain in South-East Asia*, pp. 136–42, 147–50.
73. Hall, *History of South-East Asia*, p. 517.
74. Ibid., p. 518.
75. Ibid., pp. 519–20.

76. J. F. Cady, *A History of Modern Burma* (Cornell U.P., Ithaca, 1958), p. 69.
77. Ibid., p. 69.
78. Ibid., pp. 72–3.
79. Ibid., p. 74.
80. Ibid., p. 78.
81. Ibid., p. 79.
82. Ibid., pp. 85–6.
83. Ibid., p. 86.
84. Ibid., p. 89.
85. Hall, *History of South-East Asia*, p. 523.
86. Ibid., p. 524.
87. Ibid., p. 527.
88. On piracy, see ibid., and N. Tarling, *Piracy and Politics in the Malay World* (F. W. Cheshire, Melbourne, 1963).
89. Hall, *History of South-East Asia*, pp. 530–1. On the Brookes, see S. Runciman, *The White Rajas* (Cambridge U.P., Cambridge, 1960), and N. Tarling, *Britain, the Brookes, and Brunei* (Oxford U.P., Kuala Lumpur, 1971).
90. Hall, *History of South-East Asia*, p. 533.
91. Ibid., pp. 553–4.

Chapter 2

1. For an admirable survey of the Tokugawa era, see G. B. Sansom, *The Western World and Japan* (Cresset Press, 1950), pp. 167–309. For two important studies of social developments, see R. P. Dore, *Education in Tokugawa Japan* (Routledge & Kegan Paul, 1965), and C. D. Sheldon, *The Rise of the Merchant Class in Tokugawa Japan, 1600–1868*, reprint edn, (Russell and Russell, New York, 1973).
2. For an engrossing account of the Jesuit view of Japan, see M. Cooper, *This Island of Japan : J. Rodrigues' Account of Sixteenth-Century Japan* (Kodansha International, Tokyo, 1973).
3. For an excellent study of the relationship between internal upheavals and the western powers in fusing together to constitute the revolutionary period of the 1850s and 1860s, see W. G. Beasley, *The Meiji Restoration* (Stanford U.P., Stanford, 1973).
4. See W. G. Beasley, *Select Documents on Japanese Foreign Policy, 1853–1868* (Oxford U.P., 1955), pp. 21–58.
5. W. G. Beasley, *Great Britain and the Opening of Japan, 1834–1858* (Luzac & Company, 1951), pp. 3–5.
6. Ibid., p. 28.
7. Ibid., p. 97.
8. G. Fox, *Britain and Japan, 1858–1883* (Clarendon Press, Oxford, 1969), p. 12.
9. Beasley, *Great Britain and the Opening of Japan*, pp. 116–17, 121, 127.
10. Fox, *Britain and Japan*, pp. 43–4.
11. For a useful brief assessment of the more conservative approach, as revealed in the views of Saigo Takamori, see I. Morris, *The Nobility of Failure : Tragic Heroes in the History of Japan* (Secker & Warburg, 1975), pp. 217–75.
12. Fox, *Britain and Japan*, p. 57.

13. Ibid., p. 54.
14. Cited ibid., p. 67.
15. See G. Daniels, 'Sir Harry Parkes : British Representative in Japan, 1865–1883' (unpublished D.Phil. thesis, Oxford, 1967), p. 46.
16. Ibid., p. 47.
17. Fox, *Britain and Japan*, p. 123.
18. Ibid., pp. 117, 119.
19. See Daniels, 'Sir Harry Parkes', pp. 1–22.
20. Ibid., p. 29.
21. Ibid., p. 82.
22. Ibid., p. 95.
23. Ibid., pp. 98–9. See also G. Daniels, 'The British role in the Meiji restoration : a re-interpretive note', *Modern Asian Studies*, 2 (1968), 293–4.
24. For their memoirs, see Lord Redesdale, *Memories*, 2 vols (Hutchinson, 1915), and E. Satow, *A Diplomat in Japan*, (ed.) G. Daniels (Oxford U.P., Tokyo, 1968).
25. Daniels, 'Sir Harry Parkes', pp. 121–2, and Daniels (ed.), *A Diplomat in Japan* pp. 141–55.
26. For relations between France and Japan, see R. L. Sims, 'French policy towards Japan, 1854–1894' (unpublished Ph.D. thesis, London, 1968).
27. Daniels, 'Sir Harry Parkes', p. 131.
28. See G. Daniels, 'The Japanese Civil War (1868) – a British view', *Modern Asian Studies*, 1 (1967), 241–63.
29. Daniels, 'Sir Harry Parkes', p. 157.
30. Daniels, *Modern Asian Studies*, 1, 263.
31. Daniels, 'Sir Harry Parkes', pp. 170–1.
32. Daniels, *Modern Asian Studies*, 2, (1968), 295.
33. W. C. Costin, *Great Britain and China, 1833–1860* (Clarendon Press, Oxford, 1937), p. 118.
34. Ibid., p. 118.
35. Ibid., pp. 119–20.
36. Ibid., p. 149.
37. Cited J. Y. Wong, 'Sir John Bowring and the question of treaty revision in China', *Bulletin of the John Rylands University Library of Manchester*, 58 (1975), 220.
38. The traditional view is illustrated in Costin, *Great Britain and China*. For the revisionist interpretation, see J. Y. Wong, 'The building of an informal British Empire in China in the middle of the nineteenth century', *Bulletin of the John Rylands University Library of Manchester*, 59 (1977), 216–37.
39. The most thorough work in English dealing with the history of the Taiping movement, including massive documentation, is to be found in F. Michael *et al., The Taiping Rebellion*, 3 vols (University of Washington Press, Seattle, 1966–71). See also V. Shih, *The Taiping Ideology* (University of Washington Press, Seattle, 1967) and S. Y. Teng, *The Taiping Rebellion and the Western Powers* (Clarendon Press, Oxford, 1971). There is an excellent short assessment by P. A. Kuhn in J. K. Fairbank (ed.), *The Cambridge History of China*, vol. 10, Pt 1, *Late Ch'ing, 1800–1911* (Cambridge U.P., Cambridge, 1978), pp. 264–317.
40. Cited Wong, *Bulletin of John Rylands University Library of Manchester*, 58 (1975), 220.
41. For a discussion of British attitudes to the Taiping movement, see J. S. Gre-

gory, *Great Britain and the Taipings* (Routledge & Kegan Paul, 1969).

42. Cited Wong, *Bulletin of John Rylands University Library of Manchester*, **58** (1975), 232.

43. Cited ibid., (1975), 231.

44. Costin, *Great Britain and China*, pp. 180–94.

45. For a careful re-examination of the *Arrow* incident, see J. Y. Wong, 'The Arrow incident : a reappraisal', *Modern Asian Studies*, **8** (1974), 373–89. See also J. Y. Wong, 'Harry Parkes and the "Arrow War" in China', *Modern Asian Studies*, **9** (1975), 303–20.

46. See Wong, *Modern Asian Studies*, **9**, and S. Lane-Poole and F. V. Dickins, *Life of Sir Harry Parkes*, 2 vols. (Macmillan, 1894).

47. Wong, *Modern Asian Studies*, **8**, 378–9.

48. Cited Costin, *Great Britain and China*, p. 212.

49. Ibid., p. 219. See also K. Bourne, *The Foreign Policy of Victorian England, 1830–1902* (Clarendon Press, Oxford, 1970), p. 83.

50. For an important reassessment of Yeh, see J. Y. Wong, *Yeh Ming-ch'en : Viceroy of Liang Kuang (1852–8)* (Cambridge U.P., Cambridge, 1976).

51. Costin, *Great Britain and China*, p. 227.

52. See Wong, *Yeh Ming-ch'en*, pp. 193–7.

53. J. K. Fairbank, 'The creation of the treaty system' in Fairbank (ed.), *Cambridge History of China*, vol. 10, Pt 1, p. 249.

54. See G. S. Graham, *The China Station: War and Diplomacy, 1830–1860* (Clarendon Press, Oxford, 1978), pp. 336–7, 342, 348.

55. Fairbank in Fairbank (ed.), *Cambridge History of China*, vol. 10, Pt 1, p. 251.

56. Cited Costin, *Great Britain and China*, pp. 279–80.

57. Ibid., p. 289.

58. Cited ibid., p. 296. For details of the naval operations, see Graham, *The China Station*, pp. 368–78.

59. Costin, *Great Britain and China*, p. 296.

60. Ibid., pp. 315–16.

61. Fairbank in Fairbank (ed.) *Cambridge History of China*, vol. 10, Pt 1, p. 257.

62. Costin, *Great Britain and China*, pp. 338–9.

63. Fairbank in Fairbank (ed.), *Cambridge History of China*, vol. 10, Pt 1, pp. 259–60.

64. On Lay, see J. J. Gerson, *Horatio Nelson Lay and Sino–British Relations, 1854–1864* (Harvard U.P., Cambridge, Mass., 1972). On Hart, see S. F. Wright, *Hart and the Chinese Customs* (Mullan, Belfast, 1950) and the magnificent collection of Hart's correspondence in J. K. Fairbank, K. F. Bruner and E. M. Matheson (eds.), *The IG in Peking : Letters of Robert Hart, Maritime Customs, 1861–1907*, 2 vols. (Belknap Press, Harvard U.P., Cambridge, Mass., 1975).

65. N. Tarling, *Imperial Britain in South-East Asia* (Oxford U.P., Kuala Lumpur, 1975), pp. 142, 155–6.

66. Ibid., pp. 144–5, 150–51.

67. Ibid., p. 174.

68. Ibid., p. 175.

69. Ibid., p. 175.

70. Ibid., pp. 175–6, 198.

Chapter 3

1. This is one of the themes pursued in an admirable comparative study, W. D. McIntyre, *The Imperial Frontier in the Tropics, 1865–75 : a Study of British Colonial Policy in West Africa, Malaya, and the South Pacific in the Age of Gladstone and Disraeli* (Macmillan, 1967). See also C. D. Cowan, *Nineteenth-Century Malaya : the Origins of British Political Control* (Oxford U.P., 1961).
2. C. M. Turnbull, *The Straits Settlements, 1826–67* (Athlone Press, 1972), p. 24.
3. On dislike of Ord, see C. N. Parkinson, *British Intervention in Malaya 1867–1877* (University of Malaya Press, Singapore, 1960), p. 104.
4. Cited McIntyre, *The Imperial Frontier*, p. 160.
5. For the development of Russian interest in Asia during the nineteenth century, see D. Gillard, *The Struggle for Asia, 1828–1914* (Methuen, 1977).
6. For a discussion of French policy, see J. F. Cady, *The Roots of French Imperialism in South-East Asia* (Cornell U.P., Ithaca, 1954).
7. McIntyre, *The Imperial Frontier*, p. 42.
8. Ibid., p. 174.
9. Ibid., p. 175.
10. Ibid., p. 184.
11. Ibid., p. 189.
12. Ibid., p. 191.
13. Ibid., p. 193.
14. Ibid., p. 198.
15. Ibid., p. 199.
16. Ibid., p. 202.
17. Ibid., p. 203.
18. Cited ibid., p. 205.
19. Ibid., p. 207.
20. Cited ibid., p. 209.
21. Cited ibid., p. 209.
22. Ibid., p. 271.
23. Ibid., p. 294.
24. Ibid., p. 299.
25. Ibid., p. 306.
26. Cited ibid., p. 306.
27. Ibid., p. 307.
28. Ibid., p. 308.
29. Ibid., p. 308.
30. On the conduct of Birch, see Parkinson, *British Intervention in Malaya*, pp. 222–3.
31. McIntyre, *The Imperial Frontier*, p. 373.
32. D. G. E. Hall, *A History of South-East Asia*, 3rd edn, (Macmillan, 1968), p. 556.
33. Ibid., p. 558.
34. E. Thio, *British Policy in the Malay Peninsula, 1880–1910*, vol. 1 (University of Malaya Press, 1969), pp. 4–6.
35. Ibid., p. 7. See also P. L. Burns, 'The constitutional history of Malaya with special reference to the Malay states of Perak, Negri Sembilan and Pahang, 1874–1914' (unpublished Ph.D. thesis, London, 1965).

36. Thio, *British Policy in the Malay Peninsula*, vol. 1, pp. 69–74.
37. Ibid., pp. 91–2.
38. For Swettenham's retrospective views, see his *Footprints in Malaya* (Hutchinson, 1942) and *British Malaya : An Account of the Origin and Progress of British Influence in Malaya*, revised edn (Allen & Unwin, 1948).
39. Thio, *British Policy in the Malay Peninsula*, vol. 1, pp. 120–39.
40. Ibid., pp. 163–4.
41. Ibid., p. 164.
42. Ibid., p. 165.
43. Ibid., pp. 169–70.
44. Hall, *History of South-East Asia*, pp. 700–1.
45. Thio, *British Policy in the Malay Peninsula*, vol. 1, pp. 206, 235.
46. Ibid., pp. 252–4.
47. Hall, *History of South-East Asia*, pp. 566–7.
48. For the history of the North Borneo Company, see K. G. Tregonning, *Under Chartered Company Rule (North Borneo, 1881–1946)* (University of Malaya Press, 1958).
49. Hall, *History of South-East Asia*, pp. 570–1.
50. J. F. Cady, *A History of Modern Burma* (Cornell U.P., Ithaca, 1958), p. 96.
51. Cady, *History of Modern Burma*, pp. 97–9.
52. Ibid., p. 106.
53. Ibid., pp. 107–08.
54. Ibid., p. 110.
55. Ibid., pp. 116–7.
56. See E. Chew, 'The withdrawal of the last British residency from Upper Burma in 1879', *Journal of South-East Asian History*, **10** (1969), 259.
57. Cited ibid., 263.
58. Cady, *History of Modern Burma*, pp. 116–17.
59. Ibid., p. 117.
60. Ibid., p. 119.
61. See Hall, *History of South-East Asia*, pp. 666–78. See also V. G. Kiernan, 'Britain, Siam, and Malaya, 1875–1885', *Journal of Modern History*, **28** (1956), 1–20 and 'The Kra canal projects of 1882–5: Anglo–French rivalry in Siam and Malaya', *History*, **41** (1956), 137–57. See in addition J. S. Brider, 'International rivalry in Siam, 1843–1909 : the Kra canal project' (unpublished Ph.D. thesis, Manchester, 1977), and J. Chandran, *The Contest for Siam, 1889–1902* (Penerbit Universite Kebang Saan, Kuala Lumpur, 1977).
62. Hall, *History of South-East Asia*, p. 689.
63. Ibid., p. 689.
64. Ibid., pp. 690–1.
65. Ibid., p. 691.
66. Ibid., pp. 692–3.
67. Ibid., p. 696.
68. Ibid., p. 698. See also J. A. S. Grenville, *Lord Salisbury and Foreign Policy* (Athlone Press, 1964), pp. 109–10.
69. See M. C. Wright, *The Last Stand of Chinese Conservatism : The Tung-chih Restoration, 1862–74* (Stanford U.P., Stanford, 1957).
70. J. K. Fairbank (ed.), *The Cambridge History of China*, vol. 10, Pt 1, *Late Ch'ing, 1800–1911* (Cambridge U.P., Cambridge, 1978), p. 477.
71. See S. Y. Teng and J. K. Fairbank, *China's Response to the West : a*

Documentary Survey, 1839–1923 (Harvard U.P., Cambridge, Mass., 1961), pp. 85–132.

72. For an excellent study of the relationship between the government and the merchants, see N. A. Pelcovits, *Old China Hands and the Foreign Office*, reprint edn (Octagon Books, New York, 1969), pp. *vii–ix*.
73. Ibid., pp. 14–15, 18–19, 20–3.
74. Ibid., p. 30.
75. See B. Dean, *China and Great Britain : the Diplomacy of Commercial Relations, 1860–1864* (Harvard U.P., Cambridge, Mass., 1974), p. 13.
76. Pelcovits, *Old China Hands*, pp. 16, 70.
77. Ibid., pp. 53–4.
78. Ibid., pp. 129–30.
79. Ibid., p. 103.
80. Ibid., p. 133.
81. Ibid., p. 133. See also G. C. Allen and A. Donnithorne, *Western Enterprise in Far Eastern Economic Development : China and Japan* (Allen & Unwin, 1954), pp. 107–8.
82. Pelcovits, *Old China Hands*, p. 158–60.
83. Cited D. McLean, 'Commerce, finance, and British diplomatic support in China, 1885–6', *Economic History Review*, 2nd series, **26** (1973), 469.
84. Ibid., 468.
85. Ibid., 469.
86. Fairbank in Fairbank (ed.), *Cambridge History of China*, vol. 10, Pt 1, p. 263.
87. J. K. Fairbank, K. F. Bruner, E. M. Matheson (eds.), *The I.G. In Peking : Letters of Robert Hart, Chinese Maritime Customs, 1868–1907*, 2 vols. (Belknap Press, Harvard U.P., Cambridge, Mass., 1975) vol. 1, pp. 192–3, 205–06.
88. Ibid., vol. 1, pp. 692–3.
89. Ibid., vol. 1, p. 84n.
90. Cited ibid., vol. 1, pp. 120–1.
91. Ibid., vol. 1, pp. 593, 603, 604.
92. P. A. Cohen, *China and Christianity : the Missionary Movement and the Growth of Chinese Antiforeignism, 1860–1870* (Harvard U.P., Cambridge, Mass., 1963), pp. 272–3. For the wider background of Christian activities in China, see K. S. Latourette, *A History of Christian Missions in China* (Society for the Promotion of Christian Knowledge, 1929).
93. See the illuminating chapter by P. A. Cohen, 'Christian missions and their impact to 1900', in Fairbank (ed.), *Cambridge History of China*, vol. 10, Pt 1, pp. 543–90.
94. Cohen in Fairbank (ed.), *Cambridge History of China*, vol. 10, Pt 1, pp. 554–55.
95. Cohen, *China and Christianity*, p. 78.
96. Cited ibid., pp. 78–9.
97. Cohen in Fairbank (ed.), *Cambridge History of China*, vol. 10, Pt 1, p. 555.
98. Ibid., vol. 10, Pt 1, p. 565.
99. Cohen, *China and Christianity*, pp. 45–9.
100. Cited ibid., p. 194.
101. See D. Steeds and I. Nish, *China, Japan, and 19th Century Britain : Commentaries on British Parliamentary Papers* (Irish Academic Press, Dublin, 1977), p. 40.
102. Ibid., pp. 40–1.

103. E. Hornby, *Sir Edmund Hornby : an Autobiography* (Cassell, 1928), pp. 249–50, as cited in Steeds and Nish, *China, Japan, and 19th Century Britain*, p. 41.
104. Steeds and Nish, *China, Japan and 19th Century Britain*, p. 41.
105. Ibid., pp. 43–4.
106. For two thorough surveys of economic developments in Japan, see G. C. Allen, *A Short Economic History of Japan*, 2nd edn (Allen & Unwin, 1962) and W. W. Lockwood, *The Economic Development of Japan* (Princeton U.P., Princeton, N. J., 1970).
107. For the situation in the tumultuous 1870s, see G. B. Sansom, *The Western World and Japan* (Cresset Press, 1950), pp. 310–489. See also J. Hirschmeier, *The Origins of Entrepreneurship in Meiji Japan* (Harvard U.P., Cambridge, Mass., 1964) and K. Yamamura, *A Study of Samurai Income and Entrepreneurship* (Harvard U.P., Cambridge, Mass., 1974).
108. For a valuable assessment of Saigo Takamori, see I. Morris, *The Nobility of Failure : Tragic Heroes in the History of Japan* (Secker & Warburg, 1975), pp. 217–75.
109. For political developments, see R. M. Scalapino, *Democracy and the Party Movement in Prewar Japan* (University of California Press, Berkeley, 1953) and G. Akita, *The Foundations of Constitutional Government in Modern Japan 1868–1900* (Harvard U.P., Cambridge, Mass., 1967).
110. For a discussion of the Japanese army, see R. F. Hackett, *Yamagata Aritomo in the Rise of Modern Japan, 1838–1922* (Harvard U.P., Cambridge, Mass., 1971). For the early British impact on the Japanese navy, see G. Fox, *Britain and Japan, 1858–1883* (Clarendon Press, Oxford, 1969), pp. 250–73.
111. See G. Daniels, 'Sir Harry Parkes : British Representative in Japan, 1865–1883' (unpublished D.Phil. thesis, Oxford, 1967), p. 192.
112. Ibid., p. 374.
113. Steeds and Nish, *China, Japan, and 19th Century Britain*, p. 50.
114. Cited I. Nish, *Japan's Foreign Policy, 1869–1942* (Routledge & Kegan Paul, 1977), p. 12.
115. For a succinct discussion of the background in Japanese government in the early 1870s, see Nish, *Japan's Foreign Policy*, pp. 12–25.
116. Nish, *Japan's Foreign Policy*, p. 30.
117. Ibid., p. 33.
118. Cited ibid., p. 271.
119. Ibid., p. 48.
120. Ibid., p. 17.
121. Ibid., p. 34.
122. See J. Ch'en, *Yuan Shih-k'ai, 1859–1916*, 2nd edn (Stanford U.P., Stanford, 1972), pp. 8–28.
123. Nish, *Japan's Foreign Policy*, p. 38.
124. See Chapter 6 below.
125. See Fox, *Britain and Japan*, pp. 537–8.
126. Ibid., pp. 314–16. On the Blue Funnel line, see F. Hyde and J. R. Harris, *Blue Funnel : a History of Alfred Holt and Company of Liverpool, 1865–1914* (Liverpool U.P., Liverpool, 1957).
127. Fox, *Britain and Japan*, pp. 316–17. For an illuminating account of life in the treaty ports, see J. E. Hoare, 'The Japanese treaty ports, 1868–1899 : a study of the foreign settlements' (unpublished Ph.D. thesis, London, 1971).
128. Fox, *Britain and Japan*, p. 326.

129. Ibid., pp. 328–9. See also Allen and Donnithorne, *Western Enterprise in Far Eastern Economic Development*, p. 35.
130. Fox, *Britain and Japan*, pp. 330, 334.
131. Ibid., p. 333.
132. Ibid., p. 341.
133. Ibid., p. 345.
134. Ibid., pp. 353–4.
135. Ibid., pp. 358–9.
136. Ibid., p. 363.
137. Ibid., p. 366.
138. Ibid., p. 366.
139. Ibid., pp. 368–9.

Chapter 4

1. See J. A. S. Grenville, *Lord Salisbury and Foreign Policy* (Athlone Press, 1964), pp. 127–47 for a discussion of the evolution of British policy. For Chamberlain's attitude, see J. L. Garvin and J. Amery, *Life of Joseph Chamberlain* (Macmillan, 1934), vol. 3, pp. 241–346.
2. For the views within the China Association, see N. A. Pelcovits, *Old China Hands and the Foreign Office* (Octagon Books, New York, 1969), pp. 216–17, 235, 264–8.
3. Cited L. K. Young, *British Policy in China, 1895–1902* (Oxford U.P., 1970), p. 66.
4. Cited ibid., p. 70.
5. Ibid., pp. 77–9.
6. W. R. Braisted, 'The United States and the American China Development Company', *Far Eastern Quarterly*, **11** (1952), 147–65.
7. *The Times*, 31 May 1898, cited in Young, *British Policy in China*, p. 82.
8. Young, *British Policy in China*, p. 85.
9. Ibid., p. 85.
10. Ibid., pp. 88–9.
11. Ibid., p. 90.
12. Ibid., p. 91.
13. Ibid., p. 95.
14. Ibid., pp. 96–7.
15. For the ideas of K'ang Yu-wei, see I.C.Y. Hsu, *The Rise of Modern China* (Oxford U.P., 1970), pp. 430–54 and S. Y. Teng and J. K. Fairbank, *China's Response to the West : a Documentary Survey, 1839–1923* (Harvard U.P., Cambridge, Mass., 1961), pp. 147–64. See also M. E. Cameron, *The Reform Movement in China, 1898–1912* (Stanford U.P., Stanford, 1931).
16. Young, *British Policy in China*, pp. 108–09. For a concise survey of the Boxer movement, see V. Purcell, *The Boxer Uprising* (Cambridge U.P., Cambridge, 1963).
17. Young, *British Policy in China*, pp. 109–10.
18. J. K. Fairbank, K. F. Bruner, and E. M. Matheson (eds.), *The I.G. in Peking : Letters of Robert Hart, Chinese Maritime Customs*, 2 vols. (Belknap Press, Harvard U.P., Cambridge, Mass., 1975), vol. 2, pp. 1214–15.
19. Young, *British Policy in China*, p. 117.

20. Ibid., p. 119.
21. Cited ibid., p. 120.
22. Ibid., p. 128.
23. Cited ibid., p. 133.
24. Ibid., p. 133.
25. Ibid., p. 137.
26. Ibid., p. 154.
27. Ibid., pp. 157–8.
28. Cited Fairbank *et al, The I.G. in Peking*, vol. 2, p. 1235.
29. Cited Young, *British Policy in China*, p. 194.
30. Ibid., p. 194.
31. Ibid., p. 205.
32. Cited ibid., p. 219.
33. Cited ibid., p. 241.
34. M. C. Wright (ed.), *China in Revolution : the First Phase, 1900–1913* (Yale U.P., New Haven, 1968), pp. 1–3.
35. I. H. Nish, *The Anglo–Japanese Alliance : the Diplomacy of Two Island Empires* (Athlone Press, 1966), p. 124.
36. Ibid., p. 216.
37. Ibid., p. 131.
38. Cited ibid., pp. 156–7.
39. Ibid., pp. 158–9.
40. Ibid., p. 163.
41. For a full discussion of developments in Japan, see ibid., pp. 163–74.
42. Nish, *The Anglo–Japanese Alliance*, pp. 181–2.
43. Ibid., p. 186.
44. Ibid., p. 189.
45. Ibid., pp. 195–6.
46. Ibid., pp. 204–10.
47. Cited ibid., p. 216.
48. Ibid., p. 263.
49. Cited ibid., p. 265.
50. Ibid., p. 267.
51. Cited ibid., p. 274.
52. Ibid., pp. 279–80.
53. For a succinct discussion of the issues involved, see E. W Edwards, 'The Japanese alliance and the Anglo–French agreements of 1904', *History*, **42** (1957), 19–27.
54. Nish, *The Anglo–Japanese Alliance*, p. 291.
55. For a short account of the war, see D. Walder, *The Short Victorious War* (Readers Union, Newton Abbot, 1973). See also J. A. White, *The Diplomacy of the Russo–Japanese War* (Princeton U.P., Princeton, N. J., 1964) and S. Okamoto, *The Japanese Oligarchy and the Russo–Japanese War* (Columbia U.P., New York, 1970).
56. Cited Nish, *The Anglo–Japanese Alliance*, p. 294.
57. Ibid., pp. 295–6.
58. This theme is explored in Okamoto, *The Japanese Oligarchy and the Russo–Japanese War*. For the relationship between the *genro* and the government in this period, see T. Najita, *Hara Kei in the Politics of Compromise, 1905–1915* (Harvard U.P., Cambridge, Mass., 1967).
59. Cited Nish, *The Anglo–Japanese Alliance*, p. 299.
60. Ibid., pp. 299–300.

61. Cited ibid., p. 301.
62. Ibid., p. 303.
63. Ibid., p. 304.
64. Ibid., p. 310.
65. Cited ibid., pp. 331–2.

Chapter 5

1. See I. H. Nish, *Alliance in Decline : a Study in Anglo–Japanese Relations, 1908–1923* (Athlen Press, 1972), p. 30. See also E. W. Edwards, 'Great Britain and the Manchurian railway question, 1909–10', *English Historical Review*, **81** (1966), 740–69.
2. Nish, *Alliance in Decline*, pp. 22–7 and R. Storry, *Japan and the Decline of the West in Asia, 1894–1943* (Macmillan, 1979), pp. 87–9.
3. See E. W. Edwards, 'The far eastern agreements of 1907', *Journal of Modern History*, **26** (1954), 340–55 and Edwards, *English Historical Review*, **81**, 740—69.
4. I. H. Nish, *The Anglo–Japanese Alliance : the Diplomacy of Two Island Empires, 1894–1907* (Athlone Press, 1966), p. 359.
5. Nish, *Alliance in Decline*, p. 19.
6. Ibid., pp. 19–22.
7. Ibid., pp. 31–2.
8. See P. Lowe, *Great Britain and Japan, 1911–15 : a Study of British Far Eastern Policy* (Macmillan, 1969), pp. 18–19.
9. Ibid., p. 21.
10. Ibid., p. 19.
11. Ibid., pp. 20–1.
12. Ibid., pp. 40–2.
13. Cited ibid., p. 42.
14. Ibid., pp. 44–5.
15. Ibid., pp. 274–5.
16. Ibid., p. 47.
17. For two valuable studies of Yuan Shih-k'ai, see J. Ch'en, *Yuan Shih-k'ai, 1859–1916*, 2nd edn, (Stanford U.P., Stanford, 1972) and E. P. Young, *The Presidency of Yuan Shih-k'ai : Liberalism and Dictatorship in Early Republican China* (University of Michigan Press, Ann Arbor, 1977).
18. For a wide-ranging assessment of the changes in Chinese society in this period, see M. C. Wright (ed.), *China in Revolution : the First Phase, 1900–1913* (Yale U.P., New Haven, 1968). See also J. Gray (ed.), *Modern China's Search for a Political Form* (Oxford U.P., 1969).
19. Cited Lowe, *Great Britain and Japan*, p. 61.
20. See Young, *The Presidency of Yuan Shih-k'ai*, pp. 27–49.
21. Lowe, *Great Britain and Japan*, p. 68.
22. For this aspect, see M. B. Jansen, *The Japanese and Sun Yat-sen* (Harvard U.P., Cambridge, Mass., 1954).
23. See M. Ikei, 'Japan's response to the Chinese revolution of 1911', *Journal of Asian Studies*, **25** (1966), 213–27.
24. Lowe, *Great Britain and Japan*, p. 66.
25. For studies of Sun Yat-sen, see H. Z. Schiffrin, *Sun Yat-sen and the Origins of the Chinese Revolution* (University of California Press, Berkeley, 1968),

and M. Wilbur, *Sun Yat-sen : Frustrated Patriot* (Columbia U.P., New York, 1976).

26. Cited Lowe, *Great Britain and Japan*, p. 69.
27. Cited ibid., pp. 71–2.
28. Ibid., pp. 71–2.
29. Ikei, *Journal of Asian Studies*, **25**, 222–3.
30. Cited Lowe, *Great Britain and Japan*, p. 78.
31. Ibid., p. 124.
32. See ibid., pp. 132, 141–2.
33. *The Economist*, 28 September 1912, cited Lowe, *Great Britain and Japan*, p. 137, n. 3.
34. Cited Lowe, *Great Britain and Japan*, p. 143 n.
35. See Young, *The Presidency of Yuan Shih-k'ai*, pp. 50–137.
36. Lowe, *Great Britain and Japan*, pp. 90–1.
37. Ibid., p. 93.
38. Young, *The Presidency of Yuan Shih-k'ai*, pp. 117–18.
39. See Jansen, *The Japanese and Sun Yat-sen*, pp. 161–2.
40. Lowe, *Great Britain and Japan*, p. 96.
41. Ibid., p. 103.
42. Cited ibid., p. 104.
43. Cited ibid., p. 105.
44. Ibid., p. 106.
45. Ibid., p. 107.
46. Ibid., p. 108.
47. Cited ibid., pp. 107–08.
48. Ibid., pp. 112–13.
49. Ibid., p. 113.
50. See Jansen, *The Japanese and Sun Yat-sen*, Ch. 4 and I. H. Nish, 'Japan's indecision during the Boxer disturbance', *Journal of Asian Studies*, **21** (1961), 449–61.
51. Lowe, *Great Britain and Japan*, p. 150.
52. Ibid., pp. 152–3.
53. Ibid., p. 155.
54. Cited ibid., p. 156.
55. Ibid., p. 156.
56. Ibid., p. 157.
57. Cited ibid., p. 158.
58. Ibid., p. 159.
59. Ibid., p. 159 n.3.
60. Ibid., pp. 160–1.
61. Ibid., p. 161.
62. Cited ibid., pp. 161–2.
63. *The Times*, 4 May 1914, cited in Lowe, *Great Britain and Japan*, p. 162.
64. Cited Lowe, *Great Britain and Japan*, p. 163.
65. Ibid., p. 164.
66. For the views of Sir John Jordan, see Lowe, *Great Britain and Japan*, p. 165.
67. Cited Lowe, *Great Britain and Japan*, p. 166.
68. The naval scandals erupted when information was taken from the files of the German firm of Siemens-Schukert and released to the press. This showed that lucrative bribes had been accepted by high Japanese naval officers in

return for ordering the firm's products. The British firm of Vickers was also rumoured to be involved. The resulting furore in Tokyo brought about the government's downfall; the position was delicate for the government, since the prime minister was an admiral.

69. For an assessment of Kato's influence see I. H. Nish, *Japan's Foreign Policy, 1869–1942* (Routledge & Kegan Paul, 1977), pp. 83–104.
70. Lowe, *Great Britain and Japan*, p. 171.
71. Ibid., p. 172.
72. Ibid., p. 173.

Chapter 6

1. See P. Lowe, *Great Britain and Japan, 1911–15* (Macmillan, 1969), p. 180.
2. Ibid., p. 180.
3. Cited ibid., pp. 181–2.
4. See C. N. Spinks, 'Japan's entrance into the World War', *Pacific Historical Review*, 5 (1936), 304–5 and I. H. Nish, *Japanese Foreign Policy, 1869–1942* (Routledge & Kegan Paul, 1977), pp. 93–6.
5. Lowe, *Great Britain and Japan*, p. 185.
6. Cited ibid., pp. 185–6.
7. Cited ibid., p. 187.
8. Cited ibid., pp. 188–9.
9. Ibid., pp. 190–1.
10. Cited ibid., p. 191.
11. Ibid., p. 198.
12. See ibid., pp. 203–04.
13. Cited ibid., p. 204.
14. Ibid., p. 206. See also W. R. Louis, *Great Britain and Germany's Lost Colonies, 1914–1919* (Clarendon Press, Oxford, 1967).
15. For a reassessment of Coronel, see J. Sweetman, 'Coronel : anatomy of a disaster', in G. Jordan (ed.), *Naval Warfare in the Twentieth Century* (Croom Helm, 1977), pp. 70–89.
16. For a discussion of the origins of the demands, see Lowe, *Great Britain and Japan*, pp. 220–8. See also Nish, *Japanese Foreign Policy*, pp. 96–104.
17. Lowe, *Great Britain and Japan*, pp. 221–2.
18. Cited P. S. Dull, 'Count Kato Komei and the twenty-one demands', *Pacific Historical Review*, 19 (1950), 156.
19. See M. B. Jansen, *The Japanese and Sun Yat-sen* (Harvard U.P., Cambridge, Mass., 1954), pp. 180–2 for discussion of the role of the *Kokuryukai*.
20. Cited Lowe, *Great Britain and Japan*, p. 229.
21. Ibid., p. 230.
22. Ibid., p. 232.
23. Ibid., p. 234.
24. Ibid., pp. 240–1.
25. Ibid., pp. 242–3.
26. Cited ibid., p. 243.
27. Cited ibid., p. 245.
28. Ibid., p. 247.

29. Ibid., p. 249.
30. See A. S. Link, *Wilson : the Struggle for Neutrality, 1914–1915* (Princeton U.P., Princeton, N. J., 1960), pp. 306–08.
31. See E. P. Young, *The Presidency of Yuan Shih-k'ai* (University of Michigan Press, Ann Arbor, 1977), pp. 210–40, and M. Chi, *China Diplomacy, 1914–1918* (Harvard U.P., Cambridge, Mass., 1970), pp. 62–84.
32. See P. Lowe, 'Great Britain, Japan, and the fall of Yuan Shih-k'ai, 1915–1916', *Historical Journal*, **13** (1970), 706–20.
33. Chi, *China Diplomacy*, p. 76.
34. For a succinct assessment, see J. E. Sheridan, *Chinese Warlord : Feng Yu-hsiang* (Stanford U.P., Stanford, 1966), pp. 1–30. See also D. G. Gillin, *Warlord : Yen Hsi-shan in Shansi province, 1911–1949* (Princeton U.P., Princeton, N. J., 1967) and L. W. Pye, *Warlord Politics : Conflict and Coalition in the Modernisation of Republican China* (Praeger, New York, 1971).
35. Chi, *China Diplomacy*, p. 115.
36. Ibid., p. 116.
37. Ibid., p. 117.
38. Ibid., p. 118.
39. Ibid., pp. 122–3.
40. Ibid., p. 124.
41. Ibid., p. 126.
42. Cited ibid., p. 128.
43. Cited ibid., p. 130.
44. Cited ibid., p. 130.
45. See I. H. Nish, *Alliance in Decline : Anglo–Japanese Relations, 1908–1923* (Athlone Press, 1972), p. 178.
46. See F. W. Ikle, 'Japanese-German peace negotiations during World War I', *American Historical Review*, **71** (1965), 62–76, and F. Fischer, *Germany's Aims in the First World War* (Chatto & Windus, 1967), pp. 228–36.
47. Cited Lowe, *Great Britain and Japan*, p. 308.
48. Nish, *Alliance in Decline*, p. 203.
49. Ibid., p. 203.
50. Ibid., pp. 204–05.
51. Ibid., p. 206.
52. Ibid., pp. 206–07.
53. Ibid., p. 207.
54. Cited ibid., p. 208.
55. Ibid., p. 226.
56. Ibid., pp. 227–8.
57. On the complexities of the situation in Russia with particular reference to the role of the allied powers, see J. W. Morley, *The Japanese Thrust into Siberia, 1918* (Columbia U.P., New York, 1957), and R. H. Ullman, *Anglo–Soviet Relations, 1917–1921*, 3 vols. (Princeton U.P., Princeton, N.J., 1961–72).
58. Nish, *Alliance in Decline*, p. 238.
59. Cited Lowe, *Great Britain and Japan*, p. 187 n. 2.
60. Cited Nish, *Alliance in Decline*, p. 239.
61. Nish, *Alliance in Decline*, p. 239.
62. Ibid., p. 240.
63. Ibid., p. 240.
64. See C. J. Christie, 'The problem of China in British foreign policy, 1917–

1921' (unpublished Ph.D. thesis, Cambridge, 1971), p. 124. For a discussion of the activities of Semenov and other White Russians in Manchuria, see J. J. Stephan, *The Russian Fascists* (Hamish Hamilton, 1978).
65. Nish, *Alliance in Decline*, p. 249.
66. Ibid., p. 250.
67. Ibid., p. 250.
68. For Churchill's frequently extreme views on intervention, see M. Gilbert, *Winston Churchill* (Heinemann, 1975), vol. 4, pp. 219–442.
69. Christie, 'The problem of China', p. 128.
70. See Ullman, *Anglo–Soviet Relations* 3 : *The Anglo–Soviet Accord* (Princeton U.P., Princeton, N.J., 1972), pp. 397–473.

Chapter 7

1. See C. J. Christie, 'The problem of China in British foreign policy, 1917–1921' (unpublished Ph.D. thesis, Cambridge, 1971), p. 225.
2. Christie, 'The problem of China', p. 230.
3. Christie, 'The problem of China', p. 231.
4. I. H. Nish, *Alliance in Decline : Anglo–Japanese Relations, 1908–1923* (Athlone Press, 1972), p. 268.
5. See W. R. Louis, 'Australia and the German colonies in the Pacific, 1914–1919', *Journal of Modern History*, **38** (1966), 407–21.
6. Nish, *Alliance in Decline*, p. 271.
7. Ibid., p. 272.
8. Ibid., p. 272.
9. Cited ibid., p. 273.
10. Ibid., p. 273.
11. Cited ibid., p. 274.
12. Cited ibid., p. 274.
13. Ibid., p. 275.
14. For a general account of developments in China in 1919, see Chow-tse Tung, *The May Fourth Movement* (Harvard U.P., Cambridge, Mass., 1960).
15. For a full analysis of developments between 1919 and 1921, see Nish, *Alliance in Decline*, Ch. 16–22.
16. See ibid., pp. 310–11.
17. Cited ibid., p. 312.
18. Ibid., pp. 328–9.
19. Cited P. Lowe, *Great Britain and Japan, 1911–15* (Macmillan, 1969), p. 310 n.
20. Nish, *Alliance in Decline*, p. 330.
21. Ibid., p. 331.
22. Cited ibid., p. 333.
23. Cited Lowe, *Great Britain and Japan*, p. 294.
24. Cited ibid., p. 295.
25. Cited ibid., p. 295.
26. Cited ibid., p. 295.
27. Cited ibid., pp. 295–6.
28. Ibid., p. 296. For a discussion of Japanese interest in India, see D. K. Dignan, 'The Hindu conspiracy in Anglo–American relations during World War I', *Pacific Historical Review*, **40** (1971), 57–76, and T. G. Fraser, 'India in

Anglo–Japanese relations during the First World War', *History*, **63** (1978), 366–82.

29. Cited Lowe, *Great Britain and Japan*, p. 296.
30. Ibid., pp. 296–7.
31. See Nish, *Alliance in Decline*, pp. 345–9, for an illuminating summary of the misunderstandings and suspicions that marred Anglo–Japanese relations in the summer of 1921.
32. Nish, *Alliance in Decline*, p. 356.
33. Ibid., p. 364.
34. Ibid., p. 359–61.
35. Ibid., pp. 369–70.
36. Ibid., p. 373.
37. Ibid., pp. 375–7.
38. W. R. Louis, *British Strategy in the Far East, 1919–1939* (Clarendon Press, Oxford, 1971), p. 99. For a thorough discussion of naval issues, see S. Roskill, *Naval Policy between the Wars* (Collins, 1968), vol. 1.
39. Louis, *British Strategy*, p. 99.
40. On this aspect, see two excellent essays by S. Asada, 'The Japanese navy and the United States', in D. Borg and S. Okamoto (eds.), *Pearl Harbor as History : Japanese–American Relations, 1931–41* (Columbia U.P., New York, 1973), pp. 225–59, and 'Japanese admirals and the politics of naval limitation : Kato Tomosaburo vs Kato Kanji', in G. Jordan (ed.), *Naval Warfare in the Twentieth Century* (Croom Helm, 1977), pp. 141–66.
41. Cited Louis, *British Strategy*, p. 105.
42. For an admirable account of the development of the Singapore base, see I. Hamill, 'The strategic illusion : the Singapore strategy and the defence of Australia and New Zealand, 1919–1942' (unpublished Ph.D. thesis, Leeds, 1975). See also W. D. McIntyre, *The Rise and Fall of the Singapore Naval Base* (Macmillan, 1979).
43. For the attitude of the Labour governments towards the Far East, see D. Marquand, *Ramsay MacDonald* (Cape, 1977), pp. 315–17, 332; and D. Carlton, *MacDonald versus Henderson* (Macmillan, 1970), pp. 174–84.
44. See Roskill, *Naval Policy*, vol. 1, pp. 300–30.
45. See Asada in Jordan (ed.), *Naval Warfare*, pp. 141–66.
46. For further discussion of defence issues, see Ch. 8–10 below. For a valuable overall assessment of Britain's dilemma in defence, see N. H. Gibbs, *Grand Strategy* (HMSO, 1976), vol. 1.
47. For the policies of the Comintern and of the Chinese communists, see S. Schram and H. Carrere d'Encausse, *Marxism and Asia* (Allen Lane, 1969), J. Guillermaz, *History of the Chinese Communist Party 1921–1949* (Methuen, 1968), S. Schram, *Mao Tse-tung* (Penguin, Harmondsworth, 1970), and R. C. Thornton, *China : The Struggle for Power, 1917–1972* (Indiana U.P., Bloomington, 1973).
48. For a discussion of the Kuomintang in the 1920s, see P. Cavendish, 'The new China of the Kuomintang', in J. Gray (ed.), *Modern China's Search for a Political Form* (Oxford U.P., 1969), pp. 138–86.
49. Louis, *British Strategy*, pp. 124–5.
50. Cited ibid., p. 125.
51. Cited ibid., p. 125.
52. Ibid., p. 127.
53. *Morning Post*, 18 January 1926, cited in Louis, *British Strategy*, p. 128.

54. Cited Louis, *British Strategy*, p. 130.
55. Ibid., p. 131. See also H. Kane, 'Sir Miles Lampson at the Peking legation, 1926–1933' (unpublished Ph.D. thesis, London, 1973).
56. Cited Louis, *British Strategy*, pp. 131–2.
57. Cited ibid., p. 132.
58. Cited ibid., pp. 144–5.
59. Ibid., pp. 147–8.
60. Ibid., p. 151.
61. Ibid., p. 152.
62. Cited ibid., p. 153.
63. Cited ibid., p. 156. For Lampson's views, see Kane, 'Sir Miles Lampson', pp. 30–68.
64. Louis, *British Strategy*, p. 157.
65. Cited ibid., p. 158.
66. Cited ibid., p. 161.
67. Ibid., p. 166.
68. C. F. Remer, *Foreign Investments in China* (Macmillan, New York, 1933), pp. 352–3.
69. Ibid., pp. 363–4.
70. Ibid., p. 395.
71. Ibid., p. 372.
72. Ibid., p. 365.
73. Ibid., p. 365.
74. E. M. Gull, *British Economic Interests in the Far East* (Oxford U.P., 1943), p. 110.
75. Ibid., p. 113.
76. Remer, *Foreign Investments*, p. 365.
77. I. H. Nish, *Japanese Foreign Policy, 1869–1942* (Routledge & Kegan Paul), p. 167. For a concise account of the British attitude towards the London conference, see S. Roskill, *Naval Policy between the Wars* (Collins, 1976), vol. 2, pp. 37–70.
78. Nish, *Japanese Foreign Policy*, p. 168.
79. Ibid., pp. 169–72.
80. Marquand, *Ramsay MacDonald*, pp. 502–4, 506–8.
81. Roskill, *Naval Policy*, vol. 2, pp. 62–70, and Marquand, *Ramsay MacDonald*, pp. 509–17.

Chapter 8

1. For two comprehensive accounts of the origins and consequences of the Mukden incident, see S. N. Ogata, *Defiance in Manchuria* (University of California Press, Berkeley, 1964) and T. Yoshihashi, *Conspiracy at Mukden* (Yale U.P., New Haven, 1963).
2. See A. J. P. Taylor, *The Second World War* (Hamish Hamilton, 1975), p. 11.
3. For a lucid discussion of Shidehara diplomacy, see I. H. Nish, *Japanese Foreign Policy, 1869–1942* (Routledge & Kegan Paul, 1977), pp. 126–80.
4. For a cogent assessment of Chang Tso-lin and his relationship with the Japanese, see G. McCormack, *Chang Tso-lin in Northeast China, 1911–1928 : China, Japan, and the Manchurian Idea* (Dawson, Folkestone, 1977).

5. One of the clearest accounts of the tangled situation in Manchuria is to be found in the report of the Lytton Commission, *Appeal by the Chinese Government : Report of the Commission of Enquiry* (League of Nations, Geneva, 1932).

6. For two valuable analyses of Japanese nationalism, see T. R. H. Havens, *Farm and Nation in Modern Japan : Agrarian Nationalism, 1870–1940*, (Princeton U.P., Princeton, N.J., 1974), and R. J. Smethurst, *A Social Basis for Prewar Japanese Militarism : the Army and the Rural Community* (University of California Press, Berkeley, 1974).

7. For an excellent discussion of the psychology of militant nationalism in Japan in the 1930s, see R. Storry, *The Double Patriots* (Chatto & Windus, 1957).

8. For an admirable examination of the Manchurian crisis in all respects, see C. Thorne, *The Limits of Foreign Policy : the West, the League, and the Far Eastern Crisis of 1931–1933* (Hamish Hamilton, 1972).

9. *Documents on British Foreign Policy, 1919–1939*, hereafter cited as *D.B.F.P.*, 2nd series, **8**, no. 587.

10. Thorne, *Limits of Foreign Policy*, p. 150.

11. For a discussion of Stimson's policy, see A. Rappaport, *Henry L. Stimson and Japan, 1931–33* (Chicago U.P., Chicago, 1963).

12. Cited Thorne, *Limits of Foreign Policy*, p. 151.

13. Cited ibid., p. 152.

14. For a full discussion of the difficulties facing the navy, see P. Haggie, 'The Royal Navy and the far eastern problem, 1931–1941' (unpublished Ph.D. thesis, Manchester, 1974).

15. For an evaluation of foreign policy under Simon, see C. J. Hill, 'British foreign policy, 1931–1935' (unpublished Ph.D. thesis, Manchester, 1976).

16. Thorne, *Limits of Foreign Policy*, p. 187.

17. Ibid., pp. 210–11.

18. See *D.B.F.P.* 2nd series, **9**, no. 61.

19. On the past contacts between Inukai and Sun, see M. B. Jansen, *The Japanese and Sun Yat-sen* (Harvard U.P., Cambridge, Mass., 1954).

20. Cited Thorne, *Limits of Foreign Policy*, p. 206.

21. Ibid., p. 208.

22. *D.B.F.P.* 2nd series, **9**, no. 238.

23. Ibid., 2nd series, **9**, no. 238.

24. Ibid., 2nd series, **9**, no. 636.

25. Cited Thorne, *Limits of Foreign Policy*, p. 242.

26. Ibid., p. 242.

27. *Foreign Relations of the United States*, Japan, 1931–1941, 2 vols. (Government Printing Office, Washington, 1943), **1**, 83–7.

28. Thorne, *Limits of Foreign Policy*, pp. 255–8.

29. Cited ibid., p. 261.

30. Ibid., p. 252, n. 2.

31. For the conclusions and recommendations of the Lytton Commission, see *Appeal by the Chinese Government*, Chs. 9 and 10.

32. I am grateful to Dr Ian Nish for kindly allowing me to read an unpublished paper examining Matsuoka's attitude towards the League of Nations in 1932–33. This shows that Matsuoka was less hostile towards the League than most previous writers have assumed and that he viewed withdrawal from the League with considerable reluctance.

33. Thorne, *Limits of Foreign Policy*, p. 333.

34. See *D.B.F.P.*, 2nd series, **11**, no. 91.
35. Thorne, *Limits of Foreign Policy*, pp. 333–4.
36. Unpublished paper on Matsuoka by Dr Nish.
37. There is no satisfactory biography of Neville Chamberlain at present; Professor David Dilks is preparing an important new study. See K. Feiling, *Neville Chamberlain* (Macmillan, 1946), which is of some use for the extracts from Chamberlain's letters and diaries.
38. A. Trotter, *Britain and East Asia, 1933–1937* (Cambridge U.P., Cambridge, 1975), p. 36.
39. Ibid., p. 37.
40. Cited ibid., p. 40.
41. Ibid., pp. 42–3.
42. Ibid., pp. 43–4.
43. Ibid., pp. 48–9.
44. See S. Asada, 'Japanese admirals and the politics of naval limitation : Kato Tomosaburo vs Kato Kanji', in G. Jordan (ed.), *Naval Warfare in the Twentieth Century* (Croom Helm, 1977), pp. 141–66. See also S. Pelz, *Race to Pearl Harbor : the Failure of the Second London Naval Conference and the Onset of World War II* (Harvard U.P., Cambridge, Mass., 1974).
45. Cited Trotter, *Britain and East Asia*, p. 54.
46. Ibid., p. 56.
47. Ibid., p. 57.
48. Ibid., p. 57.
49. Cited ibid., p. 73.
50. Ibid., p. 73.
51. Ibid., p. 73.
52. For an extremely thorough analysis of defence issues in the 1930s, see N. H. Gibbs, *Grand Strategy* (HMSO, 1976), vol. 1.
53. For an admirable study of Hankey, see S. Roskill, *Hankey : Man of Secrets* (Collins, 1974), vol. 3.
54. Cited Trotter, *Britain and East Asia*, p. 96.
55. Ibid., p. 91.
56. Ibid., p. 92.
57. Ibid., p. 99.
58. Ibid., p. 100.
59. Ibid., pp. 103–04.
60. Ibid., p. 110.
61. Ibid., p. 110.
62. Cited ibid., p. 147.
63. Ibid., p. 148. On the Leith Ross mission, see S. L. Endicott, *Diplomacy and Enterprise : British China Policy, 1933–1937* (Manchester U.P., Manchester, 1975), pp. 102–49.
64. Trotter, *Britain and East Asia*, p. 150. For a study of Hoare, see J. A. Cross, *Sir Samuel Hoare* (Cape, 1977).
65. Trotter, *Britain and East Asia*, p. 151.
66. Ibid., p. 152.
67. Ibid., p. 154.
68. Ibid., p. 155.
69. Ibid., p. 156.
70. Ibid., p. 157.
71. Ibid., p. 159.
72. Ibid., pp. 159–61.

73. Ibid., p. 163.
74. For a discussion of Japanese policy, see J. B. Crowley, *Japan's Quest for Autonomy in East Asia* (Princeton U.P., Princeton, N.J., 1966), pp. 187–300.
75. Cited Trotter, *Britain and East Asia*, p. 166.
76. Cited ibid., p. 167.
77. Ibid., pp. 180–1.
78. Ibid., pp. 192–3.
79. D. G. E. Hall, *A History of South-East Asia*, 3rd edn (Macmillan, 1968), pp. 730–1. For a thorough discussion of British policy in Burma, see F. S. V. Donnison, *Public Administration in Burma* (Oxford U.P., 1953). See also J. F. Cady, *A History of Modern Burma* (Cornell U.P., Ithaca, 1958).
80. Hall, *History of South-East Asia*, p. 740.
81. Ibid., p. 741.
82. Ibid., p. 744.
83. J. Kennedy, *A History of Malaya, A.D. 1400–1959* (Macmillan, 1962), pp. 236–8. See also J. G. Butcher, *The British in Malaya, 1880–1941: the Social History of a European Community in Colonial South-East Asia* (Oxford U.P., Kuala Lumpur, 1979).
84. Ibid., p. 239.
85. Ibid., pp. 241–2.
86. Ibid., p. 242.
87. E. M. Gull, *British Economic Interests in the Far East* (Oxford U.P., 1943), p. 128.
88. Ibid., p. 128.
89. Ibid., p. 128.
90. Ibid., p. 128.
91. Ibid., p. 128.

Chapter 9

1. For a discussion of the outbreak of the Undeclared war, see J. B. Crowley, *Japan's Quest for Autonomy in East Asia* (Princeton U.P., Princeton, N.J., 1966), pp. 301–78, and I. H. Nish, *Japanese Foreign Policy, 1869–1942* (Routledge & Kegan Paul, 1977), pp. 209–27.
2. Cited P. Lowe, *Great Britain and the Origins of the Pacific War : a Study of British Policy in East Asia, 1937–1941* (Clarendon Press, Oxford, 1977), p. 17.
3. Cited ibid., p. 18.
4. Ibid., p. 21.
5. See B. A. Lee, *Britain and the Sino-Japanese War, 1937–1939* (Oxford U.P., 1973), pp. 40–2.
6. Lowe, *Great Britain and Origins of Pacific War*, p. 23.
7. For a discussion of Roosevelt's speech, see D. M. Borg, *The United States and the Far Eastern Crisis of 1933–1938* (Harvard U.P., Cambridge, Mass., 1964), pp. 369–98. See also R. A. Dallek, *Franklin D. Roosevelt and American Foreign Policy, 1932–1945* (Oxford U.P., 1979), pp. 144–56.
8. Cited Lowe, *Great Britain and Origins of Pacific War*, p. 31.
9. For an assessment of Roosevelt's ideas, see J. McV. Haight Jr., 'Franklin D. Roosevelt and a naval quarantine of Japan', *Pacific Historical Review*, **40**

(1971), 203–26, and L. Pratt, 'The Anglo-American naval conversations on the Far East of January 1938', *International Affairs*, **47**, (1971), 745–63. See also Dallek, *Franklin D. Roosevelt*, pp. 153–8.

10. See Pratt, *International Affairs*, **47**, 757.
11. Lee, *Britain and Sino–Japanese War*, p. 119.
12. Lowe, *Great Britain and Origins of Pacific War*, pp. 41–2.
13. Ibid., p. 43.
14. Ibid., pp. 46–50.
15. Cited ibid., pp. 51–2.
16. Ibid., p. 53.
17. Ibid., p. 55.
18. Ibid., p. 55.
19. Ibid., p. 59.
20. Ibid., p. 60.
21. Ibid., p. 60.
22. Ibid., p. 62.
23. Ibid., p. 67.
24. N. H. Gibbs, *Grand Strategy* (HMSO, 1976), vol. 1, p. 425.
25. Lowe, *Great Britain and Origins of Pacific War*, p. 69.
26. Ibid., pp. 72–3.
27. Ibid., p. 75.
28. Ibid., p. 76.
29. Ibid., pp. 76–7.
30. Ibid., pp. 79–80.
31. Ibid., p. 81.
32. Ibid., p. 84.
33. Ibid., p. 85.
34. Ibid., p. 89.
35. Cited ibid., p. 91.
36. Ibid., pp. 97–8.
37. For a discussion of Japan's relations with Germany and the Soviet Union, see J. W. Morley (ed.), *Deterrent Diplomacy : Japan, Germany and the U.S.S.R., 1935–1940* (Columbia U.P., New York, 1976), pp. 113–78.
38. Cited Lowe, *Great Britain and Origins of Pacific War*, p. 106.
39. See ibid., Ch. 4, for a discussion of the subjects briefly summarised here.
40. Ibid., p. 140.
41. Ibid., p. 140.
42. Ibid., pp. 141–2.
43. Ibid., p. 143.
44. Ibid., p. 144.
45. Ibid., pp. 148–9.
46. Ibid., pp. 151–2.
47. For two excellent studies of Wang Ching-wei and the Japanese, see J. H. Boyle, *China and Japan at War, 1937–1945* (Stanford U.P., Stanford, 1972), and G. E. Bunker, *The Peace Conspiracy : Wang Ching-wei and the China War, 1937–1941* (Harvard U.P., Cambridge, Mass., 1972).
48. Lowe, *Great Britain and Origins of Pacific War*, pp. 156–7.
49. Ibid., p. 159.
50. There is no satisfactory biography of Matsuoka in English. For a concise assessment see B. Teters, 'Matsuoka Yosuke : the diplomacy of bluff and

gesture', in R. D. Burns and E. M. Bennett (eds.), *Diplomats in Crisis : United States–Chinese–Japanese Relations, 1919–1941* (European Bibliographical Centre-Clio Press, Oxford, 1974), pp. 275–96. See also Nish, *Japanese Foreign Policy*, pp. 235–46. For a perceptive study of Konoe, see R. Storry, 'Konoye Fumimaro : the last of the Fujiwara', in G. F. Hudson (ed.), *St. Antony's Papers, no. 7 : Far Eastern Affairs, no. 2* (Oxford U.P., 1960).

51. Lowe, *Great Britain and Origins of Pacific War*, p. 174.
52. Ibid., p. 162.
53. Ibid., pp. 162–3.
54. Ibid., p. 188.
55. Cited ibid., p. 190.
56. Ibid., p. 194.
57. Cited ibid., p. 196.
58. Ibid., p. 209.
59. Ibid., pp. 209–10.
60. Ibid., p. 211.
61. Ibid., p. 212.
62. Ibid., p. 213.
63. Ibid., pp. 214–5.
64. Ibid., p. 292.
65. For a discussion of American policy, see H. Feis, *The Road to Pearl Harbor* (Atheneum, New York, 1965), pp. 101–61.
66. Lowe, *Great Britain and Origins of Pacific War*, p. 221.
67. Ibid., pp. 223–4.
68. Ibid., pp. 225–6.
69. On this interesting aspect, see I. H. Anderson, Jr., 'The 1941 *de facto* embargo on oil to Japan: a bureaucratic reflex', *Pacific Historical Review*, **44** (1975), 201–31.
70. Lowe, *Great Britain and Origins of Pacific War*, pp. 236–7.
71. Ibid., pp. 237–8.
72. Ibid., p. 239.
73. See C. Hull, *The Memoirs of Cordell Hull*, 2 vols. (Macmillan, New York, 1948), vol. 2, pp. 1017–18.
74. For the text, see *Foreign Relations of the United States, Japan, 1931–1941*, 2 vols. (Government Printing Office, Washington, 1943), vol. 2, pp. 556–7.
75. See R. J. C. Butow, 'Backdoor diplomacy in the Pacific: the proposal for a Konoye-Roosevelt meeting, 1941', *Journal of American History*, **59** (1972), 48–72. For a thorough account of the activities of Drought and Walsh, see R. J. C. Butow, *The John Doe Associates : Backdoor Diplomacy for Peace, 1941* (Stanford U.P., Stanford, 1974).
76. Lowe, *Great Britain and Origins of Pacific War*, p. 252–3.
77. Ibid., pp. 252–3.
78. Ibid., pp. 265–6.
79. Ibid., p. 272.
80. Cited ibid., p. 273.
81. Cited ibid., p. 274.
82. The text of the appeal is given in *Foreign Relations of the United States, Japan, 1931–1941*, vol. 2, pp. 784–6.

Chapter 10

1. See I. H. Nish, *Japanese Foreign Policy, 1869–1942* (Routledge & Kegan Paul, 1977), p. 249.
2. The prevailing mood of Japanese leaders emerges clearly from N. Ike (ed.), *Japan's Decision for War : Records of the 1941 Policy Conferences* (Stanford U.P., Stanford, 1967).
3. The official history of the British war effort in the Far East is to be found in S. W. Kirby *et al, The War Against Japan*, 5 vols. (HMSO, 1957–69). A shorter account of the Malayan campaign and the background to it is provided in S. W. Kirby, *Singapore : the Chain of Disaster* (Cassell, 1971). See also a stimulating account by L. Allen, *Singapore, 1941–1942* (Davis-Poynter, 1977).
4. P. Lowe, *Great Britain and the Origins of the Pacific War* (Clarendon Press, Oxford, 1977), pp. 279–80.
5. See Allen, *Singapore* pp. 121–84, 247–63.
6. Lowe, *Great Britain and Origins of Pacific War,* p. 279.
7. On this aspect, see I. Simson, *Singapore : Too Little and Too Late* (Leo Cooper, 1971).
8. For a selection of the Churchill-Roosevelt correspondence, see F. L. Loewenheim, H. D. Langley, and M. Jonas (eds.), *Roosevelt and Churchill : Their Secret Wartime Correspondence* (Barrie & Jenkins, 1975).
9. The relationship between Churchill and Roosevelt is one of the themes in C. Thorne, *Allies of a Kind : the United States, Britain, and the War against Japan, 1941–1945* (Hamish Hamilton, 1978). This is a most important work providing a comprehensive examination of Anglo–American relations with reference to the Far East and Pacific.
10. Lowe, *Great Britain and Origins of Pacific War*, p. 280.
11. Ibid., p. 280. For the frequently mordant comments of General 'Vinegar Joe' Stilwell, who was involved in the retreat from Burma, see T. H. White (ed.), *The Stilwell Papers* (William Sloane Associates, New York, 1948), pp. 43–106.
12. For a lucid account of the Japanese impact, see W. H. Elsbree, *Japan's Role in Southeast Asian Nationalist Movements* (Harvard U.P., Cambridge, Mass., 1953). For a useful documentary collection, see J. C. Lebra (ed.), *Japan's Greater East Asia Co-Prosperity Sphere in World War II* (Oxford U.P., Kuala Lumpur, 1975). See also J. C. Lebra, *Japanese-Trained Armies in Southeast Asia* (Heinemann, Hong Kong, 1977), which provides a valuable comparative survey of the Japanese impact.
13. See Lebra, *Japanese-Trained Armies*.
14. Lebra, *Japanese-Trained Armies*, pp. 1–18.
15. See Ba Maw, *Breakthrough in Burma* (Yale U.P., New Haven, 1968), for an extremely interesting account of his relationship with the Japanese.
16. Ba Maw, *Breakthrough in Burma*, Ch. 2.
17. Ibid., Ch. 4.
18. Thorne, *Allies of a Kind*, pp. 221, 608–10.
19. Ba Maw, *Breakthrough in Burma*, pp. 155–6.
20. Ibid., pp. 360–5.
21. Cady, *History of Modern Burma*, p. 483.
22. A. Short, *The Communist Insurrection in Malaya* (Frederick Muller, 1975), pp. 21–5.

23. S. Gopal, *Nehru*, (Cape, 1975), vol. 1, pp. 249–75.
24. See R. J. Moore, *Churchill, Cripps and India, 1939–1945* (Clarendon Press, Oxford, 1979).
25. Thorne, *Allies of a Kind*, pp. 170–97, 305–27.
26. Ibid., pp. 320–2, 437–9.
27. For Stilwell's acrid views of Chiang Kai-shek, see White, *The Stilwell Papers*, passim, and B. Tuchman, *Sand Against the Wind : Stilwell and the American Experience in China* (Macmillan, 1971).
28. Cited M. Howard, *Grand Strategy*, (London, HMSO, 1972), vol. 4, p. 83. For a short lucid account of the war in Burma, see R. Callahan, *Burma, 1942–1945* (Davis-Poynter, 1978).
29. Howard, *Grand Strategy*, vol. 4, p. 84.
30. Cited ibid., vol. 4, p. 86. See also Thorne, *Allies of a Kind*, pp. 155, 163.
31. See Howard, *Grand Strategy*, vol. 4, pp. 88–91.
32. Ibid., vol. 4, p. 96.
33. Ibid., vol. 4, p. 98.
34. Cited ibid., vol. 4, p. 101.
35. Ibid., vol. 4, pp. 242–3. See also Thorne, *Allies of a Kind*, p. 165.
36. Thorne, *Allies of a Kind*, p. 155.
37. Howard, *Grand Strategy* vol. 4, p. 248 and Thorne, *Allies of a Kind*, p. 166.
38. Cited Howard, *Grand Strategy*, vol. 4, p. 276.
39. Ibid., vol. 4, p. 277.
40. Thorne, *Allies of a Kind*, p. 166.
41. Howard, *Grand Strategy*, vol. 4, p. 397.
42. Cited ibid., vol. 4, p. 399.
43. Ibid., vol. 4, pp. 399–400.
44. Thorne, *Allies of a Kind*, p. 297.
45. Howard, *Grand Strategy*, vol. 4, p. 403. For Stilwell's views of Chennault, see White, *Stilwell Papers*, pp. 37, 38, 203, 204.
46. Howard, *Grand Strategy*, vol. 4, p. 405.
47. Ibid., vol. 4, p. 440.
48. Ibid., vol. 4, p. 443.
49. Ibid., vol. 4, p. 444.
50. Ibid., vol. 4, pp. 447–48.
51. On MacArthur, see D. Clayton James, *The Years of MacArthur* (Leo Cooper, 1975), vol. 2, and W. Manchester, *American Caesar : Douglas MacArthur, 1880–1964* (Little, Brown, Boston, 1978). For a discussion of the problems associated with the establishment of SEAC, see Thorne, *Allies of a Kind*, pp. 297–302.
52. Howard, *Grand Strategy*, vol. 4, p. 574.
53. Cited Thorne, *Allies of a Kind*, pp. 298–9.
54. Cited ibid., pp. 335–6, 337.
55. J. Ehrman, *Grand Strategy* (HMSO, 1956), vol. 5, p. 163.
56. Ibid., vol. 5, p. 163.
57. Ibid., vol. 5, p. 173.
58. Ibid., vol. 5, p. 188.
59. Ibid., vol. 5, pp. 191–2.
60. Thorne, *Allies of a Kind*, p. 335.
61. On Bose, see J. C. Lebra, *Jungle Alliance : Japan and the Indian National Army* (Asia Pacific Press, Singapore, 1971).

62. Ehrman, *Grand Strategy*, vol. 5, pp. 407–08 and Thorne, *Allies of a Kind*, p. 406.
63. Ehrman, *Grand Strategy*, vol. 5, pp. 441–48.
64. Cited ibid., vol. 5, p. 459.
65. Ibid., vol. 5, p. 460.
66. Ibid., vol. 5, p. 481 and Thorne, *Allies of a Kind*, pp. 412–13.
67. Thorne, *Allies of a Kind*, pp. 412–13.
68. Cited Ehrman, *Grand Strategy*, vol. 5, p. 518.
69. Ibid., vol. 5, p. 523.
70. See W. Slim, *Defeat into Victory* (Cassell, 1956), and R. Lewin, *Slim : the Standardbearer* (Leo Cooper, 1976).
71. Thorne, *Allies of a Kind*, p. 522.
72. Ibid., pp. 587–633.
73. See C. Thorne, 'The Indochina issue between Britain and the United States, 1942–1945', *Pacific Historical Review*, **45** (1976), 73–96.
74. Ehrman, *Grand Strategy* (HMSO, 1956) vol. 6, p. 257.
75. Thorne, *Allies of a Kind*, p. 523.
76. Ibid., p. 527.
77. Ibid., p. 527.
78. See G. Daniels, 'The great Tokyo air raid, 9–10 March 1945', in W. G. Beasley (ed.), *Modern Japan : Aspects of History, Literature, and Society* (Charles E. Tuttle Company, Tokyo, 1976), pp. 113–31.
79. For an examination of the political situation in Japan in 1945, see R. J. C. Butow, *Japan's Decision to Surrender, 1945* (Stanford U.P., Stanford, 1965).
80. See M. J. Sherwin, 'The atomic bomb and the origins of the Cold War', *American Historical Review*, **78** (1973), 945–68.
81. Ehrman, *Grand Strategy*, vol. 6, p. 297.
82. Ibid., vol. 6, p. 298. See also H. S. Truman, *Memoirs 1945 : Year of Decisions* (New American Library, New York, 1965), pp. 460–70.
83. Ehrman, *Grand Strategy*, vol. 6, pp. 302–03.
84. Ibid., vol. 6, p. 306.

Chapter 11

1. On this aspect see C. Thorne, *Allies of a Kind : the United States, Britain and the War Against Japan, 1941–1945* (Hamish Hamilton, 1978), pp. 520–45, 654–69.
2. See R. Minear, *Victors' Justice* (Princeton U.P., Princeton, 1971), p. 9. There is, surprisingly, only one monograph in English dealing with the International Military Tribunal for the Far East (IMTFE). This is in marked contrast to the numerous works examining the corresponding trial held at Nuremberg in 1945–46.
3. The majority of those on trial were generals or admirals. Interestingly there were no representatives of Japanese capitalism.
4. In private, MacArthur's views of the Australian war effort had been more critical than his public expression of opinion. See C. Thorne, 'MacArthur, Australia, and the British', *Australian Outlook*, **29** (April and September 1975), 53–67, 197–210.
5. See Minear, *Victors' Justice*, pp. 86–92. For an account of Nuremberg, see B. F. Smith, *Reaching Judgement at Nuremberg* (Andre Deutsch, 1977).

6. For Hankey's contemporary views, see Lord Hankey, *Politics, Trials and Errors* (Pen-in-Hand, Oxford, 1950).
7. See Minear, *Victors' Justice*, p. 172.
8. Cited in R. W. Buckley, 'British diplomacy and the allied control of Japan, 1945–1946', in G. Daniels and P. Lowe (eds.), *Proceedings of the British Association for Japanese Studies*, hereafter cited as *P.B.A.J.S.*, **2**, Pt 1, (1977), 167.
9. Buckley, *P.B.A.J.S.*, **2**, Pt 1, 174.
10. See F. C. Jones, H. Borton, and B. R. Pearn, *Survey of International Affairs : The Far East, 1939–1946* (Oxford U.P., 1955), pp. 307–08, 338.
11. Buckley, *P.B.A.J.S.*, **2**, Pt 1, 174.
12. Cited ibid., **2**, Pt 1, 175.
13. Ibid., **2**, Pt 1, 178.
14. Ibid., **2**, Pt 1, 168, 178.
15. Ibid., **2**, Pt 1, 181.
16. G. Daniels, 'Britain's view of postwar Japan, 1945–49', unpublished paper given at the Anglo-Japanese conference on Britain, Japan and the Second World War, held at the Imperial War Museum, London, in July 1979. I am most grateful to Dr Daniels for kindly allowing me to cite his paper prior to publication.
17. Daniels, 'Britain's view of postwar Japan'.
18. Cited ibid.
19. Ibid.
20. For a wide-ranging consideration of Japan's role in the world since 1945, see R. M. Scalapino (ed.), *The Foreign Policy of Modern Japan* (University of California Press, Berkeley, 1977).
21. See Thorne, *Allies of a Kind*, pp. 451, 558.
22. For developments in Hong Kong during the war, see G. B. Endacott and A. Birch, *Hong Kong : Eclipse* (Oxford U.P., Hong Kong, 1978). See also Chan Lau Kit-ching, 'The Hong Kong question during the Pacific War', *Journal of Imperial and Commonwealth History*, **2**, (1973) 56–78.
23. See Thorne, *Allies of a Kind*, pp. 440–2.
24. Cited D. C. Watt, 'Britain and the Cold War in the Far East, 1945–58', in Y. Nagai and A. Iriye (eds.), *The Origins of the Cold War in Asia* (University of Tokyo Press, Tokyo, 1977), pp. 94–5.
25. See Watt in Nagai and Iriye (eds.), *Origins of the Cold War*, p. 90.
26. See J. W. Esherick (ed.), *Lost Chance in China : the World War Despatches of John S. Service* (Random House, New York, 1974).
27. For a rigorous discussion of the situation in China, see S. Pepper, *Civil War in China, 1945–1949* (University of California Press, Berkeley, 1978).
28. See B. Porter, *Britain and the Rise of Communist China : a Study of British Attitudes, 1945–1954* (Oxford U.P., 1967), pp. 1–24.
29. Watt in Nagai and Iriye (eds.), *Origins of the Cold War*, p. 110.
30. Ibid., p. 111.
31. Cited Porter, *Britain and Communist China*, pp. 25, 28.
32. Porter, ibid., pp. 25–44, discusses the general issue of recognition.
33. Ibid., p. 29.
34. Ibid., pp. 26–7.
35. Ibid., p. 28.
36. Watt in Nagai and Iriye (eds.), *Origins of the Cold War*, p. 111.
37. Ibid., p. 112.
38. The Nixon visit to China in 1972 started to pave the way but the various

problems relating to Taiwan and to concomitant complexities in Congress prevented full recognition until granted by the Carter administration in 1979.

39. Porter, *Britain and Communist China*, pp. 87–8. See also G. Warner, 'The Korean War', *International Affairs*, **56** (1980), 98–107.

40. Cited ibid., p. 89.

41. Ibid., pp. 96–7.

42. Ibid., p. 112.

43. Ibid., p. 112.

44. Ibid., p. 119.

45. Ibid., pp. 120–1. By March 1951 the quantity of rubber sent to China from Malaya comprised 120,000 tons.

46. Ibid., pp. 121–2.

47. Ibid., pp. 126–7.

48. For a lucid account of developments in Indo-China, see D. Lancaster, *The Emancipation of French Indochina* (Oxford U.P., 1961).

49. For Eden's views, see Earl of Avon, *The Eden Memoirs : Full Circle* (Cassell, 1960), pp. 77–145.

50. Porter, *Britain and Communist China*, pp. 134–5.

51. Ibid., p. 135.

52. Ibid., p. 136.

53. Ibid., p. 139.

54. Ibid., p. 139.

55. For a succinct account of relations between Britain and China, see R. Boardman, *Britain and the People's Republic of China, 1949–74* (Macmillan, 1976).

56. See D. Wilson, *Mao : The People's Emperor* (Hutchinson, 1979), pp. 389–445.

57. On the development of Sino-Soviet relations, see J. Gittings, *Survey of the Sino–Soviet Dispute* (Oxford U.P., 1968).

58. For the views of Richard Nixon and Henry Kissinger, see R. M. Nixon, *The Memoirs of Richard Nixon* (Sidgwick & Jackson, 1978) and H. Kissinger, *The White House Years* (Weidenfeld & Nicolson with Michael Joseph, 1979).

59. *The Observer*, 28 October 1979.

60. See Boardman, *Britain and China*, pp. 136–62.

61. See Thorne, *Allies of a Kind*, pp. 661–12.

62. See W. Slim, *Defeat into Victory* (Cassell, 1956), p. 520 where Slim records his respect for Aung San and his belief that Aung San could have proved to be an 'Asian Smuts'. In a television interview apparently recorded in 1976 and shown on 27 August 1979, after his assassination by the Provisional IRA, Lord Mountbatten stated that one of his deepest regrets was that he had not forced the pace of change more rapidly in Burma in 1945, as Aung San was pro-British and Burma could then have remained within the British Commonwealth. A Burmese army officer carried one of Mountbatten's medals in the procession at the state funeral in London on 5 September 1979. Burma observed an official period of mourning for the passing of one who had been closely associated with Aung San in 1945.

63. See J. F. Cady, *A History of Modern Burma* (Cornell U.P., Ithaca, 1958), p. 532.

64. See selections from Aung San's speeches in R. M. Smith (ed.), *Southeast Asia : Documents of Political Development and Change* (Cornell U.P., Ithaca, 1974), pp. 93–6.

65. For the text, see Smith (ed.), *Southeast Asia*, pp. 87–91.
66. The Irish Free State belonged to the British Commonwealth when it came into existence as a result of the agreement reached between Lloyd George, Arthur Griffith and Michael Collins in December 1921. The Irish constitution of 1937, drawn up by de Valera, marked the decisive step towards complete independence and this was formally proclaimed by Eire in 1949.
67. For a study of Burma since 1948, see J. Silverstein, *Burma : Military Rule and the Politics of Stagnation* (Cornell U.P., Ithaca, 1977).
68. J. Kennedy, *History of Malaya, A.D. 1400–1959* (Macmillan, 1962), p. 266.
69. Ibid., p. 282.
70. Ibid., pp. 267–8.
71. Ibid., p. 283.
72. Ibid., p. 282.
73. A. Short, *The Communist Insurrection in Malaya, 1948–1960* (Frederick Muller, 1975), p. 118.
74. The most valuable account of the Emergency, resting upon an investigation of the Malayan archives, is in Short, *Communist Insurrection in Malaya*. See also R. L. Clutterbuck, *The Long, Long War* (Faber, 1966), and E. O'Ballance, *Malaya : The Communist Insurgent War, 1948–1960* (Faber, 1966).
75. See Short, *Communist Insurrection in Malaya*, pp. 39–40.
76. Ibid., p. 41 n.7.
77. Ibid., pp. 65–6.
78. Ibid., pp. 78–85.
79. Ibid., pp. 303–05.
80. Ibid., p. 336.
81. Ibid., pp. 173–456.
82. Ibid., pp. 338–44, 346, 365, 382–3.
83. Ibid., pp. 507–8.
84. K. G. Tregonning, *A History of Modern Malaya* (Eastern Universities Press, London, 1964), p. 315.
85. P. Darby, *British Defence Policy East of Suez, 1947–1968* (Oxford U.P., 1973), pp. 233–4 and Tregonning, *History of Modern Malaya*, pp. 316–17.
86. Darby, *British Defence Policy*, pp. 281–2; see also J. A. C. Mackie, *Konfrontasi : The Indonesian-Malaysia Dispute, 1963–1966* (Oxford U.P., Kuala Lumpur, 1974).
87. Darby, *British Defence Policy*, pp. 281–2.
88. Ibid., pp. 236–7.
89. Ibid., pp. 281–2.
90. Ibid., pp. 291–2.
91. Ibid., pp. 291–2.
92. For a balanced survey of the American intervention in Vietnam, see G. Lewy, *America in Vietnam* (Oxford U.P., 1978).
93. Darby, *British Defence Policy*, p. 283.

Select bibliography

Full reference to the works used in the preparation of this study is made in the end-notes. The following is a list of certain of the most valuable works, whether of a general or specific character. Section 1 comprises books of a more general nature, dealing with the British role in the world, including the Far East. Section 2 consists of significant books on more specific subjects. Section 3 comprises relevant general surveys of the history of countries or areas within the Far East.

1. General works

D. K. Fieldhouse, *Economics and Empire, 1830–1914*, (Weindenfeld & Nicolson, 1973).

G. F. Hudson, *The Far East in World Politics* (Oxford U.P., 1937).

V. G. Kiernan, *The Lords of Human Kind : European Attitudes to the Outside World in the Imperial Age* (Weindenfeld & Nicolson, 1969).

D. C. M. Platt, *Finance, Trade, and Politics : British Foreign Policy, 1815–1914* (Clarendon Press, Oxford, 1968).

A. P. Thornton, *The Imperial Idea and Its Enemies* (Macmillan, 1959).

B. Porter, *The Lion's Share : a Short History of British Imperialism, 1850–1970* (Longman, 1975).

G. Woodcock, *The British in the Far East : a Social History* (Weidenfeld & Nicolson, 1969).

2. Specific aspects

W. G. Beasley, *Great Britain and the Opening of Japan, 1834–1858* (Luzac & Company, 1951).

R. Boardman, *Britain and the People's Republic of China, 1949–1974* (Macmillan, 1976).

W. C. Costin, *Great Britain and China, 1833–1860* (Clarendon Press, Oxford, 1937).

P. Darby, *British Defence Policy East of Suez, 1947–1968* (Oxford U.P., 1973).

G. Fox, *Britain and Japan, 1858–1883* (Clarendon Press, Oxford, 1969).

M. Greenberg, *British Trade and the Opening of China, 1800–42* (Cambridge U.P., Cambridge, 1951).

W. R. Louis Jr., *British Strategy in the Far East, 1919–1939* (Clarendon Press, Oxford, 1971).

P. Lowe, *Great Britain and the Origins of the Pacific War : a Study of British Policy in East Asia, 1937–1941* (Clarendon Press, Oxford, 1977).

W. D. McIntyre, *The Imperial Frontier in the Tropics, 1865–75 : a Study of British Colonial Policy in West Africa, Malaya, and the South Pacific in the age of Gladstone and Disraeli* (Macmillan, 1967).

I. H. Nish, *The Anglo–Japanese Alliance : the Diplomacy of Two Island Empires* (Athlone Press, 1966); *Alliance in Decline : Anglo–Japanese Relations, 1908–1923* (Athlone Press, 1972).

N. A. Pelcovits *Old China Hands and the Foreign Office* (Octagon Books, New York, 1969, reprint of original 1948 edn).

B. E. Porter, *Britain and the Rise of Communist China : a Study of British Attitudes, 1945–54* (Oxford U.P., 1967).

A. Short, *The Communist Insurrection in Malaya, 1948–1960* (Frederick Muller, 1975).

N. Tarling, *Imperial Britain in South-East Asia* (Oxford U.P., Kuala Lumpur, 1975).

C. Thorne, *The Limits of Foreign Policy : the West, the League, and the Far Eastern Crisis, 1931–1933* (Hamish Hamilton, 1972); *Allies of a Kind : the United States, Britain, and the War against Japan, 1941–1945* (Hamish Hamilton, 1978).

L. K. Young, *British Policy in China, 1895–1902* (Oxford U.P., 1970).

3. Particular areas

W. G. Beasley, *The Modern History of Japan*, 2nd edn (Weidenfeld & Nicolson, 1975).

J. F. Cady, *A History of Modern Burma* (Cornell U.P., Ithaca, 1958).

J. K. Fairbank (ed.), *The Cambridge History of China*, vol. 10, Pt 1 : *Late Ch'ing, 1800–1911* (Cambridge U.P., Cambridge, 1978).

D. G. E. Hall, *A History of South-East Asia*, 3rd edn, (Macmillan, 1968).

I. C. Y. Hsu, *The Rise of Modern China* (Oxford U.P., 1970).

J. Kennedy, *A History of Malaya, A.D. 1400–1959* (Macmillan, 1962).

F. V. Moulder, *Japan, China, and the Modern World Economy: Towards a Reinterpretation of East Asian Development ca. 1600–ca. 1918* (Cambridge U.P., Cambridge, 1977).

I. H. Nish, *Japanese Foreign Policy, 1869–1942 : Kasumigaseki to Miyakezaka* (Routledge & Kegan Paul, 1977).

R., Storry, *A History of Modern Japan* (Penguin, Harmondsworth, 1976); *Japan and the Decline of the West in Asia, 1894–1943* (Macmillan, 1979).

Index